GLAMORGAN CRICKETERS

GLAMORGAN CRICKETERS
1949–1979

Andrew Hignell

HALSGROVE

First published in Great Britain in 2022

British Library Cataloguing-in-Publication Data
A CIP record for this title is available from the British Library

ISBN 978 0 85704 362 7

Halsgrove
Halsgrove House,
Ryelands Business Park,
Bagley Road, Wellington, Somerset TA21 9PZ
Tel: 01823 653777 Fax: 01823 216796
email: sales@halsgrove.com

Part of the Halsgrove group of companies
Information on all Halsgrove titles is available at: www.halsgrove.com

Printed and bound in India by Parksons Graphics Ltd

Contents

Introduction

This is the third volume in a series of books containing biographies of every Glamorgan cricketer. The first covered the period from 1889, when Glamorgan played their inaugural inter-county fixture against Warwickshire at Cardiff Arms Park, until 1920 when the final batch of Minor County Championship matches took place. The second covered the seasons between 1921 and 1948, and the years when the Welsh county developed from largely being a motley assortment of amateurs into a team who were mainly professional in both name and deed.

The metamorphosis from a team who lurched from one defeat to another into a side that won the County Championship title in 1948 was largely the result of the actions of three men – Johnnie Clay (Vol.2 p15-24), Maurice Turnbull (Vol.2 p111-124) and Wilf Wooller (Vol. 2 p269-284). Johnnie and Maurice had overseen a fund-raising campaign during the troubled years of the early 1930s as well as other actions which guaranteed Glamorgan's survival as a first-class side and ended the reliance on the generous gifts of patrons such as Sir Sidney Byass who, in 1920, had given the Club a nest-egg of £1,000 to cover the costs of securing sufficient home and away fixtures in order for the Club to be classified as first-class.

With a more secure financial footing having been established by the late 1930s Glamorgan were performing far better on the field and to the delight of both Maurice and Johnnie, opposing teams were no longer expecting a two-day victory over the Welsh county. Wilf had made his debut during these years, although at the time, the burly North Walian was known more for his outstanding exploits on the rugby field and in the red jersey of Wales. His all-round efforts in the victory over the 1939 West Indians at the Arms Park showcased his latent talents in first-class cricket, but just as the Glamorgan

Wilf Wooller (2nd left, front row) with his Championship-winning team, plus the Lord and Lady Mayoress of Cardiff, together with other City councillors at a civic function in the autumn of 1948

in the City Hall to celebrate Glamorgan's success. Also in the image are Johnnie Clay (front right), Haydn Davies (second row, first left), Emrys Davies (second row, second left), Norman Hever (second row, third left), Phil Clift (second row, fourth left), Willie Jones (third row, first left), Jim Pleass (third row, second left), Gilbert Parkhouse (third row, third left), Jim Eaglestone (third row, fourth left), Allan Watkins (third row, extreme right) and Len Muncer (fourth row centre).

officials started to plan for a bright future with the man dubbed 'The Prince of Wales', the daffodil-embossed sweaters were being swopped for the khaki, blue and grey of military uniforms as the Second World War led to a cessation in sporting activities for six long and bloody years.

These were also years which robbed the nation, as a whole, of many fine people, including Maurice who tragically gave his life to King and Country whilst serving with the Welsh Guards in mud-laden Normandy during 1944. Others endured many difficult years, with Wilf being one of thousands of Allied Prisoners of War in the Far East and it was through his fortitude and resilience that Wilf survived the horrors of life in the Changi camp and working on the notorious Death Railway.

When county cricket resumed in 1946, Johnnie was determined that Maurice's efforts would not be wasted and, with the help of Wilf, plus other pre-war stalwarts, the pair oversaw further success for Glamorgan, culminating in a wonderful afternoon on 24 August 1948 when, under Wilf's captaincy, the Welsh county defeated Hampshire by an innings at Bournemouth to clinch the Championship title. It was fitting that the final wicket in this game was taken by Johnnie, as the great off-spinner had an l.b.w. appeal upheld against Charlie Knott, but it was completely by coincidence that the presiding umpire should have been Dai Davies (Vol.2 p76-82) the former Glamorgan batsman from the 1920s and 1930s. His words "That's out, and we've won the Championship", spoken with tears of joy in his eyes, have gone down in the folklore of Welsh sport.

Their success was built on the *esprit de corps* shown by Wilf's men, some outstanding performances by the likes of Allan Watkins (Vol. 2, p294-304), Gilbert Parkhouse (Vol. 2 p319-327), Emrys Davies (Vol. 2 p98-106) and Willie Jones (Vol. 2 p254-260), plus Wilf's own willpower and determination to win as well as some outstanding fielding, especially close to the wicket. "There may be better batting and bowling sides in the country," he said to one journalist reflecting on his team's success, "but none could match our fielding and we were undoubtedly the best group of catchers in the County Championship."

It was a potent mix and, fuelled by the heady feelings of patriotism and national identity, there were hopes that Wilf's team could taste further glory in the subsequent years. As this book outlines, these dreams, even by Celtic standards, were far too romantic and it was to be 21 years before the Championship pennant flew over Glamorgan's headquarters with Tony Lewis leading Glamorgan to a victory over Worcestershire at Cardiff to secure the 1969 title.

A group of Glamorgan players and friends enjoying the sunshine at Hove in 1948. Left-to-right – Willie Jones, unknown, Jim Eaglestone, unknown, George Lavis, Phil Clift, Haydn Davies, Allan Watkins and Len Muncer.

This is not to say however that this period was barren and devoid of joy as there were many days of both collective and individual success. For example, the 1950s witnessed a thrilling and largely unexpected victory over the 1951 Springboks at Swansea, besides seeing Gilbert Parkhouse and Jim McConnon win Test honours with England. The 1960s were also the most successful decade in the Club's history to date with Peter Walker and Jeff Jones making their bow in international cricket, whilst Glamorgan – or in the minds of some Wales – defeated the 1964 and 1968 Australians in historic matches at Swansea, with the events on the hallowed turf at St Helen's being totemic moments in the sporting history of Wales and rivalling the achievements of Cardiff City FC in winning the FA Cup at Wembley in 1927 and the victory by the Welsh rugby team over New Zealand at the Arms Park in 1905.

The seasons until 1979, as covered by this book, were part of a period of important change, both locally and nationally. It was a time which saw the end of the distinction between amateur and professional, with everyone from 1963 onwards being classed as a paid player. These were years which saw fundamental changes to the way county cricket was played, with these innovations in the county calendar starting, as well, in 1963 with the inauguration of the Gillette Cup. The competition was seen as cricket's version of the FA Cup and was an attempt to brighten up the county game, besides moving away from the negative tactics which had blighted many games during the 1950s.

The scorecard for Glamorgan's Sunday League match against Somerset at Sophia Gardens, Cardiff on 1 June 1969 – the first year on the 40-over competition.

For it's first two years, the maximum length of innings in the knockout competition was 65-overs before switching to 60 overs per side from 1965 onwards. It was also the first time a competition had attracted national sponsorship and the success which the razor blade and shaving company enjoyed was replicated from 1969 onwards by cigarette manufacturers John Player and Sons who sponsored a 40-overs per side competition on Sunday afternoons.

The creation of the John Player Sunday League was built on the success during the 1960s of the games staged by the International Cavaliers, a team sponsored by Rothman's, another cigarette-maker, and composed of some of the top players in world cricket and augmented by some of the overseas stars who had been hired by the counties in another and very important change in the world of county cricket. Each of the seventeen counties had matches against the Cavaliers, with the funds raised going towards their long-serving players who were enjoying Benefit Years or towards local charities. Many of these matches were televised and the excellent viewing figures which accrued prompted the BBC to cover from 1969 one match every Sunday in the new competition sponsored by John Player.

These innovations continued into the 1970s with the introduction from 1972 of an early season competition, sponsored by Benson and Hedges, with innings spanning 55 overs per side and, like the Gillette Cup, a prestigious final at Lord's. The main difference though was the creation of zonal groups, with counties clustered geographically and augmented by combined Minor County and university teams, before a batch of quarter- and semi-finals to determine who would play each other at Lord's.

Advertising boards, sponsored cars and corporate dining areas were other trappings of this early commercialism of cricket although from Glamorgan's point of view, it saw only a handful of changes at the grounds at which the Club played, whilst only a small number of capped and senior players were given motor vehicles by grateful sponsors. For some of the English counties, notably Kent and Lancashire, the introduction of one-day cricket into the domestic calendar saw a period of great success. For Glamorgan, there were occasional quarter-final appearances before a fine run of form in the Gillette Cup of 1977 saw the Welsh county defeat Leicestershire in the semi-final at Swansea prior to an appearance against Middlesex in the Cup Final at Lord's.

It had been a dramatic and unexpected turnaround for the Welsh county who had endured a truly dreadful summer in 1976, during which they lost the services of Majid Khan, their first truly great overseas player and a man who in 1969 had played a memorable and match-winnings innings against Worcestershire at Sophia Gardens to help his adopted county clinch the Championship title. Seven years later, it was very much a summer of discontent as the Pakistani and several others severed their links with the Club, only for a remarkable turnaround the following year as Glamorgan played their first-ever one-day final at Lord's.

Other changes had taken place during this period which were specific to Glamorgan Cricket, in particular their switch of ground in Cardiff from the Arms Park to Sophia Gardens. It was a move which had it's roots back in the 1950s when Wilf and others in the Club's hierarchy were eager to create a Centre of Excellence and purpose-built facilities at a ground which was owned by Glamorgan CCC. The scheme to move to an area of land in Pontcanna Fields or in Sophia Gardens failed to win the support at first of Cardiff Corporation but, in the early 1960s, a move

Majid Khan, watched by Eifion Jones, the Glamorgan wicket-keeper, is interviewed by Alun Williams of BBC Wales on the balcony of the Sophia Gardens Pavillion after Glamorgan had beaten Worcestershire to win the 1969 County Championship.

to the latter got the green light following the decision to redevelop the Arms Park rugby ground and create a National Stadium. However, Cardiff Athletic Club were the tenants of the new Sophia Gardens cricket ground, rather than Glamorgan, with the Welsh county playing for the final time at the Arms Park in 1966 before switching their activities the following year to the new ground in the Bute-owned parkland on the west bank of the River Taff.

The period covered by this book also saw two of the Club's finest players in their pomp – batsman Alan Jones and bowler Don Shepherd. Nobody has – or indeed ever will – score more runs or take more wickets than Don and Alan. Both hold a very special place in the Club's history for what they achieved with bat and ball during this period with each being integral members of the Glamorgan teams which defeated the 1964 and 1968 Australians as well as winning the 1969 County title and finishing as runners-up the following year. Neither were called upon by the England selectors to play against a Test Match nation, but to the west of Offa's Dyke, each hold a very special place in the hearts and minds of the Welsh sporting nation, many of whom still cannot fathom why with tallies of over 36,000 first-class runs and in excess of 2,000 wickets Alan and Don were ignored by the England selectors.

This *hwyl* and fervent passion displayed by the Club's supporters was one of the constants throughout this period. Whilst many changes were taking place to the look and feel of the county game, Glamorgan supporters still desired success, besides welcoming the likes of Majid and Viv into their ranks as honorary Welshmen. Another constant was Wilf Wooller, albeit in various guises, with the man who led the county to the 1948 county title remaining as the Club's captain until 1960 before performing the role of Secretary until retiring in 1977 and subsequently becoming the Club's President. The hand of W. Wooller continued to loom large over the affairs of Glamorgan CCC throughout this period

from 1949 until 1979 as well as beyond and, just like Dai Davies at Bournemouth in 1948, there were tears in the eyes of the Club's *eminence grise* as he joined the team of 1993, their supporters and sponsors at the end of the season functions to celebrate their success in winning the one-day league.

Glamorgan legends Alan Jones, Don Shepherd and Tony Lewis speak with Kent and England's Colin Cowdrey (left) plus JBG Thomas of the Western Mail (right) at a special function to celebrate the Club's Championship-winning success in 1969.

1949

If 1948 had been an outstanding year for his team, 1949 was a wonderful one for Wilf Wooller as a bowler, with the Glamorgan captain claiming 120 wickets as he enjoyed, by some way, his most successful summer with the ball during his county career. 'The Skipper' had claimed 73 scalps in 1948 and now, in the months following his marriage to Enid James, he had exceeded this tally by 47. But there was no honeymoon for his team as the reigning county champions slipped back into a mid-table position, winning seven of the 26 Championship matches.

It was always going to a hard year for Glamorgan as Wilf and his team had put many noses out of joint with their title success, and there were several opposing captains who were less than generous when it came to declarations in 1949 compared with the year before. The Welsh county were given few favours and, in several games, were expected to bowl out a team in their second innings rather being given a slightly generous declarations as in 1948.

The Glamorgan team of 1949. Back row – Phil Clift, Gilbert Parkhouse, Norman Hever, Jimmy Eaglestone, Maurice Robinson and Jim Pleass. Front row – Willie Jones, Haydn Davies, Wilf Wooller, Emrys Davies and Len Muncer.

There were other reasons behind the Welsh county's slide down to 8th place in the table. Emrys Davies (Vol. 2, p98-106) had a relatively moderate season, whilst for much of the season, Glamorgan were without Willie Jones (Vol. 2, p254-260) who had sustained an injury whilst fielding at Gravesend in June and was sidelined for many weeks. There were also absentees in the bowling ranks with work commitments in his family's business meaning that Stan Trick (Vol. 2, p362-363) whose clever left-arm spin had been a potent weapon, especially on the sand-based pitch at St Helen's was unavailable for the games at Swansea.

In his absence, there were opportunities for sixteen-year old Jim Pressdee, a right-hand batsman and slow left-arm bowler from the Mumbles who had impressed with the county's 2nd XI as under the watchful tutelage of Trevil Morgan (Vol.2, p135-140) and George Lavis (Vol.2 p155-158), a number of young colts were given opportunities in matches against Minor County opposition.

At the other end of the age spectrum, 1949 also saw Johnnie Clay (Vol. 2, p15-24) play his final County Championship with the silver-haired spinner making his last appearance against Yorkshire at Newport. His appearance in the game at Rodney Parade starting on 27 August was quite fitting given that it was for Monmouthshire that he had played against Glamorgan in Minor County games during 1920 when he was a young tearaway bowler. He had taken four wickets against Glamorgan, but twenty-nine years later, he went wicketless against Yorkshire as he bowed out of county cricket after a truly magnificent playing career.

Haydn Davies avoids being run out by his opposite number Tom Wade during Glamorgan's County Championship match against Essex at Valentine's Park, Ilford in 1949.

414
MONTGOMERY, Stanley William.

Born - West Ham, 7 July 1920.
Died - Cardiff, 5 October 2000.
RHB, RM.
Professional.
Ed – Brew Road School, West Ham.
1st XI: 1949-1953.
2nd XI: 1949-1953.
Club and Ground: 1950-1953.
Essex 1948.
Clubs: Romford, Barry Athletic, Briton Ferry Steel, Hill's Plymouth, Merthyr, Maesteg Celtic and XL Club.

Batting and Fielding Record

	M	I	NO	RUNS	AV	100	50	CT	ST
F-c	29	43	2	763	18.60	1	3	9	-

Bowling Record

	Balls	M	R	W	AV	5wI	10wM
F-c	222	10	99	6	16.50	-	-

Career-bests

First-class – 117 v Hampshire at Dean Park, Bournemouth, 1949.
3/29 v Hampshire at Dean Park, Bournemouth, 1952.

Stan Montgomery, a Cardiff City footballer, wrote his name into Glamorgan's record books by scoring a century on only his second Championship appearance, against Hampshire at Bournemouth, besides sharing a fifth wicket stand of 264 with Maurice Robinson – their efforts remain the best for that wicket for the Welsh county in first-class cricket.

A tall and upright batsman, Stan had been on the staff of his native Essex in the years immediately after the Second World War but at the time, football was his main recreation. In May 1948 he played for Essex in their two-day friendly at Fenner's against Cambridge University, but despite making an assertive 76, Stan did not secure a place in their Championship line-up.

Everything changed following a move to South Wales at the end of the 1947/48 season after Stan had agreed terms with Cardiff City. He joined Barry Athletic and soon drew the attention of Glamorgan's talent scouts. In July 1949 he made his Glamorgan debut against Derbyshire at the Arms Park and played positively in both innings against the Peakites – indeed, it was his competitive nature and tall imposing presence that impressed Wilf Wooller, especially when compared with some of the less confident members of the playing squad. However, there were occasions when he and Wilf did not see eye to eye, such as the match when a mix-up in calling saw Stan run out the fiery Glamorgan captain much to the mirth of the fielding side. After the umpire had upheld the appeal, Wilf unleashed a volley of oaths in Stan's direction before trudging off red-faced and angry back to the pavillion.

"I don't think you should get out for at least an hour or so," was the mirthful comment from one opponent to the ashen-faced Stan, who was now appreciating the gravity of his error. Fortunately, Wilf had slightly calmed down by the time Stan returned but, even so, he still had a dressing down and after play, as well as the following morning, he went back out in full kit for over half an hour with Wilf in order to practice running between the wickets. The century at Bournemouth proved to Stan's one and only first-class hundred, and he posted three other half-centuries in his 29 appearances for Glamorgan before retiring from professional cricket at the end of the 1953 and focusing on his footballing career and no doubt, a quieter life away from the Glamorgan skipper!

Stan Montgomery demonstrates one of his defensive strokes in a specially posed photograph at Cardiff Arms Park.

Stan had begun his football career playing for non-league football Romford during World War Two, besides guesting on several occasions for Southend United before agreeing terms with Hull City in 1944. The centre-half only spent a short period in Yorkshire before returning to play at Southend and making 96 appearances for them between 1946 and 1948. He then joined Cardiff City for a fee of £6,000, on the recommendation of Jimmy Nelson, a member of the Bluebirds FA Cup-winning side of 1927 and a man whose daughter Maureen, Stan later married.

He made a goalscoring debut for Cardiff City in their League match against Grimsby Town in January 1949 and duly played the remaining seventeen matches of the season. Over the course of the next seven years, Stan was a mainstay of the Bluebirds and missed few games, besides helping them secure promotion into the First Division during the 1951/52 season and on occasions the following season also leading the side.

A cigarette card of Stan Montgomery, the Glamorgan cricketer and Cardiff City footballer.

Stan left Cardiff City in 1955 and returned to non-league football with Worcester City before finishing his career in Wales with spells at Newport County, Llanelli and Ton Pentre. After his retirement from playing football, he became a sports coach and was appointed by George Swindin, then manager of Norwich City as the Canaries' first team coach in 1962. George took over at Cardiff five months later so Stan Montgomery followed him back to South Wales and to Ninian Park, where he worked again as first team coach for the next two years.

After Swindin left Cardiff City following the teams' relegation at the end of the 1963/64 season, Stan coached at Bradfield College, Cranleigh School and then in 1969 at Cardiff University, before working as a Sports Adviser to the Boys Clubs of Wales and helping Bristol Rovers as a talent scout in the South Wales area. He later had a spell as Rovers' Youth team coach, before returning to Ninian Park again during the mid-1980s on the request of manager Alan Durban to take charge of the club's trialists.

415
PRESSDEE, James Stuart.

Born – Mumbles, 19 June 1933.
Died – Edenvale, Johannesburg, 21 July 2016.
Professional.
RHB, SLA, occ WK.
Ed – Oystermouth School, Swansea.
1st XI: 1949-1965.
2nd XI: 1951-1960.
Club and Ground: 1949-1962.
Cap: 1955.
MCC 1964; North-east Transvaal 1965/66-1969/70.
Clubs: Swansea, Pontardawe, St Fagans, Llanelli, Maesteg Celtic, Springs and Mumbles.

Batting and Fielding Record

	M	I	NO	RUNS	AV	100	50	CT	ST
F-c	322	543	83	13411	29.16	12	75	344	-
List A	6	6	0	105	17.50	-	1	2	-

Bowling Record

	Balls	M	R	W	AV	5wI	10wM
F-c	21993	1095	8988	405	22.18	19	5
List A	144	4	101	3	33.67	-	-

Career-bests:

First-class   150* v Cambridge University at Ynysangharad Park, Pontypridd,1965.
9/43 v Yorkshire at St Helen's, Swansea, 1965.
List A   60 v Essex at The Gnoll, Neath, 1964.
3/46 v Somerset at Cardiff Arms Park, 1963.

Jim Pressdee was the most recent, and probably last, Glamorgan player to perform the Double of 1,000 first-class runs and 100 wickets. Besides being an outstanding all-round cricketer, Jim was Glamorgan's youngest player in post-war cricket (and second youngest overall) as he made his first-class debut in their County Championship match against Nottinghamshire at the Arms Park in 1949 when aged 16 years and 59 days.

Jim was born in the Mumbles where his family ran a thriving bakery business in Queens Road. He attended Oystermouth School and showed great promise at both cricket and football, besides leading the school's team to the Swansea Schools Shield for the first time. He also won a place in the Swansea Schoolboys side, whilst in May 1948 he appeared at left-back for Wales against Scotland in the Victory Shield schoolboy international at Ninian Park in Cardiff. The programme notes for the match neatly summed up Jim's talents as a footballer – "a most reliable full-back, who is deadly in his tackling and kicks very well. He is good with his head and his positional play leaves little to be desired."

A place on the books of Swansea Town soon followed, with Jim later having offers to join Tottenham Hotspurs. During the 1950s. Jim became involved in the transfer negotiations over the move of Arthur Willis, the England full back, from Spurs to the Vetch Field club. The London-based club agreed to Willis' move but only if Jim would move to White Hart Lane in exchange. A dispute then arose between Jim and the Swansea club over the accrued share of his benefit and the deal was shelved, before Swansea agreed in September 1954 to pay a sum of several thousand pounds for Willis' transfer.

Jim Pressdee.

Jim was also invited to play for the England Youth team against Germany at Wembley but he declined the invitation because he was playing in a 2nd XI match for Glamorgan. Nevertheless after completing his National Service with the RAF and securing a full-time contract with the Welsh county, he was able to successfully mix his sporting passions, with Jim playing for Swansea Town between 1953 and 1955, before a spell with non-League clubs including Llanelli and Brecon Corinthians.

Having played his first Championship match as a sixteen year-old, it wasn't until 1952 that he made his next appearance, and then whilst on leave from the RAF as he played against Sussex on his home turf at St Helen's. Having completed his National Service, he made four further appearances in 1953, before becoming a regular in the Welsh county's line-up.

Following further coaching from George Lavis, Jim duly developed into a gritty and stubborn middle-order batsman, with a fierce square-cut and a powerful straight drive, often on the up over mid-on. He also became a clever left-arm spinner with a low action, often floating the ball up in a slow and tempting arc. Despite not having a high, classical action like other left-armers, he proved a deft foil for Jim McConnon's cleverly flighted off-spin and, later, the parsimonious off-cutters of Don Shepherd. Both McConnon and Shepherd were miserly in their approach to bowling, so much so that frustrated batters would often fancy their chances when Jim bowled at the other end.

Jim would often start a spell by bowling quite wide of the stumps, tossing the ball up in an inviting loop. Having not got a run at the other end, batsmen now had their chance but had to stretch outside off-stump. Some chanced their arm and got away with it, but often Jim claimed an early scalp before straightening his line to further frustrate the batters before switching again to slightly wider of the crease.

Jim Pressdee demonstrates his bowling action at the Arms Park.

These subtle tactics saw Jim top the county's bowling averages in 1955 with 72 victims at a cost of just 19. It was a summer when he also scored 803 runs and held 42 catches, either in the leg-trap or gully where in both positions he made the most of his ambidextrous ability to catch with equal ease either with his right or left hand. It was no surprise that his all-round efforts in 1955 deservedly won Jim his county cap. In contrast, the next couple of years were slightly disappointing with Jim only taking 31 wickets in 1956 before struggling with injury in 1957. But he bounced back to form in 1958 with seven half-centuries followed the next year by his maiden hundred against the Indian tourists at the Arms Park.

1959 was certainly a breakthrough summer for Jim as far as his batting was concerned and followed a move up to the number three position. His hundred against the Indians was the first of a dozen first-class centuries which he scored for Glamorgan, including one against Kent at Dartford where he revealed a more attacking side to his batting, romping to three figures before lunch. He might have scored another against Kent and his thirteenth in all, during a match at Maidstone which also gave an insight into his single-minded and, at times, feisty character.

On this particular occasion, Jim had stubbornly guided Glamorgan to safety and after a long partnership with Alan Rees, he seemed set to reach three figures. But spectators at The Mote had barracked his slow batting and, in response, Jim was determined to continue in blocking mode, forsaking a chance to reach a hundred and denying the spectators the opportunity to, in time honoured fashion, applaud him on reaching three figures. Despite the fact that the bowlers were going through the motions, their innocuous deliveries were patted back as Jim remained undefeated on 97.

In more pleasing times in 1961 at the Arms Park, Jim etched his name into the Club's record books by becoming their first batsman to score a century for Glamorgan against the Australians. The summer had seen the format of the Australians tour change so that the Welsh county had two games against the men in baggy green caps, each over Bank Holiday weekends, with the first one over Whitsun in Cardiff, and the second at Swansea in the 'traditional' slot in August.

In the first game in late May, Jim duly became the toast of the Club as his hundred helped to save the game. Sublime centuries from Neil Harvey and Norm O'Neill had seen the Australians amass a big first innings total before cheaply dismissing the home batsmen and enforcing the follow-on. But Jim stoutly defended throughout the final day, with his unbeaten 118 seeing Glamorgan to a draw.

In fact, 1961 was a golden summer for Jim with the bat as he amassed in all first-class cricket a total of 1,892 runs and besides his century against Australia, he made Championship hundreds against Hampshire, Northamptonshire and Sussex. He then proved that his run-filled summer was not a flash in the pan, as the following year he went one better by compiling a career best 1,911 runs with hundreds against Cambridge University, Essex and Kent, with his unbeaten 130 at Canterbury being his best against county opposition.

It was no coincidence that in 1961 and 1962 he was not being captained by Wilf Wooller. Ossie Wheatley, the new leader, had inherited a team in which Jim was a very occasional spinner. It followed a series of disputes between Wilf and Jim, with the pair clashing swords both on and off the field about whether Jim should bowl over or around the wicket to certain batsmen. There were times as well as when Wilf wanted him to vary his pace or not bowl with such air. The mid 1950s had also seen constant bickering over the field placings Wilf would set for Jim's bowling, and after not getting the field he wanted, Jim stopped bowling and opted to concentrate on his batting.

Jim was certainly no angel himself and to colleagues, there were many times when he seemed to relish confrontation. It was said officially that he had lost confidence as a bowler – to an extent this may have been true, but the meddling by 'The Skipper' did not help matters and it was only when playing club cricket for Springs during the early 1960s in South Africa that Jim rediscovered his lost bowling arts.

With Ossie Wheatley wisely letting Jim decide on his own field and method of bowling, Jim returned to the Glamorgan attack with quite remarkable results and in 1963 he claimed his first-ever ten-wicket match haul against Kent in 1963 with figures of 11/148, before claiming 10/43 in a dramatic match against Nottinghamshire at Ebbw Vale. Jim was almost unplayable on the wicket at the Welfare Ground, returning figures of 15-12-5-6.

In all, Jim took 104 wickets in 1963 and, with 1,435 runs to his name. Jim duly completed the Double – the sixth and most recent Glamorgan player to achieve this outstanding all-round feat. He continued to enjoy much success with bat and ball in 1964, claiming 97 wickets for Glamorgan and playing a leading role in the famous victory over the 1964 Australians at Swansea.

Jim returned the outstanding figures of 6/58 & 4/65 to complete a ten-wicket haul against the tourists – the one and only time a Glamorgan bowler has achieved this feat against the Australians – with his achievement, most fittingly, coming during his Benefit season. His efforts in tandem with Don Shepherd also saw the pair of spinners end up as runners-up in *The Western Mail*'s Sportsman of the Year Awards, beaten only by long-jumper Lynn Davies who had won a Gold Medal at the Tokyo Olympics.

The St Helen's ground, just a few miles away from his birthplace in the Mumbles, saw another outstanding bowling feat from Jim in 1965 as he claimed a career-best 9/43 in Yorkshire's first innings of their match at Swansea – a game which remarkably

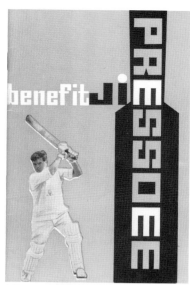

The cover of Jim Pressdee's Benefit brochure.

saw Don Shepherd also take nine wickets in the second innings – as Glamorgan secured a famous victory. His performances between 1963 and 1965 confirmed the views of many shrewd observers of Glamorgan Cricket that had it not been for the contretemps with Wilf and the apparent loss of confidence, Jim might have won honours as a Test cricketer.

1965 had also seen Jim make his career-best score as he completed an unbeaten 150 against Cambridge University at Pontypridd, but the summer proved to be his last with the Welsh county and ended in dramatic fashion following yet another spat with Wilf, this time in his guise as Club Secretary. It happened at the end of the final game of the summer at Stradey Park in Llanelli and after the Welsh county had failed to secure enough points to finish second behind Worcestershire. For much of the summer, Glamorgan had featured in the title race, so it was understandable that emotions were running high at the end of a frustrating season, but this was no excuse, on either part, for what followed as Jim tried to make his way out of the pavilion via a small office at the back of the Pavillion and through a door leading to the car park.

As usual, Wilf was using the using this office to count the gate money and, with a great deal of valuables lying around, he had already stopped some players, including Bernard Hedges from using the office as a short-cut. Jim then tried to go through with an apparent physical altercation between the two, resulting in Jim storming off to speak to the Press, who always hung around at the end of the game. On that day they had manna from heaven as Jim announced that he was leaving the Club and migrating to South Africa, before telling the journalists about what had happened.

For Jim, this may well have been the last straw that made him confirm his future lay elsewhere but, in truth, the story about his future had been rumbling on for many months whilst he had already booked his tickets to South Africa before this bust-up. The saga had begun in April, when he had told journalists "I am going to South Africa to coach again this winter and I shall probably stay there with my family." The previous year he had been in discussions, together with other senior players, with club officials about improved salaries and the hierarchy viewed his word and the threat of leaving as a lever to extract a better offer during his contract negotiations. Whatever the truth of the matter might have been, it was a sad and inglorious end to a playing career and a year when Ossie Wheatley was to describe him as amongst "the six best all-rounders in the world at the present moment."

Few would doubt that Jim was obstinate and a handful to deal with, to the extent that on one occasion when told to ring Wilf, he reversed the charges! The words of Ossie also outline how awkward Jim could be on the field – "he used to upset the other side as much as he upset his own side. He could get everyone going. He would go down the wicket and pat it down way beyond where the bowler was bowling. He would [also] back away when the bowler was in his bowling stride."

Even Wilf recognized these traits of character by referring in a tribute piece in Jim's Benefit Brochure to "the multitude of arguments which enliven existence in a dressing-room" and how "Jim Pressdee is prepared to fight tenaciously for whatever cause appeals to him." But, at the end of a summer when Glamorgan had mounted a sturdy challenge for the Championship crown, Jim's career with the Welsh county was over.

True to his word he settled in South Africa and played for North-East Transvaal until 1969/70. He also won the award of South African Cricketer of the Year in 1966 after a season when he claimed 33 wickets at just 16 runs apiece, besides striking a century. After retiring from playing at the end of the 1969/70 season, Jim focused his time on coaching at Springs High School for Boys, besides setting up a small workshop which repaired and made cricket bats.

Jim Pressdee is bowled by Peter Loader during Glamorgan's Championship encounter with Surrey in 1959.

Jim also made annual visits back to South Wales during the summer months and represented Wales in their representative matches between 1972 and 1977. His appearances included the match in June 1975 when Wales met East Africa as part of the latter's build-up for the Prudential World Cup. Despite being into his forties and not having played regular cricket for half a dozen years, Jim made an unbeaten 52 against the African cricketers.

During the 1980s, Jim returned to his native Swansea, and after a couple of seasons turning out for Mumbles he agreed to acted as captain and coach of the recently formed Glamorgan Colts side in the South Wales Cricket Association. In this capacity, he played a key role in the emergence of several players who went on to win the Sunday League under Hugh Morris' captaincy in 1993, as well as the Championship-winning team, led by Matthew Maynard in 1997, besides grooming players such as Steve James and Robert Croft who went to win England Test caps.

Jim was very much a coach of the old school. Besides strict discipline, Jim insisted on the correct dress before games and treating net sessions in the Indoor School at Neath as if they were real match situations. This meant that if you batted in full kit and if you were out, your batting practice ended there and then. On one occasion left-arm spinner Phil North made the long journey the night before back home to Newport after a 2nd XI match in Leeds. He rose early before driving to Neath for the nets. Wiping the sleep out his eyes, he walked into the nets only to be dismissed first ball. "Out you come" shouted Jim, much to Phil's consternation!

However, there was a jovial side to Jim's character, as this final tale from his career shows. It concerns another game at Llanelli, but this time in far happier times during 1964 when Glamorgan were playing Derbyshire. Ossie was trying to seek a positive outcome from a game already decimated by rain and with Glamorgan still to bat. The Glamorgan captain duly told his team that he intended to declare after one ball and asked for a volunteer to bat. Don agreed, with Jim wagering him five shillings that he couldn't score a run if he tried to bat left-handed instead of his normal right-handed grip. Derek Morgan duly lobbed the ball up, Shep scored a single and returned to much mirth and merriment in the Glamorgan changing room.

1950

Glamorgan's slide down the table continued in 1950 with the Welsh county ending up in 11th place. In their defence, they were hampered by bad weather with many games being rain-affected and nine out of the 28 Championship matches failing even to produce a decision on first innings. Despite rain delaying a start until 3.30pm on the opening day at Neath, there was still plenty of time for Glamorgan to dismantle the Derbyshire batting, with their 92-run victory over the Peakites being set-up by a seven-wicket match haul by Stan Trick.

However, the finest victory of the summer came at the Arms Park in early July where the rains stayed away for long enough to allow Glamorgan to complete their first-ever Championship victory against Middlesex. With Wilf Wooller sidelined with broken bones in his right-hand, Emrys Davies took the reins and skilfully guided the team to an 86-run victory, thanks to a fine all-round performance from Allan Watkins (Vol.2, p294-304) who made an unbeaten 98 besides taking four wickets in Middlesex's first innings.

Don Shepherd, the young fast bowler from the Gower, also took 5/74 before Glamorgan extended their lead and then set Middlesex a target of 252 in three hours. Their chase faltered against the acting captain's nagging bowling with the final wicket falling just four minutes before the close.

1950 was also a memorable year for Gilbert Parkhouse (Vol. 2, p319-327) as he won the first of seven Test caps, besides becoming Emrys Davies' new opening partner. Gilbert relished the move up the order and struck seven hundreds during the summer, including centuries in each innings against Somerset at the Arms Park. The 24 year-old followed this with another hundred against the Combined Services at Cardiff to become only the second batsman in the Club's history to score three successive hundreds, and by 17 June he had reached 1,000 runs in the shortest-ever time in the Club's history.

Emrys Davies, seen at Cardiff Arms Park in 1949.

There were other changes to the Glamorgan batting line-up in 1950 following the decision at the end of 1949 by Jimmy Eaglestone to return to London, whilst Phil Clift had contracted TB and missed the entire summer. Bernard Hedges was one of the young batsmen to be promoted into the 1st XI, whilst there were opportunities as well during 1950 in the bowling department with Wilf Wooller sidelined by injury and Johnnie Clay having retired. Jim McConnon, a former professional footballer, duly took the opportunity to stake a name for himself in county cricket before going on to win Test honours.

416
SHEPHERD, Donald John.

Born – Port Eynon, 12 August 1927.

Died – Swansea, 18 August 2017.

RHB, RFM/OB.

Professional.

Ed – Port Eynon Church School, Parkmill Elementary School and Gowerton County GS.

1st XI: 1950-1972.

2nd XI: 1948-1950.

Club and Ground: 1949-1972.

Cap: 1952; Benefit: 1960; Testimonial: 1968; Wisden Cricketer of the Year 1970.

Players 1952-1957; MCC 1953-1969/70; TN Pearce's XI 1956; South 1961;

Commonwealth XI 1967/68; International XI 1970/71.

Club: Swansea.

Batting and Fielding Record

	M	I	NO	RUNS	AV	100	50	CT	ST
F-c	647	816	241	5610	9.75	-	5	241	-
List A	73	43	20	190	8.26	-	-	18	-

Bowling Record

	Balls	M	R	W	AV	5wI	10wM
F-c	129138	7393	45571	2174	20.95	122	28
List A	3475	94	1937	99	19.56		

Career-bests

First-class –   73 v Derbyshire at Cardiff Arms Park, 1961.

9/47 v Northamptonshire at Cardiff Arms Park, 1954.

List A –   25* v Leicestershire at Coalville, 1970.

5/31 v Northamptonshire at Northampton, 1969.

Don Shepherd was the most successful bowler in the history of Glamorgan CCC, with the genial and warm-hearted cricketer taking more wickets than anyone else never to play Test cricket. Regarded by contemporaries as the finest bowler of his generation, Don claimed 2,174 wickets in a Club record 647 appearances in first-class cricket, at a shade over 20 runs apiece, with his record for the county speaking volumes for his canny skills, initially as a fast bowler and later as an off-cutter, besides his fitness and perseverance over a 23-year career with the Welsh county from 1950 until 1972.

In all, Don claimed 2,218 wickets in first-class cricket – a tally which places him 22nd on the all-time list of wicket-takers. Remarkably, he never won an England cap – something that confounded his county colleagues and legions of supporters and alike. When asked by friends about his omission, Don's answer was always the same "It didn't bother me. I never read the papers and I only wanted to play for Glamorgan".

"What's new about losing to Glamorgan" quips Barry Jarman, the Australian captain, on the balcony at St Helen's after Don Shepherd had led the Welsh county to another historic victory in 1948.

He also led Glamorgan to victory over the 1968 Australians, fittingly on his home patch at St Helen's, whilst in 1969 he was senior professional and right-hand man to Tony Lewis as Glamorgan won the Championship title. Tony put his immense success as a bowler down to Don settling "upon a style, a speed and an action that came naturally out of his mind and body: never strained, never too fast and certainly not too slow. It was as if someone had set a metronome ticking and left it running for over twenty years."

"He was a challenge for every batsman in the land, The off-cutters looked straightforward but they were a bundle of deception. He could produce the quick loop in flight, the cut of the ball into the stumps or the one which left the batsman with the identical finger action. On the very best batting pitches Don was a model of accuracy: frugal bowling that often prompted the suicide of fine stroke-makers... with a Commonwealth tour side to Pakistan he silenced a full house of over 20,000 spectators in steaming hot Multan by trapping the great Hanif Mohammad l.b.w. They said it had never happened before to Hanif at home."

In domestic cricket, Shep was fortunate to be assisted by a line of outstanding wicket-keepers, including Haydn Davies, David Evans and Eifion Jones each of whom were razor-sharp in their glovework and attentive enough to detect the way Don slightly dropped the angle of his bowling arm to subtly change his line of attack and, more often than not, extract an edge which they or the ring of close fielders would snaffle. With Peter Walker himself claiming 175 catches from Don's bowling alone, there were always plenty of chances for the leg-trap to feed upon, just like hungry vultures clustered around a carcass.

During the late 1960s, Don was also a fine lieutenant to captain Tony Lewis, who said "Don was a perfect advisor. His understanding of the game's wrinkles and the opponent's foibles was positive and helpful. To me, he was essential: a patriot and a perfectionist." Ossie Wheatley, Don's captain between 1961 and 1966, was equally fulsome in his praise "Don was a terrific chap off the field and it was a privilege to play with him. He was one of the greats of Welsh sport, and someone who played at a time when the BBC frequently televised the games Glamorgan played at home; he would have been a familiar face in everyone's front room across the country. In the newspapers in those days there would be a match report of at least half a page in both the morning and evening editions. He gave so much to cricket and Wales."

Don Shepherd, as seen in 1950.

Born in August 1927, he was the first of three children born to Jack and Lillian Shepherd who lived at Well Cottage in the village of Port Eynon on the Gower Peninsula. His maternal grandfather was the scorer for the village's cricket team, and it was George Howell who introduced young Don to cricket, with George proudly having his infant grandson sat alongside him on Saturday afternoons, and gleefully changing the tins on the rudimentary scoreboard in return for a toffee or other sweets from his doting grandfather.

Aged six or seven, young Don would also run up and bowl to the Port Eynon cricketers as they waited their turn to bat alongside the small hut they used as a Pavillion and hung their coats and other work clothes. Don had no formal coaching, and as befitted the title of his biography "Born to Bowl", he honed his mastery of line and length by bowling for hours on end with a tennis ball on the beach at his beloved Three Cliffs Bay – a place where he and his young friends would also run out into the water with nets during the evening in a bid to catch fish or instead swim in the balmy waters under the moonlight.

In 1935 Don's parents, now with Brian (born 1930) and Mavis (born 1934), moved to the village of Parkmill, 7 miles nearer Swansea to run the village shop which Don's paternal grandfather had created during the 1890s and to which had added a tearoom from which his grandmother had served refreshments to the thousands of visitors who flocked to the Gower each year. Don's father had initially been a miner before becoming the driver of the local mail van and bus.

Running the village shop and tea rooms was a very different matter for the Shepherd's, but to make things easier a new house, *Waterway,* was built alongside, whilst the original wooden structure was replaced by a more substantial brick property. As soon as they were old enough Don and his brother Brian undertook the daily delivery of newspapers. Little did he know that in the summers of late 1930s when running around with the papers containing the reports of the bowling feats of the likes of Clay and the two Davies', Emrys and Dai, that Don was building up his physique and strength that would help him erase their efforts from Glamorgan's record books.

There was plenty of time for Don to also further hone his cricketing skills, bowling at friends stood against a wicket, marked out in chalk, on a low wall outside the family's store – although in order not to upset his grandfather, a devout Wesleyan, no games were played on Sundays. Don also had plenty of opportunities to play informal games of cricket at Gowerton County Boys Grammar School, to which he had won a scholarship. Initially these happened at lunchtime, but extra play sessions arose during the afternoons as a result of shortened school hours and other disruptions associated with the air raids over Swansea. He also got an opportunity to play in a few formal games, with the opposition comprising other schools as well as RAF teams containing young airmen eager to take their minds off the more weightier matters on their minds

Don Shepherd practices his new bowling action, as an off-cutter, in the indoor nets along the corridor of the rugby stand at Cardiff Arms Park ahead of the 1956 season.

Despite his school having a proud rugby heritage, Don also played plenty football during the winter months and, as a youngster, was good enough to play for the Swansea Schoolboys team. He later had trials together with John Charles for Leeds United, with the pair spending a week in a bed and breakfast establishment in Elland Road. Legions of Glamorgan supporters were eternally grateful that it was John who got the nod and for Don, it was professional cricket that was to become his life.

But not before National Service and time initially in the Navy, with rounds of square bashing in Skegness and further training in Wigan before training as an air mechanic with the Fleet Air Arm. Don then undertook training on aircraft maintenance before joining the naval section at RAF Defford in Worcestershire. It was here during 1947 that his journey into professional cricket began, with Don's abilities as a fast-medium bowler in games for the airbase attracting the attention of officials from the Midlands county.

Worcestershire officials made contact with Don after he had impressed their former captain Maurice Jewell whilst he was umpiring the game between RAF Defford and the Gentlemen of Worcestershire in a match at Pershore. A trial duly followed one evening at New Road where he impressed other officials. The view was that the young Welshman could be the eventual replacement for Reg Perks, their seam bowler, who was poised to enter the latter stages of his successful county career

The offer of a place on the Worcestershire staff, plus a year on the MCC groundstaff duly came and with Don, at the time, having never seen a county game or any links with Glamorgan, he agreed terms. But news that a young Welshman was heading to Lord's came to the attention of Wilf Wooller. With the Welsh county seeking new bowling resources, Wilf arranged for George Lavis to meet up with Don, with the highly respected coach gently persuading Don that there was really only one county for which a proud Welshman could play. George also spoke with Worcestershire officials who were decent enough not to stand in Don's way and, after being demobbed, the twenty-year-old headed up to London as a young Glamorgan cricketer.

1948 saw Don continue his cricketing apprenticeship by playing in MCC out-matches, besides bowling to MCC members and visiting players in the pristine nets on the Nursery Ground. A week after the Welsh county had won the 1948 Championship title, Don was released from his groundstaff duties at Lord's to make his 2nd XI debut for Glamorgan in their Minor County Championship match against Devon at Exeter. He duly came on as second change with his raw pace surprising colleagues to the extend that Jack Rippon, the wicket-keeper from Swansea CC, having to leave the field with a damaged hand after misjudging how close he should stand to the debutant!

A few weeks later he was invited to attend some of the special functions arranged to celebrate the success of Wilf Wooller and his team. It gave him a chance to meet and mingle with the Championship-winning team, besides boosting his aspirations of playing alongside them in 1949. But the latter year saw Don continuing to learn his trade with Glamorgan 2nd XI. With Norman Hever and other seam bowlers staying fit, to say nothing of the indestructible nature of Wilf himself, the only opportunity which arose that summer was a place in the county's team for the two-day friendly against the RAF at Maindy Barracks.

Undeterred, Don spent the winter months in the makeshift indoor nets at Cardiff Arms Park, and it was here along the main corridor of the North Stand that, under the watchful gaze of George Lavis, he added a sharpness and finesse to his seam bowling. This was recognized by the correspondent of *The South Wales Evening Post* whose preview ahead of the 1950 season highlighted how "the most gratifying feature is the big improvement of Don Shepherd of Parkmill, who has been bowling as well as anyone in the nets. He has developed a good length and is making the ball move."

Don was duly rewarded at the end of April with a place in the Glamorgan line-up for their opening match of the season against Surrey at The Oval – a ground which in 1972 was to also see his final appearance in Championship cricket with Don leading the Glamorgan side in his last first-class game. Returning to

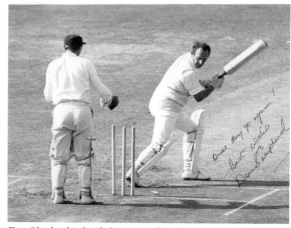

Don Shepherd is bowled in a match at Swansea.

events of 1950, it had been an inauspicious start for Don as play did not commence until three o'clock on the second day. Don then went wicketless in ten overs before being dismissed for a duck. His first victim eventually came during the fourth match of the summer, against Leicestershire at Pontypridd where, on a spin-friendly surface, he had Ken Smith caught behind by Haydn Davies in the visitor's second innings before clean bowling Maurice Tompkin.

In his fifth match he was entrusted with the new ball and a few weeks later he claimed a maiden five-for as Don took 5/74 at the Arms Park as the Welsh county recorded their first-ever victory over Middlesex. Nevertheless, his first two summers of Championship cricket yielded just 49 and 31 wickets respectively. Whilst he was economical, it was his ability to take wickets which needed further refinement, and after further intensive work in the nets over the winter months with George Lavis, 1952 proved to be his most successful summer in his quicker mode.

In all, he claimed 120 wickets in 1952 at just 22 runs apiece, was presented with his county cap, and was also chosen to appear for the Players against the Gentlemen at the Scarborough Festival. His breakthrough summer also saw him claim three ten-wicket hauls, starting in June with 11/101 against Lancashire at Preston – a performance which saw Don win his cap. He followed this with 10/113 against Essex at Westcliff-on-Sea plus a remarkable 10/40 in the game with Nottinghamshire at the Arms Park with Don's second innings haul of 6/18 becoming a new personal best.

His reward after an outstanding summer was an opportunity to open the bowling with Alec Bedser at the Scarborough Festival in a side led by Len Hutton. Don took four wickets in the Gentlemen's first innings and delivered the final over in a thrilling finale with the Gents needing 13 to win and the Players two wickets. Walter Robins clattered the first two balls to the boundary but the next four balls yielded just three runs. Don had held his nerve and proved he could play with the best.

In many ways, this match was the pinnacle of his career as a seam bowler as Don met with less success in the next two summers, taking 74 wickets in 1953 and 79 in 1954. However there were two standout performances in the latter season – a haul of 11/76 against Somerset at Weston-super-Mare, plus career-best figures of 9/47 against Northants in muggy conditions at the Arms Park. Don was able to extract lavish away swing in the humidity, which more than compensated for the lack of seam movement. At the time his figures were the second best in the Club's history and by a curious coincidence, the only bowler with superior figures – Jack Mercer who took all ten at Worcester in 1936 – was the visiting scorer that day with the Northants notcher one of the first to congratulate Don on his feat as the players and officials gathered for lunch.

It was though around this time that Don had started to find it difficult to regularly hit the seam. Haydn Davies had already spotted that Don's wrist had become quite floppy, just like Johnnie Clay before him. The perceptive wicket-keeper had quietly suggested during a conversation with Wilf that Don should copy Johnnie and change his mode to off-spin, but 'The Skipper' had not welcomed the idea – "Let him learn his trade first" he gruffly replied.

With Don still finding it hard to land the ball on the seam during 1955, Len Muncer having retired and Jim McConnon struggling with fitness and a series of recurring injuries, there was now an opportunity for Don to experiment with a slower style. With little at stake as the season drew to a close, Haydn spoke to Wilf again. This time his suggestion met with a favourable reply, and for the next few weeks, the captain, wicket-keeper and novitiate spinner spent time in the nets practicing and honing the new skills.

Like a Mother Superior happy that one of her charges was ready to go out into the wider world, Wilf was satisfied by late August that Don was ready to bowl in his new style. He duly bowled his off-cutters for the first time against Leicestershire at the Arms Park – a match in which a fresh-faced Tony Lewis also made his Championship debut for Glamorgan.

As Douglas Miller wrote in his superb biography of Don, "though Glamorgan lost the Leicestershire match by ten wickets, they had taken two steps that would set them on a course towards a more prosperous future. They had introduced as a seventeen year-old the man who fourteen years later would lead them once more to the Championship title, and for the first time they had encouraged Don to bowl in the style that would make him the county's most successful wicket-taker of all time. One week he was a journeyman seamer, the next he was on the way to becoming one of the great bowlers of the modern game and one of only ten cricketers to take 2,000 wickets in the post-War years."

The master craftsman at work – Don Shepherd bowling in the late 1960s and watched by umpire Arthur Fagg.

The closing game of the season, against Warwickshire at Neath saw Don dramatically reap the rewards for the change and long hours of practice. He claimed 6/40 and 4/45 – the first of 22 ten-wicket hauls in his slower style. There was no looking back as the dye was set for one of the most productive summers any Glamorgan has ever experienced since the Second World War.

1956 duly saw Don claim 168 wickets for the Welsh county, including taking more than five wickets in an innings on fifteen occasions. Amongst his outstanding innings returns were figures of 7/67 against Lancashire at Old Trafford, 7/48 against Nottinghamshire at the Arms Park and 8/33 in the game at the same ground against Hampshire, as well as match figures at Cardiff of 12/136 against Surrey.

With everything going right for Don, he no longer had to worry about his form As he recalled, "it seemed to me that I was always on hand and ready to bowl, and there were very few occasions when I didn't get wickets. I had the knowledge that I had great fielders around as well. And I always knew I was going to have a good bowl. The pressure was off, the fear of not bowling well and someone else jumping in."

His tall, flowing action, allowed him to extract both bounce and turn, plus a miserly attitude to conceding runs saw Don taking it almost as a personal affront if a batsmen freely scored runs form his bowling or horror of horrors, hit him back over his head for four or six. Indeed, his parsimony can be gauged from the fact that 7,393 of his 21,523 overs in first-class cricket for Glamorgan were maidens, with the Club's scorebooks being filled with tens of thousands of dot balls as visiting batsmen tried to come to terms with his subtle changes of pace and angle.

Over the course of the next sixteen summers, he proved to be a match-winner on turning pitches, as testified by a series of remarkable returns, including 6/5 against Nottinghamshire at Newport in 1961, 5/2 against Leicestershire at Ebbw Vale in 1965 and 7/7 against Hampshire at the Arms Park in 1966, whilst he also took a hat-trick against Northants at Swansea in 1964. Add to this, match returns of 12/76 against Yorkshire at Cardiff in 1957, 11/54 versus Warwickshire at Swansea in 1960, 10/56 in the match with Middlesex at Neath in 1960, 11/86 against Hampshire at Bournemouth in 1961, 11/51 in a very low-scoring game against Gloucestershire at Margam in 1962, 12/129 in the contest at Northampton in 1963, plus 11/83 against Northants at Cardiff Arms Park in 1965 and the final ten-wicket haul of his career – 12/89 versus Warwickshire at Edgbaston in 1970.

His finest hour as a spinner came at St Helen's against Yorkshire during June 1965, as Glamorgan recorded a 31-run victory inside two days. It was also a game which saw Don and his spin partner Jim Pressdee, each take nine wickets in an innings – the only time in a first-class match where a pair of bowlers have achieved this feat. Their remarkable performance saw Jim claim nine wickets in the first innings before Don opened the bowling and took nine in their second.

As all of these remarkable statistics show, Don was equally effective on pitches at home and away, dispelling the urban myth that Don was only the bane of visiting batsmen on the sandy pitches of St Helen's, or at the Arms Park if Wilf instructed the groundsman to use a little bit more sand than normal in his pitch preparation! There were many factors contributing to his success in bamboozling so many batsmen with his subtle wiles, not least that his off-cutters were delivered at a quicker pace than usual, with subtle variations in the angle of his arm and the release of the ball from his hand.

Don also asked his wicketkeepers – the outstanding triumvirate of Haydn Davies, David Evans and Eifion Jones – to stand back from the stumps to compensate for the additional speed compared with a traditional spin bowler where the keeper would be standing up. This explains why Haydn took 86 catches but only 7 stumpings to Don's bowling, whilst David claimed 117 catches and 6 stumpings, with Eifion making 65 catches and 5 stumpings.

Some saw this ploy of standing back as a negative tactic, but for Don, if a batsman was frustrated and tied down, he was more than likely to play a rash shot, miscue an aggressive blow or lose concentration and edge a ball into the leg-trap or into the slips. With the keeper standing back, it might that the slips could be wider, so Haydn claimed many catches diving at where a traditional spinners slip would stand, allow the likes of Gilbert

Don Shepherd, flanked by Peter Walker and Ossie Wheatley, celebrates taking his 2,000th first-class wicket for Glamorgan during the game against Worcestershire at Sophia Gardens in 1969.

Parkhouse and others to take catches at a normal second slip rather than first.

As befitted a thinking bowler, Don was a shrewd observer of opposing batsmen with his gimlet-eyed analysis swiftly identifying their strengths, weaknesses and predilections for a particular stroke. In 1960, with Gilbert Parkhouse injured and Allan Watkins preferring not to take command, Don cut his teeth as the county's captain, leading the side against Essex at Westcliff as well as in an eventful contest with Lancashire at Aigburth in Liverpool. As far as the latter game was concerned, Glamorgan were without a win in nine games whilst the Red Rose county were riding high in the Championship table and challenging Yorkshire for the title. In Bob Barber and Geoff Pullar, they had a pair of Test batsmen and with Brian Statham and Ken Higgs sharing the new ball, they had a formidable attack. Indeed, the new ball duo were soon making inroads as after Don had won the toss and opted to bat, Glamorgan were floundering at 26-5, with Bernard Hedges – Don's room-mate for so many years – the only recognised batsman remaining. But Bernard got stuck in with a fine 83 to wrest the initiative back in what proved to be a low-scoring game.

On the final day, Lancashire were left with a target of 190, but after a fine team effort by the Welsh attack, and some shrewd captaincy they fell fifty runs short. It was the first away win of the season, and having beaten a top-class side, Don was naturally pleased as punch. But, as he later recalled, "It was an exceptional effort and when you get that sort of effort from everybody it makes it all worthwhile. I got on the phone to Cardiff hoping to keep us together for the next game but I got a flea in my ear from Wilf over some matter or other, and instead was told that six of the team had been dropped for the next game!"

Don had few pretentions as a batsman, and adopted a quite rustic style, opting for blows using the long-handle rather than tentative prods. In 816 innings, he scored 5610 runs and struck five first-class fifties, including a career-best 73 against Derbyshire at the Arms Park in 1961. He also had a record of 156 ducks to his name in all cricket, but in 1964 he struck a six from the last ball to give Glamorgan a one-wicket win in their Gillette Cup match with Worcestershire at Newport As with his bowling, his greatest moment with the bat also came at his beloved St Helen's where against the 1961 Australians, he entered the record books as a batsman as, to the delight of a packed St Helen's, he equaled the world record for the fastest fifty in first-class cricket, racing to his half-century in just fifteen minutes and all whilst sporting a black eye having top-edged a ball from Gloucestershire's David Allen into his eye in the previous match at Pontypridd. In the modern era, with head injury assessments and the like, Don would probably have been told to take a rest and miss the tourist game, but these were very different days and, with the help of a few aspirins, Don duly took his place in the team, despite having his eye still half-shut.

Typically, he did not want to let the team down and, to the delight of a packed crowd, he raced to his fifty with six massive sixes, each struck in his typically no-nonsense way. As the consummate team man and senior professional, Don was never one to boast about his personal achievements either with bat or ball. "I just had a bit of luck and a good old swing with the bat that day," he would modestly say when asked about events that August afternoon at Swansea in 1961. Whereas other players take great delight in bragging about their performances, Don would just unashamedly smile, with the glint in his eye being the only additional sign about how he felt about his place in the game's batting records.

Another couple of his proudest days in Glamorgan's ranks came at Swansea where in 1964 Shep claimed nine wickets during the victory over the Australians, before four years later, he acted as the stand-in captain for Tony Lewis, as he led the county to their historic double over the men in baggy green caps, with the 79-run victory being a tribute to his subtle tactics and shrewd bowling changes as he set the Australians a target of 360 on the final day.

1969 was great year for Wales with the investiture of the Prince of Wales and for the man dubbed in the press as "The Prince of Wiles", Don enjoyed a wonderful summer

Don Shepherd, as seen in 1972 – his final summer as a Glamorgan player.

himself as Glamorgan's vice-captain and senior professional as the Club won the County Championship, sealing victory by defeating Worcestershire at Sophia Gardens. It was very special game for Don as he claimed his 2,000th wicket in first-class cricket – with Jim Yardley departing most fittingly 'c Walker b Shepherd' - in the visitors' first innings before in the second dismissing Brian Brain, the Worcestershire tail-ender, to clinch the victory which sealed the Championship title for Glamorgan.

Captured by the BBC Wales television cameras, the black and white footage, with Wilf Wooller's jubilant commentary, has provided iconic images for Welsh sporting history, as well as reminders of the simple and joyful days without any histrionics or high-fives by fielders and bowlers as in the modern era. Rather than any over-the-top celebrations at having taken the wicket to clinch the title, Don calmly walked across to mid-wicket to shake hands and hug his captain and great friend Tony Lewis.

A regular selection for the Players against the Gentlemen at the Scarborough Festival, Don had been chosen for the MCC against the 1957 West Indians in a game regarded as something of a trial for the forthcoming Tests. However, he went wicketless and probably set in train the misguided notion that he was only successful on helpful Welsh pitches.

International honours never came his way, leaving many speechless and confounded about the way the England selectors never gave Don the nod. His exclusion puzzled contemporaries in whom he was held in the highest of esteem. "Had he been an Australian," Richie Benaud once said, "he would have played for his country many, many times," whilst John Arlott, the doyen of broadcasters and journalists during Don's long and distinguished career, when asked to write an article on the best XI never to play for England, described Don's regular omission as "simply inexplicable."

Don's outstanding efforts with Glamorgan were however recognized by Wisden for whom he was one of their Cricketers of the Year in 1970, whilst he toured Pakistan with a Commonwealth XI in 1967/68, as well as visiting Ceylon and the Far East with the MCC in 1969/70 alongside Tony Lewis and Alan Jones. Despite constantly being overlooked Don was never bitter about not getting a chance to play Test cricket. "It never worried me not playing for England," he said in a special programme broadcast on BBC Wales to celebrate his 90th birthday. "There were so many terrific off-spinners around – Fred Titmus, David Allen, John Mortimore, Ray Illingworth – and they could all bat, while I was a bit of a slogger. I was happy enough doing what I did and what happened to me through my life."

Don Shepherd receives a special presentation from members of the Metropolitan Cricket Club in Lusaka during Glmaorgan's end of season tour to Zambia in 1972.

Late in his career came the fresh challenge of regular one-day cricket. Since 1963 there had been the small number of Gillette Cup matches, but from 1969, there were regular 40 overs matches on a Sunday. It put an end to the Benefit matches, the rounds of golf or strolls around the Gower with his young family which had filled previous Sundays. But Don took to the new format like a duck to water, claiming 5/31 in the inaugural John Player Sunday League game at Northampton before regularly returning economical figures to prove, that for one of the finest bowlers of his generation, the new format was simply business as usual.

When Glamorgan did not renew his contract at the end of the 1972 season, there was speculation that he might see out his years playing in the Lancashire Leagues. But instead, Don returned to his roots on the Gower and ran the family's shop in Parkmill for the next two decades. For many Glamorgan supporters, a visit to the Gower was not complete without visiting Shepherd's to buy an ice-cream or some sweets from the iconic Welsh cricketer, and having a quick chat with the Glamorgan legend.

Don also acted as a commentator and summariser on both television and radio, besides writing for local and national newspapers, with his mellow tones and perceptive analysis alongside his great friend Edward Bevan, the BBC Wales cricket correspondent, bringing a huge audience for "Sunday Spin" as a new generation of Glamorgan cricket fans were able to share Don's wisdom during radio coverage of the Welsh county's one-day matches.

During the late 1980s Don also acted as Glamorgan's bowling coach and, in his typically unassuming way, acted as a mentor for aspiring spinners such as Robert Croft, besides helping Steve Barwick to also switch from seam to off-cutters. Indeed, Don was summoned one afternoon during a match against Somerset as the public address announcer at Taunton, said "Please could Mr Don Shepherd make his way to the Away Changing Room!" He swiftly answered the call and carefully advised Barwick and the Glamorgan captain about the fielding positions needed for his new style of off-cutters.

In the truest sense of the word, Don was a gentleman, and whilst contemporaries described him as a hard and tough professional with ball in hand, off the field you could not wish for a more kind and gentle soul, and someone who put family values at the top of his agenda, and someone who always had time for others as befitted the proud husband of Joan Evans, who he had married in September 1953, the father of Mark (who himself was a fine bowler in club cricket and for Glamorgan 2nd XI) plus daughters Vicky, Debbie and Mandy, as well as six grandchildren.

In 2009 Don received a Lifetime Achievement Award from BBC Wales, with the 40th anniversary of the 1969 County Championship win being marked by Don receiving the award from Majid Khan, the Club's great overseas player that summer and now a TV executive in Pakistan. His final appearance at a Glamorgan match came on 3rd August 2017 when he, together with colleagues from the Championship-winning team of 1969, were at Sophia Gardens to join the guard of honour ahead of the Welsh county's Twenty20 match against Gloucestershire as the Welsh county celebrated fifty years of county cricket at the Cardiff ground. Eleven days later, he celebrated his ninetieth birthday, before entering hospital for what should have been a short stay and a routine operation. On being admitted to the ward, the sister came round to check details and, after asking Don his date of birth , she said "Ah, so you are eighty-nine," to which Don replied "No, I'm ninety," and then after a short pause "not out!"

Sadly, Don died in hospital a few days later with confirmation of his passing coming late on the evening after the champagne corks had been flying at Sophia Gardens with Glamorgan clinching a home quarter-final in the NatWest T20 Blast. His death was greeted on social media with a flood of warm tributes from Glamorgan players past and present with Robert Croft leading the heartfelt comments by saying "a light has gone out with the passing of the Great Don Shepherd. Some never meet their heroes. I did and Shep was 100 times more."

The next day on BBC Radio's Test Match Special, Geoff Boycott, the former Yorkshire and England batsman, paid the following tribute – "Don was a wonderful bowler, and not the easiest to read. Glamorgan were an unfashionable county at the time and Don deserved on merit to have played for England." Sky's cricket commentator and former England batsman David Lloyd also said "Don was one of the great men of the game," whilst cricket writer Scyld Berry said in the *Sunday Telegraph* "Don was a lovely, lovely man – the sport in its richness is so fondly recalled because of the likes of Shep."

In the *Sunday Times*, their correspondent Simon Wilde described Don as "A giant of Welsh cricket who would have thrived in England colours – a brilliant bowler and a true gentlemen. Nobody has taken more first-class wickets than he did without playing Test cricket and in eras when England were less well-blessed than they were in the 1950s, it is hard to imagine he would not only have played but thrived due to his tireless accuracy."

The day before the Welsh county appeared at Twenty20 Finals Day at Edgbaston, Don's funeral took place at All Saints' church in Oystermouth, with the Glamorgan legend being given a highly fitting send-off by family, friends and colleagues. Canon Keith Evans, who officiated at the service, summed up everyone's feeling about the man, as well as the outstanding cricketer, by saying: "Don was one of life's true gentlemen; despite being a giant of the sporting world he was always very grounded and modest. Your presence here, in such large numbers, is probably the greatest tribute that can be paid to Don and reflects the respect in which he was held." He then finished by reading a most apt statement from Don's family: "He had time and a smile on his face for everyone. He loved people and would spend time chatting to everyone. He used to say, 'a smile costs nothing'. He was such a lovely man. We are the lucky ones to have had him. What a privilege it was. He was our hero."

417
McCONNON, James Edward

Born – Burnopfield, County Durham, 21 June 1922.
Died – Altrincham, 26 January 2003.
Professional.
RHB, OB.
Ed – Broome School, Durham.
1st XI: 1950-1961.
2nd XI: 1950.
Club and Ground: 1949-1961.
Cap: 1951.
England 1954 (2 Caps); Cheshire 1962-1964.
Clubs: Burnopfield, Newport.

Batting and Fielding Record

	M	I	NO	RUNS	AV	100	50	CT	ST
F-c	243	350	38	4514	14.70	-	13	143	-

Bowling Record

	Balls	M	R	W	AV	5wI	10wM
F-c	35901	1584	15656	799	19.59	49	12

Career-bests
First-class – 95 v Middlesex at Cardiff Arms Park, 1958.
     8/36 v Nottinghamshire at Trent Bridge, 1953.

Spin bowler Jim McConnon played a leading role in Glamorgan's dramatic win over the 1951 Springboks at Swansea – one of the most remarkable victories in the Club's history.

The South Africans were chasing what seemed a quite modest victory target of 147 and, at tea on the second day, they appeared to be well on course at 54 without loss. But captain Wilf Wooller and wicket-keeper Haydn Davies were convinced that all was not lost, with parts of the wicket starting to crumble. During the interval, they chivvied the softly spoken off-spinner – "Just remember to drop the ball on that rough spot on the wicket Jim, and we'll win" were their words of advice. With plenty of vocal support from Haydn, Jim responded with an astonishing spell of 6/10, including a hat-trick as in the space of three quarters of an hour the South Africans collapsed to 83 all out as Glamorgan became the only county side to defeat the Springboks on their tour.

Jim McConnon, as seen in 1950 following his switch to professional cricket.

1951 was Jim's second summer of Championship cricket, having made his county debut the previous season, at the age of twenty-eight. His rather late entry into the first-class game was the result of the Durham-born sportsman having previously been a professional footballer with Aston Villa. The Birmingham-based football club also had a cricket team which played games against a variety of opponents in the West Midland, including an annual friendly against Worcestershire and in August 1939 Jim claimed five wickets with his seam bowling at New Road. In 1945 he also appeared for a Northamptonshire XI against a Birmingham Festival XI at Edgbaston.

The centre-half subsequently signed for Lovells Athletic in the Welsh League, but a knee injury forced Jim to give up football. Just as one door closed, another opened, as Jim's cricketing career with Newport CC blossomed, and his abilities as an attacking batsman and tall seam bowler drew the attention of Glamorgan's talent scouts.

During the winter of 1948/49, he was invited to the county's makeshift nets along one of the corridors of the North Stand at the Arms Park, where under the wise guidance of Glamorgan's coach George Lavis, Jim transferred his bowling talents into off-spin, fully utilizing his height, flowing natural action and exceptionally long fingers.

As winter turned into spring, Jim had sufficiently impressed George for an offer of a contract with the Welsh county. Terms were agreed in a rather unconventional way one evening during a practice session in the North Stand. A message came from Wilf Wooller for Jim to pop up to his flat in Westgate Street, overlooking the Arms Park. As Jim later recalled, "I went in, wondering what he might be able to offer me, and I heard this sizzling noise. And there was Wilf, with a frying pan, cooking up some bacon and eggs for the two of us. 'Now look,' he said, 'why don't you come down and have some games with us?' " The pair then discussed the terms of a contract with Glamorgan and a few days later, everything was agreed and signed.

1949 saw Jim continue his apprenticeship in the Glamorgan 2nd XI, as well as in the Club and Ground side, where he played some decent innings including 70 against the South Wales and Monmouthshire League side at Gowerton, as well as 77 against Swansea CC. Later in the summer he also appeared in Glamorgan's two-day friendly against the RAF at Maindy Barracks.

Jim McConnon, seen bowling during 1954.

He made his first-class debut for Glamorgan against Surrey at The Oval at the start of the 1950 season, ironically in the same match as Don Shepherd, then a fiery fast bowler. Jim though was still a work in progress and having taken 33 wickets in his maiden season, Jim spent many long hours in the Indoor School, further perfecting his new arts. The extended practice paid off as he claimed 136 wickets during 1951 besides proving himself to be a fine fielder in the gully.

As witnessed by the dramatic victory over the Springboks, Jim formed a potent partnership with Len Muncer. Jim's return including figures of 6/10. Given his physique and sharp powers of spin, comparisons were made to Johnnie Clay, another tall and gaunt off-spinner who had admirable flight that deceived opposing batsmen. As Allan Watkins' observed Jim "didn't have to float it, it floated naturally because he was so tall."

That summer Jim also found a soul-mate in Willie Jones, another insecure character who like Jim would doubt his abilities and was racked at times by nerves. Fortunately, Wilf Wooller had swiftly recognized these traits and whilst being short, explosive and even dismissive when dealing with other bowlers, 'The Skipper' would be gentle, supportive, understanding and quite thoughtful when dealing with the man, dubbed by colleagues as 'Jimmy Mac'.

A re-occurrence of his old knee injury led to Jim missing much of the 1952 season, but he soon made up for lost time the following summer by taking 97 wickets, including a career best 8/36 against Nottinghamshire at Trent Bridge. He might have even made it past the 100-mark had he not become reluctant to bowl on unresponsive surfaces, such as the one at Grace Road as Glamorgan ended the season at Leicester. As Phil Clift recalled "we'd had a glorious spell and the wicket was concrete hard and Wilf said to Jim 'Come and have a bowl'. But Jim replied 'No Skipper, it's no good to me!' "

Despite these self-doubts and quirks of character, Jim's name was increasingly being mentioned as a potential England player. Wilf Wooller, the Glamorgan skipper, regarded Jim as a match-winning spin bowler, and there was confirmation that Jim was an aspiring Test player when he was selected for the Commonwealth side on their tour to India in 1953/54. Sadly, Jim's knee injury flared up again whilst in the sub-continent, and he was forced home early, but he was fit again by the start of the 1954 season, and further added to his growing reputation by taking 105 wickets. His hauls that summer included 5/16 against Northamptonshire at the Arms Park, 9/68 against Leicestershire at Swansea, 7/96 against Nottinghamshire at Trent Bridge and 7/23 against Surrey at The Oval.

In 1954 the off-spinner duly made his England debut in the Third Test against Pakistan at Old Trafford – in so doing he became the sixth Glamorgan cricketer to win Test honours and the first professional spin bowler. He began in confident vein, taking 3 for 12 in a six-over spell, before retaining his place for the Fourth Test at The Oval. This time he returned figures of 9-2-35-0 and 14-5-20-1 with several half chances going abegging. Shrewd commentators observed that had he been bowling like that in a county game, Glamorgan's outstanding leg-trap would have snaffled the chances without any fuss.

Jim McConnon in his England blazer during the MCC's tour to Australia and New Zealand in 1954/55.

Another Jim – Surrey's Laker – was also in the frame for the tour that winter to Australia and New Zealand, but the England selectors had been wooed by the superb flight of the Glamorgan bowler, and it was this natural attribute which saw Jim head Down Under in the winter of 1954/55. But like Gilbert Parkhouse before him, it proved to be an unhappy time in the Southern Hemisphere.

All seemed well at first as Jim began the Australian leg of the tour with 6/57 against a Western Australian Country XI, followed by some promising spells in the matches against state teams. But then came two nasty injuries – firstly, Jim spent a week in hospital after being struck a painful blow on the lower body whilst fielding at silly mid-on, then shortly after Christmas he badly fractured the little finger of his right hand during a match at Hobart. The medical opinion was that it would take several weeks to heal properly and, with Jim unlikely to be fit until the final two weeks of the tour in New Zealand, the tour management agreed that it would be best for the off-spinner to return home without further adding to his number of Test caps.

In fact, he never played in international cricket again, besides suffering from further niggling injuries. His lack of confidence also become something of a hindrance with Jim, when fit, still fretting about bowling on good wickets. Bernard Hedges remembered how, if a right-handed batsman started to go after Jim, he would murmur "This is a left-handers pitch" as he walked past his colleagues. Others reflected on observations from Jim's time in the England camp when it had been said by some that in the heat of battle, nerves let him down.

With Wilf Wooller's patience starting to run thin over Jim's injury record, Glamorgan's officials became uncertain about offering a contract unless he underwent a full medical. In response, Jim – who was always concerned about how he was going to financially look after his family – told the Glamorgan committee that he intended to quit county cricket and having agreed terms with Burnley would be playing in the Lancashire Leagues in 1957. The Glamorgan Yearbook noted "he has terminated his meteoric rise to fame in the cricket world in an equally rapid manner."

He enjoyed a memorable summer as Burnley won the League, with Jim taking 52 wickets at 6.8 apiece, besides gaining almost gladiatorial status with posters proclaiming

'Jim McConnon versus Everton Weekes' when the club met rivals Bacup. Away from the pressure cooker environment of county cricket, Jim had enjoyed himself once again with ball and bat in hand, but most important of all he had proved to those who had doubted it that he was fit enough to play the game. With his family still living in Newport, he was delighted when Glamorgan approached him about a return to the Welsh county in 1957.

He duly formed a highly successful partnership with Don Shepherd, who had converted to spin from seam the previous summer. To colleagues, he also appeared to thrive on a little bit of rivalry with his spin partner. At the start of the summer, Wilf would usually throw the ball to Jim ahead of Don, but after his meteoric summer the previous year and further wicket-laden spells in 1957, it was Shep who became regarded as the senior spinner. Allan Watkins remembered Jim often making a bid for the end offering more assistance to the spinners." 'Why aren't I at that end', he would often say to Wilf." But the

A group of Glamorgan cricketers seen relaxing outside the Diglis Hotel in Worcester in 1956 – left to right, Don Shepherd, Peter Walker, Gilbert Parkhouse and Jim McConnon.

captain's tactics seemed to get the best out of Jim as he took 99 wickets in 1957, followed by 113 at just 18 apiece in 1959.

It may have been no coincidence that around this time Jim also developed into a forceful late order batsman, striking a career-best 95 against Middlesex at the Arms Park in 1958. Jim seemed to enjoy batting at the Cardiff ground as three years before, he had hit 28 runs in an over during the county's match against Sussex, smashing two sixes and four fours in a whirlwind assault on Ian Thomson's bowling that also saw Jim pull a ball from the Sussex bowler onto the roof of an 80-foot high block of flats that adjoined the ground.

Jim took a Benefit Year in 1961, and then retired from Championship cricket. For the next six years played Minor County cricket for Cheshire besides coaching at Stonyhurst, before subsequently working for Guinness alongside Brian Statham. Jim, and his wife Pauline, had three children, Michael, Catherine and Christopher.

418
HEDGES, Bernard.

Born – Pontypridd, 10 November 1927.
Died – Mumbles, 8 February 2014.
RHB, RM.
Ed – Pontypridd County Boys School.
Professional.
1st XI: 1950-1967.
2nd XI: 1949-1967.
Club and Ground: 1951-1962.
Cap: 1954; Benefit: 1963.
RAF 1948; Wales 1969.
Clubs: Pontypridd, Neath, Pontarddulais, Glamorgan Nomads and Ynysygerwn.

Batting and Fielding Record

	M	I	NO	RUNS	AV	100	50	CT	ST
F-c	422	744	41	17733	25.22	21	84	200	-
List A	7	7	1	250	41.67	1	1	4	-

Bowling Record

	Balls	M	R	W	AV	5wI	10wM
F-c	572	24	260	3	86.67	-	-
List A	228	13	134	8	16,75	-	-

Career-bests

First-class 182 v Oxford University at Oxford, 1967.
 1/16 v Oxford University at Oxford, 1967.
List A 103* v Somerset at Cardiff Arms Park, 1963.
 2/17 v Somerset at Cardiff Arms Park, 1963.

Bernard Hedges had an eighteen-year career in first-class cricket, sandwiched between Glamorgan's two Championship-winning seasons, during which time he amassed 17,733 runs with his tally putting him in seventh place on the all-time list of run scorers for the Welsh county, besides writing his name into the Club's record books by scoring their first-ever century in a one-day game with an unbeaten 103 against Somerset in their Gillette Cup match at Cardiff Arms Park.

During his outstanding career between 1950 and 1967, the top-order batsman struck 21 centuries in first-class cricket for Glamorgan – all on uncovered wickets and a total exceeded by only eleven other batsmen for the Club – with a Championship best score of 141 against Kent at Swansea in 1961, as well as 144 against the 1962 Pakistanis at the Arms Park.

No surprise therefore that he was described by his contemporaries as a real street-fighter, and a most technically correct batsman in whatever circumstances. Yet despite these attributes and his consistency, there were no England call-ups or selection on a

Bernard Hedges, seen on the balcony of the Pavillion at Swansea.

Bernard Hedges pulls a ball to the boundary whilst batting in a Championship match at Neath.

winter tour with the MCC. For much of his career, Glamorgan were an unfashionable county with their highest position during his playing career being 1963 when, under Ossie Wheatley, they were runners-up in the County Championship. He was missing from their line-up through illness when the Glamorgan team defeated the 1964 Australians at Swansea, and he had retired to take up a job with Barclaycard by the time the Welsh county repeated the trick four years later at St Helen's.

Nevertheless, he was a loyal servant of the daffodil county and developed into a reliable and brave opening batsman who forged vibrant and successful opening partnerships, initially with Gilbert Parkhouse and subsequently with Alan Jones. He never shirked away from the challenges of facing the pace and fury of bowlers such as Fred Trueman, Frank Tyson or Brian Statham who, armed with a shiny new ball thrived on the green, damp and occasionally spiteful wickets in these days when batsmen played without helmets and relied on a good eye, swift reflexes plus a calm head.

Bernard possessed all of these attributes as well as a range of powerful strokes, to the extent that he often outscored his more illustrious partners. Like many short men – he stood at around 5 foot 7 inches – Bernard's armoury of strokes included a rasping square cut, plus savage pulls, sweetly-timed straight drives off the front foot, as well as punched drives off the back foot to any deliveries short of a length outside off stump.

His level-headed temperament and sound technique also helped him counter the wiles of the spin bowlers who reveled in this era of uncovered pitches, with Bernard employing the sweep stroke to good effect on many occasions, especially in the second innings of these three-day games when the instructions from Wilf Wooller were to go for quick runs in order to set-up a run-chase later in the day.

Known for his stiff-legged walk to the wicket, he played without any flamboyance with the simplicity and purity of his method being also reflected in his honest approach, always walking if he edged the ball into a fielder's hands, never waiting around for the umpire to uphold an appeal. On more than one occasion, he even made the unprecedented move to start walking off when an l.b.w. appeal was being made – in his own mind, he was out, simple as that and although other colleagues may have questioned his actions, that was the way Bernard played the game – a true Corinthian and a gentleman professional whose approach was akin more to the amateurs rather than his colleagues in the paid ranks.

He was in prime form during the early 1960s, amassing 2,026 runs in 1961 to become only the second batsman in Glamorgan's history to reach this notable milestone, with his tally just 45 runs short of the Club record set two years before by his opening partner Gilbert Parkhouse. He proved that his efforts in 1961 were not a flash in the pan by making 1,851 runs the following year. In all, he passed a thousand runs every season between 1956 and 1963 and a hallmark of his consistency at the top of the order was that in the latter season, he reached this milestone without scoring a century.

Bernard was born in Pontypridd in November 1927 – the eldest of eight children born to Jack and Gwen Hedges and raised in a small council house in the Rhydyfelin district of the former iron-making centre of South Wales. His family's roots lay in North Cardiff where his great-grandfather had been mine host of the Royal Exchange Public House in Llandaff North. His grandfather had initially worked at the Melingriffith Tin Works at Whitchurch before heading north up the Taff Valley to Pontypridd to work as an engine driver.

Besides working at local collieries Jack Hedges had played as a scrum-half for Pontypridd. He named his first son after his own brother who had died fighting in the Great War for the King's Shropshire Light Infantry and whose body was never found. Four sisters and three brothers duly followed as Bernard progressed from the local primary school to Pontypridd County School for Boys. He commenced his secondary education shortly after the start of the Second World War, and despite the call-up of several young and agile masters, there were sufficient teachers, as well facilities, to encourage and satisfy the sporting desires of Bernard and his friends.

The winter saw Bernard play both rugby and association football for his school, as well as the local youth club, whilst in the summer, it was cricket. His batting prowess saw Bernard chosen in the Welsh Secondary Schools side for their match against a Glamorgan Colts side at Cardiff Arms Park in 1945, besides being invited to the Indoor Nets in the North Stand at the Arms Park, where George Lavis – the man who subsequently put him name forward for a summer contract with Glamorgan – taking a shine to the young man from Ponty.

1946 saw Bernard round off his schooling by captaining the County School's 1st XI, besides playing again for the Welsh Secondary Schools. He then undertook his National Service with the RAF. Whilst at the County School, he had regularly attended the ATC

Squadron Summer Camps at the St Athan airbase where he had undertaken basic training besides taking part in further games of rugby and football. Indeed, in May 1946 he had captained the Wales ATC rugby team against England ATC, whilst he also represented Great Britain ATC in football at an international tournament held in Switzerland.

Having commenced his National Service, Bernard was initially based at St Athan – a very convenient arrangement as he could gain leave to regularly visit his family back in Rhydyfelin, as well as playing at either fly-half or full-back in the Pontypridd 1st XV. In June 1947 he was promoted to an administrative position at RAF Halton in the Vale of Aylesbury in Buckinghamshire where he continued to mix his military duties with plenty of sport.

After impressing as a batsman during inter-camp matches, Bernard was invited to a trial in May 1948 for the full RAF side. All went well and in July he had the thrill of appearing at Lord's in the match between the RAF and the Royal Navy. From London, the RAF team then travelled up to Newcastle for their next game against the Minor Counties – a game which saw the young Welshman make 143 and receive telegrams of praise from his doting coaches back in Cardiff.

Further decent innings followed for various RAF teams during 1949 before at the end of the year being offered a summer contract of £6 and 10 shillings a week by Glamorgan. Without any other work offers on the horizon, Bernard agreed terms and on 3rd June 1950 he made his first-class debut against Somerset at the Arms Park. His selection stemmed from injuries to both Allan Watkins and Wilf Wooller leading to a vacancy in the batting line-up. Having played well in 2nd XI games, a message was sent to Bernard who was on tour in South Devon with the Glamorgan Nomads. He duly travelled on a late evening train from Plymouth and reached Cardiff during the early hours of the

Bernard Hedges stands alongside Wilf Wooller in 1950.

morning – not the most ideal preparation for a Championship debut, but it proved to be a very low-key affair with Bernard making 3 in his only innings.

Things were very different at the end of the month as Bernard, having retained his place in the side, struck a maiden Championship century with 103 in three and a half hours against Sussex at Chichester. In all he struck, 13 fours and one six, besides sharing in a seventh wicket stand of 153 with Wilf who had returned from injury and was greatly impressed by the youngster resolve and fleet of foot running in between wickets.

Although it was almost three years to the day before he would score his next hundred, Bernard remained in the side and continued his steady development in the middle order. He also learnt to cope with the antics of some of his more experienced opponents and bowlers who were keen to put him off his game with their ribald comments. An example came in a match with Essex where he was announced as "Edges" over the tannoy as he made his way to the middle. He had a rather shaky start and played the ball several times from Trevor Bailey through the slip cordon. After yet another ball had disappeared down to third man, the England all-rounder stood arms akimbo in mid-pitch and loudly said, for all to hear, 'They gave you the right name didn't they!'

Bernard had heard worse on the rugby pitches and he continued in his unflappable and phlegmatic approach which had stood him in good stead since his earliest days on the sports fields of Pontypridd. It was an approach which was to last throughout his playing career and as his son Stephen wrote "He duly approached the vagaries of the cricket season in quite a philosophical way, and did not get as visibly stressed as Willie Jones sometimes did. To those around him, Bernard seemed to accept and balance the success that came with his ability as well as recognising its limits. His approach could be summed up in the phrase that he used often when discussing the game or other aspects of life. 'It happens' he would say. His pithiness was no accident. He was a man who did not relish social occasions and was never one to regale friends and family with stories or verbal embellishment."

The 1950s saw Bernard continued to mix amateur rugby with professional cricket and, after a series of excellent performances at full-back for Pontypridd, he featured on 4th November 1950, in a final Welsh Trial. The game at Pontypridd's home ground saw Bernard appear in the Possibles XV but, for once, he did not impress. He had shone with some strong line-breaking bursts in club rugby and he tried this tactic against Probable, but on rain-sodden turf, his ploy never worked and other names went down in the selectors notebooks.

Nevertheless he continued to play for Pontypridd until the 1951/52 season, before switching to Swansea RFC for whom he was their regular full-back in 1952/53, with his move resulting from Bernard having fallen in love with a Swansea girl called Jean Davies. In order to see more of his sweetheart, Bernard secured lodgings in the Copperopolis and spent the rest of his rugby career with the All Whites.

Whilst happily in love, Bernard's progress as a county cricketer then took a temporary blow as he suffered a severe bout of kidney stones. He only appeared in four first-class games in 1953 and during May went into hospital for an operation to remove the painful obstructions which went on to trouble him for the rest of his life. Thankfully, he was restored to form and fitness for 1954, and with Emrys Davies nearing the end of his career, Bernard was moved up the order to the number three spot, with Wilf having more than half an eye on Bernard becoming Emrys' replacement. Indeed, in a couple of matches when Gilbert Parkhouse was indisposed, Bernard opened with Wilf himself.

Bernard continued to flourish up the order, adding 195 for the third wicket with Willie Jones in the match against Derbyshire, whilst at Trent Bridge he made 129 against a lively Notts attack and shared a stand of 164 with Allan Watkins which laid the foundations for a 40-run victory over the East Midlands side. His doughty efforts duly saw Bernard being presented with his county cap during the match against Warwickshire at Llanelli.

He duly made the number three spot his own for the next few summers and in 1956 featured in an ill-tempered game at Hove where, after Wilf had been involved in some verbal spats with the opposition and crowd, the instructions were to shut up shop and bat out for a draw. Like a dutiful soldier, he duly carried out the orders to the letter, and in his phlegmatic way ignored the barracking the Glamorgan team received from the disgruntled Sussex supporters.

The following year he was involved in another incident, this time as a fielder during Glamorgan's game against Surrey at The Oval. Peter May, who at the time was the captain of England, miscued a ball low to mid-on where Bernard was fielding. To many, it looked like Bernard had held the ball just above the surface, so the Surrey batsman started to walk back to the Pavillion. But Bernard thought otherwise and, always placing honesty above all other values, he indicated to the umpire that the ball hadn't carried. Seeing Peter out of his ground Wilf told Bernard to throw the ball to him, whereupon the Glamorgan captain – who ironically was an England Test selector at the time – threw the ball to Haydn Davies who removed the bails, and ran out Peter.

The batsman later told Wilf he should not have left his crease, but up in the Press Box, Wilf's actions were viewed by the journalists as an act of premeditated gamesmanship. No blame was attached to Bernard in what had taken place, but the next morning, the back pages of the national newspaper had plenty of coverage

Bernard Hedges, in his civvies, demonstrates his on-drive in the nets in the North Stand at Cardiff Arms Park.

of the match at The Oval and critical comments about Wilf's actions which it was felt had rubbed up against the spirit, if not the rules, of the game. Bernard wisely kept his counsel – he knew of Wilf's foibles, but as an established and well-respected member of the side, he was not going to add grist to the mill by publically criticizing his captain. As at Hove, and for some years in the RAF, he was merely following orders and was content for those charged with leadership to undertake the decision-making.

The summer of 1957 also saw Bernard and Gilbert become Glamorgan's regular opening pair, following a successful experiment against Leicestershire at Coalville in the first week of June. Bernard duly made 128 as Glamorgan romped to a victory by an innings and 52 runs, and later in July against Nottinghamshire at Stradey Park, the duo added 156 for the first wicket with Bernard going on to make 139 and completely master the bowling of Australian spinner Bruce Dooland. His contemporaries in the Glamorgan side regarded this as his finest hundred in Glamorgan colours, with Bernard time and again, sweeping and cutting the Test bowler.

The pair went on to share a number of other outstanding first wicket stands, including 181 against Middlesex in 1958 at Cardiff Arms Park with their efforts still remaining as a record for that wicket. Their contrasting styles and characters perfectly complemented each other, with Stephen Hedges writing "Whereas Gilbert appeared sweat free and unruffled, Bernard would often look bathed in sweat, hair splayed across his scalp like the spiked fur of a drenched house cat. Batting was hard work and Bernard approached it in that light. He was the artisan to Gilbert's artist, the perfect battling foil to the clean rapier of the Test batsman. The two gained a great reputation for their running between the wickets, putting pressure on the fielding side and constantly forcing bowlers to have to readjust their line of attack."

1961 proved to be the high water mark in Bernard's distinguished career as he amassed 2,026 runs and, in the process, went past the career landmark of 10,000 runs. Two of his finest innings that run-filled summer came during the away match at Northampton. In the first innings he made an unbeaten 134 and shared a stand of 206 in even time with Jim Pressdee, before in the second innings sharing an opening stand of 165 in just an hour and a quarter with Gilbert, with their whirlwind efforts giving Glamorgan the perfect start as they chased a target of 214 in two and a quarter hours. Whilst Gilbert made what remains the fastest authentic hundred in the Club's history, Bernard saw the Welsh county through to victory with Alan Rees, remaining unbeaten on 95 and typically being satisfied to drive the ball back past the bowler for a single to see his side home rather than attempting a lusty blow for six in order to complete a century.

However, he did open his shoulders during the closing game of the summer, away to Surrey having arrived at The Oval with his seasonal tally 95 runs short of 2,000. By this time Euros Lewis was having a trial as an opener with Gilbert with Bernard occupying the number four berth. He could have been excused for wondering whether he might never reach the landmark as the first day saw Surrey's batsmen limp along before being dismissed for 262. But Bernard was not to be denied as he reached his personal target before completing a hundred by hoisting Tony Lock high over mid-wicket for six! There was plenty for Glamorgan's team to toast that night in London, as well as on their train journey back home the following night as after cheaply dismissing Surrey for a second time, they eased to an emphatic victory.

1961 had also seen Bernard open the innings with Alan Jones, the man who was to be his regular first-wicket partner for the rest of his career. Their relationship on the cricket field had begun though back in 1956, and had nothing at first to do with batting. Instead, it was because of their inside-leg measurement and similar shoe size! The match in question was the visit of the Australians to Swansea, and with both Jim Pressdee and Gilbert getting injured, Alan was pressed into service as an emergency fielder. He had gone to the ground to watch so didn't have any kit. After answering the SOS call over the tannoy, the schoolboy put on Bernard's spare kit and proudly went out to field for the first of so many times for Glamorgan.

Alan and Bernard first opened three years later when Gilbert was on England duty at Headingley against the 1959 Indians. Glamorgan were at Edgbaston with Bernard and Alan facing a Warwickshire attack which included two men who later played for the Welsh county, Ossie Wheatley and Tom Cartwright. The pair had occasional outings together in the next few years before opening on a regular basis from early June 1963 when Surrey played at St Helen's and Gilbert was absent with arthritis and a back strain

– ailments that were to end both his distinguished career and the pairing with Bernard which had lifted the hearts of so many Glamorgan supporters.

1963 was also Bernard's Benefit year as well as being the year when he sustained a nasty facial injury during the match against the West Indian tourists at Swansea. With one of his children ill in hospital, Bernard was rested for the game, but a series of injuries saw Bernard come on as twelfth man and field in the gully – a position in which he rarely appeared. He had only been on the field for one ball when Willie Rodriguez square-cut a ball from Ossie Wheatley straight into Bernard's face. There was blood everywhere with the blow also smashing Bernard's dentures. Don and Jim Pressdee helped him off the field, with blood all over his shirt and his head held back to restrict the flow of blood. With his mouth stuffed with cotton wool, he told a journalist who was enquiring about his health before being taken to a dentist, "If Glamorgan want me for the next match at Northampton, I'll be ready." He was duly patched up and made a typically gutsy 78 on a lively and quick surface.

The summer of 1963 had also seen the introduction of the Gillette Cup into the fixture list, with Bernard marking the advent of one-day cricket into the summer programme by becoming the Club's first-ever centurion in List A cricket. It came against Somerset at the Arms Park with the new format being a surprise to everyone, including Tony Lewis with whom Bernard shared a century stand for the third wicket. As Tony recalled, "Bernard and I said 'how do we play this?' One of us has got to stay here while the other one needs to get some runs. I was [acting] captain so I said 'I'll tell you what. I'll do you a favour. I'll try and stay here and you play all of your shots.' I thought it was going to be short but it was 65 overs, almost a first-class innings, much longer than we thought. We stayed there. I blocked and we stayed there a long time."

Charles Barnett (right) presents Bernard Hedges with his Man-of-the-Match Award after Glamorgan had beaten Somerset at Cardiff Arms Park in 1963 to win their inaugural match in the Gillette Cup in 1963.

Bernard duly reached three figures in the 64th and penultimate over of the innings, but his day's work was not over as he then had a rare spell of seam bowling, taking 2/17 in eight accurate overs. It was something of a makeshift attack with both Don and Ossie being rested but as Tony recalled "I knew Bernard could bowl because of his work at the Indoor School in Neath. He wasn't on the list to bowl but I looked at how the pitch was playing and who we had. The ball didn't bounce very much. I knew he could bowl straight. That was the main thing."

Besides his phantom medium pace, Bernard also held a steepling catch so it was no surprise that he got the nod from the adjudicator to win the inaugural Man-of-the-Match Award. It was a great way as well for Bernard to start his Benefit Year and although his

Benefit Match was rained off, he garnered the decent sum of £4,402 at the end of the year – something which Bernard shrewdly invested as at the age of thirty-six, he started to think about life after cricket. Indeed, 1963 was the last year in which he reached 1,000 runs, and although he carried on playing until 1967, it was the beginning of the end.

Another bout of kidney stones, brought on by eating strawberries, saw him miss the final month of 1964, including the historic victory over the Australians at Swansea, as well as part of 1965. Around this time, Bernard, as a concerned family man and eager to look after his wife and two sons, was also involved in discussions, together with Don and Jim Pressdee, with Wilf and the Glamorgan committee about enhanced salaries for the established players.

Bernard Hedges sprints off the field at Cardiff Arms Park after scoring a century against Somerset in 1963 tin Glamorgan's first-ever List A one-day match.

Some of the discussions were quite heated, but nothing compared to what happened at Llanelli at the end of the 1965 season, after the Welsh county had failed to secure enough points in their game with Essex to finish second behind Worcestershire. For much of the summer, Glamorgan had been in the title race so emotions were running high in the home dressing room. Bernard, like the others was keen to head for home, and he tried leave via a small office at the back of the Pavillion and then through the door leading to the car park. The office though was being used by Wilf to count the gate money. He stopped Bernard from using the office as a short-cut, pushed him back through the door and threw his cricket bag into the corridor. Shortly afterwards, the fiery Jim Pressdee tried to leave by the same route, but an even more physical altercation took place between the pair, who for years had never seen eye-to-eye, before Jim stormed off to speak to the Press to announce that he was quitting the Club and migrating to South Africa.

The Glamorgan committee, concerned about a perceived lack of discipline within the team, subsequently held an enquiry, with Bernard being asked to give his version of events. Naturally, he was quite upset at what had happened, especially as he had the highest respect for Wilf, but his pride had been dented and he was even more annoyed when he subsequently received a letter severely reprimanding him for his behavior. It was clear that Wilf had taken affront to personal challenges to his authority, and the committee's decision to side with their captain in sending a reprimand to Bernard may also have been influenced by the contract discussions the previous year.

Bernard tried to appeal against his reprimand, and also to speak to the officials, but all to no avail and he entered 1966 feeling let down by the Club. It was no coincidence that what followed was his least successful with just 659 runs at an average of 18.30 and only a couple of fifties. The nadir of the season came during August when Glamorgan played

Yorkshire at Scarborough. Bernard was hit in the box whilst batting and subsequently missed the last two weeks of the summer as he had an operation to remove a damaged testicle.

At the end of the season, he was only offered a one-year contract for 1967 and with preference going to the younger players, he did not appear in the 1st XI until the beginning of June when the Welsh county met Oxford University at The Parks. He duly made a career-best 182 and, soon after, returned to the Championship line-up. But he continued to enjoy a lean time with his 422nd and final match coming against Worcestershire at New Road in the final week of July. Glamorgan were left on the final afternoon with the unlikely target of 51 in just sixteen minutes. Bernard opened with Peter Walker and was caught on the boundary for five in the first over, before the match ended in a draw.

The following week at Swansea, Majid Khan hit a stunning 147 in the space of 89 minutes for the Pakistanis against the Welsh county. A few weeks later, Wilf Wooller was able to announce the signing of the gifted batsman for 1968 and beyond. It was also announced that Bernard's contract had been terminated.

During the autumn he secured a position with Barclays Bank, and after a short spell coaching in the Indoor School at Neath, Bernard played for various clubs in the South Wales Cricket Association, besides in 1969 captaining Wales against the International Cavaliers at Colwyn Bay, and scoring a century against the star-studded line-up. But Bernard saw little of his former colleagues on a regular basis, especially with his work promoting Barclaycard seeing him and his family move to the West Country and then the Home Counties following his promotion to become Area Manager for the South-East Area office of Barclaycard based in Woking.

He was sad about his treatment to end his playing career, but never bitter or resentful. He had enjoyed a decent career, yet despite offers and encouragement from the likes of Don Shepherd, with whom he roomed for most of his career, Bernard rarely attended the annual gatherings of the Glamorgan Former Players Association. In 1982 he played for a Glamorgan Past and Present XI against an Old England side at Swansea, but this was a rare sighting of a man who had played with such distinction for the Club.

His aloofness surprised several of his former team-mates but, for Bernard, his life had moved on. He had little interest in the modern game – in fact, he held little interest in anything of the late twentieth century, preferring simple food, traditional music plus the TV and radio staples of the 1950s and 1960s. As his son Stephen wrote in his outstanding biography of his late father, "his unwillingness to embrace the modern World was, at turns, endearing and frustrating for those around him."

He had been the first person from Pontypridd to win a regular place in the Glamorgan line-up and fittingly he was inducted in 2004 into the Rhondda Cynon Taf Sporting Hall of Fame alongside other sporting legends of the valleys including rugby players Bleddyn Williams, Tom David and Neil Jenkins. After retiring, Bernard moved back to Wales and settled in the Mumbles. It was here, just a few miles away from Don Shepherd, his long-standing room-mate and long-standing friend, that Bernard passed away in February 2014 after a long and noble fight against cancer.

LEWIS, Kenneth Humphrey.

Born – Penygladdfa, Newtown, 10 November 1928.

Professional.

RHB, RFM.

Ed – Newtown GS.

1st XI: 1950-1956.

2nd XI: 1950-1956.

Club and Ground: 1949-1956.

Worcestershire 2nd XI 1949; Montgomeryshire 1948-1965; North Wales 1960.

Clubs: Newtown, Neath, Llanelli, Swansea, Ammanford, Welshpool and Clydach.

Batting and Fielding Record

	M	I	NO	RUNS	AV	100	50	CT	ST
F-c	36	48	14	312	9.17	-	-	15	-

Bowling Record

	Balls	M	R	W	AV	5wI	10wM
F-c	4170	126	2044	55	37.16	-	-

Career-bests

First-class –   34 v Hampshire at Cardiff Arms Park, 1956.

4/25 v Kent at Cardiff Arms Park, 1953.

Ken Lewis was a brisk right-arm seam bowler who, when on National Service, had taken 10/21 for the Royal Artillery in a match against Charterhouse. He subsequently enjoyed a seven-year career in county cricket but, owing to a series of injuries, was never able to command a regular place in the Glamorgan side.

Born and raised in Newtown in Mid-Wales, Ken's success in Services cricket during the late 1940s led to trials with both Worcestershire and Glamorgan during 1949. Like Don Shepherd before him, Ken subsequently rejected overtures from the West Midlands club and joined Glamorgan's staff in 1950.

After some promising performances in 2nd XI and club cricket, Ken made his first-class debut in Glamorgan's three-day friendly against the Combined Services at the Arms Park in June 1950. He opened the bowling with Norman Hever and claimed three wickets, besides showing that he was capable of bowling genuinely fast spells. This led to him keeping his place for the next Championship match, against Gloucestershire at the Wagonworks ground in Gloucester. Ken went wicketless as the Welsh county defeated their West Country neighbours and it was in the following game, against Derbyshire at The Gnoll in Neath that he claimed his maiden Championship scalp, beating Charlie Elliott for sheer pace and clean bowling him.

He played in the next three games but failed to claim a clutch of wickets and returned to the 2nd XI. A leg injury then restricted his activities during1951, with Ken's next first-class appearance not coming until May 1952, again against the Combined Services

Ken Lewis.

at the Arms Park, followed by a couple of Championship appearances, each in away games at the Wagon Works again as well as at Westcliff-on-Sea against Essex.

Ken was fit enough to appear in a dozen games during 1953 – a season which saw him claim career-best figures of 4/25 against Kent at the Arms Park, but he broke down again early in 1954 before being injured on his comeback against Worcestershire at Dudley and taking no active part in the match. Fortunately he was able to make eight appearances during 1955 and secure a contract extension for the following summer, but after six further first-class matches he sustained a serious leg injury in 1956 and was forced to retire, ironically shortly after having also played for L.C. Steven's XI against the RAF in the Eastbourne Festival and a match when his tally of wickets included that of Raman Subba Row, later of England.

Ken duly returned to Powys and rejoined the Newtown club. He also worked as an insurance agent before securing employment in a local garage. His final major match was for North Wales against Glamorgan at Colwyn Bay in 1960. During this period, he also played as a professional for Welshpool, besides appearing for Montgomeryshire as well as guesting for the Shropshire Gentlemen.

Whilst attached to Glamorgan, Ken had played in club cricket for Neath, Clydach, Ammanford, Llanelli and Swansea, besides during the winter months playing football for Newtown FC. He was a talented footballer, playing mainly at inside left, and was in the Newtown side which defeated Chirk to win the Welsh Amateur Cup in April 1955. In recent years, Ken has proudly served as President of Newtown Cricket Club.

420
WATKINS, William Martin DFC.

Born – Swansea, 18 January 1923.
Died – Sketty, Swansea, 15 March 2005.
RHB, LBG.
Amateur.
Ed – Dynevor GS, Swansea.
1st XI: 1950.
2nd XI: 1950.
Club: Swansea.

Batting and Fielding Record

	M	I	NO	RUNS	AV	100	50	CT	ST
F-c	1	1	0	3	3.00	-	-	-	-

Career-bests
First-class –   3 v Hampshire at St Helen's, Swansea, 1950.

Bill Watkins, who was awarded the DFC as a teenage pilot of Lancaster bombers during the Second World War, had an outstanding career in club cricket in the Swansea area and played once for Glamorgan during August 1950 when Gilbert Parkhouse was a late withdrawal from the Welsh county's line-up for the Championship match with Hampshire.

Despite his late call-up Bill opened the batting with Emrys Davies against the visitor's lively new ball attack but, as befitted someone who had taken part in 31 missions and 121 hours of sorties, many of them at night, over industrial targets in Germany during 1944, he was not overawed by the occasion.

Born in Swansea and educated at Dynevor Grammar School, Bill had enlisted with the RAF on leaving school and, after initial training at Hendon Flying School, he became a member of 514 Squadron based at RAF Waterbeach in Cambridgeshire.

When hostilities were over, Bill returned to his native Swansea, and after marrying Eileen Evans during 1945, he worked as a metallurgist for British Aluminium and ALCOA. He had a fine record as an opening batsman with Swansea CC,

Bill Watkins, seen in his military uniform.

besides being a decent rugby player for the town club and the Swansea schoolboys team. Bill's talents with the oval ball also led to trials with the Wigan rugby league team, but he turned down offers to turn professional and remained in South Wales.

421
DAVIES, Dr David <u>Roy.</u>

Born – Llanelli, 12 August 1928.
Died – West Clandon, Guildford, 14 July, 2013.
RHB.
Ed – Llanelli GS, Llandrindod Wells GS, Oswestry HS and Cardiff University.
1st XI: 1950.
2nd XI: 1946-1951.
Club and Ground:1949-1950.
Clubs: St Fagans.
Squash for Wales.
Adopted brother of HG Davies.

Batting and Fielding Record

	M	I	NO	RUNS	AV	100	50	CT	ST
F-c	1	1	0	7	7.00	-	-	-	-

Career-bests
First-class –   7 v Somerset at Weston-super-Mare, 1950

Roy Davies played once for Glamorgan in 1950. Born in Llanelli, he was the younger brother of Glamorgan wicket-keeper Haydn Davies, with his sole appearance at first-class level coming at Clarence Park in Weston-super-Mare in 1950 when he appeared against Somerset, making 7 in his only innings.

Haydn and Roy lost both their parents during World War Two, so Haydn, who was 27 at the time, adopted eleven year-old Roy as his son. Roy subsequently attended Llandrindod Wells Grammar School and Oswestry High School, where he captained the school's 1st XI and showed great promise as a stylish right-handed batsman and an alert fielder. After completing his National Service, Roy read Chemistry at Cardiff University and played regularly for the St Fagans club, besides appearing for Glamorgan 2nd XI.

Roy Davies.

After graduating, Roy moved to the Manchester area to work for Unilever. He duly worked for the company for 32 years as an industrial chemist and fuel technologist, besides rising to the position of Technical Head of their European operations. Like Haydn, Roy was an outstanding squash player and represented Wales on a number of occasions.

1951

Glamorgan climbed up to 5th place in the Championship table during 1951, but their finest hour came in early August during their match at Swansea against the touring Springboks. Chasing a target of 147, the tourists had reached 54-0 at tea, with some in the estimated crowd of 24,000 at St Helen's deciding that they had seen enough and, fearing traffic problems along the Mumbles Road, they made their way to the car parks, bus and train stops close to the ground to start an early journey home.

They duly missed one of the greatest passages of play in the Club's history as the South Africans were dismissed for 83 in the hour or so after tea as Len Muncer (Vol.2, p365-369) took four wickets whilst Jim McConnon claimed 6/10, including a hat-trick – the Club's first-ever against a Test-playing side.

Some breath-taking catches were also taken close to the wicket, including one by Wilf Wooller himself, standing at silly mid-on as, after deflecting a firm on-drive from Clive van Ryneveld, he then clutched onto the rebound having almost been knocked off his feet by the blow from the batsman. Gilbert Parkhouse, who was fielding as substitute for Emrys Davies, also held two fine catches despite nursing a wrist injury.

Glamorgan's improved form in the County Championship was the result of several

A dapper Wilf Wooller, wearing a neckerchief and his Glamorgan team, as seen at Edgbaston for the County Championship match against Warwickshire in 1951. Back row (left to right) – Bernard Hedges, Phil Clift, Norman Hever, Jim McConnon, Gilbert Parkhouse and Allan Watkins. Front row – Willie Jones, Haydn Davies, Wilf Wooller, Emrys Davies and Len Muncer.

batsmen enjoying a handsome season. In all, six batsmen scored over 1,000 first-class runs – the first time that so many batsmen from the Welsh county had passed this landmark. The top-order also had a field day against Derbyshire at Cardiff Arms Park as Glamorgan declared on 587-8 after posting the highest total in the first-class history. All of the top six – Emrys Davies, Phil Clift, Gilbert Parkhouse, Willie Jones, Allan Watkins and Wilf Wooller – passed the fifty-mark before Jim McConnon took 7/69 and 7/84 to spin his team to an innings victory.

422
SHAW, George Bernard.

Born – Treharris, 24 October 1931.
Died – Port Pirie, South Australia, 1 August 1984.
Professional.
RHB, OB.
Ed – Quaker's Yard Grammar school.
1st XI: 1951-1955.
2nd XI: 1951-1969.
Club and Ground: 1948-1954.
Clubs: Ebbw Vale, Briton Ferry Town and Hill's Plymouth.

Batting and Fielding Record

	M	I	NO	RUNS	AV	100	50	CT	ST
F-c	16	20	13	30	4.28	-	-	4	-

Bowling Record

	Balls	M	R	W	AV	5wI	10wM
F-c	1376	36	706	26	27.15	2	1

Career Bests

First-class –   11 v Combined Services at Cardiff Arms Park, 1952.
5/38 v Combined Services at Cardiff Arms Park, 1952.

George Shaw, who made sixteen appearances for Glamorgan, was an off-spinner who never fulfilled his early promise. The pupil at Quaker's Yard Grammar School had shown rich potential in junior cricket and in 1948 the seventeen year-old made his debut for the county's Club and Ground side, largely on the recommendation of Club coach George Lavis who had been impressed by George's ability to spin the ball and an action modelled on his boyhood hero Johnnie Clay.

George was the youngest of three children born to John and Elizabeth Shaw, with his father running a highly successful bakery business in Merthyr Tydfil. Despite his youth, George also had a full set of false teeth – top and bottom – and his contemporaries on Glamorgan's junior staff still remember how his teeth would clatter together whenever he laughed. George progressed onto Glamorgan's full-time staff in 1951 having completed his National Service and that summer he made his first-class debut against the Combined Services in their contest at Pontypridd.

It was in the corresponding game in 1952 that George had

George Shaw.

his finest hour in Glamorgan ranks, with figures of 5/67 and 5/38 against a Services team led by Alan Shirreff and containing Jim Parks, Ray Illingworth, Keith Andrew and Roly Thompson, all of whom went on to regular places in county sides. Sadly, this was not to be for the young and enthusiastic spinner whose high slow loop imparted plenty of spin on the ball, but he struggled for accuracy against seasoned professionals. Despite a return of 4/45 against Hampshire at Bournemouth later in 1952, George did not feature during 1953 and remained as an understudy to Jim McConnon. He re-appeared in six games in 1954 and the following year took 4/76 in the game with Northamptonshire at the Arms Park but with Don Shepherd's successful conversion to off-cutters, George – who had modest pretensions as a batsman – left the Glamorgan staff at the end of the summer.

He continued to play, with some success in club cricket for Ebbw Vale, whilst he joined his late father's bakery business. He later went into business with Ossie Wheatley and ran a restaurant, appropriately known as The Pygmalion in Wellfield Road in Cardiff, before emigrating to Australia during 1978. Tragically, George was killed in a car crash six years later near Adelaide.

1952

The 1952 season began in dramatic style as Glamorgan recorded their first-ever Championship victory at Lord's as they comprehensively defeated Middlesex by 131 runs, and with further victories during the first half of the season, Wilf Wooller's team threatened to repeat their achievements of 1948. But their title bid was thwarted by an injury to Jim McConnon, the emerging off-spinner, whilst other batsmen – notably Willie Jones – lost form and confidence. Five batsmen passed the 1,000-run mark, whilst Emrys Davies achieved the remarkable feat of scoring 1626 runs without posting a Championship hundred.

In McConnon's absence, Len Muncer showed that he had lost none of his old skills as the veteran all-rounder became only the second player in the Club's history to achieve the Double. He also proved to be a match-winner in three of the victories which Glamorgan recorded at home, starting with an innings victory over Kent at Pontypridd with Len claiming a match haul of 9/67. This was followed by a haul of 8/76 against Leicestershire as the East Midlands side also slumped to an innings defeat at Neath, before Len took 8/42 as Northamptonshire were beaten by seven wickets at the Arms Park.

The Glamorgan squad which played Warwickshire at Edgbaston in 1952. Back row (left to right) Jim Pleass, Bernard Hedges, Phil Clift, Jim McConnon, Don Shepherd, Gilbert Parkhouse, Willie Jones. Front row – Allan Watkins, Emrys Davies, Wilf Wooller, Haydn Davies and Len Muncer.

Len also shone with the bat in the narrow two-wicket win at Derby during mid-August. The game proved to be a real dogfight with runs hard to come by in bowler-friendly conditions which saw seventeen wickets tumble on an eventful second day. On the final morning, Glamorgan were left chasing a target of 139 and having slipped to 57-6, Derbyshire appeared to be in the driving seat. But Len overcame a thigh strain to defend stoutly against the pace of Les Jackson, the lively seam bowling of Derek Morgan and the clever leg-breaks of Dusty Rhodes.

With the doughty support of Jim Pleass (Vol. 2, p374-380), the seventh wicket pair took the score to 99 whereupon Jim was bowled, shortly before Haydn Davies was caught behind. With 31 needed, and just one batsman left in the Pavillion, Len switched to a more aggressive approach and he gallantly saw Glamorgan home without any further alarms.

423
DAVIES, John Anthony.

Born – Pontypridd, 3 February 1926.
Died – Llantrisant, 1 April 2005.
RHB, LBG.
Ed – Pontypridd County Boys School.
Amateur.
1st XI - 1952.
2nd XI - 1950-1953.
Herefordshire.
Clubs: Pontypridd, St Fagans, Cowbridge, Ludlow, MCC, XL Club.

Batting and Fielding Record

	M	I	NO	RUNS	AV	100	50	CT	ST
F-c	1	2	0	11	5.50	-	-	-	-

Career-bests
First-class –   11 v Worcestershire at Cardiff Arms Park, 1952.

John Davies, known to all as "J.A.", played once for Glamorgan in 1952 and had an outstanding career as a batsman in club cricket in South Wales and the Marches.

Born and raised in Pontypridd, John was the son of an artist who supplied cartoons for, amongst others, the *South Wales Echo* and their popular *Football Echo*. He picked up the cricket bug at a young age and together with his younger brother Douglas – who inherited his father's artistic talents – played cricket in the back garden of their home in Pontypridd or on the nearby common. Their next-door neighbour was the town's Postmaster, besides being the President of Pontypridd CC (as well as the father of Johnny Morris – the BBC presenter of *Animal Magic*) so he was very understanding if balls flew over the wall or, as on one famous occasion, smashed their lounge window. His benevolent attitude was in contrast to another neighbour, Mr Parry, the town's station master, was confiscated the Davies' ball when it landed in his back garden or amongst his prized blackcurrants!

In 1939 John won selection for the Pontypridd Under 15 team which won, to their father's pleasure, *The South Wales Echo and Western Mail* Schools Shield. The following year there was an even broader smile on the face of Mr Davies senior as the Pontypridd team, under the captaincy of J.A., retained the title.

On leaving the County Boys School, John joined the Army and served as a sergeant in the South Wales Borderers. Amongst his postings was a spell in Germany but he still found plenty of time to play cricket and it was on German soil that he scored his first-ever hundred in a Services match. After being demobilized he returned to Pontypridd and began his long and successful career with the Midland Bank. He also played regularly for Pontypridd and secured a regular berth in their 1st XI after a century for their second string against Penarth.

John Davies (left) seen with Phil Clift at a Glamorgan Former Players Association annual gathering at Sophia Gardens.

1951 was an important year for J.A. following a promotion to a bank in Cowbridge. His move saw him transfer his allegiance to the town's club and after some further impressive innings for Cowbridge, he made his debut for Glamorgan 2nd XI. The following year John struck half-centuries against Worcestershire 2nd XI and Somerset 2nd XI before posting 112 against Gloucestershire 2nd XI at Bristol. Johnnie Clay was also in the Cowbridge side and after this fine run of form for the county's 2nd XI, plus an unbeaten 132 against Brecon, the Glamorgan stalwart recommended to Wilf Wooller that J.A. should be given a chance to play in Championship cricket.

'The Skipper' agreed and after John secured leave at the end of August, he made his debut in the Welsh county's closing Championship match against Worcestershire at the Arms Park. Batting at number four, he made 11 as Glamorgan were bundled out for 117 in their first innings. Batting for a second time, J.A. was caught behind by Hugo Yarnold for a duck as he gloved a sharp lifting delivery from the veteran Reg Perks as the Welsh county lost by 139 runs.

He appeared for Glamorgan 2nd XI again in 1953 but the match with Worcestershire proved to be his sole appearance at first-class level as he won further promotion with Midland Bank at branches in Shropshire. He became a leading light with the Ludlow club, as well as appearing in Minor County cricket for Herefordshire – all whilst serving as Manager of several branches of the bank.

Had he opted not to go into the world of finance, John would probably have secured a place on Glamorgan's professional staff and appeared alongside Bernard Hedges, another product of the Pontypridd County Boys School and one year his junior. After retiring from the Bank and returning with his wife Judy to live in Cowbridge, J.A. continued to play for the town club, as well as the Wales Over 50s team and the Forty Club. At the time of his death in 2005, John was President of Cowbridge CC.

1953

Glamorgan, yet again, flattered to deceive during the first half of the season. Having won their first two Championship games, against Worcestershire at Swansea and Kent at the Arms Park, Wilf Wooller's team were still unbeaten in early June when they recorded two more back-to-back victories on home soil as they defeated Essex at Llanelli and Derbyshire at Pontypridd. But their form fell away during the closing six weeks and they did not win another match during Coronation Year after defeating Warwickshire by four wickets at Ebbw Vale during mid-July.

Their early season success came as no surprise to Wilf who, in a tub-thumping interview with local journalists ahead of the season, had described the squad of 1953 as being better than the one which had lifted the county title in 1948. He had largely based his comments on the fact that Jim McConnon had returned to fitness. "He's the ace in my pack because Jim's a real match-winner" were Wilf's words to the scribes and in the opening game of the summer at St Helen's, the off-spinner duly claimed five wickets in Worcestershire's first innings

But Wilf was nearly made to eat his words in Worcestershire's second innings as the visitors mounted a dramatic late rally. The game entered the final half hour, with Worcestershire needing 55 to win and Glamorgan four further wickets as Jim was introduced into the attack. But John Whitehead struck him for a couple of massive sixes, with his lusty blows looking like tipping the balance towards the visitors. Despite a couple of wickets falling, Whitehead carried on attacking Jim, but with four runs needed, he was well caught on the boundary edge by Gilbert Parkhouse as he attempted another huge blow against Len Muncer. Don Shepherd then bowled Hugo Yarnold with the fourth ball of the final over to seal a dramatic one-run victory.

This had been the narrowest Championship victory in the Welsh county's history and came during a season where, for once, there were no new faces bloodied by the Glamorgan selection committee, and a year that saw the Club take first-class cricket to Margam as the newly-completed sports complex owned by the Steel Company of Wales hosted the three-day friendly against the Gentlemen of Ireland.

The Glamorgan team mingle with the Gentlemen of Ireland at Margam in 1953. On the back row is Gilbert Parkhouse (2nd left) and Norman Hever (4th left), in the middle row are Jim Pleass (1st left), Stan Montgomery (2nd left), Don Shepherd (3rd left), Jim McConnon (6th left), Phil Clift (2nd right) and Willie Jones (far right), whilst in the front row are Haydn Davies (2nd left), Wilf Wooller (3rd right) and Allan Watkins (far right).

1954

Glamorgan showed that their resurgence during the first half of 1953 had not been a flash in the pan as they bounced back from losing their opening game of 1954 by an innings against Lancashire, to record eleven victories in the 28 Championship matches and rose up the table from tenth to fourth place.

It was a red-letter summer for Wilf Wooller and Allan Watkins as both completed the coveted Double in all first-class cricket. The pair combined with good effect in the thrilling ten wicket victory against Leicestershire at Swansea, with Allan making a career-best 170* before Wilf took 6/28 as the East Midlands side fought hard to avoid an innings defeat after interruptions earlier in the game for rain. But their stubbornness was to no avail as Wilf, bowling with a typical combination of fire and determination, dismissed three of the last four batsmen in the space of eleven balls, and all without conceding a run. His efforts meant Glamorgan needed thirteen to win in a shade over ten minutes, before Gilbert Parkhouse settled the issue with some typically sublime boundaries in the opening over.

Gilbert's finest moment, and to some extent Wilf's as well, had come in July at Lord's as Glamorgan posted their second victory on Middlesex soil. The 22-run victory was underpinned by a superb 182 from Gilbert with the Swansea-man also benefiting from the decision of umpire Harry Elliott to recall the Glamorgan opener on 99 after he had been adjudged caught behind. But the Derbyshire man realized that the sound had been Gilbert's bat hitting the turf and, shortly afterwards, the former England batsman celebrated his recall by completing his century.

A gaggle of schoolboys look on as Haydn Davies chats with Bill Edrich at Swansea in 1954.

Some probing seam bowling then allowed Glamorgan to secure a decent lead, which they duly extended with Wilf, opening the batting and posting a combative half-century before setting Middlesex a target of 251 to win. Jack Robertson responded with a classic century, but wickets fell at regular intervals at the other end as Wilf scythed his way through the home batting, claiming 7/65 including the final scalp of John Warr who holed out to Don Shepherd attempting to strike the Glamorgan batsman in the direction of Buckingham Palace!

424
EDRICH, Brian Robert.

Born – Cantley, Norfolk, 18 August 1922.
Died – Padstow, Cornwall, 31 May 2009.
LHB, OB.
Professional.
1st XI: 1954-1956.
2nd XI: 1954-1962.
Club and Ground: 1954-1957.
Kent 1947-1953; Oxfordshire 1966-1970; Minor Counties 1967.
Clubs: Heacham, Buckingham, Maesteg Town, Maesteg Celtic, Hill's Plymouth, Briton Ferry Steel and Swansea.

Batting and Fielding Record

	M	I	NO	RUNS	AV	100	50	CT	ST
F-c	52	80	8	1246	17.30	-	3	34	-

Bowling Record

	Balls	M	R	W	AV	5wI	10wM
F-c	48	3	12	0	-	-	-

Career-bests
First-class –   74 v Leicestershire at St Helen's, Swansea, 1954.

Brian Edrich was a member of the famous cricketing clan from Norfolk who could raise a family XI of both genders and take on all who dared. As the youngest of four sons born to Bill Edrich senior, Brian matched his elder brothers for ability and enthusiasm. Whilst he failed to win international honours, Brian enjoyed a three-year career with Glamorgan having previously played for Kent either side of the Second World War.

He grew up on the family's farm near Lingwood in Norfolk as well as in East Yorkshire when the family moved briefly north in 1932, before returning to live near Heacham. By his mid-teens Brian was playing for the Heacham 1st XI and, after impressing with the bat in an Edrich family team during 1938, he was recommended to Kent who duly offered him a junior contract for the following summer without having ever seen him play.

Brian duly played for Kent's second string during 1939 before returning to work on the family's farm shortly after the outbreak of War. He also helped in the construction work for an airfield near Bircham Newton before becoming a trainee pilot with the RAF during March 1942. Whereas his more famous brother Bill took part in daring low-level raids in Blenheim bombers on enemy vessels in the North Sea and English Channel, Brian won his wings in Canada, before flying Vultee Vengeances in India, followed by work on air-sea rescue missions in Ceylon. With the War having ended in Europe, Brian was keen to return home in 1946 and applied for B-class demobilization to return to agricultural work in Norfolk. His application was successful, but it precluded him from resuming his fledgling career as a professional cricketer until 1947.

Brian Edrich, seen at Canterbury in the early 1950s.

Brian accepted the situation and, as he later reflected, "I had nowhere near learnt my trade before the War and I would not have been happy to go straight into county cricket after playing so little. Indeed, I doubt if it would have done me any good. I was still only twenty-four and I felt there was plenty of time."

He duly arrived at Canterbury in the spring of 1947 believing that he would gradually ease himself back into day-to-day cricket with some Club and Ground games, plus further matches for the 2nd XI. However, after a net against Doug Wright, Ray Dovey and Fred Ridgway he was parachuted straight into the 1st XI for their opening Championship fixture at the St Lawrence ground the following weekend against Derbyshire. It proved to be a baptism of fire as Brian was struck on the pad first ball by Bill Copson. The umpire turned down the appeal but the visiting fast bowler was indignant at the end of the torrid over – "That was f***** plumb" he growled at Brian who retained his composure and went on to eke out 24 on his first-class debut.

Brian appeared in a further nine games and ended the season with a very modest batting average of 9.68, plus three expensive wickets at a cost of 86. But Kent persevered with the left-handed batsman and off-cutter who took his aggregate to 324 runs in 1948 plus thirty wickets, before enjoying a fine summer with both bat and ball during 1949. His success began in early June at Southampton where he removed the first five Hampshire batsmen before Brian finished with the splendid figures of 7/41.

In the final week of the month, he led a rearguard action against Sussex at Tunbridge Wells after Kent had been forced to follow-on. His efforts with Fred Ridgway also saw the pair share a new Kent record partnership of 161 for the ninth wicket. Their stand began when Kent were still 53 runs in arrears and with just reserve wicket-keeper Geoff Ward left to bat, a Sussex victory looked on the cards.

But Ridgway settled in as Brian reached his maiden hundred after 130 minutes at the crease. His partner then opened his shoulders with great effect, smashing 4 sixes and 10 fours against the tiring attack. Brian also took toll of some weary bowling as he went past 150. Ridgway was eventually dismissed by the Langridge brothers before Ward also dropped anchor as Brian moved into the 190s. But three runs later his valiant and career-best innings came to an end as his partner was caught. Brian had struck 29 fours in his unbeaten 193 and although Sussex successfully chased 135 in an hour and a half, Brian's efforts won him his county cap.

He ended the summer with 893 first-class runs and might even have reached a thousand had he not missed several games during the second half of the summer. Such were the vagaries of county cricket during the immediate post-War years that some of the professionals made way for the talented amateurs during July and August. As Brian recalled "The amateurs inevitably pushed me lower down the order. Personally I didn't resent this at all. They were good players and were now available because of their holidays from work. I was also prone to muscle strains, presumably after the years of under-use and I missed the odd game through that as well."

Brian failed to score another hundred in 1950 – a summer which saw him amass just 409 first-class runs with his finest performance that summer coming at Lord's against Middlesex and elder brother Bill. On the final morning of an enthralling contest, the pair locked horns as Brian looked to extend Kent's lead, but with five wickets having fallen, the Middlesex bowlers were looking to make further inroads. Brian had other ideas though and staunchly defended, as his brother resorted to a series of short-pitched deliveries in a bid to end the innings. But Brian ducked and weaved before top-edging a hook against Bill which sent the ball first bounce over the wicket-keeper's head and into the sight-screen. "Good shot, Brian," said Jim Sims, causing everyone except for Bill to double-up in mirth. But it was Brian who had the last laugh as Kent went on to win by 32 runs.

He returned to form in 1951 with an aggregate of 1,267 runs and a tally exceeded by just Arthur Fagg and the young Colin Cowdrey. During the summer, he scored two hundreds, including 104 against Glamorgan at Swansea in an innings that was to prove even more important to him than he realized at the time. Despite a shoulder injury, he added another hundred against the Welsh county in 1952 and shared a fine stand of 221 in a shade over three hours with Dickie Mayes. But this proved to be his last fine innings for Kent as the following year, his shoulder continued to play up and prevented him from bowling. Having tightened up his defensive technique during 1952, Brian was promoted up the order and had a spell at number three. The experiment didn't work and by mid-July he was out of the side and at the end of the summer his contract was not renewed.

The committee's decision came as a huge surprise and Brian was still in a state of shock a few days later when he had a phone-call from Bill. "How do you get on with Wilf Wooller?" he asked before Brian replied "All right." Bill then explained that he had met Wilf at a cricket dinner and had asked what Brian was planning on doing now that his career with Kent was over. Bill had explained that he wasn't sure, to which the Glamorgan captain said "He always gets runs against us. We're interested in him." A phone-call duly took place between the pair with Brian explaining that his shoulder would not allow him to bowl any more, but Wilf explained that with Emrys Davies coming towards the end of his career, they wanted him as a batsman."

Brian duly made the first of 52 appearances for the Welsh county against Surrey at Pontypridd at the end of

An older Brian Edrich seen whilst playing club cricket in South Wales in 1958.

May 1954. He recorded a trio of fifties during the summer and took time to adjust to the slower surfaces in South Wales. However, his jovial personality meant that he was a popular figure with other players and, most importantly, with Wilf himself who found through chats with Brian that he was a good judge of an opposing batsman and could swiftly assess their strengths and weaknesses. Indeed, it was these talents that led to the start of the second phase of Brian's career with Glamorgan and followed a couple of barren summers with the bat where he got no further than 46 and had endured another failed spell at the top of the batting order.

The sudden and tragic death of George Lavis in July 1956 had left a vacancy in the Club's coaching staff and during Glamorgan's visit to Weston-super-Mare to play Somerset, Wilf had a chat with Brian. Fearing that he was about to hear bad news, Brian was pleasantly surprised when Wilf suggested that he joined the coaching staff, assisting Phil Clift, leading the Club's 2nd XI and helping to promote cricket throughout Wales. Having recently secured his MCC coaching certificate, Brian accepted the offer, besides agreeing to play at weekends for Maesteg Celtic in the South Wales and Monmouthshire League – a position which besides financially benefitting him, allowed Brian a chance to run his eye over aspiring young players.

He also helped out with umpiring several of the 2nd XI matches and swiftly adapted to his new role. By showing the same careful and considerate manner towards coaching as his late predecessor, Brian was able to get the best out of his young charges. As Peter Walker recalled, "while a seriously committed performer on the field, Brian was a joyful companion off it in the days when having several beers with opposition players and umpires at the end of a day's play was considered *de rigueur*. Brian ingrained in me the importance of sportsmanship and how to accept the lows in life as well as its highs. He had enjoyed his share of both, but always handled these with an engaging laugh and a mischievous smile. He played the game in the same way."

He remained with Glamorgan until 1963 – officially, it was said that financial cutbacks had led to his departure, but with Gilbert Parkhouse coming towards the end of his illustrious career, the Club were also looking to restructure their coaching set-up, besides giving Wilf, who by now had also retired, a new challenge. Brian subsequently secured a coaching post at St Edward's School, Oxford besides an opportunity to play Minor County cricket for Oxfordshire. He duly turned out for them between 1966 and 1971, besides winning a place as an opening batsman in the Minor Counties representative side which met the 1967 Pakistanis at Swindon.

That summer Brian also played in the Gillette Cup for Oxfordshire against Cambridgeshire at Wisbech. Once again, he opened the batting and met with little success, but during his final match of note, and second List A match, Brian made 30 batting at first wicket down for Oxfordshire against Worcestershire at the Morris Motors Sports Ground in Cowley. It was clearly a difficult wicket on which to bat, but he drew on all of his experience from his stints in county cricket with Kent and Glamorgan before being dismissed by Norman Gifford as his side ended their 60 overs on 99-9.

After retiring from coaching, Brian moved to live in Padstow in Cornwall. He stoically endured a difficult time during his last five years, but always welcomed former colleagues and opponents alike and, in his kind and thoughtful way, was happy to recall both the good and bad days of his playing career.

425
WARD, Donald John.

Born – Trealaw, 30 August 1934.
Professional.
RHB, OB.
Ed – Haverstock School, Chalk Farm.
1st XI: 1954-1962.
2nd XI: 1951-1962.
Colts: 1958.
Club and Ground: 1955-1962.
Cap: 1961.
Clubs: Shepherd's Bush, Briton Ferry Town, Pontarddulais, Gorseinon, Maesteg Celtic, Gowerton, Pontardawe, Neath, Maesteg Town, Tondu and Porthcawl.

Batting and Fielding Record

	M	I	NO	RUNS	AV	100	50	CT	ST
F-c	135	206	33	2496	14.42	-	6	65	-

Bowling Record

	Balls	M	R	W	AV	5wI	10wM
F-c	10778	448	4987	187	26.67	5	-

Career-bests
First-class –   86 v Somerset at Cardiff Arms Park, 1956.
7/60 v Lancashire at Stanley Park, Blackpool, 1962.

Don Ward, who played 135 times for Glamorgan between 1954 and 1962, was one of the unsung heroes of the Welsh county's team. Rarely grabbing the headlines, the diminutive right-handed batsman and off-spin bowler, was known to some as the 'Tonypandy Tot' and like many an actor who has made brief or cameo appearances, is remembered for having been in a film, rather than playing a starring role.

Indeed, Don chipped in with bat on many occasions, and played some fearless and attractive innings which together with others efforts helped Glamorgan to victory. As an understudy, initially to Jim McConnon and subsequently Don Shepherd, his off-spin was a useful weapon in the armoury of various Glamorgan captains. Like many bowlers who are short in stature, Don's flight and brisk trajectory made him quite difficult to play at first, compared with the more classical loop and spin of the taller spinners. His quicker style of spin meant that he hit the bat harder than other colleagues and his use in, quite literally, short spells added variety to the attack.

Don Ward.

Another of Don's greats assets was his fielding, whether it be close to the wicket or in the outfield. In each area, he showed great prowess, snaffling many chances in the leg-trap and swiftly running and gathering any balls that were sent into the deep. He was also a safe catcher on the boundary's edge, and allied to his tenacious batting and useful bowling, Don was a valued part of the Glamorgan team.

Born near Tonypandy, Don's family moved to Acton in 1942 and he first came to prominence during 1949 after England's demise the previous summer in the Ashes series. Under the guidance of EM Wellings, the correspondent of the now defunct London paper, the *Evening News*, Don was one of the schoolboys selected in a project called the Evening News Colts who received coaching at Alf Gover's Indoor School in a bid to unearth fresh talent and prevent further heavy defeats to Australia. Besides attending the coaching sessions, Don also played for the Colts against the Cross Arrows at Lord's, before winning a place as a batsman and off-spinner in the English Schools Cricket Association side in 1950 and appeared that summer against his Welsh counterparts at the Arms Park.

On leaving school, Wilf Wooller helped Don to secure a place on the MCC groundstaff at Lord's in 1951 before undertaking his National Service with the Army and representing them in matches against the likes of the Royal Navy and RAF during 1953 and 1954. By this time, he had a wealth of experience of 2nd XI cricket having first played for Glamorgan's second string in 1951, and shortly after completing his National Service, Don made his first-class debut in July 1954 for the Welsh county against Essex at Colchester. It proved to be a rain-affected draw but nevertheless Don had a chance to display his bowling talents, mopping up the Essex tail with figures of 3/15 from 9.5 overs.

He featured regularly during 1955 and 1956, and in the former year was a member of an all-Welsh born Glamorgan side which defeated Warwickshire by an innings and 80 runs at Neath. 1956 also saw him make his highest first-class score with a valiant 86 against Somerset at the Arms Park. It was also his maiden half-century in county cricket having arrived at the wicket with his team 140-6 and facing a sizeable deficit on first innings. His sprightly efforts saw Glamorgan to 313 and a decent first innings lead of 72 before trying to press for victory.

The game at Cardiff duly ended in a draw and it was to be five years before Don posted his next fifty. By this time, Jim Pressdee was bowling less so the Welsh county opted for an off-spinning triumvirate of Shepherd, McConnon and Ward to exploit the turning wickets of South Wales and further afield. The upshot was that Don got an extended run in the county's 1st XI and he responded with five half-centuries, a series of smart catches in the leg-trap plus 50 wickets. His reward was his county cap, plus a contract for 1962. This however proved to be his final summer in the county cricket, despite bowling Glamorgan to victory at Blackpool with figures of 7/60 in what ironically proved to be his penultimate county game.

With Glamorgan only prepared to offer Don another one-year contract, he decided to retire and gain greater job security initially with a transport company in South Wales before running a general store in Garth near Maesteg. He continued to play in the South Wales Leagues and during August 1972 represented Wales in their Triple Crown fixture against Ireland at Swansea.

This particular Donald John might have enjoyed a longer and more successful county career had it not been for the presence of another Donald John in Glamorgan's ranks. Nevertheless, his record of 187 wickets at just 26.67 apiece, with five-wicket hauls against Lancashire, Nottinghamshire, Surrey, Worcestershire and Yorkshire places him in the upper echelons of off-spinners to have represented the Welsh county.

Allan Watkins (left) and Don Ward walking out to bat.

426
DAVIES, William George.

Born – Barry, 3 July 1936.
Died – Llandough Hospital, 17 July 2022.
RHB, RM.
Ed – Barry Boys School.
1st XI: 1954-1960.
2nd XI: 1953-1961.
Club and Ground: 1957-1960.
Clubs: Barry, Clydach and Maesteg Celtic.

Batting and Fielding Record

	M	I	NO	RUNS	AV	100	50	CT	ST
F-c	32	58	0	674	11.62	-	2	14	-

Bowling Record

	Balls	M	R	W	AV	5wI	10wM
F-c	1312	50	646	16	40.37	-	-

Career-bests
First-class –   64 v Somerset at Bath, 1960.
                   2/23 v Warwickshire at Edgbaston, 1960.

Billy Davies took a wicket with his first delivery in county cricket, against Surrey at The Oval during 1957. Coming on as first change, the former pupil of Barry Boys School had Tom Clark caught in the gully by Jim Pressdee with his maiden delivery in first-class cricket for Glamorgan – a feat which had been achieved only once before by Jack Johns against Somerset at Cardiff during 1922.

Whilst pleased at this place in the Club's bowling annals, Billy was more of batsman and only really a back-up bowler. Four years before, he had made his Championship debut for the Welsh county. A series of promising innings in club cricket for Barry had seen Billy win selection for the county's 2nd XI during 1953 before the following summer, after further decent scores for the county's second string and for Barry, Billy made his first-class debut during late August for Glamorgan, opening the batting with Gilbert Parkhouse against Warwickshire at Edgbaston.

Billy also played in the next Championship match against Derbyshire at Chesterfield, which saw the Welsh county win by ten wickets, but his development as a county cricketer

was abruptly halted by his National Service in Germany. It meant that Billy did not play Championship cricket again until 1957 – a season when in thirteen appearances, he opened the batting again with Parkhouse as well as with Wilf Wooller.

He duly compiled his maiden Championship half-century by making 58 against Kent at Gravesend, besides entering the Club's record books at The Oval with the first of sixteen wickets for the Welsh county. This followed a winter coaching alongside Peter Walker in Johannesburg in South Africa but injury restricted Billy to a solitary appearance during 1959, followed by eight more during 1960. In the opinion of his friend and colleague Peter Walker, Billy though was never the same batsman as before his National Service – "When we were first on the staff, Billy looked to have a very promising career ahead of him as an opening batsman, but he was ruined by his compulsory

Billy Davies, as seen during 1958.

two years of National Service where some bad habits in his batting technique became indelibly ingrained. On his return, his youthful promise had evaporated."

1960 saw Billy make 64 against Somerset at Bath, but at the end of the season, he left the Glamorgan staff to take up a job with Refuge Assurance. His final appearance in the Championship had been in mid-August against Warwickshire at Edgbaston where, now batting at number eight, Billy made 4 and 7. He had more to remember though in his penultimate Championship appearance where he came face-to-face with England and Yorkshire fast bowler Fred Trueman in a remarkable encounter at Bradford Park

Avenue. Their meeting, however, took place in the Glamorgan changing-room where, in his typically garrulous way, Fred wandered in to meet old friends and adversaries besides sowing a few seeds of doubt into the newcomers and fresh faces such as Billy.

With Wilf Wooller absent, Gilbert Parkhouse was leading the side so after the stand-in leader had gone out to the middle for the toss with Vic Wilson, in bounded Fred who then sat on a table in the centre of the room. After Billy and the other novices had been introduced to the fast bowler by Bernard Hedges, Fred directed a series of comments in the direction of his new acquaintances – "I 'it Peter May on 'is ead last week, tha' knows. Aye! An' that Colin Cowdrey. Wun int' block-ole and wun in't Adams apple. Ah'll tell thee. That Tom Graveney E's a front foot player but 'ee never get's on front foot t'me, tha' knows. Ee knows ah'd pin 'im like a moth t'bluddie sightscreens!".

Seeing a nervous smile on Billy's cherubic face, Fred then rattled off a few more pithy comments about other county players until the door opened again and in returned Gilbert – "Sorry chaps, We've lost the toss. Vic's put us in and it's a bit green but oh! Hello Frederick!" he said realizing that the pace bowler was up to his usual trick of trying to unsettle the young players. "Good day, Gilbert, he replied, "So it's me who as t'bowl is it?" before getting up and turning in the direction of Billy and saying "Well, it's reet nice to welcome you young lads to cricket in Yorkshire. I'll be comin' down the 'ill from that 'igh red wall a bit sharpish. Good luck t'ya lads. Ah'll see thee art there in t'middle then – wun by bloody wun!"

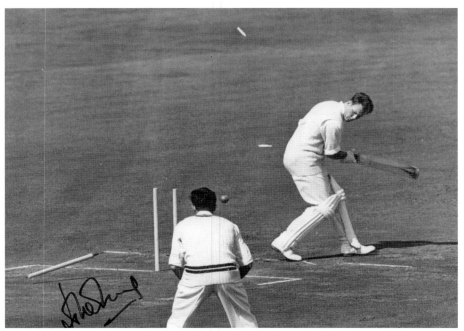

Billy Davies is bowled!

After this not-so-subtle piece of kidology, Billy only made 1 and 0, but it was Ray Illingworth who was bowling seamers who dismissed him in both innings, rather than 'Fiery Fred'. In fact, the England paceman nearly ended up on the losing side as Yorkshire scraped home by one wicket after being set a target of 173 on the final day against an attack missing Allan Watkins and Brian Evans who were both unable to bowl. In their absence Peter Walker switched from spin to left-arm seam and shared the new ball with Billy who cheaply dismissed Ken Taylor before Don Shepherd joined the attack and bowled in tandem with Walker for the rest of the innings.

By lunch, the pair had reduced Yorkshire to 98-6 with some of the home crowd venting their frustration by making ribald comments in the direction of the White Rose batsmen as they returned to the Park Avenue Pavillion. But Illingworth remained resolute and after the interval shared what proved to be a match-winning stand with Don Wilson, with the pair adding 49 before Walker struck again. Trueman then struck a few lusty blows before being snared, like so many, at short-leg by Walker off Shepherd's canny bowling. "Perhaps he should have spent more time practicing his batting in the nets rather than being in our room!" quipped one Glamorgan player as Trueman departed for the Pavillion whilst another joked "He would have heard far worse if The Skipper had been here! Anyway, come on boys, we can win this!"

With four runs needed and the tension mounting, David Evans spilled an edge from Illingworth, but two runs later Jimmy Binks was run out leaving the game on a knife-edge. However, Illingworth settled things in his team's favour as he fiercely square-cut Walker to the boundary ropes to complete a match-winning fifty and break Welsh hearts.

Billy continued to play in club cricket during the 1960s for Hill's Plymouth and Barry, in addition to appearing for Wales against the International Cavaliers at Colwyn Bay in 1969, as well as in their Triple Crown matches in 1971. The following summer he led the Welsh side against Ireland, Jamaica and the Orange Free State.

1955

After their return to winning ways during 1953 and 1954, the Welsh county plummeted to 16th place in the table as a series of fault lines also started to open up within the Glamorgan camp.

The retirement the previous summer of Emrys Davies led to a rejigged batting line-up with Wilf Wooller continuing to act as Gilbert Parkhouse's opening partner. No-one could question his resolve or purpose with the bat, but it was his bowling which, for once, was definitely his weaker suit as his prowess with the ball seemed to be on the wane after his Herculean efforts the previous summer.

Wilf was not the only bowler who seemed a shadow of their former self as Don Shepherd also lacked his previous penetration with the new ball and took only 59 Championship wickets at the relatively expensive return of 30 runs apiece. Jim McConnon was also beset with injury after his brief flirtation in Test cricket with England and an unhappy winter tour in Australia. It was therefore quite comforting that Allan Watkins, yet again, passed the 100-wicket mark in Championship cricket whilst Jim Pressdee made great headway as a left-arm spinner.

It was not just Wilf's bowling that was a worry for the Glamorgan committee as his captaincy during 1955 also attracted criticism, with accusations of the Welsh county being intent on playing negative cricket, with batsmen under orders to go-slow or bowlers being told to deliver balls short of a length on or around leg stump and with a defensively set field. The committee were also concerned that gate receipts had fallen by £2,000 and, compared with the heady years of the late 1940s and early 1950s, there were some terse conversations as the officials started to plan for 1956 and beyond.

A Glamorgan 2nd XI team group from 1955 including in the back row Alan Jones (2nd left), Frank Clarke (3rd left), Peter Gatehouse (4th left), David Parry-Jones (5th left) and Howard Morgan (far right) whilst in the front row are Peter Walker (third left) and George Shaw (4th left).

427
DAVIES, Hugh Daniel.

Born – Pembrey, 23 July 1932.
Died – Cardiff, 2 December 2017.
Professional.
Ed – Llanelli Boys GS and Cardiff College of Education.
1st XI: 1955-1960.
2nd XI: 1951-1959.
Colts: 1956.
Club and Ground: 1949-1956.
Clubs: Llanelli, Barry, Hill's Plymouth, Neath, Clydach and SCOW Margam.

Batting and Fielding Record

	M	I	NO	RUNS	AV	100	50	CT	ST
F-c	52	70	26	247	5.61	-	-	16	-

Bowling Record

	Balls	M	R	W	AV	5wI	10wM
F-c	6619	214	3659	115	31.81	4	-

Career-bests

First-class – 28 v Essex at Westcliff-on-Sea, 1958.
6/85 v Yorkshire at Bramall Lane, Sheffield, 1957.

Hugh Davies made 52 appearances for Glamorgan between 1955 and 1960. After retiring from teaching, he also acted as the Chairman of Cricket Wales, having earlier served on the Glamorgan committee. From 1993 until 2001 Hugh acted as Chairman of the Club's cricket committee – a period which saw the Welsh county win one-day silverware as well as the Championship title.

Born in Pembrey during July 1932, Hugh was the second son of Henry and Mary Davies who kept the Red Lion Inn in Llanelli. He duly attended the town's Boys Grammar School where he shone at cricket and rugby, and his talents were recognized with selection for the Welsh schoolboys in both sports.

Hugh's ability as a brisk right-arm seam bowler drew Glamorgan's attention, especially given the fact that the Welsh county were looking to nurture home-grown talent following their success in winning the County Championship in 1948. However, before Hugh could join the county's staff he had to complete his National Service

Hugh Davies.

with the RAF, and it was not until 1953 that he was able to become a professional cricketer.

Hugh made the first of his 52 appearances in first-class cricket against Gloucestershire at Swansea during June 1955 and he duly opened the bowling with the Welsh county's legendary captain Wilf Wooller. Hugh went wicketless in a bowling attack which also featured Allan Watkins, Jim McConnon and Jim Pressdee.

The Welsh-speaking bowler claimed his maiden wicket during his second game for Glamorgan, away to Yorkshire at Harrogate where he dismissed Frank Lowson, the opening batsman, besides catching Norman Yardley, the Yorkshire and England captain. Hugh's finest hour in professional cricket came two years later on Yorkshire soil where he played a key role in Glamorgan's seven-wicket victory at the Bramall Lane ground in Sheffield. Hugh claimed 6/85 in Yorkshire's second innings with his career-best tally including the scalps of the first five Yorkshire batsmen – Lowson, Bryan Stott, Vic Wilson, Ray Illingworth and Ken Taylor.

But just when Hugh had secured a regular place in the Glamorgan's line-up, he sustained a knee injury. Hugh had hoped that Glamorgan – or more correctly Wilf Wooller – would offer him a two-year contract, but with doubts about his long-term fitness this was not forthcoming and Hugh only appeared in nine further Championship matches after 1957. In modern times, a more gentle approach by the Glamorgan hierarchy would have embraced a period of rehabilitation and further medical screening in the hope that the fast bowler would regain fitness. But Hugh played in different times and for a Club where Wilf, in essence, made all of the decisions.

During to the closing years of Hugh's county career, he had embarked on a teacher training course at Cardiff College of Education and only played on an occasional basis during the late 1950s with his final first-class appearance coming at Lord's in May 1960 with Hugh claiming four wickets in Middlesex's second innings to take his final tally of wickets to 115 at 31 runs apiece.

Hugh Davies (far right) seen in 1997 as work starts on the creation of the National Cricket Centre at Sophia Gardens. On the left is Ossie Wheatley, plus Steve Watkin, Mike Powell, Steve James and Matthew Maynard.

He subsequently became a successful PE teacher, besides coaching at Glamorgan's Indoor Schools in Neath and Ebbw Vale. By the time, Hugh became a senior PE advisor for Mid-Glamorgan in 1982 he had become a member of the Glamorgan committee, besides being a summariser for BBC Radio Cymru during their Welsh language coverage of the county's games. In subsequent years, Hugh rose to the position of Chairman of Cricket with Glamorgan CCC, besides working for the Cricket Board of Wales from its inception in 1997, and serving as its Chairman between 2002 to 2011.

During his playing career, Hugh played club cricket for, amongst others, Llanelli, Neath, Barry and the Steel Company of Wales, whilst his son Adam also had a spell on Glamorgan's playing staff in the early 2000s before following his father onto the Club's committee.

428
REES, Alan Henry Morgan.

Born – Port Talbot, 17 February 1938.
Died – Morriston, 17 March 2022.
RHB, RM.
Professional.
Ed – Glanafan Grammar School.
1st XI: 1955-1971.
2nd XI: 1954-1970.
Cap: 1963.
Clubs: Maesteg Town, Briton Ferry Town, Dafen, SCOW Margam, Port Talbot and Ammanford.
Rugby Union for Maesteg, Aberavon, Llanelli and Wales (3 caps).
Rugby League for Leeds.

Batting and Fielding Record

	M	I	NO	RUNS	AV	100	50	CT	ST
F-c	216	372	53	7681	24.07	2	36	113	-
List A	17	15	1	207	14.78	--	1	5	-

Bowling Record

	Balls	M	R	W	AV	5wI	10wM
F-c	567	11	398	6	66.33	-	-
List A	6	0	2	0	-	-	-

Career-bests
First-class – 111* v Lancashire at Cardiff Arms Park, 1964.
　　　　　　　3/68 v Kent at Cardiff Arms Park, 1960.
List A – 　　　50 v Essex at The Gnoll, Neath, 1964.

Alan Rees was amongst the finest fielders in first-class cricket during the 1960s. A livewire at cover point or mid-wicket, his athletic fielding resulted in many dismissals, most notably during Glamorgan's back-to-back victories over both the 1964 and 1968 Australians at Swansea with Alan proudly playing a key role in both of these historic victories over the men in baggy green caps.

His fielding and steady batting in both games confirmed the belief that one of Alan's strengths was being able to produce the goods at the right time. Although he only averaged a shade over 24, Alan – at 5 foot and 7 inches – had the reputation of being a real fighter with the bat and a man, as befitted a rugby international, who was a fierce competitor and a fine natural athlete. The victory over the 1964 Australians also came during a purple patch for Alan who, a fortnight before, had posted back-to-back centuries with 106* against Kent at Maidstone followed next game with an unbeaten 111 against Lancashire at the Arms Park.

Although Alan never reached three figures again in his career, the middle-order batsman played two important innings in the victory over the 1964 Australians with scores of 48 and 47 helping his side to leave the tourists with a target of 268 on the wearing surface at St Helen's. By the close of play, Australia had chiselled away at the target and were 75-1 and seemingly well poised to maintain their unbeaten record in the county games, and against a team who had recorded just three wins from twenty Championship matches so far that summer.

An autographed photo of Alan Rees.

But the following morning, the Welsh county side fought back in grand style with Don Shepherd giving little away during a superb spell of bowling. Alan's razor-sharp fielding also stifled the Australians attempts to break free from the shackles which Don's nagging off-cutters had imposed. Tony Lewis also took a superb running catch in the deep, before Alan took a stunning waist-high catch at mid-wicket off Jim Pressdee's bowling to remove Bill Lawry just as it seemed the Australian opener was set to play a successful role as the anchorman in the run-chase. His departure left the tourists on 207-6 with Barry Jarman only having the bowlers to help him score the remaining 62 runs.

Despite the intense heat, and a touch or two of cramp, Shepherd and Pressdee continued to infuriate the visitors and as further wickets tumbled, the Glamorgan side – and the crowd of nearly 15,000 – held their breath as history beckoned. With 37 runs still to make, Eifion Jones caught Neil Hawke, before what seemed like half the population of the Principality surged onto the outfield and took part in an unscripted, but very Celtic celebration. As the songs grew louder and louder by the minute, it became clear to any doubters that it wasn't just Glamorgan who had beaten the Australians, it was Wales too!

Four year later, these joyous scenes at the St Helen's ground were repeated with Alan, yet again, playing a key role with the bat and in the field in a second piece of Welsh sporting history. Although he was dismissed by John Gleeson in the first innings for a duck, Alan again rose to the occasion with an unbeaten innings of 33 during which he helped to marshall the lower order and help guide Glamorgan to an impressive lead of 365 by the close of the second day.

With clear blue skies, the Swansea ground was packed to the rafters shortly before the start of the last day's play, with everyone hoping that the Glamorgan side could record another famous victory. It was not long before Alan was in the spotlight, as with the total on 35, the Australian openers set off for a quick single, but Alan, at cover, swooped on the ball before making an accurate underarm throw at the stumps at the striker's end to beat the desperate lunge of Ian Redpath who kept on running in the direction of the Swansea Pavillion, much to the delight of the large and partisan crowd.

After the victory in 1964, several of the Australians had told journalists that they had rarely seen a better fielder in county games, and perhaps remembering these plaudits, their team of 1968 were wary again of taking quick singles to the Port Talbot-born fielder.

Alan's fielding plus the clever tactics of acting captain Don Shepherd, helped to keep a rein on the tourists progress. As wickets tumbled, every ball that Alan intercepted at cover point and swiftly returned into the gloves of wicket-keeper Eifion Jones was accompanied by loud and passionate applause. His efforts rubbed off on his team-mates who enthusiastically held every chance that came their way, and when Dave Renneberg's holed out to Majid at cover, Glamorgan had won another memorable game by 79 runs.

Alan's reputation as one of the finest cover fielders in county cricket had also seen him summoned as an emergency fielder to Headingley in July 1964 for the Third Test of the Ashes series. With Glamorgan not playing over that period, Alan Jones also made his way to Yorkshire as another substitute fielder and the pair spent time together on the field after Peter Parfitt and Ken Taylor had each sustained injuries. Alan duly made

Alan Rees.

a smart catch to remove Peter Burge for 160 off the bowling of Fred Trueman and end the tourist's innings after the tourists had amassed a lead of 121 runs. His efforts though could not prevent an Australian victory as after dismissing England for a second time, Bobby Simpson's team eased to a seven-wicket win.

It was quite fitting that Alan should have his county colleague alongside him when appearing in Test cricket as well as playing at the Leeds ground where he was also playing rugby league, giving the rare distinction of playing both cricket and rugby at Headingley.

The two Alans – Jones and Rees – had played together in schools and colts cricket before, as junior professionals on Glamorgan's books in the late 1950s, sharing a bedsit in Richmond Road in Cardiff, thereby overcoming the need to return each night after play or practice at the Arms Park to their homes in Port Talbot or Clydach.

In 1967, the two Alan's had also opened the batting in Glamorgan's inaugural game at Sophia Gardens against the Indian tourists following the re-development of the Arms Park and the creation of the National Stadium. It was a bit of a soggy encounter with rain washing out the scheduled first day and despite the fact that the building work at their new home in the Welsh capital was yet to be completed, the pair walked out from the new Pavillion on 25 May 1967 as a new chapter in the history of the Welsh county unfolded. After the first ball bowled by Sadanand Mohol had escaped the gloves of Farokh Engineer and sped away for a bye, Alan Jones duly scored the first run at Glamorgan's new home before Alan Rees struck the first boundary.

Two years before, Alan Rees had also entered the cricket record books in rather unusual circumstances at Lord's during Glamorgan's Championship match against Middlesex. The game during mid-August 1965 had seen the Welsh county being set a target of 286 by Fred Titmus and after half-centuries by Peter Walker and Tony Lewis, a further 68 runs were needed in 35 minutes when Alan went down the wicket to the off-spin of Titmus only to over-balance and palm down the ball with his left glove as he fell over. As he later recalled "I was getting bogged down by Fred Titmus so I decided to give him the charge. Titmus saw me coming and bowled it a little quicker and wider of the leg stump. With John Murray sniffing a stumping, I put my left hand out and stopped the ball. After a deathly hush, Titmus appealed to umpire Ron Aspinall culminating in me being told I had to go." Alan duly departed as only the thirteenth player in cricket history to be dismissed 'handled the ball' and the first in English cricket since 1907.

Having shone as a schoolboy batsman and playing with success for the Welsh Schools, Alan had joined the Glamorgan staff during the mid-1950s. The right-handed batsman made his first-class debut against Somerset at Weston-Super-Mare in 1955, but with his studies at Loughborough University and National Service with the RAF, it was almost four years before Alan's next Championship appearance, against Warwickshire at Neath during 1959. Four years later, Alan won his county cap in 1963 having become a regular in the Welsh county's middle-order, besides becoming one of the finest cover points in Championship cricket.

His most productive season was in 1964 when the modest and stylish batter scored 1,206 runs in first-class cricket, and by which time Alan had also represented Wales at rugby union before pursuing a career in rugby league. After playing as a junior for Aberavon, Alan had joined Maesteg RFC and captained their side during 1961/62. His performances at fly-half led to three Welsh caps in 1962 with Alan playing against England, Scotland and France and scoring one drop goal. He had also been sounded out about a tour with the British Lions, but he declined a potential invitation owing to his burgeoning cricket career. He might also have played more times for Wales but, ahead of the 1962/63 season, Alan opted to turn professional in the oval ball game and play rugby league for Leeds

Alan Rees glances Ron Hooker to the ropes at Lord's during Glamorgan's County Championship match against Middlesex at Lord's in 1965.

giving him a rare chance to play both rugby and cricket at the historic Leeds ground. However, he was just settling into the team when he suffered a badly broken nose during an ill-tempered match against Oldham and spent many weeks on the sidelines. Within two years, Alan hung up his rugby boots with his talents largely unfulfilled at the highest level.

The softly spoken and modest Alan left Glamorgan's staff at the end of the 1968 season to become a sports development officer for Afan Borough Council. Given his place in the Club's history, and the back-to-back victories over the Australians, it was surprising that his departure – hastened to allow the signing of overseas batters – did not coincide with the award of a Benefit Year. However, he continued to play club cricket in the South Wales Cricket Association, and having been offered a match contract for one-day games, Alan re-appeared in Gillette Cup matches for Glamorgan during 1970 and 1971, as well as playing in Sunday League games during 1972. Whilst he fielded with his usual vigour and athleticism, he met with little success with the bat.

After leaving Afan Borough Council, Alan became a sales co-ordinator at a car dealership and garage in Port Talbot, in addition to taking up squash and winning a number of competitions for Welsh veterans. However, for Glamorgan supporters, Alan will always be remembered as one of their finest fielders and the man who featured in the memorable victories over the 1964 and 1968 Australians.

429
LEWIS, Anthony Robert CBE.

Born – Uplands, Swansea, 6 July 1938.

RHB, LBG.

Ed – Neath GS and Christ's College, Cambridge.

1st XI: 1955-1974.

2nd XI: 1954-1974.

Club and Ground: 1957.

Cap: 1960.

England 1972-1973 (9 Tests); Cambridge University 1960-1962 (Blue all three years);
Combined Services 1958-1959; Gentlemen 1962, Commonwealth XI 1967/68.

Clubs: Neath, South Wales Hunts, I Zingari, Arabs, Cambridge Quidnuncs, Heartaches,
MCC, Old England and The Lord's Taverners.

Rugby for Neath, Gloucester, Cambridge University and Pontypool.

Batting and Fielding Record

	M	I	NO	RUNS	AV	100	50	CT	ST
F-c	315	546	52	15003	30.37	21	81	155	-
List A	93	90	4	2061	23.96	-	12	27	-

Bowling Record

	Overs	M	R	W	AV	5wI	10wM
F-c	331	3	306	4	76.50	-	-
List A	14	0	60	0	-	-	-

Career-bests

First-class –   223   v Kent at Gravesend, 1966.

3/18   v Somerset at The Gnoll, Neath, 1967.

List A –   96   v Hertfordshire at St Helen's, Swansea, 1969.

In 1972/73 Tony Lewis became the first Glamorgan player to lead England in an overseas tour. This coveted honour crowned a highly successful playing career during which Tony also led Glamorgan to their second Championship title in 1969.

Tony was a man of many talents – a stylish and elegant batsman who, in the words of Christopher Martin-Jenkins could "drive the ball impeccably, cut well and could work the ball anywhere on the leg-side with easy timing." In modern parlance, Tony was very much a touch player and often seen at his best on the faster pitches on the county circuit, rather than the more turgid surfaces in Wales. He also possessed all of the attributes associated with the best of captains – tactically astute, besides playing the game with a smile on his face and always capable of getting the best out of his colleagues. Like his predecessor Ossie Wheatley, he was always prepared to gamble on a declaration even if there was a chance that Glamorgan might not win the game.

In many ways, he was unfortunate to be playing at a time when England possessed a number of fine captains, especially Ray Illingworth. However, in 1972/73, Tony eventually had the chance to lead England on the tour of India and Pakistan – he did not disappoint and led the MCC team to a series win.

After retiring from playing (prematurely in many people's eyes), Tony made the seamless progression from changing room to commentary box, working in various guises in the spoken and written media for almost thirty years. He had never really seen cricket as a career and, for several years, had mixed playing with journalism and broadcasting, with his interest in the latter being fuelled by a friendship with Richie Benaud and a series of conversations with the Australian during the Commonwealth XI's tour to Pakistan during February and March 1968.

As a commentator on both TV and radio, Tony had a rich and mellifluous voice, making shrewd analysis of proceedings out in the middle, as would be expected from a man who successfully captained both the Welsh county and England. His comments were never dry or turgid with his commentaries always full of puckish wit and Welsh whimsy. Indeed, a smile was never far away from his face when broadcasting or eloquently talking about cricket.

Born in Swansea, Tony was brought up in Neath with his semi-detached home in Bracken Road, just a stone's throw away from The Gnoll. It was here and the town's grammar school where his sporting instincts were nurtured, along with his musical talents. For a while, it looked as if Tony might follow his sister Heather – a talented pianist – into the musical world as he progressed from lessons with a young schoolmistress in Neath to securing a place as a violinist in the National Youth Orchestra of Wales. Shortly after his seventeenth birthday, Tony had to decide whether to accept an offer to take part in the Orchestra's summer course and concerts or to make his first-class debut for Glamorgan – the invitation with the daffodil embossed letterhead won the day.

Rugby was another of Tony's passions as he played at various positions in the backs for Neath Grammar School and the town's Schoolboys team, besides donating his front teeth to a rugby pitch in the Amman Valley courtesy of an opponent's toe-cap when in his early teens. But on Tuesdays, from the age of thirteen until eighteen, Tony had been given leave of absence from his afternoon lessons to catch the bus to Cardiff and take part in the evening net sessions staged in the rudimentary nets, assembled by the Glamorgan coaches along the second floor corridor of the North Stand at the Arms Park, with Tony and an assemblage of other aspiring talent, batting and bowling on a 22-yard strip of ship's linoleum.

There was no heating in the nets, nor hot water in the changing rooms for the youngsters, but this was surpassed by plenty of passion and a desire to impress the county's coaches, led by George Lavis, a man who was always smartly turned out in his Glamorgan blazer and neatly pressed whites. It was a lesson for the aspiring colts that no matter what the occasion, there was pride in wearing the daffodil blazer.

For Tony, the route he had taken from Cardiff General Railway Station to the Arms Park in Westgate Street for four winters, also became the route he took, aged seventeen, for his first-class debut during August 1955 having accepted the offer to play at Cardiff against Leicestershire, as well as appearing in the following, and closing, game of the summer on his home patch at Neath against Warwickshire. He had sporadically played 2nd XI cricket since the age of fifteen and had audaciously cover-driven for four the first ball he ever faced for the Welsh county bowled by Gloucestershire's Tom Goddard at the Nylon Spinners' ground in Pontypool. But this had been in front of a handful of spectators and with several thousand expected at the Arms Park and a team from the East Midlands chockful of experienced and talented players, this was an entirely different matter.

It was with a mix of excitement and trepidation that the callow youth politely knocked on the door of the home dressing-room and walked in. It was full of noisy voices as Haydn Davies, Allan Watkins, Willie Jones and Gilbert Parkhouse exchanged words with Wilf Wooller on several issues, but as Tony entered, 'The Skipper' broke off from these debates and said "Hello Tony, welcome to the madhouse!"

It was a very different place several hours later as Tony's first innings ended in a first-ball duck, having been trapped l.b.w. by the Australian spinner Jack Walsh, with the schoolboy returning to a silent changing room. "Bad luck Tony, Len Hutton started that way too", said Gilbert, whilst Willie added "Anyone tell you to play forward to Walsh

A youthful Tony Lewis as seen whilst playing for Cambridge University during 1958.

until you know what's going on?" Tony mumbled "No" in reply before adding "Is that what you do?" A few minutes later Wilf in his inestimable way sauntered over and said to Tony "Mark down every Leicestershire name out there. Catch up with the bastards one day, Tony and make them pay!"

Wilf duly took Tony, the only other amateur at that time, under his wing and in only in his second match, he told the schoolboy, as they headed at lunch to sit at the table reserved for the gentlemen players and committee, "You better get used to the committee table. You'll be dealing a lot with them when you are captain!" Pre-ordained it may have been by 'The Skipper', but little did the teenager know that he would duly enter the Club's annals by becoming the first, and so far, only Glamorgan captain to clinch the County Championship title on Welsh soil.

It was to be fourteen years before Tony achieved this accolade and during that time Wilf, the sporting colossus of Wales, played a guiding hand in Tony's journey into adulthood. It was Wilf who assisted Tony's transition from Neath Grammar School to reading History at Christ's College, Cambridge. Tony's original intention had been to go to Manchester University, but Wilf told Tony one day that he had written to his old tutor at Christ's and that he should expect an invitation to attend an interview at his former College. An interview duly took place with Dr Lucan Pratt, with the College's Senior Tutor welcoming Tony with the following words – "we have a letter from a certain Mr. Wilfred Wooller, but I must tell you that it is not necessarily to your benefit. Mr Wooller, I recall, was a very destructive gentleman and the last time he called in to my rooms, it was feet first through the ceiling from a party in the room above!" Nevertheless, Tony received a favourable offer and, after completing his National Service with the RAF, he went up to Cambridge, much to Wilf's delight, for the Michaelmas Term of 1959.

One aspect though of Tony's sporting development in which Wilf did not play a role had been his debut at full-back for Neath during March 1958. At the time, Tony was a cadet in the RAF and at home on a week-end pass. Finding themselves one man short for the visit to Gloucester, Tony was a late replacement with the team bus pulling up outside his home so that a member of the selection committee could knock on the door and ascertain his availability. It did not take Tony long to answer in the affirmative.

Whilst based at RAF Innsworth, Tony had also spent a season with Gloucester RFC, and whilst a Freshman at Cambridge, he pipped Ian Balding, another Christ's student and later a fine trainer of racehorses, for the number 15 shirt in the Light Blues XV. Later in his first year, Tony secured a regular place in the Cambridge XI and was able to show the benefit of having played five further Championship games for Glamorgan, besides playing for the RAF and also the Combined Services against Lancashire and Somerset, as well as undertaking a short tour to Holland.

Tony's cricketing education duly continued on the well-manicured surfaces at Fenner's, so lovingly tended by Cyril Coote, who besides being groundsman acted as a shrewd coach, mentor and confidant to a distinguished linage of student cricketers, including Tony who – like so many before and after him – was only too eager to learn from the man who spent over forty years at Cambridge. It was on one of Cyril's beloved pitches that Tony duly made his debut for the Light Blues against Surrey on 27 April 1960. Batting at number three, he was bowled by Alec Bedser for 4 in the first innings before being caught and bowled by Peter Loader for 70 in the second innings.

Later that summer, Tony moved up to open the batting with Roger Prideaux, the Tonbridge-educated batsman who was on Kent's playing staff. It proved to be a productive partnership with the pair adding 198 for the first wicket at Taunton in a run-laden game with Somerset where the top three on each side each posted centuries in their team's first innings. For Tony, his 106 was his maiden first-class hundred and he followed it up with 71 second time around, and shared another century stand with Roger who went on to make 106 and steer the students to a thrilling victory. Their purple patch continued in the final game before the Varsity Match, against Colonel LC Steven's XI at Eastbourne with the pair sharing an opening stand of 215. Tony also posted another century and might have added a third had rain not washed out the final day with Tony unbeaten on 75 in Cambridge's second innings.

On 6 July 1960 Tony become a Double Blue as he walked out to open the batting in the Varsity Match at Lord's. By sheer coincidence, Dai and Emrys Davies were the two umpires at Lord's, with the two former Glamorgan stalwarts each passing on words of encouragement to the young Welshman who seemingly was set to make another century in Cambridge's second innings. "Take it easy Tony bach," cajoled Dai when Tony was at the non-striker's end having completed his half-century whilst having reached the nineties, Emrys added "Get them in singles Tony." But on 95 he charged down the wicket to the leg-spin of Worcestershire's Alan Duff and was caught by Javed Burki at mid-on. As the crestfallen Welshman returned to the Pavillion he walked past Dai who said "I should really pick up that stump and crack it across your arse. A hundred was there you for you!"

A fortnight later Tony was back in South Wales and playing for the rest of the summer with Glamorgan. The county circuit being what it is meant that news of Tony's tame dismissal at Lord's had reached the ears of Wilf and other Glamorgan players. Whereas Gilbert Parkhouse and Allan Watkins said "Bad luck" and "There'll be plenty of other opportunities", Wilf's response was "What the hell do you think you were doing. Do that for Glamorgan, and you'll be dropped for the next game!"

It was not the first time though that Wilf had reprimanded Tony as, in only the second match of his career at Neath in 1955, he had nearly made the cardinal error of running out Wilf when 'The Skipper' was on 99. With Wilf having flicked the ball behind square on the leg-side, Tony had called

A signed photograph of Tony Lewis taken at Trent Bridge during 1972.

for a run, only to see Norman Horner pounce on the ball at square-leg before the pair had crossed. As Tony recalled in his memoirs "The ball went like an arrow towards Wilf's end. The ground shook under the frantic tread of Wooller, forty-five years old, stretching for his life in his size twelves for a rare first-class century. I turned and saw the ball bounce in front of the wickets. He was a mile out. Then it skimmed over the top of the middle stump; there was no one there though. 'The Skipper' was home. He then turned and came plodding down the pitch towards me, bat raised high to acknowledge the applause and shouting to me…'Do that to me again and I'll wrap this bat right around you!' Wooller's alright, a decent sort, they were saying at Neath. Got a hundred but still got time to talk to our Tone. He had, but he had made his point."

It was probably fortuitous that Wilf was not at Edgbaston in mid-August 1960 when Tony was again dismissed when in the nineties against Warwickshire. A withering look from Gilbert on Tony's return to the Pavillion was enough for Tony who during his two months in Glamorgan's ranks amassed 616 Championship runs, with his impressive tally including vital half-centuries in each innings against Surrey at the Arms Park. Besides seeing Glamorgan to victory, it was a performance which resulted soon afterwards when Tony being awarded his county cap.

Although he had still to score a Championship century, the presentation of his cap signalled that Tony was now an integral part of the team. For Wilf – and others in the Glamorgan team – his true acceptance in the Welsh county's line-up came in more relaxed and convivial surroundings at The Flying Horse Hotel in Nottingham as the Glamorgan team celebrated Peter Walker's achievement in having won a case of champagne for his outstanding fielding. In time-honoured fashion, Peter duly shared his prize with Wilf and the rest of the squad as they assembled in one of the hotel's lounges with 'The Skipper' sitting in front of an ornate fireplace and his team gathered all around. Tony was directly opposite Wilf, and after an hour or so – and surrounded by a pile of corks and bottles of Guinness – The Skipper suddenly lent back on the mantelpiece behind him, picked up a large onyx clock, and sent it, like a scrum-half to a number ten, flying across the room towards Tony.

As he recalled, "I caught it full on the chest, with the weight knocking me over as I tumbled into another chimney recess. I heard the laughter as I disappeared. I was winded but staggered back up and winged the clock back to Wilf who plucked it out of the air and replaced it on the shelf as if it was a small travelling clock. There was applause from the team as I took a couple of sips from my glass before visiting the lavatory to answer a call of nature and check my ribcage. No sooner had I looked in the toilet's mirror and seen that all was well than I was joined by The Skipper. He slapped me on the shoulder, almost knocking me into the adjoining urinal, saying 'Bloody great that Tony. You got up and threw it back. Now they know what you're made of. Call me Wilf!' "

Tony returned to Cambridge during the autumn of 1960 as a Double Blue and a capped county cricketer, eager to build further on these achievements, but his second year at Christ's proved to be a frustrating one as he was beset by further problems with his right knee. He had already experienced discomfort the previous year and had missed several rugby games in the build-up to the Varsity match. This time, things were far worse so, on the advice of Dr Windsor Lewis, the President of the University's rugby club, Tony had the troublesome cartilage removed in January 1961 following an operation at St Bartholomew's Hospital.

This wasn't the end of the matter however, as four months after the operation, Tony badly twisted the same knee whilst fielding against Richie Benaud's Australians at Fenner's. Having missed a few games, he was able to return to the Cambridge XI and for the second year in a row, made a sublime hundred against Somerset at Taunton. But as he continued to play, the discomfort returned and after hobbling through the Varsity Match, he sought further advice in mid-July. The outcome was the end of the season as the medics advised plenty of rest and no county cricket for Glamorgan.

Happily, Tony was restored to full fitness for 1962 – a year which saw Tony lead the Cambridge side as the History undergraduate had further opportunities to hone his leadership skills against a series of county teams, which, in those days, were usually at full strength. The summer also saw Tony sign off from Cambridge with a handsome and unbeaten 103 in the Varsity Match, with his century and decent form for the University also seeing Tony being chosen for the Gentlemen against the Players at both Lord's and Scarborough, with the latter being the final match in the series which dated back to 1806.

August 1962 was also a red-letter month for Tony as, firstly, at the start of the month, he led Glamorgan against the Pakistanis at Swansea as Ossie Wheatley – who had taken over from Wilf as the Welsh county's leader – took a well-deserved rest. Secondly, Tony also made his maiden Championship hundred with an unbeaten 123 against Nottinghamshire at Trent Bridge, before at the end of the month making 151 against Sussex at Hastings and ending the summer with an aggregate in excess of 2,000 runs in all first-class games.

His success at Cambridge, as well as for Glamorgan, had also led to approaches from other counties, including Leicestershire. Their go-ahead secretary Mike Turner had met with Tony and introduced him to their Chairman who was happy to arrange work in France for his hosiery business during the winter months. But despite the frustration of playing on slow and turning wickets at Swansea and Cardiff, Tony remained loyal to Glamorgan – "Whatever the pitches, I was Welsh and felt it passionately. We had identity and something inside which would make us too proud to play badly without self-recrimination."

After coming down in 1962, Tony became a mainstay in the Welsh county's middle-order besides being appointed as Glamorgan's vice-captain. During the winter, he worked for an advertising agency in Cardiff and settled into married life with his wife Joan and raising two daughters, Joanna and Anabel. Tony also had a brief flirtation with rugby again, this time playing for Pontypool before sustaining a broken ankle against Abertillery. It prompted another ear bashing from Wilf, now in his guise as Glamorgan's secretary. "You bloody fool," was Wilf's response. "A broken bone in your ankle six weeks before the cricket season. You're half bloody mad and the only reason you're not completely bloody mad is that you were playing for Pontypool not against them!"

In 1965 the advertising agency suddenly closed with the news reaching Tony when Glamorgan were playing Essex at Leyton. He shared the bombshell that he would be unemployed at the end of the season with Michael Melford, who was there to report on the game for the *Daily Telegraph*. By the end of the day, Michael had arranged for Tony to act as a reporter on Welsh club rugby with the autumn of 1965 seeing Tony start his outstanding career as a journalist. It was not long before he was also reporting for BBC Wales, with Tom Davies, their astute Radio Sports Producer, inviting Tony for an audition at their studios in Park Place in Cardiff followed by further training sessions as he became a trainee reporter at games which he was also covering for the *Daily Telegraph*.

If his winter career was in the ascent, so was his time with Glamorgan starting with the summer of 1963 – his first full season as a professional cricketer – which saw Tony and the rest of the Glamorgan side finish as runners-up in the County Championship, besides taking part in the inaugural List A game as the Welsh county met Somerset in the Gillette Cup at the Arms Park. 1964 saw Tony gleefully being part of the Glamorgan side which defeated the Australians at Swansea besides amassing 1,339 runs without scoring a hundred. The following summer Tony was an integral part of the Welsh county's team which finished third in the Championship, besides scoring a handsome 169 against the New Zealanders at Cardiff Arms Park, plus an unbeaten 146 in the game with the South Africans at Swansea.

Tony Lewis flicks a ball to the ropes during his career-best innings against Kent at Gravesend in 1966.

1966 was however his *annus mirabilis* as he became only the second Glamorgan batsman to score 2,000 runs for the Club during a season. His tally included a career-best 223 against Kent, as well as 102 against Middlesex at Lord's, 103 against Northamptonshire on his home patch at Neath, plus home and away hundreds against Gloucestershire with 100 at the Wagonworks ground in Gloucester and 146 at the Arms Park. During the summer, Ossie Wheatley also intimated to the Club's committee that with growing business interests, he intended to stand down at the end of the season as Glamorgan's leader. After a series of discussions with the Club's hierarchy, Tony was promoted to the captaincy for 1967, thereby fulfilling Wilf's prophecy.

His elevation coincided with three glorious summers in the county's history, with a victory over the 1968 Australians at Swansea, the Championship title in 1969 with his team going unbeaten through a daffodil-golden summer and then a runners-up spot in 1970. Tony however only played a watching brief in the first of these achievements, as minor ailments caused him to sit out the game at St Helen's. His absence saw Don

Tony Lewis walks out to bat at Swansea in a posed publicity photograph staged at the St Helen's ground during 1963.

Shepherd, his most able lieutenant, lead the side to a memorable 79-run victory and a special place in Welsh sporting history. During his time as the Welsh county's leader, Tony was fortunate to have someone of Don's calibre as his right-hand man. It helped as well that the pair were good friends, unlike some counties where there was envy or jealousy within the leadership unit. This was definitely not the case with Don, besides adding tactical nous befitting a man with over 2,000 wickets to his name, always willing to help Tony with declarations, especially if the captain was out in the middle. As Tony freely admitted "I could never work out a declaration from the crease. Don Shepherd used to work out the equation of time and minutes, and then wave me in."

It spoke volumes of Tony's leadership style that he accepted Wilf's presence as the Club's unelected *general factotum*. Others may have found him overbearing or meddlesome, but Wilf was never going to change. Tony had known him since the 1950s and had survived many a verbal tirade from 'The Skipper'. It's true that Wilf's carping comments in the newspapers and on BBC commentaries ruffled a few feathers, but Tony knew where Wilf's heart lay as a passionate and proud Welshman. There were times when captain and secretary clashed swords, but, to Tony's credit, their spats took place behind closed doors – unlike those after Tony had retired during the 1970s – with the captain safe in the knowledge that, after all, he had been chosen at a very young age to step one day into Wilf's shoes, besides knowing that if arbitration was required, he could always call upon Johnnie Clay, now the Club's venerable President and the man who himself had groomed Wilf as the county's leader during the immediate post-War years.

Like many others before, and after, his form dropped having taken over the captaincy. Having averaged over 40 in 1966 with a tally in excess of 2,000, Tony scraped past the 1,000 run-mark in 1967 with a modest average of 22, whilst in 1968 he did little better with the bat, amassing 1,163 runs at 24. Unburdened by the captaincy, as on the Commonwealth XI's tour of Pakistan in 1967/68, Tony was in good form, He ended the tour, alongside county colleagues Don Shepherd and Peter Walker, as the leading run-scorer with 477 runs, including an unbeaten century against a Pakistan Board XI at Karachi.

Any feelings of ambivalence which Tony may have held over his batting form in county cricket were dispelled over the course of the next two seasons as he increased his tally to 1422 and 1693 and saw Glamorgan enjoy a purple patch, winning 20 Championship games and losing just 6 of the 48 games during 1969 and 1970. The seeds had been sown during his first two years as the Welsh captain's leader, and a time when Tony had also shown his mettle by opting for Eifion Jones as wicket-keeper, ahead of David Evans, whose glovework continued to be outstanding but whose batting had been limited. As Tony later reflected, "he was hurt. I must be honest, so was I, to have had to be the decider. He became ill: I was taught a lot about the aspirations of professional cricketers and their families"

A couple of seasons later, Tony also moved Bryan Davis, the West Indian batsman from the opener's berth with Alan Jones down to number five in the order after the Trinidadian had appeared to be unused to the new ball lavishly moving off the seam. Tony again – "he was a little resentful. It was a tumble of ego for a Test player, especially one who had come to county cricket hoping to re-establish his chances with the West Indian selectors. Relegation in Glamorgan meant diminishing chances back home."

Both decisions, however difficult they were for Tony to make, proved to be correct as the small and closely-knit squad reached their apex in 1969 and reaped rewards from the plan which he had devised together with Wilf and Chairman of Cricket, Tom Taylor (Vol. 2, pp. 199-200). With the bonus points structure favouring quick scoring in the first innings, the key message from Tony was for his batsmen to adopt a positive approach, with the captain also being fully prepared to declare in arrears, knowing that his bowlers had the skills and mental fortitude to dismiss their opponents for a second time. The key ingredients were the steadfastness of Alan Jones and Bryan Davis at the top of the order, coupled with the fast-scoring abilities of Majid Khan and Tony himself in the middle-order, an outstanding fielding unit led by the fearless Peter Walker and his equally brave side-kick Roger Davis and wicket-keeper Eifion Jones, plus the skills of Malcolm Nash and Tony Cordle with the new ball, the emergence of Lawrence Williams as a quality change bowler and the miserly attitude of Don Shepherd and his probing off-cutters.

For 'Shep' control with the ball was the key weapon in Tony's armoury and, on many evenings over a pint or two after play, he would remind Tony of his simple philosophy – "Tie 'em down, don't over-attack, make them hit the ball to our fielders. Batsmen can be idiots. They'll get themselves out half of the time." The fact that shortly after 'Shep' had claimed the final and decisive wicket in the title-clinching game against Worcestershire at Sophia Gardens, he instantly looked for Tony before the pair embraced each other, and were engulfed by members of the joyous crowd who had sprinted onto the outfield, spoke volumes for the bond of trust, loyalty and mutual respect which existed between the Glamorgan captain and his wise deputy.

Shortly afterwards, standing arms aloft on the Pavillion balcony Tony's smiling face was captured by photographers and television cameras alike, with the fact that he had bagged a pair in the game now being a distant memory. Standing that afternoon in front of thousands of jubilant supporters was the crowning moment of Tony's sporting career and in his coronation speech to the waiting journalists he heaped praise, in his typically magnanimous way, on his colleagues, stressing that it had been an outstanding effort by his small squad of players, all of whom at one time or another had produced a match-winning effort.

But we should not forget Tony's decision-making and leadership skills. As he wrote in his autobiography, "every captain brings his own personal qualities to the job. I offered independence because I never relied on Glamorgan County Cricket Club for my living; my freelance writing and broadcasting in the winter was far more profitable. I believed in encouraging an atmosphere in which players thought their own game through and enjoyed themselves."

Neither should we discount his diplomacy, as with the hullaballoo that followed the bizarre ending to the game at Bournemouth when, after a lengthy rain-delay on the final afternoon, the home team had left Dean Park believing the match was over, only for the umpires – Peter Wight and Lloyd Budd – to take to the field with the Welsh county and, in the absence of the Hampshire batsmen, awarding the game to Glamorgan. There had clearly been a misunderstanding and, with Glamorgan still riding high in the table, Tony and the rest of the Club's management did not want the season to be remembered as the year when they won the title as a result of what had happened at Bournemouth.

Hampshire's request for a court of appeal was upheld and Tony duly went up to Lord's and sat in one of the MCC's committee rooms, surrounded by a phalanx of representatives from the South Coast county, including players, lawyers and their sundry match-day officials, plus the two umpires. "In contrast, I was the sole Glamorgan advocate," as Tony recalled. "Hampshire's volatile argument lasted most of the morning but eventually, near lunchtime, I was asked for my version. I simply said that I had come only to advocate the removal of the ten points we had been awarded for that so-called win."

For 'AR', as he was affectionately known by his team-mates, he was lucky that the squad had been largely injury-free that summer, with a settled eleven augmented by leg-spinner David Lewis and Ossie Wheatley, with the emergence of Lawrence Williams compensating for the loss of Jeff Jones who had succumbed the year before to a career-ending injury. Tony was also fortunate that he could call upon the mercurial talents of Majid, the gifted Pakistani batsman.

Hungry for runs and not weighed down by other worries – as in the years when he

A proud Tony Lewis shows off a special memento from his team's Championship-winning success in 1969 to a TV cameraman watched by committee member Bill Edwards (seated) and Norman Riches during a black-tie event staged at Cardiff City Hall.

succeeded Tony – Majid's abilities to score quickly, as well as play with freedom on the most capricious of pitches had been priceless. With the square at Sophia Gardens still playing tricks and often causing the ball to either rise up sharply or scuttle through low, there were a few doubts in the minds of Tony and his batsmen, as well as the visitors. But not so, Majid – who also spent time living with Tony and his young family, besides acting as a charming baby-sitter, whose graceful and chanceless century against Worcestershire saw the Welsh county into the ascendancy and helped the team of '69 take their rightful place in the Club's annals besides earning the following tribute from Tony – "he was the finest batsman I ever partnered in the middle."

For Tony, 'Shep' and Alan Jones another reward came their way at the end of the summer as the trio of happy Welshmen were chosen in the MCC party to tour Ceylon and the Far East, with 'AR' deservedly leading the party on their month-long visit. Their itinerary may have been hastily put together in light of the cancellation of the original plan to tour East Africa, following concerns over the UK's relations with South Africa, but it was a clear sign that the game's ruling body had taken notice of the Welsh county's success and their leadership attributes of their captain, if not the Test-playing capabilities of his players.

Two and a half years later, Tony was elevated to the England captaincy following Ray Illingworth's decision not to tour India, Pakistan and Sri Lanka. Geoff Boycott also withdrew, so it was Kent's Mike Denness who was Tony's vice-captain whilst Donald Carr acted as tour manager. The Glamorgan leader duly repaid the selectors faith by steering England to victory in the First Test at Delhi, despite a tweak in his right calf muscle and a first innings duck – l.b.w. to Chandrasekhar. He fully recovered and later hit 125 in the Fourth Test at Kanpur and at a time when there was talk of an attack by the Black September movement. Despite their hotel being alive with soldiers and plain-clothes police, Tony was able to focus on the cricket and attack the home spinners for his maiden Test century.

However, when the Glamorgan captain reached three figures, there was an amusing moment – "Lots of Indians ran onto the field with garlands and handshakes. However, the century had come with a single which took me to the other end. The student avalanche therefore hit Keith Fletcher. I looked down the pitch and saw him suffocating with garlands, all dripping wet and beaten to a pulp by back-slappers. He duly walked up the pitch and said 'It's OK, but they are for you mate as I'm only five not out!' "

During his time in the sub-continent, Tony had contacted Wilf to inform that his knee problems had flared up again and that he wished to stand down from the Glamorgan captaincy. Despite a telegram from HRH Prince Charles after the Championship victory in 1969 to do the same in 1970, Tony's team had disobeyed these regal instructions as his team ended as runners-up. But this proved to be the final summer of success for Tony's team as 1971 saw them plummet down to 15th before rising up a couple of places to 13th in 1972, with Tony posting what would prove to be his 21st and final Championship hundred against Nottinghamshire – the team against whom he had posted his first. There was little joy as well in the limited-overs games as Glamorgan struggled to find the winning formula in List A games. By the time Tony returned to the UK in the spring of 1973, Majid had been appointed as his successor with the Pakistani saying at the time that he did not want the captaincy, but for the sake of Glamorgan CCC he would do it but solely only in terms of on-field matters. It give license to others to oversee (and meddle in) the off-field matters as well as matters of selection, and with other senior players finishing their careers and the results deteriorating further, it was a recipe for disaster.

After his success in the sub-continent, Tony retained his place for the opening Test of the 1973 summer against New Zealand at Trent Bridge, but Tony's contribution at Nottingham was just 2 and 2, and he lost his place for the subsequent games in the series. With his knee still giving him discomfort, Tony only managed nine games during which he hit a sole fifty. After operations to his knee and Achilles tendon, Tony achieved greater mobility during 1974, but a Championship hundred still proved elusive. Several of the Championship-winning squad had departed by this time, including Don Shepherd and Peter Walker, and life in the Glamorgan camp was markedly different with a crop of youngsters looking to make their way in the game.

Tony also found run-scoring elusive in the List A games, including the Sunday League encounter at Cardiff on 21 July 1974 against Leicestershire. It proved to be his last game in Glamorgan's ranks as a couple of days later, after being told he was being left out of the Championship

Glamorgan duo Tony Lewis and Majid Khan toss ahead of England's Third Test against Pakistan in March 1973. When published in UK newspapers, it prompted one wag to suggest that the caption should say "Has Wilf Wooller given you any instructions!"

91

team against Middlesex, Tony called time on his career and announced his retirement. As he later admitted "there was never a second thought about playing on. It was an immediate relief not to get out of bed in the morning praying that my knees were not hurting."

After retiring in 1974, Tony became a highly regarded broadcaster and cricket writer, besides playing in more relaxed surroundings for the South Wales Hunts, I Zingari, the Arabs, Cambridge Quidnuncs, Heartaches, MCC and Lord's Taverners, in addition to leading an MCC party on a tour to the United States. In 1975 he was appointed as both cricket and rugby correspondent of the *Sunday Telegraph*, besides acting for the next ten years as the presenter of BBC Radio's *Sport on Four* programme on Saturday mornings. Between 1988 and 1992 Tony served as Glamorgan's Chairman, whilst from 1998 until 2000 he acted as the President of the MCC. During these years he also acted as Chairman of the Welsh Tourist Board and the Welsh National Opera, with his outstanding work for all of these organisations leading to the fitting award of the CBE in the 2002 New Year's Honours for services to sport, broadcasting and Wales.

Tony subsequently chaired the MCC World Cricket committee between 2006 and 2011, besides overseeing Wales' bid to stage the Ryder Cup, which was eventually achieved at the Celtic Manor in Newport during 2010. The following year, Tony was appointed a Life Vice-President of the MCC as well as captain of the Royal Porthcawl Golf Club. By this time, he had reduced his broadcasting and journalism activities although from 2015 Tony has continued to contribute a perceptive weekly column for the *Western Mail*.

Many though of the modern era will remember him as a broadcaster rather than a successful county cricketer and, as a young journalist for *Wisden Cricket Monthly* recently wrote about Tony's time on BBC TV, and the end-of-play highlights, "We miss the eyebrows, the sprightly, probing, Robin Day-like, 'If I may say so' interjections. We miss the asides and the wryness. We miss him saying when a thick edge runs down to third-man, '…and it always goes for four…' We miss the owlishness. The blazer. The glint, the shoulder lean, and the rectitude."

Tony Lewis is introduced by MCC Tour Manager Donald Carr to Indian Prime Minister Mrs Indira Gandhi during the England tour of the sub-continent in 1972/73.

1956

After the brickbats which came their way the previous summer, Glamorgan Cricket was badly in need of a tonic during 1956. It duly came their way through the wonderful transformation of Don Shepherd from what had been a journeyman existence as a seam bowler into a potent and match-winning purveyor of off-cutters.

Don's haul of 168 first-class wickets more than made up for Jim McConnon's decision to regain fitness by plying his trade in the Lancashire Leagues with Don, quite remarkably, claiming his 100th wicket on 2 July. Never again would a bowler in county cricket reach this milestone so quickly and for much of the season it looked as if Johnnie Clay's Club record of 176 first-class wickets would be surpassed by the off-cutter.

The Glamorgan squad for the match against Warwickshire at Edgbaston during July 1956. — Back row (left to right) — Jim Pleass, Ken Lewis, Jim Pressdee, Peter Walker, Louis Devereux, Bernard Hedges and Don Ward. Front row — Gilbert Parkhouse, Haydn Davies, Wilf Wooller, Allan Watkins and Don Shepherd.

Through his efforts, Glamorgan rose up to 13th place and it would have been even higher had Jim Pressdee not lost confidence as his spin-bowling partner, or if both Phil Clift or Allan Watkins not lost form with the bat, as the latter failed to pass 1,000 runs for the first time since the Second World War.

Despite the success of Don in his new slower style, and Wilf Wooller's astute captaincy, The Glamorgan captain once again attracted some bad press, especially after the match against Sussex at Hove during May when, after the home side had amassed 379-9, Glamorgan scored only 143 runs in six hours and forty minutes before achieving their objective of saving the game after a marathon innings from 'The Skipper'.

Facing a barrage of criticism in the national papers, Wilf's supporters quickly leapt to his defence, arguing that with the limited resources at his command, and other batsmen out of form, what else could he have done in order to prevent Sussex from winning. But with the gate receipts yet again at the end of the summer being less than anticipated, there was a growing consensus that such negative batting was bad for cricket, and the image of Glamorgan, whatever the outcome of the match.

HORSFALL, Richard.

Born – Todmorden, 26 June 1920.
Died – Halifax, 25 August 1981.
RHB.
Professional.
1st XI: 1956.
2nd XI: 1956.
Club and Ground: 1956.
Essex 1947-1955; South of England 1948.
Club: Todmorden.

Batting and Fielding Record

	M	I	NO	RUNS	AV	100	50	CT	ST
F-c	5	9	0	76	8.44	-	-	2	-

Career-bests
First-class –   21 v Essex at Ilford 1956.

Dick Horsfall had a brief spell with Glamorgan in 1956 after a nine-year career with Essex during which he scored seventeen hundreds including a career-best 206 against Kent at Blackheath in 1951.

The Yorkshire-born right-hander had played with success in the Lancashire League for Todmorden since 1936 and had aspirations of joining his native county after the Second World War. No offers however came his way, but Essex expressed an interest in the fast-scoring batsman and during mid-June 1947 Dick made his first-class debut against Sussex at Brentwood, and made a fluent half-century.

It proved to be a successful move for Dick as the following month he made his maiden century as he struck 170 in three and three-quarter hours against Hampshire at Bournemouth and shared a stand of 225 with Frank Vigar. Three further hundreds followed in 1948 besides the award of his county cap and selection in the South of England team which met Glamorgan in a special match at Swansea in September 1948 as the Welsh county celebrated their Championship success.

The following summer Dick was restricted by back problems to just six appearances for Essex and with further niggles in 1950 some wondered if he would recover and

Dick Horsfall.

regain his place in Essex's middle-order. Fortunately, he bounced back in 1951, amassing 1,655 runs including a three-hour century against Glamorgan at Chelmsford as well as his double-century against Kent during which he shared a record-breaking stand of 343 with wicket-keeper Paul Gibb.

Dick was in good form again in 1952 striking three centuries and making 1,560 runs before having a run-laden summer in 1953 with 1,731 runs and five hundreds, including an unbeaten 151 against Kent and 140 in the game with Somerset. However, his finest innings that summer came at Edgbaston where he recorded the fastest century of the season, with a hundred in just 85 minutes against Warwickshire. But his back problems flared up again in 1954 with Dick only making one century and amassing 921 runs. 1955 was another lean summer as Dick only scored 721 runs and, with his average having dropped to 17, he was released by Essex at the end of the season.

Given his experience, and remembering his flowing hundred against the Welsh county in 1951, Glamorgan's officials were pleased to offer him terms for 1956 in the hope that his ailments would not resurface. At first, all seemed well as he made an attractive 77 against Gloucestershire during a two-day friendly, but after just five appearances, Horsfall had further health problems and lost his place in the team. Soon afterwards, he announced his retirement from professional cricket and returned to Todmorden where he played as an amateur for the next two summers.

431
DEVEREUX, Louis Norman.

Born – Heavitree, Exeter, 20 October 1931.
Died – Aberystwyth, 12 November 2016.
Professional.
RHB, OB.
Ed – Torquay Boys GS.
1st XI: 1956-1960.
2nd XI: 1959-1960.
Colts: 1956-1960.
Cap: 1956.
Middlesex 1949; Combined Services 1950-1951; Worcestershire 1950-1955.
Clubs: Gorseinon, Cardiff and Poloc.

Batting and Fielding Record

	M	I	NO	RUNS	AV	100	50	CT	ST
F-c	106	187	25	3292	20.32	1	14	60	-

Bowling Record

	Balls	M	R	W	AV	5wI	10wM
F-c	4354	224	1768	72	24.55	2	-

Career-bests
First-class – 108* v Lancashire at Old Trafford, 1957.
6/29 v Yorkshire at Acklam Park, Middlesbrough, 1956.

Louis Devereux played in 106 matches for Glamorgan between 1956 and 1960. Born in Exeter and educated in Torquay, Louis played twice as a seventeen year-old for Middlesex in 1949 in their matches against Cambridge and Oxford University having the previous year been on the MCC groundstaff and playing at Lord's alongside a youthful Don Shepherd.

In 1950 Louis joined Worcestershire, with the right-handed batsman and off-spin bowler subsequently appearing in 79 games for the Midland county. Louis enjoyed his most successful all-round season during 1953 hitting 732 runs, besides claiming 55 wickets for Worcestershire, and he remained a regular in the county's line-up until the middle of the 1955 season.

Louis joined Glamorgan in 1956 and made an immediate impact, scoring 833 runs and taking 22 wickets, including a career-best 6/29 in the first innings of Glamorgan's match against Yorkshire at Acklam Park in Middlesbrough. Louis' victims included Vic Wilson, Ken Taylor, Willie Watson and Brian Close as Yorkshire were skittled out for just 174, but play was only possible on the opening day of the contest, with steady rain on the remaining days preventing Glamorgan from forcing a victory. A fortnight later at Newport, Louis took 5/11 against Gloucestershire as the visitors collapsed in their second innings from 61-0 to 81 all out with Louis bowling in tandem with his good friend Don Shepherd, who also claimed five cheap wickets with his off-cutters. But once again, Louis' excellent efforts with the ball did not seal a Glamorgan victory. Tom Graveney had scored a double-hundred in the visitors first innings and, with the Rodney Parade wicket taking spin, Sam Cook and Bomber Wells bowled Gloucestershire to a 37-run victory. Nevertheless, Louis' steady batting in his debut season in Wales, allied to his bowling and sharp fielding duly won him his county cap.

Louis Devereux.

The following year, Louis struck an unbeaten 108 against Lancashire at Old Trafford, besides passing a thousand runs for the one and only time in his career. But 'Shep' having made a successful transition from pace bowler to off-cutter, and Jim McConnon enjoying some productive summers with his off-breaks, including 106 Championship wickets in 1959, Louis' off-spin was called upon less and less by captain Wilf Wooller.

Louis made his last appearance for the Welsh county during the first week of July 1960 at Bristol and in a game which saw Gloucestershire inflict an innings defeat on Wilf's team. Although Louis was unbeaten on 26 as Glamorgan followed-on, he lost both his place in the team, and later his place on the county's staff. The following month was a difficult one for Louis as, aware that his contract was up at the end of the summer, he fretted about his future. Discussions did take place with Wilf and others, but even so, it still came as something of a surprise for Louis to read of his release in an article in the *Western Mail* newspaper. His playing colleagues were surprised at his treatment and believed he was a wonderful fellow who never enjoyed the best of luck.

Whilst on Glamorgan's staff, Louis played club cricket for Gorseinon and Cardiff, besides coaching in South Africa and Argentina during the winter months. Indeed, during 1959/60 Louis also played in club cricket in Buenos Aires. In his youth, Louis had been a talented table tennis player and had represented England in 1949, whilst he also played cricket for the Combined Services in 1950 and 1951.

After being released by Glamorgan, Louis played for the Poloc club in Glasgow before moving back to Wales. He initially ran the Bluebell Hotel in Aberystwyth, before becoming the proprietor of the nearby Central Hotel from 1965 until 1995. During this time, he enjoyed playing golf, and successfully reduced his handicap down to one.

432
EVANS, David Gwilym Lloyd.

Born – Lambeth, 27 July 1933.
Died – Drefach, Llandyssul, 25 March 1990.
RHB, WK.
Professional.
Ed – Amman Valley GS.
1st XI: 1956-1969.
2nd XI: 1954-1969.
Club and Ground: 1956-1962.
Cap: 1959; Benefit: 1969.
International Cavaliers 1967-1968.
Clubs: St Fagans, Briton Ferry Steel and Ammanford.

Batting and Fielding Record

	M	I	NO	RUNS	AV	100	50	CT	ST
F-c	270	364	91	2875	10.53	-	-	503	55
List A	5	2	0	9	4.50	-	-	6	-

Bowling Record

	Balls	M	R	W	AV	5wI	10wM
F-c	24	0	12	0	-	-	-

Career-bests
First-class –   46* v Oxford University at The Parks, Oxford, 1961.
List A –   8 v Surrey at The Oval, 1965.

Glamorgan have been fortunate to have had a lineage of highly capable wicket-keepers in post-war cricket with David Evans succeeding Haydn Davies at the end of the 1958 season. For the next ten years, before the emergence of Eifion Jones, David maintained the high standards set by his predecessor before retiring in 1969 with over 500 dismissals to his name.

Born in London to a family who hailed from Ammanford, David was brought up in the village of Pen-y-Groes in Carmarthenshire with Welsh being his first language. He duly progressed from the Welsh Schools team into the Ammanford side and during a Benefit match for the club against Glamorgan the schoolboy's neat and unobtrusive glovework impressed the watching county officials. An invitation soon followed to play for Glamorgan 2nd XI in 1954 and the following year David joined the county's staff as the understudy to Haydn Davies.

He made his first-class debut in 1956 against the Combined Services at Cardiff Arms Park, and in his second match, against the West Indians at the same ground the following June, he committed the cardinal sin of running out Wilf Wooller with the young wicket-keeper failing to respond to his captain's call for a suicidal run. Dai Davies was one of the umpires and, as the annoyed Glamorgan captain walked off, he said, in Welsh, to David "I don't think Mr. Wooller is very happy with you. Tread carefully when you return to the changing room!" These were prophetic as a few minutes later when the Glamorgan innings was ended by Garry Sobers clean bowling Don Shepherd, David returned to the Pavillion and suffered a typically fierce rebuke from his captain – "Who the hell do you think you are? When I say run, you bloody run or you won't have a contract next year."

A cheerful David Evans as seen in 1985.

David survived this ear-bashing and duly took over behind the stumps on a regular basis when Haydn retired at the end of the 1958 season. The following summer, David won his county cap after some excellent performances behind the stumps, both standing up to the spinners and standing back to the quicker bowlers. Whereas some county wicket-keepers opted for a flamboyant and over-demonstrative approach, David was the polar opposite, preferring instead to play a quiet and unassuming role, with wonderfully soft hands with the balls almost melting into his gloves.

A posed publicity photograph of David Evans in wicket-keeping kit, staged at the St Helen's ground during 1963.

David constantly strove for perfection and during his early years on the county circuit, David was an avid watcher of play, carefully studying opponents to see if he could learn anything to make him an even better cricketer. He duly became one of the best keepers in the country during 1960s, with Ossie Wheatley believing that David only spilled two chances during the six summers when the seamer was the Glamorgan's leader – a most impressive record, given that David was keeping to a variety of fine bowlers, including the pace of left-armer Jeff Jones, Ossie's brisk away swing, the subtle off-cutters of Don Shepherd, plus the clever spin of Jim McConnon and Jim Pressdee.

His finest season was in 1963 when he claimed 89 victims and beat Haydn Davies' county record of 82 dismissals set in 1955. The following summer David suffered the first of several broken fingers with his absence behind the stumps giving Eifion Jones a chance to cut his teeth in the 1st XI. However, David's greater finesse saw him win his place back and in 1967 he took six catches in an innings against Yorkshire at Swansea to equal another of Haydn's county records. David might have also broken this record had he, in a typically unselfish way, not let another fielder run in and catch a top edge which he himself would have easily pouched.

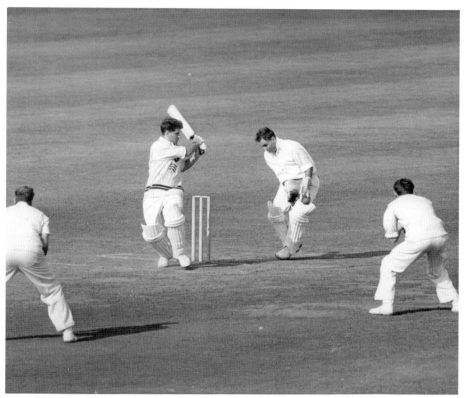

David Evans makes a smart take the stumps as Middlesex's Ted Clark swings at a delivery from Jim McConnon, watched by Peter Walker, crouching at forward short-leg and Wilf Wooller at silly mid-on.

As far as his batting was concerned, David was a courageous but limited batsman who occasionally, as a great team man, fulfilled the role of night-watchman. Regarded by some as a 'strokeless wonder', he never posted a first-class fifty with his tally of 2,875 runs being the highest by any Glamorgan batsman never to score a half-century. Had he been a more prolific batsman, David might have enjoyed a longer county career.

The news of his demotion from the county line-up at the start of 1968 did not come as a complete surprise but, nevertheless, it hit David hard. A serious-minded fellow, he had always wanted to be liked by his colleagues and his demotion from the 1st XI saw

A delighted David Evans stumps Middlesex's Bob Gale during Glamorgan's Championship encounter with Middlesex at Lord's in 1967.

David Evans, as an umpire.

David suffer from bouts of depression and anxiety. Fortunately, he had already started to think about his next career and, during the winter of 1967/68, David had been awarded a Churchill Scholarship and was able to travel to Singapore, Ceylon, Australia, New Zealand, Fiji and North America. Whilst abroad, he studied coaching methods and delivered a series of promotional lectures. David retired from the county game after his Benefit season in 1969, and initially took up coaching posts in Holland and Tasmania, but he missed the camaraderie of the county circuit and subsequently qualified as an umpire before joining the first-class list for the start of the 1971 season.

In 1979 he stood in his first One-Day International, then two years later he was added to the Test panel. He continued to stand in international games until heart problems forced him to stand down from the Test panel at the end of 1985. His first Test Match had been the remarkable game in the 1981 Ashes series at Headingley which saw Ian Botham turn the tables on the tourists after the Australians had forced England to follow-on. As David recalled after the match, "When England batted again, it seemed as if the game might finish early and I started thinking about my journey back home to Cardiff. But then Ian Botham played one of the most amazing innings I have ever seen, before Bob Willis steamed in to produce a devastating spell of fast bowling. I eventually travelled home feeling quite tired, but also very proud to have been involved in my first Test. I also started to wonder what on earth might happen in my next international!"

David also stood in the 1985 Ashes series, but shortly after the match at Lord's he was taken ill, and during September underwent heart surgery. He returned to the first-class list during 1986, albeit with a reduced schedule of county games, but he suffered further problems during the winter of 1989/90 and died the followed spring, just a few weeks before the start of the new domestic season.

433
CLARKE, Frank.

Born – Cardiff, 8 October 1936.
Professional.
RHB, RFM.
Ed – Allensbank School.
1st XI: 1956-1960.
2nd XI: 1955-1960.
Colts: 1956.
Club and Ground: 1957-1959.
Army 1958, Royal Engineers 1958 and Warwickshire 2nd XI 1961.
Clubs: St Fagans, Neath and Maesteg Town.

Batting and Fielding Record

	M	I	NO	RUNS	AV	100	50	CT	ST
F-c	31	41	15	98	3.76	-	-	10	-

Bowling Record

	Overs	M	R	W	AV	5wI	10wM
F-c	648	143	1868	50	37.36	1	-

Career-bests

First-class –   31 v Indians at St Helen's, Swansea, 1959.
          5/66 v Middlesex at Lord's, 1959.

Frank Clarke was a lively right-arm seam bowler who played for Glamorgan between 1956 and 1960. His finest moment with the ball came at Lord's in 1959 when he took a career-best 5/66 during the Championship match against Middlesex.

Born and raised in Cardiff, Frank had played with success as a schoolboy for St Fagans, and played for the county's Colts and 2nd XI in his final year at school. In 1956 Frank made his first-class debut against the Combined Services at the Arms Park, before making his Championship debut in early June against Leicestershire at Llanelli. The strapping teenager, standing at 6 foot 3 inches, impressed with his pace but claimed a solitary wicket on the benign surface at Stradey Park

Frank's county career was then stalled by his National Service with the Royal Engineers, although he was given sufficient leave to play for the Army and in 1958 played for them in their matches against Oxford and Cambridge Universities, with Frank impressing at The Parks by

Frank Clarke.

taking 5/31 against the Dark Blues. He also had the opportunity to appear at Lord's for the Army against the Royal Navy and after completing his military training, he returned to South Wales eager to claim a place in the Glamorgan side. Several shrewd judges believed that Frank could become part of a potent all-Welsh seam attack alongside Brian Evans, Hugh Davies and Allan Watkins, and during 1959 he played in 18 out of Glamorgan's 30 first-class games. Frank's pace again impressed but his sole five-wicket haul came in the end-of-season draw against Middlesex at Lord's. During the summer, he had suffered various niggling leg injuries which affected his rhythm, besides finding Wilf Wooller quite a demanding and hard task master. He was not alone in this respect but, in hindsight, a more sympathetic captain might have got the best out of the mild-mannered bowler.

His ailments continued during 1960 and restricted Frank to a solitary first-class appearance that summer against the South Africans at the Arms Park. Besides these niggles, the emergence of Jeff Jones as a hostile left-arm bowler, plus the signing of Ossie Wheatley as Wilf's replacement as captain, also meant that his opportunities would be further restricted in the future and, with doubts over his long-term fitness, Frank left the Glamorgan staff at the end of the 1960 season.

He still, however, harboured ambitions of playing county cricket and Frank had a brief trial with Warwickshire at the start of the 1961 season, but with no offer of a contract he began to train as a carpenter and cabinet maker. He subsequently moved to Sussex and set up a successful business which also saw Frank become one of the country's leading antique furniture restorers. His outstanding skills and craftsmanship have also been put to good effect during the redevelopment of the Pavillion bars and committee rooms at the Hove ground, with Frank being rightly very proud of his work at Sussex's headquarters.

434
WALKER, Peter Michael MBE.

Born – Clifton, 17 February 1936.
Died – Cardiff, 4 April 2020.
Professional.
RHB, LM / SLA.
1st XI: 1956-1972.
2nd XI: 1954-1972.
Cap: 1958.
Transvaal 1956/57-1957/58; Commonwealth XI 1959-1967/68; England 1960 (3 Tests); MCC 1960-1967; South 1961; Players 1962; Western Province 1962/63; AER Gilligan's XI 1963; International Cavaliers 1965-1966; DH Robins' XI 1969; TN Pearce's XI 1971.
Clubs: Neath, Cardiff, Maesteg Town and Llanelli.

Batting and Fielding Record

	M	I	NO	RUNS	AV	100	50	CT	ST
F-c	437	738	106	16510	26.12	12	86	656	-
List A	72	68	7	1218	19.96	-	4	32	-

Bowling Record

	Balls	M	R	W	AV	5wI	10wM
F-c	53341	2749	21652	771	28.08	22	2
List A	1840	40	1065	52	20.48	2	

Career-bests

First-class – 152* v Middlesex at Lord's, 1962.
7/58 v Middlesex at Lord's, 1962.
List A 79 v Staffordshire at Stoke, 1971.
5/21 v Cornwall at Truro, 1970.

Peter Walker – an integral member of Glamorgan's Championship-winning team of 1969 and a man who featured in the Club's historic victories over the 1964 and 1968 Australians – was undoubtedly, the finest close catcher in post-war county cricket, fully utilizing his tall frame and seemingly telescopic arms and hands when standing fearlessly at short-leg to the likes of Don Shepherd, Jim Pressdee and Malcolm Nash.

Peter Walker, seen in 1978 in a BBC publicity photograph.

In all, Peter held 656 catches for the Welsh county and set a host of fielding records which still stand today, including eight catches during the match with Derbyshire at Swansea in 1970 and a seasonal best of 67 catches during 1961 – one of four occasions when he took over 50 catches in a season. 175 of the catches during his magnificent career came from the bowling of Don Shepherd and the off-cutter duly paid Peter the following compliment – "A true great as a fielder and someone without whom I doubt I would have ever enjoyed so much success. As I developed the art of control as an off-cutter, Peter was able to safely stand at short-leg without all of the modern-day protection and safely pounce on any misjudgement that was forthcoming from the opposing batsman."

Peter had been born in Bristol during February 1936, but his father Oliver – a Cardiff-bred journalist and music critic – had emigrated during 1938 to South Africa so Peter and his younger brother Tim grew up in Johannesburg. As a pupil at Highlands North High School, Peter had shown promise as an all-rounder and had been regularly coached by Glamorgan and England all-rounder Allan Watkins, as well as occasionally by a pair of other Welsh stalwarts, Dai and Emrys Davies. These experiences fuelled Peter's ambitions to be a county cricketer but, during 1952, the sixteen-year-old ran away to sea as he joined the Merchant Navy spending time on vessels criss-crossing the Atlantic and heading to various ports in Western Europe..

When the vessels docked at Avonmouth, Peter had the chance of catching up with his maternal grandparents in Bristol. On another occasion, he decided to head by train to Cardiff to see if, by chance, he could catch up with Allan Watkins. As luck would have it,

Peter Walker and his father in South Africa circa 1952.

Peter Walker seen on the SS Aruba *as it crossed the Atlantic.*

the all-rounder was in a meeting in the Club's offices on the second floor at 6, High Street together with Johnnie Clay and Wilf Wooller. Both had known Peter's father when he had played for Cardiff and after asking Peter about life at sea, and his cricketing ambitions, they suggested that he took a stroll around the city and then come back to the office after lunch. On the recommendation of Allan, a trial immediately followed that afternoon in the makeshift nets in the rugby grandstand at the Arms Park, initially with Peter bowling his left-arm swing and spin under the watchful gaze of Club coach George Lavis. Messrs. Wooller and Clay then came over from the offices and together with Lavis they took off their jackets and bowled for a while to Peter who was wearing pads and gloves borrowed from a nearby kit-bag.

Despite the spontaneity and lack of practice, Peter impressed these grandees of Glamorgan Cricket and the offer, at £4 a week, of a summer contract for 1954 and 1955 then followed. It allowed Peter to further his cricketing education by playing for Cardiff and Llanelli, as well as the county's 2nd XI plus their Club and Ground side, and by the time Peter joined the county's full-time staff in 1956 he had developed into an assertive middle-order batsman and left-arm swing bowler.

During June 1956 Peter made his first-class debut for the Welsh county against Leicestershire at Stradey Park, Llanelli. On his earliest appearances for the Welsh county, Peter had fielded in the covers and elsewhere in the outfield, but everything was to change in June 1957 at the Arms Park after an off-the-cuff exchange with legendary captain Wilf Wooller during the match against Warwickshire. Glamorgan had been cheaply dismissed on a shirt-front pitch and with the opposition batsmen going well against the new ball attack, Wilf was poised to introduce Jim

A photograph of Peter Walker taken in 1957.

104

McConnon into the attack. Peter had been shuttling to and fro from third man to third man, so unsure where to stand for the off-spinner, he went up to ask 'The Skipper' where he should go. The exasperated Wooller turned round and said "Just spit in the air Peter and stand where it lands!"

Peter duly did what he was told and positioned himself at short-leg. To the second ball from McConnon, Peter caught at full stretch to his left an inside-edge from the bat of Norman Horner.

So began an outstanding career as a close-to-the-wicket fielder which, in Championship cricket saw Peter take 609 catches – the fifth highest total on record by any fielder in the competition and surpassed only by Frank Woolley, John Langridge, Arthur Milton and Brian Close.

He modestly attributed his success to being equally adept catching with his left or right hand, sharp reflexes allied to a knack of crouching low to the ground, keeping a watchful eye on the batsman's movements but never ever anticipating where the ball might go. He also believed that his time as a callow youth in the Merchant Navy had also helped as together with colleagues he whiled away the long hours at sea by having a catching competition throwing potatoes around the deck. As Peter wryly joked in later years "If we missed any of the flying spuds, there would be less for everyone to eat that night!"

Peter also formed an almost innate relationship with Don Shepherd, the legendary bowler who, during Peter's first year of county cricket had switched from seam to off-

Peter Walker dives to his left to catch Abbas Ali Baig during Glamorgan's match against the Indian tourists at Swansea in August 1959. Keeping wicket is David Evans whilst Jim McConnon and Jim Pressdee are in the slips.

cutters. Crouching at short-leg, Peter could sense the unease and uncertainty which the opposing batsmen felt when facing the Club's leading wicket-taker of all-time. Peter duly took 175 catches from Shep's masterful bowling with the 'c Walker b Shepherd' being the most successful fielding combination in the Club's history and contributing to a shade over a quarter of Peter's total catches during his career with Glamorgan.

Peter also took some fine catches in the slips, often standing a fraction wider than where first slip would stand, and telling his colleague alongside at second slip "You're standing too close to me," before advising that they move further along to where third slip would normally stand. There were no arguments, as on many occasions, Peter would dive low to either his left or right and comfortably take a series of catches . There were some stunners off his own bowling, such as the diving catch one-handed to his left to dismiss Abbas Ali

Baig in the game against the Indians at Swansea in 1959, whilst there were a host of amazing catches against the other bowlers. These included one at Grace Road against Leicestershire, when Maurice Hallam firmly clipped a ball off his legs against Brian Evans only for Peter at leg-slip to dive and catch the ball two handed, low to his right. There was another occasion at Pontypridd where Tom Graveney propped forward to Euros Lewis and edged a ball into his pads. The ball ballooned up into the offside

Another victim for Peter Walker as he pouches a catch from Jim Pressdee's bowling during Glamorgan game against the 1965 South Africans at Swansea. David Evans is the Welsh county's wicket-keeper.

whereupon Peter swiftly moved across from short-leg, in front of the Worcestershire batsman and completed a two-handed catch at silly point.

It should not be forgotten that, unlike the modern era of protective helmets and shinpads, the close-to-the-wicket fielders in these days only wore a box for protection. Admittedly, there were several times when Peter thought about his safety as he crouched about three yards from the bat at forward short-leg. One of these came early in his career against Nottinghamshire at Trent Bridge when Arthur Jepson was using the long handle against the Glamorgan attack. Wilf duly recalled Jim McConnon, believing that the off-spinner would cleverly end his run spree. With Peter crouching low in his usual position, Arthur continued his salvo as he sent the first delivery whizzing past Peter's right ear to the leg-side boundary.

As Peter later recalled "I decided to move back a couple of feet before the next ball got the same treatment and, this time, fizzed past by left ear. Believing my time had come,

I retreated a fraction further only for Arthur to play defensively forward to the next ball and inside edge it, via his front pad, in my direction. I dived forward but at full stretch just failed to get my right hand under the ball. As I lay there, a booming voice came from behind me at mid-on ' Stay where you are, Walker!' Wilf then came up, compared the position to which I had retreated to where I had been originally placed. He duly scratched a line with his thick heavy boots on the turf and said 'Move from there and you'll never play for Glamorgan again.' In trepidation, I dutifully moved back closer to Arthur who, thankfully, had an almighty swish at the next ball, missed and was bowled!"

Peter Walker, seen bowling spin at Lord's in 1961 for the MCC again Yorkshire in the Champion County match which was the traditional curtain-raiser to the domestic season.

Another occasion when 'The Skipper' tested Peter's mettle came at Bristol at the end of July 1957. At the time Peter was still bowling left-arm swing, and after Gloucestershire's opening pair of George Emmett and Martin Young had shared a stand of 103, Peter returned to the attack and made the breakthough. As Peter wrote in his autobiography, "five hours later I was still bowling with my eventual analysis being 50.3 overs, 10 maiden, 116 runs and 7 wickets. Not once did Wilf ask me how I was feeling or whether I wanted a rest. I think he was waiting for me to fall over with fatigue. It was his way of putting me to a test that I'm sure that he himself would have taken on, even then aged 44."

Perhaps because of this experience, Peter increasingly focused on his slower style of left-arm bowling, fully utilizing his tall frame and high natural action. Having two bowlers in one was very handy for Wilf – this may well have been his underlying thinking at Bristol – and coupled with Peter's batting and fielding skills, he had become a regular in the county's side by the end of 1957. The following July, Peter registered his maiden Championship hundred with an unbeaten 104 against Surrey at Swansea – a shade over two months after Peter had been awarded his county cap having put together a string of useful scores, a handful of wickets and some high-quality catches at short-leg which had earned Peter the nickname of 'Flypaper Fingers' by the Press.

Peter's maiden century at Swansea was a monkey off his back as the previous month he had run himself out for 99 during Glamorgan's match against Warwickshire at the Courtaulds ground in Coventry. It also followed a verbal spat with Surrey and England fast bowler Peter Loader who had returned to the attack, armed with the new ball with Peter unbeaten on 84. After edging a ball from Loader for a single, the feisty bowler walked down the pitch and said to Peter, "you're going to have to work f***ing hard if you are going to get the next fifteen runs!" He was right, as for the next half an hour,

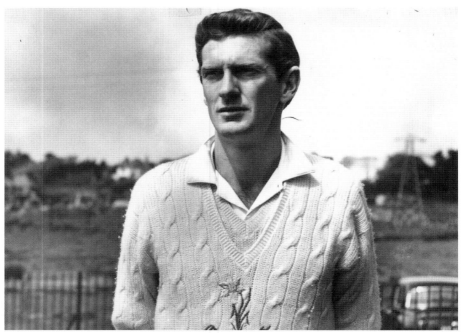

Peter Walker, as seen in 1962 wearing his capped player's sweater.

he bowled a series of boomerang-like out-swingers outside Peter's off stump leaving the youngster to scramble the runs at the other end.

Peter ended the 1958 season with 1,052 runs to his name but 1959 proved to be his breakthrough summer as he ended with 1,564 runs plus 80 wickets and 69 catches as he came the leading fielder in the country. His tally of catches also broke the Club's previous record, set by Maurice Turnbull who had held 49 catches during 1947. Peter's record-breaking 50th catch came at Swansea at the start of August at Swansea, and during Glamorgan's match against the Indians as, at gully, he held onto an outside edge from the bat of Nari Contractor from the bowling of Don Shepherd. His feat prompted Peter's father to send him a telegram with a biblical quotation – "The Lord is thy shepherd, thou shall not want!" It also led to the England selectors calling up the Glamorgan all-rounder to act as England's twelfth man for the final Test of their series against India at The Oval.

The following summer Peter was chosen to play for the MCC against the 1960 South Africans at Lord's. It may have followed some kind words from Wilf Wooller who was one of the England selectors but, at the time, with Peter having focused on left-arm, England were seeking a replacement for Tony Lock who was in the process of re-modelling his action after further instances of being called for throwing. Peter did not do his England prospects any harm by taking 3/36 in 27 overs and making 57 batting at number eight having arrived at the crease with the MCC on 126-6.

It had been a spirited performance and aware of Peter's potential he was duly included by the England selectors for the first of three Tests against South Africa, with the game taking place at Edgbaston. For the past five winters, Peter had returned to the Cape so having played against many of the Springboks in provincial cricket in South Africa, his knowledge of their strengths and weaknesses was useful to England captain Colin Cowdrey as the squad prepared the night before at their traditional eve of match dinner at The Raven Hotel in Droitwich. However, it was not until shortly after the toss that Peter knew he was making his England debut and only when Gubby Allen walked into the changing room asking him about his cap size.

Peter enjoyed a decent debut driving and sweeping with confidence, besides taking a couple of smart catches at backward short-leg off the bowling of Fred Trueman and Brian Statham, as well as delivering a tidy spell of left-arm spin in which he could have claimed the wicket of Pom-Pom Fellows-Smith caught behind by Jim Parks only for umpire John Langridge to err as the batsman stood at the crease, adamant that he hadn't feathered a catch into the wicket-keeper's gloves. John later apologized to Peter but the all-rounder still returned to South Wales on a high with John Arlott writing "Walker has all the gifts to make a Test Match all-rounder."

Colin Cowdrey introduces HRH The Duke of Edinburgh to Peter Walker whilst the Glamorgan player was 12th man for England during the Lord's Test of the 1968 Ashes series. Umpire Arthur Fagg is on the right whilst alongside Peter are a bespectacled Geoff Boycott, plus a beaming Alan Knott and a more reserved John Edrich.

With England having won at Edgbaston, Peter kept his place in the side for the second Test at Lord's where he posted a half-century at Lord's, batting at number seven during a stand with MJK Smith, besides taking five catches and delivering thirteen overs without taking a wicket as England completed a comprehensive innings victory, and with more than a day to spare. Peter played again at Trent Bridge where England won overwhelmingly by eight wickets, but it proved to be his final Test appearance and, despite England having comfortable victories in all three Tests, Peter was subsequently omitted from the Test side, as the selectors looked elsewhere.

Many felt that he might win a place on the MCC tour to New Zealand in 1960/61, but as Peter ruefully recalled "my liking for late nights and the good times off the field, probably cost Barry Knight and I a trip to New Zealand." Whether or not this is true, it was a time when there were batting options aplenty and, like his county colleague Don Shepherd, Peter faced stiff competition from other slow bowlers including Gloucestershire's David Allen, Yorkshire's Ray Illingworth and Middlesex's Fred Titmus. Although he never got another chance at Test level, at least Peter – unlike 'Shep' – got the chance to

Peter Walker receives an award from Jimmy Hill, the famous football personality, having been the leading fielder in county cricket during 1960.

wear, albeit briefly, the England cap and blazer, besides gaining a certain amount of notoriety for featuring, alongside MJK Smith and Fred Trueman in the first-ever Test Match hat-trick recorded at Lord's when each were dismissed in successive deliveries by Geoff Griffin.

His omission also came at a time when his form with Glamorgan had dropped away. Gilbert Parkhouse and his mentor Allan Watkins each spoke at length with Peter about his lack of runs and wickets for the Welsh county, in addition to what has been perceived as a less-than-professional attitude with the all-rounder appearing to be increasing paranoid to any hint of criticism, and being introverted, morose and uncommunicative with the rest of the team. Matters had become so low that during the away match with Somerset, Peter spent the night stretched out on a pew in Bath Abbey, before the following morning seeking out Wilf Wooller and saying that he wanted to resign from Glamorgan.

As Peter remembered, "I had run away to sea when I was sixteen and now, in a way, I was ready to run away again, to look for some fresh adventures. I had a face-to-face meeting with Wilf and we agreed that I would put on hold my resignation.....[Later] he and Allan Watkins helped me take a more rational line and regain some perspective. I felt ashamed at my impetuosity. If Allan could soldier on in the twilight of his career with crippling arthritis in both knees, why the hell couldn't I... I later sailed back to a winter in South Africa. I'd been told by Wilf and an understanding committee to use this as a period of reflection and to get my head straight before returning."

A tour of the West Indies with EW Swanton's XI also helped Peter to bolster his shaky confidence after the seesaw happenings of 1960, and he duly performed the Treble during 1961, scoring 1,347 first-class runs, taking 101 wickets in all games and holding 73 catches. In the history of county cricket, only Wally Hammond and Micky Stewart have bettered this outstanding seasonal return with his record-breaking efforts being achieved despite being struck in the face by Brian Statham at Neath and sustaining a nasty eye injury early in May.

Peter also followed in his father's footsteps by cutting his teeth as a journalist, and the following summer came close to the feat of scoring a century and taking ten wickets in the same match as he recorded a pair of career-best performances at Lord's. First, he confounded the Middlesex batsmen with a return of 7/58, before dispatching their bowlers to all parts of the St John's Wood ground as he struck an unbeaten 152. However, this was one feat which, for one, missed the clutches of Peter Michael Walker, as he went wicket-less in the second innings.

Despite his outstanding cricketing achievements, Peter was still restless and slightly neurotic so at the end of the 1962 summer and his marriage to Joy Trick in Newport, Peter and his new wife travelled to South Africa with the all-rounder telling the Glamorgan committee that he had resigned from county cricket to take up a business appointment in the Cape. It proved to be a brief sojourn as the Walkers returned in the spring of 1963 with Peter resuming his career with Glamorgan, his freelance journalism and settling into family life with Joy and their first child, Sarah.

It was an important decision as Peter played a key role in three of the great feats in Glamorgan's history – the Championship-winning summer of 1969 as well as the back-to-back victories over the Australians at Swansea during 1964 and 1968 – besides enjoying a decent Benefit Year in 1966, as well as hitting unbeaten centuries against Gloucestershire at Lydney in 1967, plus three figure scores against Sussex and Nottinghamshire in 1968. The latter summer also saw Peter play a major hand, quite literally, in the latter

Peter Walker, seen whilst batting at Grace Road in Leicester during 1970.

victory as the Australians were set a target of 365 on the final day by acting captain Don Shepherd. Like a Grand Master at chess, the wily off-cutter cleverly rotated his bowling as the tourists watchfully accumulated against the enthusiastic Glamorgan team. But for a while in late afternoon, it looked as though Shep's efforts would be trumped by Paul Sheahan, the tourist's number four batsman, who led a counter-attack with a fighting century.

Peter then had a spell at the Pavillion End and, with one of the worst balls he ever bowled, Peter ended Sheahan's defiance as the Australian – on 137 – drilled the ball back in the air just to the right of the non-striking batsman. Peter was not going to miss out, throwing himself full length to his right and gleefully pouched the ball. His catch turned the game in favour of the Welsh county and, with the lower order exposed, besides the ball starting to lavishly turn, there was a flurry of further wickets before Peter ended the contest as Dave Renneberg drove him into the hands of Majid Khan at cover, and Glamorgan had won by 79 runs.

The following year Peter was a member of the Glamorgan team which won the 1969 Championship. He failed to add to his tally of centuries, but posted nine invaluable fifties besides holding 29 catches in a predatory leg-trap augmented by Roger Davis. His adaptable and level-headed batting helped to dig Glamorgan out of trouble in a couple of instances, whilst at other times his quick-thinking and ability to garner fast runs helped Tony Lewis to reach declaration targets. He also claimed 61 wickets at 23 runs apiece and proved an admirable and dependable foil to Don Shepherd's off-cutters. "A fine team man and someone whose efforts with both bat and ball, and in the field, played an important and often understated role in our success" was Tony Lewis' summary of Peter's efforts during 1969.

By the time of the heady and very Welsh victories over the 1968 Australians at St Helen's and the Championship success of 1969, the county calendar also included limited-overs cricket following the introduction in 1963 of the Gillette Cup and six years later the John Player Sunday League. Little did Peter know it at the time of his first appearance for Glamorgan in the 40 overs competition on 27 April 1969 at Northampton, the Sunday League was to subsequently play a major part in the next phase of Peter's superlative career in the cricket world.

After the euphoria of the Championship-winning summer, and a runner's-up spot the following year, the tight-knit Glamorgan squad started to break up. Bryan Davis returned to the West Indies whilst Ossie Wheatley retired. Even though Peter had increased his journalistic work to include duties with BBC Wales and a rugby columnist for several national newspapers, many felt that Peter would take over from Tony Lewis as the county's leader for 1973, but the Club – or rather Wilf Wooller – opted for Majid Khan instead.

Peter Walker as seen in 1969 at Sophia Gardens.

Peter, like so many others, had enjoyed a love-hate relationship with Wilf Wooller who was now the Club's secretary and *general factotum*. Grateful for the chance he had first given him aged seventeen as a footloose teenager, plus the advice and encouragement which Wilf had given him throughout his career, Peter had also clashed swords with Wilf, especially during the early 1970s when the question of player's remuneration and contracts was raised. Peter was the player's representative on the cricket committee and was viewed by some of the officials and Wilf, quite incorrectly, as something of a shop steward. Mindful of player power at a time when cricket was still being run along the lines of an amateur sports club and still to embrace commercialism, Wilf's preference for the Pakistani was approved, much to Peter's disappointment. Just to rub salt into Peter's wounds, he was only offered a match-by-match contract for 1973. He rejected the terms and played what proved to his final Championship game in the closing week of August 1972 against Middlesex at Sophia Gardens.

It had been a disappointing summer for Peter, who at the age of thirty-six, had claimed only 29 wickets in nineteen games and scored just 370 runs, compared with his tally of 1971 which had stood at 1,120 and included centuries against Lancashire and Hampshire. Don Shepherd's career also came to a close that summer as the committee looked to rebuild and nurture the next generation, but Peter was very hurt at both he and Don being overlooked as Tony's successor. As he wrote in his autobiography, "Don was pensioned off at the same time as me and, as result of this loss of experience, the short-sighted Glamorgan committee managed to plunge the club into a deep downward spiral from which it took well over fifteen years to resurface. The fact that I was denied the chance to shepherd the new generation of Glamorgan youngsters into a more successful future remains a sad memory."

Ironically, Glamorgan's sole Championship victory during 1972 was at Portsmouth when Peter was acting captain. He duly led his team to victory over Hampshire by four wickets, with Alan Jones posting a match-winning century after Bob Dudley-Jones and Majid Khan had shared eight-wickets between them in Hampshire's first innings. Second time around, Peter was amongst the wickets, mopping up the tail with 3/27 before being at the wicket with Eifion Jones when the target was reached. He had first captained

Peter Walker, seen in 1975 during his new career as a broadcaster with BBC Radio Wales.

Glamorgan during 1970 against Oxford University and on several occasions, Peter had acted as Tony Lewis' deputy in the Sunday League competition, but the Glamorgan committee opted to look elsewhere.

It was not long before a significant offer of work came Peter's way and one that was to be the focus of his life for the next twenty years or so. The previous summer he had impressed BBC personnel when being an interviewee at Cardiff during a rain-affected John Player League game.

At the time, there was library of videotape material for Frank Bough, the presenter of the *Sunday Cricket* programme to draw upon so Peter, who had worked for several years for BBC Wales, was both a willing and eloquent subject for a lengthy interview as the rain fell at Sophia Gardens.

At the end of the 1972 season, Frank told Bill Taylor, the producer of the *Sunday Cricket* programme that he wanted to cut back on his heavy schedule of presenting and, aware of Peter's position – or lack of it – with Glamorgan, suggested that Peter took over as the new presenter. Remembering Peter's impressive stint at Cardiff and aware of his work for BBC Wales, Bill duly met with Peter and the outcome of their chat was that Peter succeeded Frank as the anchorman of the BBC's coverage of the Sunday League.

It proved to be a masterstroke as Peter drew on his first-class and international experience to undertake a series of perceptive interviews during the tea intervals with contemporary players and officials. A natural raconteur and gifted interviewer, Peter excelled in his new role and duly published a compilation of these interviews called *Cricket Conversations* during 1978.

The programme, screened weekly from 1.55pm on BBC Two, was a masterpiece of outside broadcasting in the days before satellite and computer technology, and at the end of the 1976 season Peter, his cameraman and a representative from John Player holding the competition's trophy, famously spent a couple of hours hovering up and down the M4 in a helicopter during September 1976, uncertain as to the destiny of the title. For a while they were close to the Severn Bridge as it looked as if Somerset would defeat Glamorgan to clinch their first piece of silverware but the Welsh county turned the tables on the West Country side and the intrepid BBC crew just made it in time to The Mote at Maidstone where Kent had defeated Gloucestershire, improved their net run rate and finished on top of the table. After the helicopter had landed on the outfield, Peter had barely sixty seconds in which to wrap up the programme but, in his unflappable

Peter Walker, seen at Hastings in 1978, whilst working as a broadcaster on the BBC TV's Sunday Cricket *programme as Doug Insole of the TCCB makes a special presentation to umpire John Langridge, the former Sussex batter.*

style, he perfectly performed the combined duties as master of ceremonies and presenter, as surrounded by a gaggle of enthusiastic Kent supporters, the Sunday League trophy was handed over to the Kent captain.

Besides his work for BBC Two and BBC Wales, Peter continued to write for several national newspapers including the *Sunday Telegraph* and later the *Mail on Sunday* as well as, from 1974, acting as Chairman of the Professional Cricketers Association, working closely with the likes of Jack Bannister, Mike Brearley and others to improve the lot of the county cricketers, besides working tirelessly with a number of accountants and financial advisors to provide adequate insurance cover for the hard-working professionals. Peter's hard work for the Association during the 1970s and 1980s helped to lay the

Peter Walker interviews footballer Arfon Griffiths during the BBC Wales Sports Personality of the Year Award programme in 1975, watched by Wales manager Mike Smith, plus John Toshack.

foundations on which the current Association exists, running training sessions as well as a host of welfare and lifestyle courses, besides helping players move seamlessly into new careers after their days in the summer sun have ended.

Peter's stock as a TV presenter had also risen sufficiently by the late 1970s for him to undertake a stint as a reporter on *Nationwide*, the popular early evening programme which followed the national and regional news. Amongst Peter's assignments was an invitation to appear in a light-hearted celebrity event at The Horse of the Year Show with Peter, after tuition from Debbie Johnsey, the well-known show-jumper who lived at Chepstow, riding a former Irish steeple-chaser over a series of obstacles at Olympia!

By the mid-1980s, Peter was also the father of two boys, Daniel and Justin, as well as the husband of a second wife, Susan. Around this time he also heard that like others, his freelance contract with BBC Wales was unlikely to be extended. The upshot was that Peter and fellow broadcaster David Parry-Jones founded Merlin Film and Video Limited. Together with several other freelancers from the BBC, Peter and David saw Merlin become, within two years of its creation. the largest and most successful independent production company in Wales, besides creating a number of outstanding programmes for the BBC, HTV and S4C, overseeing coverage of many of Glamorgan's matches and participating in the very lucrative fields of corporate programmes, commercials and media training

In 1996 Peter's career took another direction as he and David sold their business with Peter returning to the world of cricket, and acting as the first-ever Chief Executive of the Cricket Board of Wales. He duly oversaw the introduction of a nationwide coaching framework across Wales, besides helping plan the development of the National Cricket Centre at Glamorgan's headquarters at Sophia Gardens. It was the first phase of the ground's transformation into the modern stadia, and although not always seeing eye to eye with everything that happened in subsequent years, Peter proudly served as Glamorgan President in 2009 and 2010.

In 2006 Peter had his memoirs, entitled *It's Not Just Cricket* published by Fairfield Books with the book recounting some of the adventures of his youth, hunting crocodiles, roaming the streets of New York without two pennies to rub together and surviving an attempted murder in the Suez Canal. It also recounted more grim times in his life such as the days during October 1966 when he joined the rescuers in the aftermath of the Aberfan pit disaster, as well as in more recent times when he successfully fought a battle with colon cancer and the removal of six inches of his lower intestine.

Peter Walker seen at Buckingham Palace in 2011 after being presented with his MBE.

Peter was awarded the MBE for his services to cricket in the New Year's Honour's List of 2011. Sadly, during the late 2010s he struggled with dementia before having a stroke during early April 2020 and passing away in the University of Wales Hospital in Cardiff.

1957

As the anti-Wooller lobby continued to sharpen their knives, Glamorgan made headway on the field, rising up into ninth place in the Championship table. Ten matches were won and it might have been eleven had not rain washed out play at Ynysangharad Park in Pontypridd with the Welsh county poised to defeat Derbyshire.

The summer saw a return to form by most of the senior batsmen with Gilbert Parkhouse, Allan Watkins and Bernard Hedges each passing the 1000-run mark. Jim McConnon was also restored to the county's ranks after his northern sojourn the previous summer, and together with Don Shepherd, the two purveyors of off-breaks shared 195 wickets between them in the County Championship.

There were some encouraging signs as well from the youngsters with Alan Jones being rewarded for consistent batting performances in the 2nd XI with a first-class debut. Hugh Davies and Peter Walker also added youthful zest to the seam bowling department and helped to take some of the pressure off Wilf Wooller and Allan Watkins.

The only major area of concern appeared to be the state of the pitches at the Arms Park. Of the six matches staged at the Cardiff ground during 1957, only one went into the third day with all of the others ending inside two. The further loss of revenue through gate receipts and the quality of the surfaces themselves led to talk of possibly playing fewer matches in the future in the heart of the Welsh capital. Comments by Wilf and others opened up some old wounds with the leading officials of Cardiff Athletic Club, especially those who had previously clashed swords with the Glamorgan captain about the possible move to a new ground in Pontcanna Fields or Sophia Gardens. The upshot of these discussions over the future of the Arms Park meant that the anti-Wooller faction gained fresh and key supporters within the corridors of power.

435
DAUNCEY, John Gilbert.

Born – Ystalyfera, 9 April 1936.
RHB.
Professional.
1st XI: 1957.
2nd XI: 1954-1959.
Colts: 1958.
Club and Ground: 1954-1958.
Clubs: Swansea, Mumbles, Pontardawe, Clydach and Metal Box.

Batting and Fielding Record

	M	I	NO	RUNS	AV	100	50	CT	ST
F-c	2	4	0	54	13.50	-	-	1	-

Career-bests

First-class –   34 v Gloucestershire at St Helen's, Swansea, 1957.

Gilbert Dauncey, who played twice for Glamorgan during 1957, had a fine record as a top order batsman in League cricket in South Wales.

The diminutive opening batsman had first played for the county's 2nd XI during 1954 before commencing his National Service and spending time in South-east Asia where he played for Malaya against Hong Kong during 1955/56.

After returning home, he played some impressive innings in club and 2nd XI cricket, and was selected in two Championship games during 1957, each time with Gilbert Parkhouse, against Gloucestershire at Swansea and Kent at Neath. Allan Watkins had been unavailable for both games, and although Gilbert batted capably on each occasion, he was the one to make way for the England all-rounder when he returned to the Glamorgan side.

Gilbert Dauncey, as seen during 1956.

Gilbert played at various times in club cricket for Swansea, Metal Box, Pontardawe, Clydach and Mumbles.

436
GATEHOUSE, Dr Peter Warlow.

Born – Caerphilly, 3 May 1936.
Professional.
RHB, LFM.
Ed – Caerphilly GS and University College, Cardiff.

1st XI: 1957-1962.
2nd XI: 1953-1961.
Colts: 1958.
Club and Ground: 1953-1960.
Clubs: Caerphilly, Cardiff.

Batting and Fielding Record

	M	I	NO	RUNS	AV	100	50	CT	ST
F-c	19	23	8	85	5.67	-	-	3	-

Bowling Record

	Balls	M	R	W	AV	5wI	10wM
F-c	2854	84	1551	53	29.26	3	1

Career-bests

First-class – 20 v Derbyshire at Stradey Park, Llanelli, 1960.
7/94 v Middlesex at Lord's, 1958.

Peter Gatehouse was a fast left-arm bowler who appeared in nineteen first-class matches for Glamorgan between 1957 and 1962, during which time he was also a postgraduate student at Cardiff University.

An autographed photo of Peter Gatehouse.

He made his 2nd XI debut for Glamorgan shortly after his seventeenth birthday during 1953 and, after completing his first degree, the tall bowler – who stood at six foot, three inches – made his first-class debut against Nottinghamshire at Llanelli. He duly opened the bowling with Hugh Davies and claimed 3/27, including the visitors top three in quick succession. Nottinghamshire never recovered from this bad start and although Peter went wicketless during the second innings, Glamorgan secured an innings victory.

His postgraduate studies allowed Peter to play throughout the second half of the 1958 season, and in what was only his third-ever Championship appearance, the left-armer took 7/94 against Middlesex at Lord's. Peter did not play in 1959 but appeared in six games in 1960. After gaining his doctorate, he decided against a career in professional cricket and instead pursued a career in pharmacy. However, with injuries to other bowlers, Glamorgan kept Peter's registration for 1962 and he duly re-appeared in two games during August against the Pakistani's at Swansea as well as against Kent at Canterbury.

Peter continued to play club cricket for many years, and captained Cardiff in their Centenary season in 1967. Peter had also played rugby for Caerphilly RFC.

437
JONES, Alan MBE.

Born – Velindre, 4 November 1938.
Professional.
LHB, OB.
Ed – Clydach CS.
1st XI: 1957-1983.
2nd XI: 1955-1987.
Colts: 1956-1991.
Club and Ground: 1955-1996.
Cap: 1962.
Army 1958-1959; Combined Services 1959; Western Australia 1963/1964; Australian XI 1963/1964; MCC 1965-1969/70; England v Rest of the World 1970; International XI 1975; DH Robins' XI 1975-1976; Northern Transvaal 1975/1976; Natal 1976/1977.
Wisden Cricketer of the Year 1978.
Club: Clydach.

Batting and Fielding Record

	M	I	NO	RUNS	AV	100	50	CT	ST
F-c	610	1102	71	34056	33.03	52	186	276	-
List A	287	283	21	7156	27.31	2	42	74	-

Bowling Record

	Balls	M	R	W	AV	5wI	10wM
F-c	353	15	249	1	249.00	-	-
List A	33	0	27	3	9.00	-	-

Career-bests

First-class – 204* v Hampshire at Basingstoke, 1978.
           1/41 v Worcestershire at Worcester, 1970.
List A –   124* v Warwickshire at Edgbaston, 1976.
           3/21 v Northamptonshire at Wellingborough, 1975.

Despite starting his first-class career with a duck, Alan Jones was, by whichever yardstick you wish to judge the merits of batsmen, undoubtedly the finest produced by Glamorgan of all time with a tally of over 40,000 runs to his name in all forms of the game for the Welsh county – an aggregate which no other player is likely to surpass.

    Short, compact and possessing an exemplary technique, Alan benefitted from years of coaching by George Lavis, Phil Clift and Wilf Wooller, After serving his apprenticeship in the middle order, Alan became a fearless opening batsman, time and again, hooking and pulling the finest of county and international bowlers, and only wearing – for much of his career – his Glamorgan cap. Possessing admirable powers of concentration, Alan was also quick and nimble on his feet, deservedly becoming renowned as an outstanding,

Alan Jones, as seen in 1957.

A youthful Alan Jones, seen in 1959.

and elegant, player of spin bowling. Alan passed over a thousand runs on 23 consecutive summers – an achievement that is even more impressive considering that most of these were days of uncovered pitches. At the time of his retirement, Alan's record of 52 first-class centuries was the best-ever for the Club. This feat has subsequently been equalled by Hugh Morris in 1997 before being surpassed by Matthew Maynard during 2004 but, in the modern era, few batsmen are likely to get anywhere near Alan's tally.

Given his outstanding record, and consistency year after year, it was remarkable that the England selectors overlooked the Welsh-speaking left-hander. Some say that Alan's fielding counted against him, with a shoulder injury preventing him from throwing in the ball. "You could always take the extra run, and it probably counted against him," said his great friend Don Shepherd and another man who people believe suffered from a supposed prejudice against players from the less glamorous teams, including the Welsh county.

But as Stephen Hedges wrote in his biography of his father Bernard, one of Alan's opening partners, "what is not in doubt is Alan's wholehearted commitment to Glamorgan and Wales. He saw the high points, being part of the Championship winning side in 1969 and the low points of the late 1970s when the County finished bottom of the competition twice in four seasons from 1976 to 1979. He took over the captaincy of the side for a brief period and was the senior professional who helped guide many players through the difficult waters of establishing themselves in the professional game."

With the Welsh-speaker having been an integral part of Glamorgan's Championship-winning team during 1969, the England selectors finally gave Alan the nod during 1970 for the opening match of the hastily arranged series against the Rest of the World following the cancellation of the series with South Africa. Alan appeared in the opening match at Lord's and, like all of other participants in the match and the watching spectators, he believed the game to have Test status and gratefully accepted the blazer and cap which was given to him. He made 5 and 0 but was dropped for the remaining games of the series, before subsequently hearing that the games had been downgraded by the ICC, with Alan's status as an England international being lost.

However, on the fiftieth anniversary of that game at Lord's – 17 June 2020 – Alan was awarded with England cap number 696 in a virtual ceremony involving ECB Chair Colin Graves, plus England Men's Test captain Joe Root, Glamorgan's Chief Executive Hugh Morris, as well as Tony Lewis, his former captain and teammate. It was a worthy presentation for a man whose tally of 36,049 runs in first-class cricket stands as the 35th

highest of all time and someone who was named as one of Wisden's Five Cricketers of the Year in 1978 after leading the Welsh county to the Gillette Cup at Lord's the previous summer.

In making the award to Alan, ECB Chair Colin Graves said: "Alan's achievements on and off the cricket field are something to be celebrated, so I'm delighted that we can mark the 50th anniversary of his England appearance in this way. While the record books may not show Alan as a capped international cricketer, the ECB wanted to recognise his England appearance and celebrate his remarkable career as a player, coach and administrator by awarding him England cap number 696. My congratulations go to Alan, as well as my thanks and respect for all he has done for the game of cricket in the last six decades, especially in his native Wales."

Alan Jones walks out to open the batting for England with Kent's Brian Luckhurst at Lord's in 1970 during their match against the Rest of the World.

Such a scenario could scarcely have been in the most wildest of dreams Alan had as a young boy, growing up in the close-knit community of Velindre, near Swansea surrounded by seven brothers, as well as two older sisters. His father and elder brothers worked underground at the Graig Merthyr Colliery in Pontarddulais with Alan, like his younger siblings and their friends enjoying ball games on the patch of rough pasture opposite their home, It was here that Alan first honed his talents with his acquaintances in imaginary Test Matches with younger brother Eifion being Denis Compton and Alan being Neil Harvey.

Alan's choice was a shrewd move as in 1956, during the Australians match against Glamorgan at St Helen's, he had to leave his group of family and friends as a message came over the tannoy that any junior member of the Welsh county's playing staff should report to the Swansea pavillion. With a squad of just twelve players, the nominated twelfth man was already acting as a substitute fielder when Gilbert Parkhouse was forced off the field, and when Jim Pressdee damaged his thumb and departed for treatment, the SOS went around St Helen's for further manpower. Alan duly answered the call and, in kit hastily borrowed from Bernard Hedges, he gleefully took to the field as his schoolboy idol was still batting. Stationed at mid-off, it wasn't long before the young colt was in the action as Harvey drove a ball to him with all the power and poise associated with the man who won 79 Test caps for Australia.

Alan had joined Glamorgan's junior staff in 1955, and all at the princely sum of £5 a week for twenty-two weeks of cricket. It followed several summers during which he had impressed for Clydach as well as some promising sessions in the Indoor School in Neath which he had attended since 1952 together with a crop of excited young talent. His elevation onto the summer staff in 1955 saw Alan make his 2nd XI debut and after some promising innings over the course of the next couple of years, Alan duly made his first-class debut against Gloucestershire at Bristol in 1957.

It was a game which saw Alan dismissed without scoring in his first innings and although he made twelve in the second innings, he remembers the game at the end of July more for the run out of Bobby Etheridge and his first-ever rollicking from Wilf Wooller – "During Gloucestershire's first innings, I made a successful shy at the stumps at the

bowler's end and effected a run out but as the rest of the Glamorgan team gathered around to congratulate me Wilf came up and said 'You're a fit young man – you should have run to the ball much quicker and then thrown it to Haydn at the other end to run out Tom Graveney instead!" Wilf was certainly a hard man and he was, in hindsight, probably right but I owed a lot to what he had done as I honed my technique in the Indoor School at Neath. As a youngster, I had struggled at times against swing bowling. Wilf had picked this up but he took a lot of time in showing me exactly what I had to look out for, running in to bowl and saying 'You watch my body. For the in-swinger, I get round into this position so watch my wrist.' I will always be grateful for his advice about my batting and the time he spent with me when I was a junior on the staff."

A signed photo of Alan Jones from 1963.

Alan was also very grateful for the help 'The Skipper' provided when his development as a young cricketer was, in theory, going to be put on hold during two years of National Service with the Welsh Regiment in Cardiff. Fortunately, his arrival at Maindy Barracks followed a letter to the Commanding Officer from Wilf in which he outlined Alan's potential and stated his wishes that he hoped the youngster would be able to avail himself of all the sporting opportunities on offer. Fortunately, Wilf's request did not fall on deaf ears and the youngster, who had been presented with his first-ever bat by the local Chapel minister, had plenty of chances to further his cricketing education.

In his final year as Glamorgan's leader in 1960, and Alan's first full summer with the Welsh county after his National Service, Wilf also set the left-hander a challenge. "If you get 1,000 runs this year we'll cap you," were his words and knowing that this accolade would result in a rise in his salary and cement his place in the team, Alan did his best to achieve this goal, but in 23 Championship outings he only managed 855 runs and batted in a variety of positions in the order. He continued his development under the equally astute but less dogmatic captaincy of Ossie Wheatley from 1961, and after several near misses, most notably a fine 92 against the 1962 Indians at the Arms Park, Alan posted his maiden hundred against Sussex at Hastings.

By this time, Alan had moved up the order to regularly open the batting with Gilbert Parkhouse. It was also a time when other uncapped players on the county circuit were left to work out things for themselves with older colleagues fearing their place in the side if they gave their younger rivals too many words of assistance. But this was not the case with the former England batsman, who despite a phlegmatic exterior, was ever ready to assist Alan, especially with his mind-set at the top of the order as well as the importance of crease occupation and batting time. As Alan recalled "there were many occasions in my early days as an opening batsman when Gilbert would amble down the wicket, put his hand on my shoulder and say 'Look son, that was a poor shot. You are playing at balls that are far too wide. Leave them alone. Think about your cricket, let the bowlers get tired and then there will be more balls in the right area to score from.' "

Gilbert's words of advice certainly did the trick on 29 August 1962 as Alan scored his maiden Championship century at Hastings, shared a mammoth stand of 238 with Tony Lewis and was presented with his Glamorgan cap by Ossie Wheatley. Alan and Tony had come together after barely fifteen minutes play on the first morning, on a green pitch which was giving the Sussex bowlers plenty of assistance. But with Tony's encouragement and Gilbert's advice ringing in Alan's ears, the pair toughed it out before lunch before reaping the rewards for their diligence after lunch as the shine disappeared and the ball got softer. Their efforts saw the Welsh county to 404-6 and, as Alan recalled in his biography, "We really struggled at first but as the shine went off the ball the bowling became easier. Although I was out for 121 leaving Tony to help himself to a magnificent 150, I was a happy man. I had my century. I also had my county cap and I don't mind admitting, Tony and I had a few beers that night!"

However, the turning point in Alan's career came the following year against Somerset at Glastonbury when he became only the third batsman in Glamorgan's history – after Eddie Bates in 1927 against Essex at Leyton and Gilbert in 1950 against the West Country team at Cardiff – to score a hundred in each innings. Alan's feat followed a lean spell at the top of the order and, whilst travelling by coach with the rest of the team to

Somerset, Ossie Wheatley had spoken to Alan and told him that he had been dropped, with Bernard Hedges restored to the opener's position with Gilbert. But the latter was taken ill overnight with Alan opening in his place and making unbeaten scores of 187 and 105, besides being on the field of play for the entire match.

His achievement came during a year when Glamorgan ended up as runners-up to Yorkshire in the Championship with his efforts at the Moorlands Ground, and in the shadow of the famous Tor, helping to cement Alan's place at the top of the order. The left-hander duly finished the year with a tally of 1,857 runs, in stark contrast to his aggregates of 1,261 and 1,286 during the two previous summers. Besides having greater experience, Alan attributed the reason for his marked improvement to the emergence of Jeff Jones as a genuinely quick bowler, with the hostile left-arm bowler adding an extra dimension to the Club's net practices, especially his ability to get the ball to lift menacingly off a length.

Facing the man who later that winter, whilst on tour with the MCC, made his England debut, taught Alan some important lessons about playing fast bowling and ones he put to good use at Swansea during the match at St Helen's against the 1963 West Indians. It was Alan's first encounter with Wes Hall, the Caribbean pace ace, who during his opening salvo sent down a couple of bouncers which Alan nonchalantly hooked for four. At the end of the over, Alwyn Harris walked down from the non-striker's end and quietly said to Alan "Take it easy on him Alan, because otherwise he'll take it out on me!" In Hall's next over, he unleashed another ferocious bouncer – the fastest delivery Alan ever faced during his county career. Instinctively, he ducked and felt the draught of the ball as it whizzed past his right ear. Once again Alwyn wandered down the wicket and said to Alan "Gee that was close," to which the doughty left-hander replied "No Alwyn, that was bloody close!"

As well as facing Jeff Jones in the nets and Indoor School, Alan was also fortunate to be able to hone his skills against slower bowlers in practice session by facing legendary off-cutter Don Shepherd – a man who rarely bowled a bad ball in the nets and treated practices as if they were the real thing. As Alan admitted, " I improved my leg-side shots because of Shep, because he knew that my strong point was off stump or just outside. When he and the likes of Jeff Jones and later Malcolm Nash bowled at me in the nets, they played the only way they knew how – they were intent on bowling me out. This simply had to be good practice and I was able to work on my game and improve my play; as a result, I played my best cricket in the years from 1963 to 1973."

Alan's success during 1963 was not a flash in the pan as it was the first of seven successive summers when the left-hander exceeded the 1,500-run mark with 1966 being his most productive season with 1,865 runs to his name, and a pair of hundreds. Alan continued to surpass the 1,000-run mark every season during the 1970s with Alan – at the age of thirty-seven – enjoying something of a renaissance in 1976 during what collectively was a dreadful season for the Club, with the opening batsman ending the summer with an aggregate of 1,692 runs and at a best-ever average of 44.76.

During the winter of 1963/64 Alan had been invited by the Western Australia Cricket Association to spend time in Perth and whilst 'Down Under' he had a taste of Shield

Alan Jones, standing alongside Richie Benaud, as he meets various dignitaries whilst acting as 12th man for an Australian XI during his winter down under in 1963/64.

cricket, playing under the captaincy of Garth McKenzie, the Test fast bowler. Besides giving Alan further invaluable experience on the fast, pitches against a series of genuinely quick bowlers, his winter sojourn also saw him appear for an Australian XI against the touring Springboks. He also had a few chances to display his rarely seen off-spin and during the match against Queensland at Perth, Alan dismissed Sam Trimble, thanks to a fine catch at slip by Terry Jenner. The news of his rare wicket soon reached the ears of Peter Walker and when Alan returned to the pre-season nets at Cardiff, his county colleague ensured that he had a new nickname of 'Sam'!

It was almost six years later when Alan claimed the second wicket of his career and his only one for the Welsh county. It came at New Road during 1970 after the Welsh county had enforced the follow-on, only for Alan Ormrod and Ron Headley to share a second wicket stand of 134 and blunt the efforts of Don Shepherd and Peter Walker to press for a Glamorgan victory. The game eventually petered out in a draw after a token second innings declaration but not before Alan had broken the second wicket stand and also claimed the wicket of Headley who danced down the wicket only to midjudge the flight of the ball and be smartly stumped by Eifion Jones – a rare occasion when a pair of brothers have shared a wicket for Glamorgan.

Some of Alan's finest innings came against the touring teams with his unbeaten 161 against the 1966 West Indians at Swansea, who again boasted the fearsome pace attack of Wes Hall and Charlie Griffiths, before being followed two years later at the same ground by 99 against the Australians. After the victory over the men in baggy green caps four years earlier, a bumper crowd turned up at St Helen's eager to witness a repeat. They were not disappointed and also saw one of Alan's best knocks on Welsh soil.

As he later recalled – "it was a perfect St Helen's wicket with beautiful weather throughout the three days. The large enthusiastic crowd were treated to an absorbing game which was great to play in. When I was batting, the runs were coming easily, especially from the off-drives and I enjoyed the occasional hook and square-cut. I was looking for my century. It would also be a timely reminder to the selectors. I was in the nervous nineties and to add to the jitters the scoring rate had slowed down and Eifion was now rather uncertainly settling in at the other end. The Australians' tails were up with a counterattack being led by their spin trio. I reached ninety-nine at last, but I knew the Aussies were hell bent on preventing that single. Ashley Mallett then produced the ball that deceived me. Giving it more air, its flight into the leg-side enticed me to go for a shot that should have brought a boundary. Moving down the wicket I failed to reach the pitch of the ball. I mis-timed the shot and followed the ball every inch of the way into Neil Hawke's safe clutches at deep mid-on."

As in 1964 – and at Cardiff in 1969 following the Championship success – Alan was part of the joyous celebrations that went on long into the night and into the small hours next morning following Glamorgan's victory by 79 runs over the 1968 Australians. Several of Alan and Eifion's friends from the Pontarddulais Male Voice Choir hurried down to St Helen's to join in with the celebrations after watching coverage of the game on BBC Wales TV. Members of the Australian tour party were supposed to have caught the 7.30pm train back to London that night but, instead, they took part in the signing and jollities and ended up being on the 8.30am service the following morning!

If his innings against the 1968 Australians was amongst his best, Alan is in no doubt about where the following years stand in his career – "1969 was the greatest year of my cricketing career. It was my privilege to be in such a great cricket team, with so many tremendous players and nice people. We had matured together. There was a relaxed atmosphere about the dressing room with no fidgeting or other evident expressions of worry. We really wanted to play for each other." He duly posted three centuries that summer – all in away games with 104 at Derby, 119 at Northampton and an unbeaten 122 at Northampton, besides a series of important contributions in other games, especially in second innings run chases.

Alan Jones on-drives the ball during Glamorgan's match against Warwickshire at Sophia Gardens during August 1973. Barry Flick is the wicket-keeper.

Alan's career also saw him register Championship centuries against sixteen of the seventeen counties with Middlesex being the one team against whom he never reached three figures, with his best in 28 matches being 92 at Lord's during 1971. Nevertheless, Alan still managed to record fourteen Championship fifties against Middlesex but his failure to convert these into a three-figure score and in front of influential people in the corridors of power, may be another reason for the way the England selectors overlooked the otherwise prolific Welshman.

Despite being overlooked, Alan continued in fine fettle in subsequent seasons and in July 1980 – his Testimonial Year with the Welsh county – Alan registered his career-best score of 204* against Hampshire at Basingstoke. It came during a drawn game at May's Bounty and against a full-strength Hampshire attach which boasted Australian paceman Shaun Graf, supported by a wily seam battery of Keith Stevenson, Tim Tremlett and

Trevor Jesty, plus the potent spin combination of John Southern and Nigel Cowley. It meant much to Alan that after slumping into his seat in the changing rooms, Bernard Hedges should wander into the changing rooms – now an area manager of Barclaycard – but previously the man who had guided Alan as an opening batsman The bond which had united the pair over so many years was now the unspoken gel which brought the pair back together at May's Bounty.

Alan only scored one Championship hundred during 1981, before hitting three in 1982 against Worcestershire, Kent and Nottinghamshire, followed in 1983 by his 52nd and final century in Glamorgan's ranks against Sussex at Sophia Gardens. By this time, and Alan's retirement at the end of the 1983 season, he had opened the batting for Glamorgan with a host of other fine players, including Bernard Hedges, Gilbert Parkhouse, Roger Davis, Bryan Davis, Roy Fredericks, Alan Lewis Jones and John Hopkins, as well as short spells with others including Geoff Ellis and Kevin Lyons.

All had their own attributes and nuances, with Gilbert and subsequently Bernard helping Alan to initially establish himself at the top of the order. As Alan recalled, "Bernard and I complemented each other really. Bernard used to cut and he used to pull. He was very strong there in that area. I was a driver and, obviously, a left and a right-handed batsman was useful. Because Bernard was cutting and pulling, the bowlers would tend to pitch the ball up and then when I went down the other end they couldn't change their length so I would get a few away. It worked out very well. Not only that, when you are an opening partnership, it means that you've got to have a good understanding and Bernard was always very good at running singles. He was quick between the wickets and there was not very often he would refuse a single. A quick call and you would be off."

After Bernard's departure from the county scene, the two Davies – Roger and Bryan – became Alan's opening partners. Roger was a brave and homegrown batsman whilst Bryan arrived from the West Indies with a handsome reputation in domestic cricket and eager to regain his place in the Caribbean Test team. The duo, at differing times, acted as Alan's opening partner for their Championship-winning summer during 1969, before Geoff and 'AL' became his partner during the 1970s with John assuming this mantle and sharing some outstanding partnership with Alan during the twilight years of his outstanding career.

As pleasing as it was for Alan, as a proud Welshman, to share substantial partnerships opening the batting with homegrown players, it was the pairing with Roy Fredericks during the early 1970s that brought most joy to the left-hander. Roy had replaced Bryan in Glamorgan's line-up with the left-handed Guyanese being very different in style and approach to the Trinidadian – a flamboyant and enthusiastic opening batsman who seemed willing to play every shot in the coaching manual, and sometimes more, compared with the technically correct and more watchful approach adopted by Bryan. As Alan recalled, "the partnership with Roy was very enjoyable, although admittedly we had our problems initially, especially with our calling. Nevertheless, a friendship rapidly developed which extended beyond the field of play. His quick-scoring and willingness to attack – almost from the off – took the pressure off me and I was able to accumulate in my own way"

Alan Jones plays a ball square of the wicket against Northamptonshire during 1978. Allan Lamb, the England batter, is in the background.

Roy and Alan's partnership extended off the field with the pair becoming room mates on away trips, and at the end of August 1972, they shared – during the course of four and three-quarter hours at a sun-kissed Swansea – a record opening stand of 330 against Northamptonshire with Alan playing the anchor role as the West Indian posted an unbeaten double-century. It said much for Glamorgan cricket at that time, as the re-building began, that they ended up losing the game by 29 runs, with a dramatic collapse during the final afternoon seeing the visitors secure a victory which for most of the game had seemed out of their grasp and undoing all the hard work which Roy and Alan had achieved with their record-breaking partnership.

Alan's skillful century against Northants had, however, been yet another outstanding innings at Swansea, yet despite this and those against touring teams at St Helen's, Alan considers his best-ever innings in Glamorgan ranks occurred in Cardiff during mid-August 1967 against Lancashire, and during Glamorgan's first-ever season at Sophia Gardens after their move from the Arms Park. It came at a time when his name was being mentioned by several journalists – and not just those west of Offa's Dyke – as a potential batsman for the 1968 Ashes series and there was excitement in Glamorgan ranks when Alec Bedser – one of the England selectors – arrived at the Cardiff ground for the first day. "He's come to have a look at you," said Lancashire's Ken Higgs to Alan, with the Welshman suggesting in reply that Bedser was probably checking up on Higgs and another Jones ahead of the MCC winter tour to the West Indies.

As it turned out there was just five minutes play on the opening day before rain stymied events for the day. However, both captains – Tony Lewis and Jack Bond – were keen to have a game and, after a series of declarations on days two and three, Glamorgan were left chasing 178 in 130 minutes. It seemed a stiff target given the indifferent light and the capricious nature of the wicket at Sophia Gardens, but Alan proceeded to make a mockery of the equation as he anchored the chase with a superb and unbeaten 95 as the Welsh county reached their target with four wickets in hand. He proudly returned to the two-storey pavillion, acknowledging the applause from both the home supporters and the Lancashire team for his match-winning efforts, but Alan's feelings of elation at steering his side to a superb victory then took a dent as he learnt that Bedser had returned to London and had not waited around to watch him bat. One can only wonder how different history might have been had he stayed in Cardiff until the end of the game.

Alan Jones, as seen at Swansea in 1979.

In addition, to a prolific record in Championship cricket, Alan matured into a successful batsman in limited overs games, and during 1978 he hit Glamorgan's first-ever Sunday League century with an unbeaten 110 against Gloucestershire at Sophia Gardens. By this time Alan, had also become Glamorgan's captain and had proudly led the Welsh county against Middlesex in the Gillette Cup Final during September 1977. His elevation to the captaincy followed a sorry series of seasons under Majid Khan, who during 1969 had played a series of audacious innings, with the Pakistani's ease of playing the fast bowlers being something that Alan admired, besides a desire to dominate opposing bowlers.

However, matters had changed by the mid-1970s and in Alan's words Majid's "casual, almost lazy approach to batting was the reasons behind his abrupt and unhappy end with Glamorgan. As a person, he was likeable and liked by the players. He was a gentleman cricketer. He unfortunately became a disillusioned captain who allowed his casual manner to influence his professional attitudes, even to the neglect of his commitment to the team, the county and his fellow professionals." His departure during the long, hot summer of 1976 followed plenty of other upheavals, and the net result was that just four of the Championship-winning side of 1969 played at Lord's eight years later – Alan, Eifion, Tony Cordle and Malcolm Nash.

During these turbulent years, a series of young and homegrown players were given their chance, but only a handful, including John Hopkins, lasted the course with the Maesteg-born batsman being Alan's opening partner at Lord's on that historic day in north-west London when a host of Glamorgan supporters – dubbed Alan Jones' Daffodil Army – descended on the historic ground in St John's Wood hoping that Glamorgan could turnover Middlesex for their first-ever one-day silverware. It was not to be as Middlesex won by five wickets but, as Alan remembered, "our pride had returned, pride as a team and pride as individuals. As I stood on the balcony with the rest of the team [for the trophy presentation] you would have thought Glamorgan were the victors, the thousands of Glamorgan supporters singing in a large choir. The scene was incredible. It reminded me, and the three other old stagers of the celebrations at St Helen's back in 1969. ...we may have lost the battle, but we had won the war. A great day for Glamorgan and Wales."

Throughout his career, Alan played hard and fair, and always walked if he knew he had edged the ball. His approach was in contrast to many others, as in the following example relating to a game against Yorkshire at Swansea in 1967 when Alan was erroneously adjudged caught by wicket-keeper Jimmy Binks against Fred Trueman after the England paceman had taken the new ball. The delivery which removed Alan had brushed his fore-arm but umpire Dusty Rhodes raised his finger believing that the edge had come off Alan's gloves.

Alan remained at the crease knowing that he hadn't hit the ball, yet earlier in the game Phil Sharpe and Jack Hampshire had also dwelt at the crease but only after more obvious edges, each time against Jeff Jones. After play, both Yorkshire batsmen told Alan that they knew they had hit the ball but, as they were on 93 and 94 respectively, they were not going to walk. This rankled with Alan, especially because both he and Fred Trueman knew the ball had not come off the bat. Indeed, Fred had gone into the Glamorgan dressing room at the close of play and said 'Alan, I'm terribly sorry, you didn't hit it'. It did not help a few minutes later when Dusty Rhodes also came into the room and said "Alan, can I buy you a drink," before apologizing for his mistake.

Alan's willingness to walk also led to heated words one day during 1976/77 when he spent a season playing for Natal. The match in question was against Western Province and the incident came at a time when Natal were bidding for the Currie Cup title. Alan had seen his team to 70-odd for no wicket before getting a faint nick and walking off before the umpire had raised his finger. When Alan got back into the changing room, he was lambasted by Vincent van der Bijl, the giant Natal captain, who said to the

Alan Jones seen in 1984 as Glamorgan's Head Coach.

131

left-hander 'When you're playing in Wales, I don't care if you walk but when you're playing for Natal, you don't walk!' Natal lost the game by nineteen runs but still won the provincial title

Despite these incidents, Alan remained true to his principles and walked if he knowingly got an edge to the ball. It was partly for this Corinthian, gentlemanly and fair-spirited approach, as well as his many years of loyal and outstanding service to Glamorgan that in 1982 Alan received the MBE in the Queen's Honours List. He played his final Championship match against Hampshire at Southampton at the end of the 1983 season and took over the following year as club coach. It was in this capacity that he helped Glamorgan secure the AXA Equity & Law League in 1993 – the season when his son Andrew also played for the Club - before serving as Director of Cricket when the Welsh side won the County Championship in 1997.

Alan retired the following year after a lifetime of loyal and wholehearted service to the Welsh county but continued to coach in a part-time capacity and acted as a specialist batting advisor with various age-group teams. At Glamorgan's AGM in March 2016, Alan was appointed as David Morgan's successor as the Club's President. "I'm absolutely delighted," said Alan shortly after his appointment. "I never expected this, but it is a great honour to be President of Glamorgan County Cricket Club. Cricket has been my life from being a player in the 1950s through to the 1980s and coaching Glamorgan was a great thrill. To be President is the icing on the cake."

Head Coach Robert Croft was also quick to praise the appointment of his former mentor as the Club's President. "Alan is a legend of a player, coach, captain and bloke who always has time for everyone concerned. He started the turnaround in Glamorgan's fortunes as a coach during the 1980s and 1990s and brought through a terrific batch of players."

Four outstanding opening batters for Glamorgan – seen in 1987 – Hugh Morris, Alan Jones, John Hopkins and Alan Butcher.

Alan Jones, helping to groom the next generation of Welsh cricketers in the Indoor School at Neath during the early 1990s.

1958

The tensions that had been bubbling under the surface for several summers boiled over in a spectacular way during 1958 as attempts were made to remove Wilf Wooller from his position of authority. Against the backdrop of this rather ugly palace coup, Glamorgan slumped from 9th place in the Championship table down to a lowly spot in 15th. Morale also dropped as a lot of dirty washing was publically aired and, with doubts over the future of several players, it was no surprise that from 31 May until 12 August the Welsh county only registered a solitary victory besides suffering a string of nine defeats.

A wet August only added to Glamorgan's woes as a trial was given to Tolly Burnett, a Cambridge Blue and occasional player with Sussex 2nd XI, but the Eton schoolmaster met with little success when given a chance to display his captaincy abilities. With Wilf having declined the committee's offer of a part-time engagement as a consultative adviser, the man who ten years before had been the toast of Glamorgan Cricket resigned from his position as secretary.

Wilf Wooller.

It was not long before Johnnie Clay plus other figures in the Club's hierarchy, also followed suit and, as column after column of newsprint covered these events, a special general meeting was called by the membership in a bid to sort out the sorry mess. The meeting at Bridgend during October resulted in a vote in favour of 'The Skipper' continuing both as captain and secretary. Bolstered by this support from the grassroots of the Club, as well as his long-standing friend Johnnie and other ex-players, Wilf withdrew his resignation and returned to his office to begin planning for 1959 and beyond.

However, 1958 proved to be the end of the road for other members of the Glamorgan squad, including two who had been alongside Wilf in the Championship-winning team. Willie Jones opted to retire, whilst Haydn Davies (Vol. 2 p238-247), who had become embroiled in the politicking, also called time on his career as the Club's wicket-keeper and took up a coaching post in Scotland. His departure from South Wales was an inglorious end to an outstanding career during which the man dubbed by supporters as 'The Panda' had made a record 784 dismissals.

438
EVANS, John Brian.

Born – Clydach, 9 November 1936.
Died – Grimsby, 1 May 2011.
Professional.
RHB, RFM.
Ed – Pentrepoeth CS.
1st XI: 1958-1963.
2nd XI: 1957-1963.
Club and Ground: 1958-1961.
Cap: 1960.
Lincolnshire 1965-1971; Minor Counties 1969.
Clubs: Clydach, Briton Ferry Town, Pontarddulais, Swansea, Dafen and Grimsby.

Batting and Fielding Record

	M	I	NO	RUNS	AV	100	50	CT	ST
F-c	87	129	19	1515	13.77	-	7	45	-
List A	1	1	0	0	-	-	-	1	-

Bowling Record

	Overs	M	R	W	AV	5wI	10wM
F-c	13993	508	6670	246	27.11	10	-
List A	50	1	37	1	37.00	-	-

Career-bests

First-class – 62* v Somerset at Weston-super-Mare, 1961.
8/42 v Somerset at Cardiff Arms Park, 1961.
List A – 1/37 v Somerset at Cardiff Arms Park, 1963.

Brian Evans was amongst a group of young homegrown fast bowlers who were nurtured during the 1950s by Glamorgan's coaches. Since the early 1950s, Brian had attended the Indoor School in Neath, together with Alan Jones and other enthusiastic youngsters from Clydach. Within a few years, Brian together with Hugh Davies and Frank Clarke were offered junior terms with Brian having made his debut aged seventeen for the Glamorgan 2nd XI in 1953.

Like others of his generation, Brian's development was briefly put on hold as he undertook his National Service before joining Glamorgan's full-time staff in 1957 and making his Championship debut the following May against Nottinghamshire at Trent Bridge. Whereas the other young bowlers were taller and used their height to effect, 'Ginger' or 'Cochyn' – as he was known on account of his flame-coloured hair – had the ability to make the ball skid through, and

An image of Brian Evans taken during 1963.

after coaching from Phil Clift in the Indoor School, he learnt the knack of making it move both back in and away from batsmen.

With these new weapons in his armoury, Brian enjoyed a stellar summer in 1960, claiming 87 wickets with a series of five-wicket hauls as his raw pace surprised several experienced county batsmen. After claiming his maiden 'five-for' against Worcestershire in April, Brian claimed 5/62 against Kent, 6/64 against Essex, 5/26 against Gloucestershire, 5/45 against Surrey and 5/42 against Leicestershire. These were performances which deservedly saw Brian being awarded his county cap by Wilf Wooller during his final year in county cricket. It cheered 'The Skipper' to have a brisk homegrown bowler on the books, and a bright future was predicted for the young bowler.

A further 82 wickets were added during 1961 in a summer which saw Brian produce career-best performances with both bat and ball against Somerset at the Arms Park, returning figures of 8/42 as well as striking a feisty and unbeaten 62. These performances came during a purple patch during the last week of July when Brian also took 7/32 against Leicestershire at Margam as well as 5/37 against Essex at Clacton.

It was a summer as well where he formed a new ball partnership with Ossie Wheatley, as well as sharing some feisty spells with left-arm quickie Jeff Jones. But Glamorgan's very Celtic and fiery pairing of Evans and Jones was an all too brief one as Brian was subsequently plagued with a series of injuries. Whilst Jeff went on to win England honours, Brian only took 42 wickets during 1962 and was struck down with injury mid-way through 1963. With no sign of any improvement, Brian regrettably was forced into retirement from county cricket early in the 1964 season.

Colleagues remembered him for his various mannerisms when bowling – the regular pulling up of his socks at the end of his run-up, followed by the hitching up of his trousers and then running his hands through his hair before running in to bowl.

He subsequently took up a position as a professional with a club in Grimsby, and continued to play Minor County cricket for Lincolnshire between 1965 and 1971, besides making his final

Brian Evans, seen bowling in the nets in the rugby stand at Cardiff Arms Park in 1961.

first-class appearance playing for the Minor Counties representative side against the 1969 New Zealanders at Lincoln. Brian was still able to deliver some waspish spells but the day-to-day rigour of county cricket was out of the question.

Despite being based in Eastern England, he retained a close interest in the affairs of the Welsh county, and regularly travelled from his home near Grimsby to attend the annual luncheons held by the Glamorgan Former Players Association.

439
MORGAN, Howard William.

Born – Maesteg, 29 June 1931.
Professional.
RHB, OB.
Ed – Maesteg GS.
1st XI: 1958.
2nd XI: 1955-1956.
Colts: 1956-1958.
Club and Ground: 1958.
Clubs: Maesteg Celtic, Briton Ferry Town and Neath.

Batting and Fielding Record

	M	I	NO	RUNS	AV	100	50	CT	ST
F-c	2	3	1	11	5.50	-	-	-	-

Bowling Record

	Balls	M	R	W	AV	5wI	10wM
F-c	132	4	58	2	29.00	-	-

Career-bests

First-class –   5 v Leicestershire at Rodney Parade, Newport, 1958.
1/27 v Warwickshire at St Helen's, Swansea, 1958.

Howard Morgan played twice for Glamorgan during 1958.

Born and educated in Maesteg, Howard joined Glamorgan's junior staff during the mid-1950s after showing rich promise as a right-handed batsman and off-spinner with Maesteg Celtic. He produced some useful performances with both ball and bat in 2nd XI matches. But with Jim McConnon and Don Shepherd as Glamorgan's first choice off-spinners, Howard only appeared in a couple of Championship matches in early June 1958 – against Leicestershire at Rodney Parade in Newport, and Warwickshire at Swansea.

Howard, who was known to one and all as 'H', left Glamorgan's staff at the end of the 1958 season and duly trained as a schoolmaster, teaching Geography and PE. He subsequently taught at several secondary schools in Cardiff and the Vale, besides acting as a selector for the Welsh Schools Under-19 team from 1960 until 1985, as well as overseeing the Cardiff Schools Cricket League. After leaving the Glamorgan staff, Howard played for a number of clubs in the South Wales Cricket Association, including Neath and Briton Ferry Town, besides appearing for the Association's representative team.

Howard Morgan, as seen during 1956.

During the late 1960s he joined St Fagans and played alongside his great friend and fellow schoolmaster Graham Lewis. Howard captained the club in 1969 before moving to join Cowbridge and being a member of a very successful team at The Broadshoard. He led the Cowbridge side between 1973 and 1976, besides coaching the emerging players.

440
BURNETT, Anthony Compton.
(later changed name to Anthony Compton-Burnett)
Born – Chipstead, Surrey, 26 October, 1923.
Died – Wexham Park, Slough, 31 May, 1993.
Amateur.
Ed – Lancing College and Pembroke College, Cambridge.
1st XI: 1958.
Cambridge University 1949-1950 (Blue 1949); Sussex 2nd XI 1949-1954; MCC 1950-1951.
Clubs: Lancing Rovers, Yellowhammers.

Batting and Fielding Record

	M	I	NO	RUNS	AV	100	50	CT	ST
F-c	8	11	0	71	6.45	-	-	1	-

Career-bests
First-class –   17   v Leicestershire at Loughborough, 1958.

Tolly Burnett was the Eton schoolmaster who was given a brief trial in 1958 as Glamorgan captain as certain members of the Welsh county's committee believed that he had the attributes to replace the legendary Wilf Wooller who had indicated that he was prepared to stand down as the county's leader. It was a highly contentious decision, not least that the Cambridge Blue had never played regular county cricket.

Tolly's cricketing career began at Lancing in the late 1930s, and after serving in the Second World War, he read science at Pembroke College in Cambridge. In 1949 he made a career-best 79* for the Light Blues against Middlesex in 1949, followed by half-centuries against the Free Foresters and The Army, and fifties in each innings against Somerset. Later that summer, Tolly made his debut for Sussex 2nd XI, for whom he scored 65 against Kent 2nd XI, before making 108* against Kent 2nd XI the following summer.

On coming down, Tolly accepted a position teaching science at Eton, but he continued to play for Sussex 2nd XI and the MCC, who considered the right-hander to be a suitable candidate to lead a county side. In 1954 Northamptonshire made enquiries about Burnett's form with Sussex 2nd XI after hearing of his decent record in club cricket. Four years later, it was the turn of the Glamorgan committee to enquire about Tolly's capabilities,

In many ways, Tolly was the innocent victim of what unfolded during a period which not even the most imaginative of scriptwriters could have dreamt up and largely stemmed from an ongoing spat between Wilf and a faction on the committee who had become tired of the negative publicity and incidents which had resulted from his actions both on and off the field. In particular, Wilf had clashed swords with Norman Riches, (Vol. One, p183-188) the highly influential former Glamorgan player who at the time was both Chair of the cricket committee and Chairman of Cardiff Athletic Club over plans to take county cricket away from the Arms Park and to develop a new ground and centre of excellence instead at Sophia Gardens or in Pontcanna Fields. Norman's family had a long association with the Arms Park and during the mid-1950s, he vehemently opposed any suggestions of moving county cricket away from the city centre location.

Tolly Burnett, as seen in his days at Cambridge University during 1949.

Matters started to brew during 1957 after Wilf, aged 44, informed the committee that he was becoming more prone to niggling injuries and would be happy to stand down as captain if a suitable replacement could be found. Given the trend at the time for amateur captains, noises were made to various players at Oxford and Cambridge to see if they were interested. The knives though were being sharpened by the anti-Wooller lobby who wanted to ease Wilf completely out of the picture, arguing that it would be difficult for a young and relatively inexperienced captain to take over with Wilf still acting as Secretary.

Without any replies in the affirmative coming from any of the Oxbridge cricketers, the net was cast wider with soundings being made within MCC circles. With his name having been put forward, Tolly duly met up with Norman Riches, in his capacity as Chair of the cricket committee, and so the skullduggery began with Norman instructing Phil Thomas, the Club's Assistant Secretary, to register the Eton schoolmaster as a Glamorgan player.

News of these covert actions and an invite to play in South Wales during August 1958 eventually reached the ears of Wilf, with a row quickly erupting over how the matters had been dealt with. Eyebrows were also raised about the decision to opt for someone who had not played a first-class game since appearing for the MCC against Ireland in 1951 and had no experience of regular county cricket. Matters swiftly escalated as the committee, after lobbying by the anti-Wooller faction, only offered him a part-time consultancy role for 1959. Wilf duly tendered his resignation as Secretary with effect from the end-of-the-season – a decision described by one local journalist as "a tragic blunder made by a committee out of a combination of ignorance and personal prejudice."

It was not the sort of environment Tolly would therefore have wished to enter as he played for Glamorgan for the first time and led them against the 1958 New Zealanders at Swansea. After twenty minutes play the Kiwis were 7-2 as Don Shepherd and Peter Gatehouse struck early but Noel Harford spared the tourist's blushes and helped them recover to 306-8. Rain curtailed play on the second day, but Glamorgan collapsed in their first innings before following-on prior to further weather interruptions as the match ended in a soggy draw.

Wilf then returned for the next five matches with Tolly making his County Championship debut, aged 34, against Lancashire at Cardiff Arms Park. It proved to be an inauspicious first appearance as he was clean bowled by Brian Statham for a duck as the demoralized Glamorgan side were swiftly bundled out for just 26. Rumours of a members' revolt which had been circulating in St Helen's during the match with the New Zealanders were soon reverberating around the Arms Park and after their abject batting display against the Red Rose county, a petition began, calling for a special general meeting in October.

Tolly's modest form in Championship cricket, getting into double figures on just three occasions did not help to quell matters, neither did his fielding with the game against Lancashire seeing him miss what appeared to be a straightforward catch at mid-on as Don Shepherd deceived Geoff Pullar with a subtle off-cutter. The ball lobbed up into the air with Tolly barely having to move but as the ball swirled around he misjudged the catch, before picking it up from the turf and saying "Bad luck, Shepherd! It was just out of my reach!"

The end of August saw Tolly leading the Welsh county in their last two Championship matches of the summer, against Yorkshire at Swansea and Northamptonshire at Ebbw Vale. By this time all sorts of rumours had been circulating with it emerging that senior club officials had spoken to Tolly about the perceived strengths and weaknesses of other players, so with others in danger because of these manoeuvres behind the scenes, there were few offers of advice from colleagues as he tried to contain the opposition batsmen and stamp a semblance of authority on proceedings.

Tolly had a fine record as a captain in club cricket but his approach to leading the Glamorgan side and his tactics cut little ice, especially in the closing game at Ebbw Vale

A view of the Welfare Ground in Ebbw Vale during Glamorgan's County Championship fixture against Warwickshire in 1964.

where, rather than asking the spinners to exploit a wicket which usually offered turn, he persisted with the seam bowlers as Denis Brookes scored a century in Northants' first innings and Raman Subba Row an unbeaten one in their second. Just to rub salt into the wounds, Tolly was then one of four batsmen to be dismissed by left-arm spinner George Tribe as Northants eased to a 78-run victory with further questions being asked about the man who the committee had invited on a trial as captain.

The Special General Meeting at Bridgend Town Hall led to a referendum being held amongst Glamorgan's members to settle the issue of whether or not the Club should retain Wilf's services. 1,098 votes were in favour and 795 were against, leading to ten committee members resigning, including Club Chairman John Mayberry Bevan (Vol.1, p.329-330). Wilf duly withdrew his resignation and resumed his duties as the Club's captain and secretary for 1959. On his part Tolly returned to his teaching post at Eton, no doubt wondering what sort of hornet's nest he had unwittingly entered.

Tolly was the second cousin of Dame Ivy Compton-Burnett, the famous novelist who was regarded by several critics as one of the foremost figures in modern English fiction, specializing in exploring the complex relationships of family life. One can only wonder what she would have made of Tolly's time with Glamorgan during 1958!

Allan Watkins, fourth left, leads out the Glamorgan team from the Pavillion at Rodney Parade in Newport during June 1959 for the Championship match against Sussex. Also in the photograph are (left to right) Don Shepherd, David Evans, Gilbert Parkhouse, Frank Clarke, Jim Pressdee, Jim McConnon, Peter Walker (obscured), Louis Devereux and Don Ward.

1959

After the discord which had thwarted Glamorgan for much of the previous season, Wilf Wooller and his team bounced back by registering their most successful season since lifting the county title in 1948. They finished sixth in the Championship table and would have been runners-up to Yorkshire had the Welsh county defeated Middlesex at Lord's in the final game of the summer.

In all, a dozen Championship games were won whilst the Indian tourists were also defeated at the Arms Park where a relatively young and inexperienced team, led by Allan Watkins, won by 51 runs with Jim Pressdee completing his maiden first-class hundred and Jim McConnon giving a fine display of his match-winning prowess as an off-spinner.

Bernard Hedges and Gilbert Parkhouse flourished as opening batsmen, with their quick scoring giving plenty of time and opportunities for other batsmen to settle in and make an impact, besides providing chances for the bowlers to perform with a sizeable total on the scoreboard. Indeed, Allan and Jim Pressdee, as well as Peter Walker, each passed the 1,000-run mark with the latter also flourishing in the field with a tally of 64 catches – more than any other fielder in the country. Standing at short-leg or leg-slip, Peter formed a highly effective combination with Don Shepherd and Jim McConnon, gratefully snaffling any chance that came his way. Glamorgan's 'spin-twins' reveled at Swansea with Glamorgan winning all five of the Championship matches they staged at St Helen's during 1959.

There was great delight as well in Welsh ranks when Gilbert Parkhouse was recalled to the England team for the series against India. To many, it was a belated recall by the selectors considering his haul of 1991 Championship runs and six hundreds during 1959. Gilbert responded with 78 on his recall for the Third Test at Headingley, but after scores of 17 and 49 in the Fourth Test at Old Trafford, he was jettisoned for the final Test at The Oval and was not chosen for the winter tour to the West Indies.

441
DAVIS, Francis John.

Born – Whitchurch, Cardiff, 26 March 1939.
RHB, SLA.
Ed – Llandaff Cathedral School, Blundell's School and St John's College, Oxford.
1st XI: 1959-1970.
2nd XI: 1958-1974.
Oxford University 1963 (Blue).
Hertfordshire 1977-1978.
Clubs: Cardiff, Maesteg Town.
Brother of RC Davis.

Batting and Fielding Record

	M	I	NO	RUNS	AV	100	50	CT	ST
F-c	14	24	7	189	11.11	-	-	7	-
List A	2	1	0	4	4.00	-	-	-	-

Bowling Record

	Balls	M	R	W	AV	5wI	10wM
F-c	1401	82	674	18	37.44	1	-
List A	78	1	53	1	53.00	-	-

Career-bests
First-class –   28* v Kent at Gravesend, 1966.
               5/72 v Warwickshire at Edgbaston, 1966.
List A –   4 v Essex at Ynysangharad Park, Pontypridd, 1970.
               1/28 v Northamptonshire at Sophia Gardens, Cardiff, 1970.

John Davis, the elder brother of Roger, played occasionally for Glamorgan between 1959 and 1970 before going into teaching.

The left-arm spinner had shone as a schoolboy sportsman initially at Llandaff Cathedral School – where his mother was a teacher – before attending Blundell's School in Tiverton and showing great prowess on the cricket and rugby field. He subsequently developed his cricket career at St John's College, Oxford where he won a cricket Blue in 1963. That summer, John made a career-best 63 for Oxford University against Northamptonshire at The Parks, besides taking 5/67 against Cambridge University in the Varsity Match at Lord's.

John had made his Glamorgan debut in 1959 against the Indian tourists at Swansea, and after coming down from Oxford he joined the county's full-time staff. He duly made a further thirteen appearances for Glamorgan with his best performance coming at Edgbaston in 1966 when he took 5/72 against Warwickshire.

John left the world of professional cricket at the end of 1967 and commenced his teaching career at Berkhamsted School. However, he re-appeared for the Welsh county in a couple of List A matches during 1970.

Brothers Roger (left) and John Davis.

1960

It seemed during May 1960 that Wilf Wooller would be signing off in a blaze of glory before retiring and focusing his efforts instead on his duties as the Club's Secretary. The summer began with a victory over Worcestershire at Pontypridd before he and his team inflicted an innings defeat on Leicestershire at Swansea. But Glamorgan's form fell away during June and July with a demoralizing period of nine matches without a victory.

The Welsh county eventually ended the season in 11th place in the Championship table but the potential for much better was clearly there, as highlighted during August during the home and away games with reigning champions Yorkshire. The match at Bradford had been a real dog fight and was

Wilf Wooller (second right) and Johnnie Clay (second left) inspect the pitch at Cardiff Arms Park during a match in 1960.

finely poised with the Tykes two runs short of their target with their last pair at the crease. Mick Cowan was then baffled by a delivery from Don Shepherd which shaved the off stump. However, the bails did not drop and next over Ray Illingworth struck the winning runs. Glamorgan made amends the following week at Swansea as they defeated Yorkshire by 87 runs with Don taking 5/52 before joining forces with Don Ward to dismiss the visitors for 144 on the final afternoon.

One of the reasons for the slide down the table was that the batting mis-fired. After their successes in 1959, only four hundreds were recorded, whilst Jim McConnon and Peter Walker also lost form with the ball. The latter's demise was quite curious, as earlier in the summer he had made his England debut in the series with South Africa. However, after returning to the county circuit, his batting and bowling fell away, although Peter remained an agile fielder close to the wicket and set a Club record of 69 catches.

Brian Evans, as seen in 1960.

Another plus was the emergence of Brian Evans and Jeff Jones as each flourished in their outings in the seam attack, whilst Tony Lewis, who had enjoyed an outstanding time as a Freshman at Cambridge, emerged as a consistent run-scorer in Glamorgan's middle-order.

442
JONES, Ivor Jeffrey.

Born – Dafen, 10 December 1941.
Professional.
LHB, LF.
Ed – Stebonheath School, Llanelli.
1st XI: 1960-1968.
2nd XI: 1960-1968.
Club and Ground:1962-1964.
Cap: 1965.
England 1960-68 (15 Tests).
Clubs: Pontarddulais, Dafen, Bridgend, Briton Ferry Town, Llanelli, Briton Ferry Steel, Felinfoel and Trostre.

Batting and Fielding Record

	M	I	NO	RUNS	AV	100	50	CT	ST
F-c	157	180	69	395	3.55	-	-	36	-
List A	9	6	3	20	6.67	-	-	2	-

Bowling Record

	Balls	M	R	W	AV	5wI	10wM
F-c	3904.4	979	9583	408	23.48	16	-
List A	675	24	319	22	14.50	-	-

Career-bests

First-class –   20 v Sussex at Cardiff Arms Park, 1965.
                8/11 v Leicestershire at Grace Road, Leicester, 1965.
List A –   7 v Northamptonshire at Northampton, 1968.
                4/12 v Northamptonshire at Northampton, 1966.

Jeff Jones won 15 Test caps for England, and during the 1960s was one of the first names on the selector's team sheets when England played abroad on fast and bouncy wickets. Had it not been for a serious elbow injury sustained early in the 1968 season, the strong and burly left-arm fast bowler would surely have played many more times for England.

Jeff had progressed from club and junior cricket in the Llanelli area onto Glamorgan's junior staff in 1958, with a sign of his prowess coming during his first year where, in a 2nd XI game against North Wales, Jeff produced a spell of 8 wickets for just 8 runs and prompted coach Phil Clift to later write in the Club's Yearbook "we may well have a fine young bowler of the future."

The left-arm quickie duly made his first-class debut in 1960 against Kent at Blackheath, and within two years, and with 44 first-class wickets under his belt, Jeff became the county's new ball bowler and formed a potent pairing with captain Ossie Wheatley. The closing month of the season also saw the twenty-year-old quick bowler record a split hat-trick in the Championship match against Yorkshire at Harrogate as he ended the Tykes

A jovial Jeff Jones, as seen in 1963.   *Jeff Jones, seen bowling at Swansea during 1964.*

first innings in successive balls by having Don Wilson caught behind by David Evans before clean bowling Mel Ryan, and then doing the same to Ken Taylor with the first ball of the second innings.

He continued his development by taking 58 first-class wickets during 1963 with his potential being recognised by the England selectors, who chose the quick bowler for the winter tours, initially to East Africa and later to India. He was still to be capped by Glamorgan but on 21 January 1964, Jeff made his England debut in the second Test of the series with India at Bombay. The left-armer had bowled a lively spell in the MCC's match against West Zone at Ahmedabad which preceded the game at the Brabourne Stadium but his call-up into the Test side was primarily the result of a stomach virus which left the 15-man party four short ahead of the toss. This soon became five as Mickey Stewart succumbed at tea and took no further part in the contest. Jeff duly came on as first change after the new ball had been shared by Barry Knight and David Larter, but he went wicketless in the contest, and with Colin Cowdrey and Peter Parfitt joining the squad for the Third Test at Eden Gardens, the game at Bombay proved to be Jeff's only taste of international cricket in the sub-continent.

Some wondered, especially the patriotic Welsh, if Jeff would feature in the Ashes series of 1964 but a series of niggling injuries, especially to his right ankle, ended such fanciful ideas as he ended the year with just 19 wickets to his name. He also completed a rather unwarranted batting record as, together with his closing scores from the previous summer, Jeff recorded 11 successive scores of either 0 or 0* for Glamorgan in first-class cricket.

Jeff more than made up for this disappointments of 1964 by enjoying a breakthrough summer the following year, claiming 84 wickets at a shade under 16 apiece – a performance which deservedly won Jeff his Glamorgan cap. August 1965 also saw Jeff produce one of the most lethal spells of bowling by any Glamorgan player with his efforts on the final day of a rain-affected game at Leicester coming at a time when the Welsh still harboured ambitions of mounting a bid for the county title. With just two hours play being possible on the opening day, it was going to take something exceptional on the final day for the visitors to claim a victory. But up stepped Jeff, having not taken a wicket in Leicestershire's first innings, as he fully exploited the damp green surface at Grace Road to complete his career-best figures.

At the start of his spell he bowled three successive and quite terrifying deliveries to Maurice Hallam, the experienced Leicestershire opener. The first leapt up off the surface and whizzed past Maurice's nose before thudding loudly into the gloves of David Evans. The wicket-keeper immediately consulted with the slip cordon and everyone moved back a good ten yards. Next ball, another ferocious ball lifted up off the green and firm pitch before striking Maurice high on his torso with the batsman collapsing in a heap. The fielders behind the wicket also winced as the batsman was felled, but fortunately Maurice was swiftly back on his feet, and rubbing his chest as Jeff turned around and headed back to his mark.

David Evans and the slip fielders looked at each other again and moved back for a second time before Jeff ran in and for the third successive time produced a real snorter which this time Maurice managed to edge, before turning to the slips and shouting "catch it". To his relief, Peter Walker at first slip leapt up high, stretched out his telescopic left arm and completed an amazing one-handed catch. Maurice duly smiled in David's direction and said "I'd rather be an alive coward than a dead hero!"

An action photograph of Jeff Jones, taken during 1965.

Brian Booth and Peter Marner swiftly followed, both edging the ball into David's gloves before Jeff removed the Ceylonese duo of Stanley Jayasinghe and Clive Inman, but not before the former was also struck a fearsome blow on his left hip before collapsing onto the ground with a wail of agony. After a few minutes of writhing around on the ground, the slender batsman stood up and took a pair of cricket socks out of his left pocket saying "Do you know! Damn ball missed my thigh-pad!"

Jeff had now taken five wickets for no runs and, for the lower order, it must have been a terrifying sight to watch the Welshman decimate the Leicestershire top order. David Constant bravely offered some resistance but Jeff added three more victims to his tally to end with the astonishing analysis of 13-9-11-8. It might well be an apocryphal tale that as one of the lower order batsmen edged the fiery left-armer into the safe hands of a fielder, the batsman said "Thank you" and motioned as if to shake the fielders hand as he returned, in one piece, back to the Grace Road pavillion.

After performances such as this, it was no surprise that Jeff won selection on the 1965/66 MCC tour to Australia and New Zealand. With captain MJK Smith and manager Billy Griffith eager for England to play some aggressive cricket, the Welshman fitted the bill perfectly, besides giving variety with his line as a left-armer. With the England selectors looking for successors to the likes of Brian Statham, Frank Tyson and Fred Trueman, Jeff prospered on the hard and bouncy pitches and formed a decent new ball pairing with Warwickshire's David Brown. A measure of his progress at international level as well as his sustained fitness and standing within the MCC management was that the Welshman ended the tour as the leading wicket-taker with 48 wickets at 30 runs apiece, besides being compared by the Aussie media to their own left-arm bowling hero Alan Davidson.

Jeff Jones, seen in his delivery stride, during a match at Neath in 1967.

Jeff also rectified a habit of following through close to the stumps and running on the pitch, too close to the line of the stumps. Things had reached a head in an early tour game against New South Wales which had seen him removed from the attack after warnings from the umpires as he created a five-foot gash in the surface in front of the batting crease and around the line of off-stump to a right-hander. Despite having claimed 5/59 in the opening State match against Western Australia at Perth, Jeff was not chosen for the opening Test at Brisbane, but illness and injury to David Brown and Ken Higgs saw Jeff included for the back-to-back Tests at Melbourne and Sydney. He did not let the selectors down, filleting the middle-order at the MCG before removing opening batsman Bill Lawry in a feisty opening salvo at Sydney. In the Third Test he also gleefully added 55 for the last wicket with Gloucestershire spinner David Allan and in so doing completed a Test best 16.

With David Later struggling with injury, Jeff kept his place in the England side for the rest of the Ashes series, as well as the New Zealand leg of the tour, with the left-armer having a fine time with the ball in the Fourth Test at Adelaide, taking 6/118 – the best by a Glamorgan player in Tests for England – as Australia amassed 516 to lay the platform for an innings victory. His pace and lateral movement off the firm pitches also saw three of his wickets completed with the the assistance of Sussex wicket-keeper Jim Parks, who later remarked how hard Jeff consistently hit his gloves throughout his 29-over spell.

Jeff then rounded off an impressive tour with three more wickets in the drawn Fifth Test to end the series as England's leading wicket-taker, before adding four more scalps to his tally in the First Test against New Zealand at Christchurch, followed by five in the matches at both Dunedin and Auckland. After these successes 'Down Under' Jeff kept his place in the England team for the first two Tests of the series against the 1966 West Indians. He went wicketless in the opening Test at Old Trafford where the Caribbean side won by an innings and was criticized by some of the media for bowling too short. He was not alone in this and kept his place for the second game of the rubber at Lord's, but he only claimed a solitary wicket in the drawn game and was omitted for the remaining Tests as the selectors changed tack by introducing the left-arm spin of Kent's Derek Underwood.

1966 was a damp summer overall so for Jeff to finish with 52 Championship wickets at 24 runs apiece was a decent return. He responded by enjoying his best-ever summer during 1967 with 100 first-class wickets at 19 runs apiece, as well as seven five-wicket hauls in the Championship matches. Whilst he didn't make the England line-up for the series with India and Pakistan, he bowled with pace and hostility for the Welsh county with the highlight of his summer being returns of 5/34 against Warwickshire at Swansea, 5/29 against Hampshire at Portsmouth plus 6/27 against Kent on the capricious surface at Sophia Gardens.

After such an outstanding summer in the Championship, plus his record on the harder

Jeff Jones bowls to Alan Ormrod of Worcestershire during the Championship match at Swansea in 1968.

wickets overseas, Jeff's name was amongst the first to be agreed upon by the England selectors for the winter tour to the West Indies in 1967/68. The Welshman duly formed a potent and hostile attack alongside John Snow and David Brown as, for once, England possessed a faster and more effective fast bowling unit than their counterparts from the Caribbean.

Compared with his experiences in Australia, Jeff's 14 wickets in the Test series were relatively expensive at 46 runs apiece, with the left-armer also switching to first change for the Second, Third and Fourth matches of the rubber. Jeff returned to take the new ball with John Snow for the final Test at Georgetown, but it was his batting skills that grabbed the headlines in the closing stages of this dramatic contest. Jeff had very modest pretentions as a batsman, yet the number eleven successfully blocked out the final over from spinner Lance Gibbs to secure both a draw and series win for the England team.

With his star in the ascent, many believed that Jeff would play a key role during the 1968 Ashes series, but early in the domestic season he damaged shoulder and elbow ligaments in the Championship match against Essex at Ilford and sadly missed the rest of the season. Some believed that the injury was the result of his experiences in the Caribbean where he was encouraged to bowl a prolonged series of short-pitched deliveries to the West Indian batsmen. A consultant subsequently found arthritis in his elbow joint as well as a severe wearing of the bone,

In a bid to rescue his career, Jeff tried to modify his action and went on Glamorgan's tour to the Caribbean in 1969/70. But as Tony Lewis recalled it was not a successful return to the West Indies – "he began gently and worked up occasional spurts off his long run. Immediately we could see that his action had changed. There was a kink in the arm. Was it a throw or had it reset that way after the operation. Don Shepherd, Peter Walker, Ossie Wheatley and I discussed it most academically for days and we watched Jeff's bowling from all angles, but in our heart of hearts we knew that Jeff was illegally chucking the ball. He had no idea himself; he believed his arm action to be exactly as it was before the operation. I shall never forget flying home, having already fixed that I should sit next to him and tell him…He took it as nobly as anyone could. I did not know whether to cry or order a large brandy. We did neither and just sat and stared ahead, listening to the aeroplane engines grinding home the awful truth."

Jeff duly retired from professional cricket and secured a post initially as a representative for a brewery in South Wales. He later secured a post working for Llanelli Rural District Council as their sports ground supervisor, besides undertaking coaching duties in local primary schools. Jeff also appeared in charity games during the 1970s and 1980s for the Old England team, as well as the Lord's Taverners, besides playing in club cricket bowling left-arm spin. After the premature end to his career with Glamorgan and England, he took great delight to see his son Simon follow in his footsteps at county and international level, besides being a member of the Ashes-winning team of 2005.

443
HARRIS, Alwyn.

Born – Aberdulais, 31 January 1936.
Died – Glynneath, 11 March 2018.
Professional.
LHB.
Ed – Cadoxton CS.
1st XI: 1960-1964.
2nd XI: 1956-1964.
Colts: 1956.
Club and Ground: 1962-1964.
Royal Engineers 1958.
Clubs: Ynysygerwn, Briton Ferry Steel, Metal Box, Gorseinon, Hill's Plymouth,
Ammanford and Llanelli.

Batting and Fielding Record

	M	I	NO	RUNS	AV	100	50	CT	ST
F-c	49	91	3	1698	19.29	2	6	19	-
List A	1	1	0	6	6.00	-	-	-	-

Bowling Record

	Balls	M	R	W	AV	5wI	10wM
F-c	6	1	0	0	-	-	-

Career-bests
First-class – 110 v Warwickshire at St Helen's, Swansea, 1962.
List A – 6 v Somerset at Cardiff Arms Park, 1963.

Alwyn Harris.

Alwyn Harris was amongst a handful of Glamorgan batsmen to have scored a century in the county's games against touring teams when the Welsh county sercured a victory over their Test-playing opponents. He was also the Club's first batsman to face a ball in List A cricket – against Somerset at the Arms Park in 1963.

His feat against a Test team came at Cardiff Arms Park in June 1962 on the second day of Glamorgan's game against the Pakistani's. His innings of 101 saw Glamorgan match the tourist's first innings total with Alwyn sharing a second wicket stand of 195 with Alan Jones, a fellow left-hander and a good friend from their days as junior professionals. When Glamorgan drew level with the Pakistani total, captain Ossie Wheatley enterprisingly declared before taking 4/38 as the tourists were humbled for 158. Alwyn did not bat again as an unbeaten 81 from Bernard Hedges saw the Welsh county to a seven-wicket victory.

Three weeks before Alwyn had posted his maiden first-class hundred on the opening day of Glamorgan's match at Swansea against Warwickshire. However, his fine 110 did not lay the foundation of another victory as the contest ended all-square after several weather interruptions, with the game petering out into a draw as Glamorgan employed ten bowlers, including Alwyn whose single over of spin – his only one in Championship cricket – being a maiden. 1962 proved to be Alwyn's only summer of regular 1st XI cricket, but it was one which saw him pass the coveted thousand-run mark with an aggregate of 1,048 runs.

Alwyn had first played for the Glamorgan Colts whilst still at school having attracted the attention of the county's coaching staff with a series of promising performances in club cricket for Ynysygerwn. After completing his National Service with the Royal Engineers, Alwyn became a full-time member of the playing staff in 1960 and after some solid innings for the 2nd XI, he was called up to make his first-class debut in June 1960 against Kent at Blackheath.

His county career began and also ended in the Garden of England with his final appearance coming at Maidstone in 1964. In between, there were a further 47 first-class appearances, a career tally of 1,698 runs plus one other game in the 1st XI with Alwyn being a member of the Glamorgan side who won their inaugural game in the 1963 Gillette Cup, defeating Somerset at the Arms Park thanks to an unbeaten century by Bernard Hedges after Alwyn – who opened the batting with Alan Jones – had been the first Glamorgan batsman to face a ball in a List A encounter.

Alwyn, who was known as "Cha Cha" because of his liking for the dance when socializing, also coached for a season at Christ College Brecon. After leaving county cricket, he became an automotive engineer, and worked for a gearbox company in Resolven.

Alwyn Harris attempts to sweep a spin bowler during a match at Swansea in 1963.

444
WHITEHILL, William Kenneth.

Born – Newport, Mon, 13 June 1934.
RHB, WK.
1st XI: 1960.
2nd XI: 1959-1964.
Club: Newport.

Batting and Fielding Record

	M	I	NO	RUNS	AV	100	50	CT	ST
F-c	7	11	3	60	7.50	-	-	8	-

Career-bests

First-class –   16 v Gloucestershire at Bristol, 1960.

Willie Whitehill was Glamorgan's reserve wicket-keeper during the early 1960's.

He had kept for Newport since his teens and first played for the county's 2nd XI in 1959. Willie duly joined the Glamorgan staff as the understudy to David Evans and during 1960 when David was injured, Willie appeared in seven first-class matches, with his debut coming against Worcestershire at Stourbridge.

He found few other opportunities following David's return to fitness, as well as the emergence of Eifion Jones as a capable wicket-keeper and a very useful batsman. Willie continued to play for Glamorgan's 2nd XI until 1964, but did not play again in first-class cricket.

Willie Whitehill.

445
LEWIS, David Wyndham.

Born – Roath, Cardiff, 18 December 1940.
Ed – Wycliffe College.
RHB, LBG.
1st XI: 1960-1969.
2nd XI: 1959-1969.
MCC v Denmark 1961; Transvaal 1972/73.
Clubs: Cardiff, Gowerton, SCOW, Radyr and South Wales Hunts.

Batting and Fielding Record

	M	I	NO	RUNS	AV	100	50	CT	ST
F-c	12	17	6	107	9.72	-	-	3	-

Bowling Record

	Balls	M	R	W	AV	5wI	10wM
F-c	1716	58	901	21	42.90	-	-

Career-bests

First-class – 29* v Northamptonshire at St Helen's, Swansea, 1968.
4/42 v Oxford University at The Parks, Oxford, 1968.

David Lewis was a highly successful leg-spinner in club cricket in South Wales who was a member of Glamorgan's Championship-winning squad in 1969, before having a brief stint in domestic cricket in South Africa.

The son of music empresario Wyndham Lewis, David was brought up in the Rhiwbina district of Cardiff and shortly after leaving Wycliffe College, he made his 2nd XI debut for the Welsh county during their North Wales tour in 1959. The following year, the law student made his first-class debut against Northamptonshire at the Arms Park. He

David Lewis.

appeared in a further three county games over the course of the next two years before his lawyer's duties took precedence and restricted David to club cricket for St Fagans plus occasional games for the county's 2nd XI and the MCC.

He returned to 1st XI cricket during 1968 before making a couple of Championship appearances during the title-winning summer of 1969, against Yorkshire at Swansea, as well as Sussex at Hastings. David also played against the 1969 West Indians at St Helen's and went on the Welsh county's tour to Bermuda and the West Indies during 1969/70 before moving to live and work in South Africa.

Whilst in the Transvaal, he set up a fabric blinds company as well as a waste disposal business. In all, David spent seven years in South Africa and during 1972/73 David played in first-class cricket for Transvaal. After returning to Wales, David followed in his father's footsteps by becoming a concert organiser and amongst other events was responsible for setting up the World Choir Concerts at the National Stadium, Young Voices and later the Welsh Proms in St David's Hall.

He continued to be a potent leg-spinner in club cricket for Cardiff, besides representing Wales against Ireland in 1979 and making further appearances for the MCC and South Wales Hunts. David also served on the Glamorgan committee and for a while was Chairman of the cricket committee. He subsequently retired to live in Pembrokeshire.

1961

Glamorgan marked their new era, under the captaincy of Ossie Wheatley, by completing the double over Surrey for the first time in the Club's history, but it was a summer which saw the Welsh county slide down to 14th spot in the Championship table.

One of the reasons for this slippage was the injury crisis which affected the Club. Ossie must have been wondering what he had let himself in for as, firstly Tony Lewis sustained a season-ending knee injury whilst up at Cambridge before, during early June, Allan Watkins announced his retirement after a bout of illness. Soon afterwards, Jim McConnon suffered another injury and followed the all-rounder into retirement, whilst Brain Evans and Jeff Jones also picked up a series of niggling ailments.

It was heartening though for the new captain that Bernard Hedges and Gilbert Parkhouse were in vintage form, with the former scoring over 2,000 runs in all first-class games. Peter Walker also came close to completing the Double for Glamorgan, ending the summer with 1204 Championship runs and 84 wickets to his name. Jim Pressdee also bounced back after a lean year by becoming the first Glamorgan batter to score a hundred in matches against the Australians.

His feat came at the Arms Park over the Whitsun Bank Holiday and, in the second game against the 1961 Australians later in the year at Swansea, Don Shepherd wrote his name into the record books by racing to 50 in just a quarter of an hour. The off-cutter also enjoyed a wicket-laden summer, claiming 122 Championship wickets and producing a remarkable performance against Nottinghamshire at Rodney Parade where he claimed six wickets without conceding a run during an eleven over spell. His magnificent efforts saw the visitors bundled out for 86 in reply to Glamorgan's first innings total of 316-8 and helped to lay the foundations for an emphatic victory by 155 runs.

WHEATLEY, Oswald Stephen CBE.

Born – Low Fell, 28 May 1935.

RHB, RFM.

Ed – King Edward's School, Birmingham; Gonville and Caius College, Cambridge.

1st XI: 1961-1970.

Club and Ground: 1961-1962.

Cap: 1961.

Free Foresters 1956; Cambridge University 1957-1958 (Blue both years); Warwickshire 1957-1960; Gentlemen 1958-1962; MCC to Brazil and Argentina 1958/59; EW Swanton's XI to the West Indies 1960/61.

Clubs – Harborne, MCC.

Batting and Fielding Record

	M	I	NO	RUNS	AV	100	50	CT	ST
F-c	206	227	87	799	5.70	-	-	75	-
List A	21	11	4	20	2.85	-	-	6	-

Bowling Record

	Balls	M	R	W	AV	5wI	10wM
F-c	37575	1989	13356	715	18.67	37	4
List A	1206	43	613	29	21.13	-	-

Career-bests

First-class –   30 v Oxford University at The Parks, Oxford, 1961.

         9/60 v Sussex at Ebbw Vale, 1968.

List A –   4* v Lancashire at Southport, 1969.

         3/30 v Northamptonshire at Northampton, 1969.

To succeed Wilf Wooller as Glamorgan captain was always going to be a monumental job for anyone, but this is precisely what Ossie Wheatley did in 1961, and with much success over the course of the next five years with the Cambridge Blue at the helm as the Welsh county defeated the 1964 Australians – a feat which his outspoken and garrulous predecessor had never achieved during his own distinguished playing career.

Ossie brought a different style of leadership to Glamorgan Cricket compared with the Wooller way as well as a different type of personality in general. He was more suave and debonair than the more rugged and bellicose Wilf: an Adonis rather than a Titan, and someone who was essentially a right-arm fast-medium swing bowler and tail-end batsman with quite modest

Ossie Wheatley, as seen in 1968 when in semi-retirement from playing county cricket.

capabilities, rather than an in your face all-rounder who was quite prepared to open the batting as well as the bowling.

He was also not as impulsive or demonstrative in the field as Wilf, but beneath Ossie's calm and more jolly demeanor lay the same steely determination for Glamorgan to win. As Peter Walker once said, "Ossie helped to put the smile back on our faces. We had been involved in some real battles on the field during Wilf's closing years in charge as he almost waged war with several opponents and continued to have personal vendettas with some captains. But Ossie was different and we laughed again on the field besides, and quite importantly, still managing to win…In both victory and defeat Ossie insisted on nothing less than one's best effort and he led by example."

In the words of Tony Lewis, Ossie "felt strongly that cricket matches were there to be won; always go for the ten points to win and then they would be interesting to watch and to play. The two points for a first innings lead did not appeal. By his warm approach to opposing captains he persuaded them also to approach the game in his way. His declarations were fair and he would call for a spurt from any batsman if he felt their efforts were not dovetailed to the whole purpose."

Born near Gateshead during May 1935, Ossie's family – who owned a furniture-making business – moved to Birmingham when he was still at primary school. The youngster duly won a place at King Edward's School where he subsequently won a place in the XI, ostensibly as an opening batsman. In these early days he was also known as 'Steve' before a metamorphosis – following his National Service with the Royal Artillery – in both his name and cricketing skills saw Ossie win a place in the Cambridge XI as an away swing bowler.

Having won a Blue in 1957, the following year saw Ossie create a new Cambridge record with a haul of 80 wickets in eighteen matches for the university, and chiefly on the

Ossie Wheatley, sitting second left, in the King Edwards School, Birmingham 1st XI team photograph.

shirt-front pitches at Fenner's. At the time, the Light Blues could field a stronger team than many counties and, in Ted Dexter, boasted a captain who went on to lead England. Day in, day out from April until June, Ossie and his fellow students played against the cream of county talent and, as Ossie remembers "no one was allowed to go back to his college until he had had a drink with the opposition."

The main weapon in Ossie's bowling armoury was his away swing: as Ted Dexter later recalled "Ossie was not the fastest of bowlers, but he had a no-fuss run-up and delivery from near to the stumps and bowled a consistent line. Initially he made the occasional ball jag back in but after advice and plenty of practice at Cambridge, he developed a potent out-swinger." As Tony Lewis recalled, he learnt to deliver this without a major change in his action – "Ossie was unathletic and lumbered in to bowl, head rolling, but at the crease he had the perfect sideways-on action, the strong pivot on a taut front leg and the perfect wrist position to bowl his stock away-swinger. His inswinger, or rather the ball that drifted in late, was performed with exactly the same arm action but just a late, hardly perceptible roll of the wrist."

By this time, he was playing county cricket for Warwickshire with his presence being a very welcome reinforcement to their attack as the likes of Tom Pritchard moved towards retirement. His first-class debut had come for the Free Foresters, ironically against Cambridge University during 1956 before the following August making his Warwickshire debut against the Combined Services at Edgbaston with his County Championship debut happening immediately afterwards in the away match with Essex at Southend-on-Sea.

By 1959 Ossie was a regular member of the Warwickshire side, and during August he also shared in a remarkable tenth wicket partnership during the match against Northamptonshire at Edgbaston as the Warwickshire batsmen faced the fiery pace of Frank Tyson plus the clever seam bowling of George Tribe. Together with MJK Smith, Ossie added 78 for the last wicket with his partner reaching a fine and unbeaten 142 as his own contribution crept, just, into double figures. "Mike took Tyson, I took the medium-pacers" was his typically honest post-match summary of events.

By the end of 1960 Ossie had claimed 237 first-class wickets for Warwickshire at 25 runs apiece and had won his county cap, but the amateur was looking was fresh challenges. When the Welsh county made an approach about a move to South Wales for 1961 and a chance to take over the Glamorgan captaincy, Ossie was very amenable to the approach. His name had been first put forward by none other than John Arlott, the esteemed broadcaster and journalist who was a close friend of Wilf's. With the Glamorgan committee in agreement with the suggestion, Wilf made the initial contact with Ossie and the wheels were duly set in motion for Ossie's transfer to the Welsh county.

Yet even before he had pulled on a Glamorgan sweater, Ossie was involved in a heated dispute between the Welsh county, or more specifically Wilf Wooller, and the MCC over the terms of Ossie's 'employment'. It was probably a blessing that at the time Ossie was on a month-long tour of the West Indies with Jim Swanton's XI having secured a post in Cardiff with TWW – the new independent television franchise for Wales – as a public relations officer.

Following negotiations with Glamorgan, it had been proposed that Ossie would also be allowed to play cricket full-time for the Club during 1961 and 1962 on an amateur basis, besides acting as their captain and spearheading a campaign to recruit a further 2,500 members. A sticking point however in the negotiations lay in the proposed payment of £650 per annum by Glamorgan for Ossie's services and during April Wilf was told by Ronnie Aird, the MCC Secretary that the Amateur Status Standing Committee could not accept Glamorgan making such a payment if Ossie was to remain playing as an amateur. Given that Ossie's transfer from Warwickshire was already the subject of an application by Glamorgan for special registration, Ronnie added that it would be necessary for him to make the MCC's Registration Committee aware of this arrangement.

It provoked an angry response from Wilf who argued that Ossie was already working in South Wales for TWW and, given that part of his role with Glamorgan was to increase the membership of the Club and its supporters club, he would – in essence – pay for himself. Wilf's letter then contained a threat that he would resign from all MCC committees and sub-committees on which he served and would make make his objections public, before firing off a final salvo – "no committee I know has brought such ridicule to the game [as the Amateur Status Standing Committee] when it can least afford it and

Ossie Wheatley, the newly-appointed Glamorgan captain tosses the coin with his opposite number, John Clay of Nottinghamshire, at Newport ahead of their Championship match at Rodney Parade in 1961.

when it contains such glaring anomalies as the undercover payments to certain players, to say little of the sums earned by Trevor Bailey, Peter May etc. for advertising, writing etc."

The formal MCC reply from Ronnie assured Wilf that there would be no objection to Ossie's employment, provided that he was being paid based on the results of his promotional work. In a personal letter to Wilf, Ronnie added that "no other county secretary has ever written to me in the terms that you so often do, and I hope that you will discontinue this practice…The suggestion about resigning from sub-committees and reserving the right to make your views known publicly is the statement of a 'small man' which you are not… I have always valued your friendship and would like it to continue, so please do not make it difficult for me by writing any more offensive letters."

Wilf duly apologized to Ronnie and agreed that Ossie would be put on commission by Glamorgan rather than a fixed salary. This outcome was duly reported to the MCC's Registration Committee who gave the green light for Ossie to make his Glamorgan debut against Essex at the Arms Park on 3 May 1961.

The Glamorgan supporters soon took a shine to their new leader with the six foot tall, blond-haired bowler being christened 'Dai Peroxide'! Unlike previous summers, 1961 went off without a major spat with any opposing captains – several were keen to test out the Welsh county's new captain, but they soon discovered that he was not from the Wooller mould. Whilst finding him to be genial company after play, they also quickly found out that, through a mix of charm and authority, Ossie was no push over when setting a field or negotiating a possible run chase.

Whilst also being both affable and approachable to his team-mates, Ossie's colleagues were left in no doubt who was in charge and woe betide anyone who didn't do what he asked. An example came at Edgbaston during his first season as Glamorgan met Warwickshire, who had Jim Stewart in their ranks. It was common knowledge that Jim was quite a nervous fellow and would need to have a few words with the opposing fielders in order to calm his nerves. During the first innings, Jim struck up several conversations with Peter Walker at short-leg and made a decent half-century. He was determined that there was to be no repeat in the second innings so before taking to the field, Ossie told his team "if anybody in this side talks to Jimmy Stewart, even to say 'good day', they won't play for three games!"

The Warwickshire man duly arrived at the crease with Peter positioned, as normal, at bat-pad, "Hello Peter," said Jim as he prepared to take guard, "how's it going?" There was no reply. Jim tried to strike up a conversation at the end of the over, with Peter glancing in Ossie's direction. A stony-faced glare from the Glamorgan captain reminded him of the instructions so nothing was said. Jim tried for a third time but still got no response and shortly afterwards he sparred at a ball from Ossie and was caught by Billy Slade for 2.

Ossie Wheatley catches a dog which had strayed onto the outfield at Swansea during a match at St Helen's in the 1960s.

Some had wondered whether such an archetypal Englishman would fit into the Glamorgan dressing room and be accepted by the fiercely partisan Welsh supporters. His Warwickshire friends had also warned him about joining an ageing Glamorgan, whilst others said that he would find the pitches a pace bowler's graveyard. Ossie had never played a game in Wales before joining Glamorgan, but these comments about the pitches and personnel merely spurred him on, and made him relish the challenge even more.

Ossie soon found that there was something special about Glamorgan – "Unlike the English counties, it had this extra identity," he once said. "It wasn't just a group of people who happened to be drawn together, or playing under a flag of convenience." Ossie also swiftly earned the wholehearted respect and support of the team, both for his undoubted skills as a swing bowler as well as the subtle tactics he often employed, especially when compared with the more blunt methods of his predecessor. An example came in the match against Hampshire who had the swashbuckling Roy Marshall in their line-up. The West Indian was a destroyer of bowling attacks and Ossie knew that he didn't rate him as a bowler. Therefore Ossie, purposely bowled a little bit slower and wider of off stump than normal, and sent down a series of away swingers. Ossie also knew that Roy was quite impatient, so after letting a dozen or so balls pass by outside off stump, he launched himself at a wide ball, but ended up slashing the ball high in the air and being caught at third man.

His excellent inter-personal skills also helped Ossie to swiftly integrate into the Glamorgan dressing room. As Alan Jones recalled "Ossie was the type of bloke who made you believe in yourself. He had a way with all the players, making you believe you were better than you really were. He had that gift." These skills also allowed Jim Pressdee to rebuild his confidence, with Ossie successfully persuading Jim to bowl again and form a potent partnership with Don Shepherd who besides being the main spinner also acted as Ossie's senior professional.

After two undistinguished seasons, Glamorgan ended up as runners-up to Yorkshire in the 1963 Championship. Eleven of the 28 Championship games were won as Ossie's mantra of playing bright and positive cricket reaped its rewards, with innings victories over Somerset at Neath and Lancashire at Swansea.

The summer of 1964 was a memorable one for Ossie – first, during July he married Christine Godwin, the attractive TWW announcer and presenter of programmes on the channel such as 'Croeso Christine' which was a series teaching Welsh to learners. The following month he had the pleasure of leading Glamorgan to their first-ever victory, and a wholly unexpected one, over the 1964 Australians. Since 1912 only Surrey had beaten an Australian touring team and with Bobby Simpson's team already one-up in the Test series, and Glamorgan enjoying a modest season, it looked odds-on that the men in baggy green caps would maintain their unbeaten record in the shires, especially when Ossie opted to rest several of his senior players.

The rest, as they say, was the stuff of Welsh legend as Don Shepherd and Jim Pressdee spun their way through the cream of Australia's batting talent, cheered on by their loyal supporters and hundreds of others who were spending time at the historic Swansea ground having attended the National Eisteddfod was being staged a mile or so down the road from the St Helen's ground. During the Australian's second innings, Ossie kept attacking with Don and Jim, despite both suffering from cramp in the intense heat, but his tactics paid off as they continued to infuriate the visitors.

As the seventh, eighth and ninth wickets fell, the Glamorgan side – plus the crowd of nearly 15,000 – held their breath as history beckoned before, with 37 runs still to make, Eifion Jones caught Neil Hawke before what seemed like half the population of the Principality surged onto the field and took part in an unscripted, but very Celtic celebration to rival anything that had taken place on the Eisteddfod field the previous weekend. The champagne corks popped as speeches were made by Ossie – "this is like winning a Test series" the jubilant Glamorgan captain said on the balcony as the triumphant Welsh melodies grew louder and louder. "Ossie's tamed the Aussies" proclaimed the *Daily Express* the next morning as the newspaper's sub-editors had a field day in drafting the headlines for their cricket pages. Even the *Church of Ireland Gazette* contained a leading article entitle 'Welsh Rarebit' in which it pithily pointed out that the Australians were still undefeated in England, and had had to come to Wales to have their colours lowered by Ossie and his young men!

The joyous Glamorgan squad which defeated the 1964 Australians at Swansea celebrate the following day in the changing room at the Arms Park with Club physiotherapist John Evans. The players from left to right are back row – Euros Lewis, Alan Jones, Billy Slade, Eifion Jones and Alan Rees. Front row – Jim Pressdee, Ossie Wheatley, Tony Cordle, Tony Lewis and Don Shepherd.

To their captain's delight, Glamorgan showed that this totemic victory at St Helen's was no flash in the pan and for much of 1965 they were in contention for the Championship title. They led the table during late June and early July, before ending up in third place, only twelve points behind Worcestershire and were left to rue batting collapses in their closing games. It also didn't help that a quixotic declaration by Hampshire's captain enlivened a dead match at Bournemouth, allowing Worcestershire to seize their chance and record an unlikely victory and with it the county title.

As Don Shepherd reflected "It didn't quite work out for us in 1965, and this was rather sad for Ossie because he'd given a lot to the side with his attitude. I don't think he ever turned down what you'd have called a ridiculous challenge. Perhaps Wilf might have said

'That's not on, don't bother', but Ossie was never one to turn down a challenge, and I think that rubbed off on Tony [Lewis] because that was the attitude we had when we won the Championship in 1969."

Many had hoped that Glamorgan would build on their success during 1965 and mount another title bid in 1966. But it proved to be a disappointing season for the team. The ugly and unfortunate incident at Llanelli at the end of 1965 had seen Jim Pressdee return to South Africa and his departure affected the balance of Ossie's team. Once again, he tried his best to conjure up a series of victories, but it wasn't to be and 1966 will perhaps be remembered most for the fact that Ossie recorded nine ducks in a row whilst batting for Glamorgan.

With his interests outside the game growing and exciting opportunities presenting themselves with an advertising company, he handed over the captaincy to Tony for 1967. "It was the right thing to do," he later reflected. "Tony had come down from Cambridge with a fine reputation and having established himself in the middle-order, the time was right for him to take over as Glamorgan captain."

Ossie only played in four matches during 1967 as he further developed his career outside cricket, besides being hampered by trouble with his Achilles tendon, probably caused by having to return to play on hard surfaces while short of match practice. But when he was able to play, Ossie proved to be a more than able lieutenant for the new captain and was quick to offer words of advice to Tony if things threatened to go awry. An example came in a match where the opposing tail started to have a merry spree, hitting the ball in the air just over the head of the fielders or into unexpected corners of the ground. As shoulders started to droop amongst the Glamorgan fielders, Ossie wandered in from the outfield and suggested that he and Don Shepherd should return to bowl, despite having had lengthy spells earlier in the session. As Tony recalled "Ossie immediately restored order. He bowled outside off-stump to a blanket off-side field... Out of the chaos, order came and the fielders were keen again."

Ossie Wheatley practices his slip fielding during 1968.

Ossie, once again agreed to play the odd game here and there for Tony Lewis' team in 1968, but with injuries to other bowlers, especially Jeff Jones, Ossie played in sixteen matches and ended with a haul of 82 wickets at just 12.95 runs apiece. It was a summer when he also claimed a string of wickets in Glamorgan's games at Swansea. As he later admitted "I never used to bother hardly at all about bowling there before. I could not get the spinners on quickly enough!" His reward was topping the national bowling averages and selection as one of Wisden's Five Cricketers of the Year.

With his business interests flourishing Ossie informed the Glamorgan officials during the winter of 1968/69 that he was going into semi-retirement

163

but would still be happy to help out Tony Lewis if any injuries arose. As it turned out Ossie appeared in seven of the games and played a major role in the Championship success with the most famous pick up and throw in the Club's history as the Welsh county secured a last-ball victory against Essex at Swansea which took Glamorgan to the verge of the Championship title.

Not renowned as a fielder *par excellence*, Ossie struck with deadly precision as the visitors needed three off the final delivery to win a nail-biting the game. John Lever played the ball down to third man, with his last wicket partner Ray East setting off in pursuit of a last gasp victory. Seeing Ossie lumber towards the ball, John set off to complete a second and tie the game, but Ossie returned the ball over the stumps to wicketkeeper Eifion Jones who whipped off the bails with John short of his ground. As Ossie later recalled, "I remember thinking whatever I do, it does not have to be particularly quick, but it has to be as straight as I could throw it. Not having done much fielding practice for many years, I managed to wing it in. There was only a long single in it in all fairness. You could have rolled it in as Drake's last bowl if you like!"

Ossie duly kept his place in the Glamorgan side for the title-deciding match against Worcestershire at Sophia Gardens, with the former captain returning the fabulous figures of 22-10-20-2 in the visitor's first innings as he opened the bowling with Malcolm Nash. Right from the outset, Ossie's controlled efforts gave Tony Lewis and his colleagues the upper hand in this crucial match – a position they did not yield and on the third afternoon, as well as later into a memorable evening, Ossie took great delight in the jolifications and champagne-quaffing which followed Glamorgan's second title success.

He bowed out of first-class cricket during Glamorgan's celebratory tour of the West Indies, with Ossie playing his final game in early April 1970 against the Windward Islands at Roseau. Some speculated as to whether Ossie might continue to appear in the Sunday League matches – he had played in the majority during 1969, but he opted instead to make a clean break from the game.

One-day cricket had been introduced into the county calendar during Ossie's watch, but the Club initially showed an element of indifference to the new format, with Ossie agreeing to rest several players for the inaugural match in the Gillette Cup in 1963. By 1966 and three summers of little success, there was pressure from the committee for the Club to perform better in the competition, now trimmed to 60 per overs per side, so on the eve of their first round match at Northampton, Ossie called a team meeting in the hotel lounge with all of the players sitting in a circle to discuss a game plan. "I want every one of you to share your views on how we ought to bowl at the Northants batsmen, and the field placings, and how we ought to bat against them." Everyone chipped in before Don, as senior professional had the closing words. With a twinkle in his eye, he whimsically said "Well boys, I know how we're going to win the Gillette Cup. They're going to have to raffle it, and we're going to have to buy all the tickets!"

Ossie subsequently played a number of administrative roles within the game, besides acting as a Test Match selector, and diversifying his business interests to include the running of a Spanish-style wine bar and restaurant in Oxford Arcade in Cardiff. He also returned to Glamorgan Cricket in 1976 and took over as Chairman from Judge Rowe Harding after a dreadful summer which had seen, amongst many unfortunate events, the departure of Majid Khan and the Welsh county making the headlines in local and national newspapers for all the wrong reasons. He served in this capacity until 1984 with his grace and gravitas helping to restore order, in the same way that his bowling had done the previous decade. It was therefore no coincidence that in 1977, with morale restored and Alan Jones in charge, Glamorgan reached the final of the Gillette Cup at Lord's.

This is not to say however that Ossie always had the Midas touch, as the decision to bring Robin Hobbs, the former England and Essex leg-spinner out of retirement to lead Glamorgan in 1979 led to some heated exchanges as the Club went through the summer without a victory in the Championship. Ossie – together with coach/manager Tom Cartwright - had been determined to bring an England Test cricketer to the Club, believing that an experienced international player would help to lift the young players. After Robin's appointment, harsh words were exchanged between Ossie and Wilf, with 'The Skipper' resigning from the Club's committee.

Ossie Wheatley seen during Glamorgan's friendly against a team from Broadmoor Prison. On the far left is the prison chaplain, whilst either side of Ossie are Bill Edwards and Tom Taylor.

Others felt that the lack of Championship victories was not Robin's fault and that the lack of depth, or quality, in the bowling attack was the real reason behind the poor results in 1979. Few though could take issue with the way the committee addressed these issues and the subsequent decision overseen by Ossie to hire top-class overseas players. Javed Miandad duly delighted the crowds with his quick-silver batting and, had it not been for a serious back-injury, Ezra Moseley might have developed into the high-quality fast bowler the Club had been lacking for so many years.

Ossie also served as a wise Chair of the Test and County Cricket Board's Cricket Committee, besides acting as Chair of the Sports Council of Wales and helping to oversee a number of enhancements in recreational facilities throughout Wales, especially at grassroots level. Ossie also served in a similar capacity for the Cricket Foundation and it was no surprise that in 1997 he was awarded the CBE in the New Year's Honours List for services to cricket.

SLADE, William Douglas.

Born – Briton Ferry, 27 September 1941.
Professional.
RHB, RM.
1st XI: 1961-1967.
2nd XI: 1959-1968.
Club and Ground: 1962-1964.
Wales 1979.
Clubs: Swansea, Dafen, Pontyberem, Pontarddulais and Briton Ferry Town.

Batting and Fielding Record

	M	I	NO	RUNS	AV	100	50	CT	ST
F-c	67	116	11	1482	14.11	-	3	100	-
List A	4	4	0	52	13.00	-	-	2	-

Bowling Record

	Balls	M	R	W	AV	5wI	10wM
F-c	3027	146	1493	32	46.45	-	-
List A	54	2	38	0	-	-	-

Career-bests

First-class –   73* v Derbyshire at St Helen's, Swansea, 1963.
                4/144 v Middlesex at Lord's, 1962.
List A –   28 v Warwickshire at The Gnoll, Neath, 1963.

Billy Slade was a member of the Glamorgan team which defeated the 1964 Australians at Swansea. When Bobby Simpson and his fellow Australians arrived at St Helen's only one county – the mighty Surrey side of the 1950s – could claim to have beaten an Australian touring team since 1912. The tourists were already one-up in the Test series, and with Glamorgan enjoying a modest season, it looked odds-on that they would maintain this unbeaten sequence. But an inexperienced side, under captain Ossie Wheatley, turned the form book upside book.

Few in the crowd of around 20,000, must have fancied a Glamorgan win as the Welsh county were dismissed for 197 in their first innings, but after a short shower had freshened up the St Helen's wicket, Don Shepherd and Jim Pressdee produced a magnificent spell of bowling as Australia slumped to 39-6. Billy took a pair of smart catches in the leg-trap as the cream of their tourists batting talent was sent packing by Glamorgan's spin-twins.

The National Eisteddfod was being held just a mile down the road from the Swansea ground, and with the organisers showing great enterprise in arranging for a few televisions to be placed around the tented village, the back-and-white screens drew an ever-increasing crowd as word spread around the 'maes' of Glamorgan's fightback.

The following evening the two teams visited the Eisteddfod, with Billy and the other young Welshmen being greeted by a thunderous ovation as they gathered on stage. Buoyed by this hwyl, the Glamorgan bowlers then dismissed Australia for 101, before Tony Lewis and Alan Rees batting freely as the tourists were left with a tricky target of 268 on the wearing surface. They began well, but on the final morning the Welsh spinners, supported by some outstanding fielding, steadily worked their way again through the Australian batting with Billy adding another smart catch to his tally.

Despite the intense heat, and a touch or two of cramp, the spinners continued to infuriate the visitors. As wickets continued to tumble, Billy and his colleagues – plus the crowd of nearly 15,000 – held their breath as history beckoned. With 37 runs still needed, Eifion Jones caught Neil Hawke, and the celebrations began!

This was one of 67 first-class matches, plus a quartet of List A games, in which Billy played for Glamorgan between 1961 and 1967. Billy had first played for the Club's 2nd XI in 1959 when only seventeen and two years later he made his County Championship debut against Hampshire at Swansea. During his career in county cricket, Billy proved to be a capable middle-order batsman, scoring 1,482 runs with his career-best score of 73* also coming at St Helen's against Derbyshire during 1963.

Billy was also rated by Don Shepherd as one of the finest close-to-the wicket fielders he had ever seen, and in the match with Hampshire at

Billy Slade.

Bournemouth in 1961 the youngster held four catches, all off the legendary off-cutters bowling. Their combined efforts saw the Welsh county to an emphatic victory by 183 runs, with Billy's first catch to remove Jimmy Gray earning rich praise from the watching journalists. Writing in the *Western Mail*, Basil Easterbrook commented how "the batsman struck the ball like a projectile towards the youngster but Slade stood his ground and completed a seering catch as if Gray had gently tossed him an apple!"

During his career, Billy played club cricket for Briton Ferry Town, Swansea, Dafen, Pontyberem and Pontarddulais. He also coached at Marlborough School, besides running a pub in Resolven, whilst in 1979 he captained Wales in the ICC Trophy.

448
JONES, Eifion Wyn.

Born – Velindre, 25 June 1942.
RHB, WK.
Professional.
Ed – Clydach Secondary School.
1st XI: 1961-1983.
2nd XI: 1959-1984.
Club and Ground: 1972-1983.
Cap: 1967.
Clubs: Clydach, Swansea, Llanelli and Neath.
Rugby for Pontarddulais.

Batting and Fielding Record

	M	I	NO	RUNS	AV	100	50	CT	ST
F-c	405	591	119	8341	17.67	3	26	840	93
List A	295	227	66	2241	13.91	-	1	257	43

Bowling Record

	Balls	M	R	W	AV	5wI	10wM
F-c	3	0	5	0	-	-	-
List A	12	1	10	0	-	-	-

Career-bests
First-class – 146* v Sussex at Hove, 1968.
List A –   67* v Hertfordshire at St Helen's, Swansea, 1969.

Many Glamorgan supporters believe that Glamorgan's Championship-winning team of 1969 contained their best-ever homegrown batsman in Alan Jones, their greatest bowler in Don Shepherd and their finest wicket-keeper in Eifion Jones. That summer Eifion claimed 74 dismissals – more than anyone else in the country – and the stocky Welsh speaker came very, very close to winning a place on England's tour to Australia and New Zealand in 1970/71.

Eifion was the youngest of nine boys and two girls born to Evan and Beatrice Jones of Velindre, a small village in the Swansea area, with Evan and most of his boys working underground at the Graig Merthyr Colliery in the adjoining valley.

The Jones brothers, as seen in 1976 – Alan (left) and Eifion.

From a young age, Eifion would also join his elder brothers in playing cricket on a piece of rough pasture called Y Waun opposite their home in Maesgwyn. Whereas Alan opted to be Neil Harvey of Australia in these imaginary Test matches, Eifion always wanted to be Denis Compton revealing that first and foremost, he thought himself to be as a batsman.

Weight of runs in the South Wales Cricket Association saw Eifion play as a teenage batsman in Glamorgan's 2nd XI before following Alan onto the county's full-time staff in 1961. By this time he had added another string to his bow having kept wicket for the second string and his immense promise behind the stumps, as well as superior batting talents led to him replacing Willie Whitehill as David Evans' understudy. His switch to keeping wicket however came purely by accident and was the result of Phil Clift's astute eye as coach. As the former Glamorgan batsman remembered, "Eifion had come to us as a brave and bonny batsman, but one day we were short of a wicket-keeper in the second team. I'd noticed that he was a pretty good catcher and had good hand-eye co-ordination, fielding in the slips and catching almost everything that came his way. I duly said to him 'Have you ever kept wicket?' His response was 'No' so I asked if he would like to have a go. 'All right' he said, and so I arranged to get some gloves for him."

Eifion Jones keeping wicket-keeping at Swansea in a specially posed photograph at the St Helen's ground.

So began the career of a man whose 933 dismissals still stand as a Club record and a man reputed to have rarely dropped a chance either standing up to the spinners or standing back to the quicker bowlers and the clever off-cutters of Don Shepherd. Contemporaries noted how the ball rarely made a sound going into his gloves and whereas with other wicket-keepers there would be a thud as the ball was caught, it almost melted into his gauntlets, probably the result of years of practice catching a boulder and learning to brace his hands and arms on impact. His stocky frame and alert reflexes also made him a natural, and the novice impressed with his glovework on his Championship debut against Nottinghamshire at Trent Bridge during June 1961.

For the next couple of years, Eifion continued to develop his skills behind the stumps, as well as his batting prowess, and he appeared as a specialist batsman during 1963. The following year Eifion was gleefully behind the stumps as Glamorgan defeated the 1964

Australians at Swansea before some extended opportunities during 1966 and 1967, prior to taking over from David at the start of the 1968 season. As Wilf Wooller noted, "he was a trifle fortunate that his batting carried the day as David Evans was keeping as well as ever. The County however were short of runs in the middle order."

The 1963 Glamorgan team, seen during late April at the Arms Park. Standing (left to right) – Alan Jones, Jeff Jones, Peter Walker, Jim Pressdee, Euros Lewis, David Evans and Eifion Jones. Sitting – Tony Lewis, Don Shepherd, Ossie Wheatley, Gilbert Parkhouse and Bernard Hedges.

His batting skills soon came in handy during 1968 during an ill-tempered contest against Sussex at Hove in early June. There was tension right from the outset as Glamorgan captain Tony Lewis complained about one of the boundaries being only 36 paces away from the square, and the mood did not improve when Ken Suttle, the Sussex batsmen refused to walk after being caught at bat-pad off the bowling of Euros Lewis. The umpires had been unsighted, but all of the fielders close to the wicket had heard the tell-tale sound of bat on ball. The Sussex man however stood his ground, much to the annoyance of Tony and his team, and the upshot was that after this display of bad sportsmanship, he told his batsmen that they would not be setting Sussex a target on the final day.

With instructions to simply occupy the crease for the rest of the game, Alan Jones and Ian Morris began the Glamorgan second innings with forty-five minutes remaining on the second evening, but without a run on the board, the latter was run out after a mix-up in calling. As Alan later recalled "Eifion came in as night-watchman intent on seeing Tony's instructions carried out to the letter. We survived until the close and then continued our partnership the following morning. Eifion really batted well, as I knew he could, and steadily grew in confidence. By lunchtime, the two of us realized that if we kept going during the afternoon, Eifion would score his maiden century so that became our target. As he approached three figures, Eifion took the dominant role, before ending up unbeaten on 146. A few harsh words were said by the Sussex supporters as we walked off having added 230, and batting throughout the day together, but it was one of the most satisfying partnerships of my career."

Eifion Jones runs out Middlesex's Mike Smith during the Championship match at Lord's in 1969.

Eifion's efforts saw him register the first-ever century by a Glamorgan night-watchman and the first by a specialist wicket-keeper for the Welsh county since Tom Brierley had struck 101 against the same opponents in 1937. Later that summer, he also played a small part – albeit from behind the stumps – in events at Swansea as Garry Sobers became the first man to hit six sixes in an over. After the West Indian had launched Malcolm Nash for his fifth successive maximum in the over, Eifion turned to Garry and said "Bet you can't hit this one for six as well." The all-rounder grinned in response before letting his bat do the talking as he struck Nash for the record-breaking sixth six.

Eifion's efforts with the bat more than justified the difficult decision which Glamorgan had made ahead of the 1968 season for him to replace David Evans as the Club's wicket-keeper. Few questioned David's abilities behind the stumps but his limitations with the bat were well-known. Eifion duly slotted into the number eight slot in the order and as Peter Walker recalled "Brought a steely resolve to this key batting position, there to support a top-order batsman if needed or to shepherd and protect the tail-enders who followed him."

His skills with the gloves were not in doubt and, to the delight of the Glamorgan selectors, he flourished in his new role as first-choice keeper, standing up on the slow wickets at Swansea to the Glamorgan spinners, and even off-cutter Don Shepherd and nonchalantly taking the deliveries which had pitched on or around off stump and had wickedly spun down the leg-side. Eifion enjoyed a vintage summer in 1969 with 74 victims – more than any other keeper on the county circuit – besides making 102 against Somerset at Glastonbury and playing a match-winning cameo with the bat as Glamorgan defeated Middlesex at Swansea. Shortly after tea, a Glamorgan win had seemed unlikely but Malcolm Nash led a counter-attack. He received good support from Eifion but as the game entered the final over with the result still in doubt. But the doughty Welshman settled things by drilling Ron Hooker for a magnificent six over extra-cover to see Glamorgan to a vital three-wicket victory.

In July 1978 Eifion also struck a massive six high over mid-wicket against Geoff Arnold to clinch a two-wicket victory against Sussex in the Sunday League game at Hastings, whilst in 1977 he shared a match-winning stand with Gwyn Richards as Glamorgan defeated Leicestershire at St Helen's in the semi-final of the Gillette Cup. In the final at Lord's, Eifion also caught Mike Brearley off Malcolm Nash's opening delivery in the contest, but we have to return to events at Swansea during the 1960s for Eifion's finest moments in a daffodil sweater – being part of the Glamorgan teams which defeated the 1964 and 1968 Australians, and effecting the run-out which gave the Welsh county a stunning last-ball victory against Essex in 1969 as the Welsh county secured a thrilling win which put them on the verge of the Championship title

A man of few words, Eifion later summed up Ossie Wheatley's unexpected nimble pick-up and throw from third man by simply saying "Straight into the gloves. Never in doubt." When asked about how far short was John Lever, the Essex batsman, in going for the tie, he phlegmatically replied "Short enough!"

It was appropriate that Eifion's career highlights should come at St Helen's as he was very much a man of the west, also playing rugby for Pontarddulais RFC as well as having many friends in the town's famous choir. On many occasions, he and Alan would take members of county and international teams visiting Swansea to the Fountain pub in the 'Bont' where they would revel in listening to, and joining in with, the delightful Welsh harmonies.

An action photo of Eifion Jones, seen during the Sunday League match against Sussex at Hastings in 1978.

Eifion also took a leading role in the singing which echoed out from the Sophia Gardens Pavillion in September 1969 after Glamorgan had beaten Worcestershire to secure the Championship title. From his own point of view, it had not been the easiest of matches as he was struck on the head by a vicious lifting delivery from Vanburn Holder during Glamorgan's second innings and was forced to retire hurt early on the third morning of the game and received medical treatment. The doctor's diagnosis was that he should not take any further part in the match. "Perhaps you should get someone to drive you home where you can rest up," said the medic to which the dazed and bruised Eifion simply replied "No – I'm staying here!" He certainly wasn't going to miss out on the Championship-clinching celebrations and remained with a bandage on his head, watching from the pavilion balcony as Majid Khan took over behind the stumps when the visitors batted for a second time. The subsequent mixture of champagne, beer and Welsh song proved to be the perfect tonic for the popular gloveman, with Eifion, leading the singing with gusto!

Described by Tony Lewis as "a pugnacious competitor and a clear cricket thinker", some felt that Eifion might take over the Glamorgan captaincy in 1976 following Majid Khan's departure from the Club, but it was brother Alan who secured that honour, with Eifion continuing to be the Welsh county's regular gloveman until 1982. During this period,

Eifion Jones, as seen in 1983 at Glamorgan's annual photocall at Sophia Gardens.

he also had spells batting higher in the order and in 1979 recorded another Championship hundred with 108 against Warwickshire at Swansea.

Eifion retired at the end of the 1983 season with a Club record of 933 dismissals to his name, as well as several other entries in the Club's annals, including 94 victims in first-class cricket during 1970 and seven dismissals in an innings against Cambridge University at Fenner's, also in 1970. Eifion also holds the record for the most number of appearances for the Welsh county in the Sunday League competition, playing on 212 occasions, during which time he claimed a further 223 dismissals to take his overall tally in every form of cricket to over a thousand – a worthy reward for his years of loyal service to the Welsh club.

After retiring from county cricket, Eifion continued to play in the South Wales Cricket Association, besides going into business as a builder and decorator, specializing in buying up old properties and converting them into flats. His son Gareth also played for Glamorgan 2nd XI during 1995 and 1996.

449
LEWIS, Euros John.

Born – Llanelli, 31 January 1942.
Died – Llanelli, 23 June 2014.
LHB, OB.
1st XI: 1961-1966.
2nd XI: 1958-1966.
Colts: 1958.
Club and Ground: 1958-1961.
Cap: 1965.
Sussex 1967-1969; MCC.
Clubs: Dafen, Llanelli, Pontarddulais, SCOW, Llangennech and Ammanford.

Batting and Fielding Record

	M	I	NO	RUNS	AV	100	50	CT	ST
F-c	95	150	10	2169	15.49	-	11	53	-
List A	6	5	0	117	23.40	-	1	1	-

Bowling Record

	Balls	M	R	W	AV	5wI	10wM
F-c	7785	363	3821	151	25.30	7	-

Career-bests

First-class –   80 v Sussex at Cardiff Arms Park, 1965.
               8/89 v Kent at St Helen's, Swansea, 1965.
List A –   78 v Worcestershire at The Gnoll, Neath, 1963.

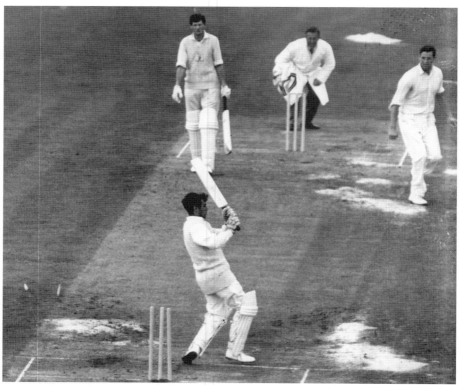

Euros Lewis is bowled by Richard Jefferson of Surrey during the Championship match at The Oval in 1965. Peter Walker is the non-striker.

Euros Lewis had a short, successful and, at times, turbulent career with Glamorgan during the 1960s.

The left-handed batsman and off-spin bowler made his Championship debut for the Welsh county in 1961 against Somerset at Weston-super-Mare, and initially it was his bold, free hitting as an opening batsman that secured a regular place in the side. He also worked hard at his spin bowling, and, as a result, his off-breaks augmented the first-choice spin partnership of off-cutter Don Shepherd, plus left-arm spinner Jim Pressdee.

1963 proved to be a red-letter year for the emerging all-rounder as his developing skills were recognised by the MCC who selected him in their side to play the West Indians at Lord's. Later in the year, Euros also returned career-best figures of 8/89 against Kent at Swansea and was presented with his Glamorgan cap.

In 1964 Euros was also a member of the Glamorgan side which defeated the Australian tourists at Swansea, as the Welsh county recorded their first-ever victory over the men in baggy green caps, as Euros and the other spinners fully exploited the dry and dusty wicket at the St Helen's ground with the Llanelli-born spinner removing Norm O'Neill in the Australian's second innings.

He played regularly during 1965 but the following summer proved to be a difficult one for both the Club and Euros. It had begun with the MCC selecting Euros for their fixture at Lord's against the West Indians, but it ended with a parting of the ways as the Glamorgan officials tired of his relish for the game's social side. He duly joined Sussex for 1967 chiefly on Jim Parks' recommendation and recollection of his career-best 80 at the Arms Park in June 1965, plus the way Euros in the space of fourteen balls had claimed four wickets to remove the Sussex tail.

Euros Lewis.

A measure of his regard initially on the South Coast was that Euros supplanting Alan Oakman, the former England cricketer, as the county's principal off-break bowler. It seemed the correct decision as Euros' first season with Sussex saw him enjoy his best-ever year, taking 85 wickets, recording four five-wicket hauls, and making thirty catches, largely in close to the wicket positions. His reward was a Sussex cap, but his wicket-taking fell away as his form became erratic.

Euros was released at the end of 1969 and returned to club cricket in South Wales, initially with Llangennech CC from 1970 to 1974, and then with Dafen Welfare CC through to 1991. Following several highly successful seasons in the South Wales Cricket Association, there was speculation that he might return to the Glamorgan ranks, especially in one-day cricket. This was not to be, and the rather self-effacing all-rounder never re-appeared for the Welsh county and continued his new career as a coach driver based in Carmarthenshire.

1962

The summer started well as Glamorgan defeated Lancashire during the first week of May by six wickets at the Arms Park. But the Welsh county had to wait until mid-June, and their next games at the Cardiff ground for their next victories as they defeated Yorkshire by five wickets before recording a seven-wicket success over the 1962 Pakistanis with Alwyn Harris, posting a century before Ossie Wheatley enterprisingly declared when his side drew level with the tourists. The Glamorgan captain then took 4/38 as the Pakistanis were humbled for 158 before an unbeaten 81 from Bernard Hedges saw the Welsh county home.

Euros Lewis (right) walks out to bat with Alwyn Harris.

This fine victory though proved to be the only bright spot during the second half of the season as Glamorgan ended up, again, in 14th place in the Championship table. Seven batsmen scored over a thousand runs during the summer with the younger brigade of Alan Jones, Alan Rees and Euros Lewis all giving glimpses of promise. But overall the batting never gelled as a unit and, at times, the Glamorgan line-up proved quite brittle, as testified by the fact that they failed to reach the 100-mark on no less than six occasions.

With Brian Evans affected by injury and Jeff Jones still learning his trade, the bowling relied heavily on Ossie and Don Shepherd. Each took over 100 Championship wickets whilst Peter Walker weighed in with 85 scalps. Jim Pressdee amassed 1,911 runs but claimed just one victim whilst Don Shepherd claimed a solitary ten-wicket haul as he returned figures of 5/19 and 6/32 against Gloucestershire at Margam. With their wafer-thin resources, Glamorgan rarely threatened to bowl sides out twice, especially on unhelpful pitches where bat dominated ball.

For the first time in several seasons, there were also some financial concerns by the end of the summer as gate receipts fell to £5,500 – their lowest in the post-war era. This fall in income came at a time when the Club's expenditure rose in excess of £36,000 with Glamorgan using six outgrounds – Llanelli, Neath, Pontypridd, Newport, Ebbw Vale and Margam – in addition to the traditional grounds at the Arms Park and St Helen's. This rise in expenditure prompted an investigation into ways of reducing costs, whilst a membership drive was commenced.

450
HUGHES, Gwyn.

Born – Mynachdy, Cardiff, 26 March 1941.
Ed – Viriamu Jones Primary School, Cardiff High School, University College, Cardiff
and Queen's College, Cambridge.
RHB, SLA.
1st XI: 1962-1964.
2nd XI: 1959-1966.
Club and Ground: 1963.
Welsh Secondary Schools 1956-59; MCC 1964; Cambridge University 1965 (Blue);
Surrey 2nd XI 1967.
Clubs: St Fagans, Briton Ferry Town, Buccaneers.
Rugby for Cardiff HSOB, Cambridge University and London Welsh Dragons.

Batting and Fielding Record

	M	I	NO	RUNS	AV	100	50	CT	ST
F-c	17	22	4	228	12.67	-	1	17	-

Bowling Record

	Balls	M	R	W	AV	5wI	10wM
F-c	1308	75	560	12	46.67	-	-

Career-bests
First-class – 92 v Australians at Cardiff Arms Park, 1964.
3/20 v Cambridge University at Fenner's, Cambridge, 1964.

Gwyn Hughes.

Gwyn Hughes was a steady left-arm spinner and right-handed batsman who played in 17 matches for Glamorgan during the early 1960's. The Cardiff-born cricketer also spent a year at Queen's College, Cambridge and represented the university at rugby during 1964, besides winning a cricket Blue in 1965.

The son of a bus conductor, Gwyn was born and raised in Mynachdy, a large council estate in North Cardiff before securing a place at Cardiff High School. It was here that his cricketing talents and ambidextrous skills were first nurtured with the youngster initially bowling chinamen and googlies. A chance conversation between his father and Stan Montgomery led to the twelve-year-old attending Glamorgan's indoor nets in the corridor of the North Stand at the Arms Park. It was here, under the tutelage of George Lavis and Phil Clift that he was duly encouraged to switch from wrist spin to orthodox left-arm, as well as joining the St Fagans club.

Gwyn duly made his debut for St Fagans at the age of fifteen, under the watchful and generous captaincy of Ernie Tyerman besides winning a place in the Welsh Secondary Schools team. He played in the Welsh side from 1956 until 1959 and, during the latter, Gwyn also made his 2nd XI debut for Glamorgan. After leaving school, Gwyn read Economics and History at Cardiff University, besides continuing to appear for the county's 2nd XI where he continued to impress with his left-arm spin as well as his solid batting which had seen him open the batting on several occasions.

In August 1962 Gwyn made his first-class debut against the Pakistanis at Swansea, before making his Championship debut against Kent at Canterbury in the following match. However, Gwyn joined the Glamorgan staff at a time when Jim Pressdee, the first choice left-arm spinner, had regained confidence in his bowling abilities under Ossie Wheatley's captaincy. Gwyn had an extended run in the Glamorgan side during 1964, but was often playing as an extra batsman and had few opportunities to stake a place in the 1st XI as a frontline spinner.

However, the match against the 1964 Australians saw Gwyn recorded a career-best 92 in the contest at the Arms Park, with the correspondent for the local newspaper writing how "the blond-haired youngster attacked the tourists bowling with glee and abandon. The Australians' attack had proved too much for other county batsmen earlier in the tour but not for the twenty-three-year-old uncapped batsman."

Gwyn Hughes, watched by wicket-keeper Wally Grout, pulls a ball for four whilst batting against the 1964 Australians at Cardiff Arms Park. Bob Cowper is at slip.

By his own admission though, Gwyn had been lucky to survive a simple chance at short square-leg before he had scored having arrived at the crease with his side on 124-5. After the interval, he reasoned that attack was the best form of defence and hit 13 fours, chiefly through the off-side and seemed poised to score a remarkable century against the tourists when he fell to a brilliant low catch by Brian Booth in the slips as he edged Alan Connolly whilst attempting a square-cut. Later that summer, Gwyn was Glamorgan's 12th man when they defeated the Australians in the return match at Swansea but, apart from carrying out drinks to Ossie Wheatley's team, he never got a chance to act as the substitute fielder during this historic victory.

At the end of the 1964 season, Gwyn went up to Cambridge to undertake a postgraduate Diploma in Education. Having been a talented full-back whilst at Cardiff High, Gwyn won a place in the Queen's XV, besides playing on one occasion for the Light Blues against Blackheath. It was a time when rugby was flourishing at the College and amongst his contemporaries at Queen's were Dr Mike Gibson, the Irish international and British Lion, as well as Geoff Frankcom, the English international centre who had a fine career with Bath RFC, and with whom Gwyn is still very friendly.

Gwyn also won a cricket Blue during 1965, and claimed 4/31 for Cambridge against the New Zealanders at Fenner's. It was a game which saw the tourists follow-on against the students, with Gwyn bowling 49 consecutive overs against the Kiwi's as they batted throughout the rest of the match to save the game. With the departure of Jim Pressdee from the Glamorgan staff at the end of the season, some wondered whether or not Gwyn might succeed the all-rounder in the Welsh county's 1st XI. However, having completed his teaching practice at Reed's School in Cobham, Gwyn had decided instead to become a schoolmaster and duly accepted an offer to teach Economics and Politics at St Paul's.

Gwyn Hughes bowls to Vic Pollard during the game in 1965 between the New Zealanders and Cambridge University at the Fenner's ground in Cambridge.

Glamorgan however kept his registration and during 1966 Gwyn played in a handful of games for the county's 2nd XI during his school holidays. The following year, the Welsh county also gave him special dispensation to play for Surrey 2nd XI against Northamptonshire 2nd XI. It proved to be his final appearance at county level but the game at Northampton saw Gwyn dismissed for nought, whilst he did not bowl in either innings. Given his cricketing commitments at St Paul's, Gwyn subsequently played during his summer holidays for the Buccaneers, a wandering club with a strong fixture list against leading clubs in Surrey and Kent.

During his undergraduate days Gwyn had played rugby for Cardiff High School Old Boys, and following his move to the London area, he subsequently played for the London Welsh Dragons. In all, Gwyn spent thirty-seven years teaching at St Paul's until retiring in 2001. Throughout this time, he was master in charge of cricket at the school, besides coaching their 1st XV for fourteen years and acting in a pastoral role as Head of Year, or Undermaster, for the Year 7 and 8 pupils.

1963

Glamorgan enjoyed a handsome summer, ending the year as runners-up to Yorkshire. Overall, the Club had its most productive summer since the Championship-winning year of 1948 with the financial worries of the previous summer being erased by a doubling in membership.

The turnaround in fortunes was the result of many factors – Ossie Wheatley's positive captaincy, the tireless efforts of Don Shepherd, the return to bowling form of Jim Pressdee who completed the 'Double' in all matches, plus the emergence of Alan and Jeff Jones as quality cricketers. The latter won a place on the MCC winter tours to East Africa and India as the England selectors sought to find fresh fast bowling talent, whilst the former struck a pair of unbeaten centuries against Somerset at Glastonbury, besides making an imperious 92 opening the batting against the West Indians at Swansea.

The Glamorgan team which played Surrey at The Oval in 1963. Standing – Alan Rees, David Evans, Jeff Jones, Peter Walker, Euros Lewis, Alan Jones. Sitting – Jim Pressdee, Don Shepherd, Ossie Wheatley, Gilbert Parkhouse and Bernard Hedges.

Glamorgan were also grateful that Peter Walker, who had apparently returned to South Africa at the end of the previous season, had a change of heart about going into business and returned to play county cricket in South Wales. He continued to pouch a number of fine catches close to the wicket, whilst behind the stumps David Evans prospered from the probing bowling of Jeff and Ossie and took 89 victims – a new wicket-keeping record for the Club.

Tony Lewis and Bernard Hedges each enjoyed decent summers with the bat, with the latter scoring a fine hundred in the Gillette Cup encounter against Somerset at the Arms Park as one-day cricket entered the county calendar. However, 1963 also saw the end of Margam as a first-class venue after the final day of the game against Cambridge University had been played on a ground completely deserted. Just £70 had been taken in gate receipts on the first day, £35 on the second and nothing at all on the last.

MILLER, Dr Hamish David Sneddon.

Born – Blackpool, 20 April 1943.
Died – USA (whilst on an internal flight) 24 April 1997.
RHB, RM.
Professional.
Ed – Rondesbosch HS, University of Cape Town, University of Wales and University of
Newcastle-upon-Tyne.
1st XI: 1963-1966.
2nd XI: 1963-1967.
Club and Ground: 1964.
Western Province 1962/63; Orange Free State 1969/70-1970/71; South African Country
Districts 1972/73.
Clubs: Ebbw Vale, St Fagans, Briton Ferry Town, Ponteland.

Batting and Fielding Record

	M	I	NO	RUNS	AV	100	50	CT	ST
F-c	27	40	3	433	11.70	-	1	15	-
List A	2	2	1	16	16.00	-	-	1	-

Bowling Record

	Balls	M	R	W	AV	5wI	10wM
F-c	3086	126	1350	48	28.12	1	-
List A	132	0	89	1	89.00	-	-

Career-bests

First-class –   81 v Gloucestershire at Cheltenham College, 1964.
           7/48 v Nottinghamshire at Trent Bridge, 1964.
List A –   13* v Somerset at Cardiff Arms Park, 1963.
           1/31 v Somerset at Cardiff Arms Park, 1963.

Hamish Miller was amongst the first wave of overseas cricketers to play in English county cricket during the 1960s. Whereas others moved to the UK for cricketing reasons, the South African all-rounder played for Glamorgan having secured a place on a course at the University of Wales.

Hamish grew up in Cape Town and attended Rondesbosch High School, one of the oldest and most revered schools in South Africa, before starting his first degree at the local university. After a decent record as an all-rounder at the famed school, Hamish won a place in the Western Province side as a nineteen-year-old, and made his first-class debut on 7 December 1962 against Natal at Newlands. He took 4/32 in the visitors' second innings but could not prevent them from winning by four wickets. Nevertheless, the seam bowler enjoyed a decent first season in state cricket, claiming 18 wickets at 24 runs apiece before heading to the UK to continue his studies at the South Wales and Monmouthshire School of Mines at, what was then known as, the Glamorgan College of Technology at Treforest.

With Alan Watkins having retired and other bowlers struggling with injuries, the presence of the young all-rounder was welcomed by the Glamorgan officials, despite the fact that his availability was limited by the demands of his course. Hamish duly made his debut for the Welsh county during May 1963 against Hampshire at Swansea, and soon proved himself to be a capable all-rounder, besides appearing in the inaugural Gillette Cup match that summer against Somerset at the Arms Park. However, his studies limited him to just five Championship appearances during 1963 plus nine the following year during his summer vacation. However, August 1964 proved to be a decent month for the mining student as in back-to-back Championship matches he struck a forthright 81 against Gloucestershire at Cheltenham, besides claiming 7/48 with his lively seam bowling against Nottinghamshire at Trent Bridge.

Hamish Miller.

Hamish played in nine further matches in July and August 1965, including Glamorgan's match against the touring Springboks at Swansea, before making four further appearances during 1966 with his final match in the Welsh county's ranks coming against Essex at Swansea in late July. He returned to the Cape after completing his studies that summer at Treforest, and in 1969/70 and again in 1970/71 played in the Currie Cup for the Orange Free State before focusing his efforts on his career as a mining engineer. Nevertheless, he still played club cricket and between 1971 and 1973 he opened the bowling for the South African Country Districts team in their annual game against Argentina at Buenos Aires.

He returned to the UK during the late 1970s and secured a Ph.D. from the University of Newcastle-upon-Tyne in 1980 having completed his thesis entitles "The Stability of Excavations and the design of mining layouts in a deep level potash mine," based on work he had undertaken at Boullby Mine, a 200 hectare site in north-west Yorkshire which is run by Cleveland Potash Limited and produced, when opened in 1973, around half of the UK's output of potash – a valuable agricultural fertiliser. Whilst studying at Newcastle he also played for the Ponteland club in the Northumberland and Tyneside Senior League

He subsequently returned to South Africa, before securing a post in the United States. However, in 1997 Dr Miller died whilst on an internal flight from Albuquerque in New Mexico to Salt Lake City in Utah.

452
CORDLE, Anthony Elton.
(birth registered as Elton Anthony Cordle)
Born – Bridgetown, Barbados, 21 September 1940.
Professional.
1st XI: 1963-1982.
2nd XI: 1962-1980.
Club and Ground:1972-1976.
Cap: 1967.
Clubs: Cardiff, Pontyberem.

Batting and Fielding Record

	M	I	NO	RUNS	AV	100	50	CT	ST
F-c	312	433	76	5239	14.67	-	9	141	-
List A	211	158	37	1627	13.44	-	2	62	-

Bowling Record

	Balls	M	R	W	AV	5wI	10wM
F-c	42083	163	19281	701	27.50	19	2
List A	9462	216	5870	221	26.56		

Career-bests

First-class –   81 v Cambridge University at Margam, 1972.
             9/49 v Leicestershire at Colwyn Bay, 1969.
List A –   87 v Nottinghamshire at Trent Bridge, 1971.
             5/24 v Hampshire at Portsmouth, 1979.

Tony Cordle, as seen during 1966.

Glamorgan have always been known as a good social team, with many fine singers in their ranks. During the 1930s George Lavis (Vol.2, p155-158) had led the team after they had been invited to sing on stage at several seaside resorts. Their repertoire before the Second World War always featured a number of traditional Welsh melodies but, by the 1960s and 1970s, the sing-songs included a series of West Indian calypsos, thanks to the input of Tony Cordle, the Club's first overseas fast bowler with the Bajan long after retiring from playing, continuing to delight with his lilting voice – albeit in Canada!

Tony was brought up in the Deacon's Housing Area, just outside Bridgetown and played a decent standard of club cricket in Barbados. His half-brother Frank King had been a Test fast bowler, whilst his father had captained a strong team in the Barbados Cricket League competition. However, Tony was still a novice as far as cricket was concerned when, shortly after his 21st birthday, he decided to follow the example of his older brother Steve and move to the United Kingdom.

He initially worked for London Transport, but after ten days – "the most frightening ten days of my life" he later admitted – he decided to move to Cardiff where his brother and sister were now based. A few days later, he went to the Labour Exchange in Westgate Street ostensibly to secure a job with British Railways. Whilst walking up the stairs he looked out on the Arms Park cricket ground. "I saw the green turf and the scoreboard – the first friendly sights I had seen in Britain." Having fond memories of playing cricket in Barbados, Tony contacted Cardiff CC, little realising that his decision in February 1962 would dramatically transform his life.

Wyndham Lewis, the Cardiff secretary, was soon impressed – so were Wilf Wooller and Phil Clift, the captain and coach respectively of Glamorgan's 2nd XI and later that summer Tony made his debut for Glamorgan's second string, claiming four wickets against Warwickshire at Ebbw Vale.

After a clutch of wickets in club cricket, besides frightening opponents with his sheer pace and fast arm, Tony received further coaching from the Glamorgan staff, plus captain Ossie Wheatley who taught him important lessons about variations of pace and swing. "I could spray it around at first," he admitted. "Direction and getting things right against the professionals used to worry me, but I cut down a bit on pace and learnt how to move the ball around both ways. I worked at it endlessly until it all came right. It was then I realized that bowling quick was not everything and that made me a more effective bowler." He could still however produce an express delivery and one of his happiest recollections in a Glamorgan sweater had been clean bowling Hampshire's Barry Richards almost before the great South African batsman could pick his bat up!

He agreed professional terms with Glamorgan for 1963, although he continued to work in the shunting yards at the Canton depot during the winter months for British Railways in addition to playing football for Grange Quins in the Cardiff and District League. In mid-June 1963 Tony made his first-class debut against Cambridge University in their friendly against Glamorgan at the Steel Company of Wales' sports ground at Margam. It was not the most august of surroundings for Tony to achieve his ambition of being, in his own words, "a proper cricketer" but, the following year he played his first major match in a Glamorgan sweater and was a member of the Welsh county's team which defeated the 1964 Australians in the Celtic cauldron that was Swansea when Glamorgan met the touring teams.

The St Helen's ground was also the place for another one of his early highlights, as, in 1966, he dismissed Conrad Hunte, the West Indian captain, for a pair, courtesy of a pair of fine catches by David Evans and Roger Davis. As he later recalled, "I never dreamed that one day I would be playing cricket with many of the men I had watched as a youngster standing on tiptoe behind the fence around the Kensington Oval in Bridgetown. It meant a lot to me as well to have their words of congratulation after the game as well."

Tony Cordle seen bowling from the River End at Sophia Gardens during the Championship match against Leicestershire in 1968.

By this time, Tony had also acquired the nickname of 'Speedy', courtesy of some mischievous humour led by Gwyn Hughes after the players had visited a cinema in Leicester following the early abandonment of play. One of the cartoon characters called Speedy Gonzales resembled the Glamorgan bowler and from that day 'Speedy' stuck. Having a nickname was also a sign of acceptance amongst the team, although in his early years on Glamorgan's staff, Tony was regarded largely as a back-up bowler to Jeff Jones and Ossie Wheatley as the Bajan learnt his trade in the 2nd XI.

1965 saw Tony claim an international bag of wickets as he dismissed Bob Barber, John Jameson, Tom Cartwright and AC Smith in the opening Championship match of the season against Warwickshire. Greater opportunities duly came his way to bowl with the new ball during 1966 and, with Ossie standing down from the captaincy at the end of that summer, it was no surprise that in 1967 Tony became the spearhead of Glamorgan's attack, claiming 74 wickets at 21 runs apiece besides winning his county cap, and being presented with this badge of honour together with wicket-keeper Eifion Jones during the match with Somerset at Weston-super-Mare.

1967 also saw Tony forge an effective new ball pairing with Malcolm Nash, with his skiddy pace and clever variations of speed and movement being the perfect complement to the left-arm swing of his opening partner. The following summer Tony recorded figures of 7/43 and 4/24 against Hampshire at Sophia Gardens, besides dismissing Barry Richards in each innings as Glamorgan recorded an emphatic victory. It was a summer that Tony also registered his maiden Championship fifty, against Worcestershire at Swansea and sharing a last wicket stand of 71 with Don Shepherd, besides staying at the crease throughout the final hour of the Championship match with Northamptonshire at Swansea as he added 66 in an eighth wicket stand with Cardiff club-mate David Lewis which helped to secure a draw for Glamorgan.

That summer, Tony also struck 56 against Yorkshire at Bramall Lane. Like all bowlers, Tony also took great pride in his batting prowess and, as befitted someone raised in the sunshine of the Caribbean, he enjoyed giving the ball a bit of tap. "I'm always happiest when I'm having a slam," he admitted "but I also tried to get my head down and stay. Actually, staying was a bit of a challenge! I like to cut late or square and put it through the covers – classy shots. I like to think I can do them occasionally!" An example was at Hove in 1966 when he struck six fours as Glamorgan raced to a four-wicket victory over

Sussex with three minutes to spare. In 1970 he also struck a six and 5 fours to help clinch victory against Essex at Ilford, despite his mobility at the crease being affected by strained ankle ligaments, whilst in 1971 Tony struck a typically forthright 87 during the Sunday League fixture with Nottinghamshire at Trent Bridge.

The ever cheerful and smiling Tony was also a member of the Glamorgan team which defeated the 1968 Australians, again at Swansea although, as in the victory over their counterparts in 1964, Tony went wicketless during these two historic victories. It was not until the game at Swansea in 1977 – his Benefit Year – that Tony achieved his long-held ambition of taking a wicket against the Australians as he dismissed opening batsman Ian Davis before removing David Hookes in the tourist's middle-order.

Tony Cordle.

The West Indian was the spearhead of the county's attack which in 1969 secured the Championship title. Amongst many fine spells that season, Cordle recorded a career-best figures in mid-June against Leicestershire at the Rhos-on-Sea ground in Colwyn Bay, although it only came about after he quite curiously came on as the seventh bowler into the attack. Ossie Wheatley and Lawrence Williams had shared the new ball, before Tony Lewis switched to spin with Don Shepherd, Peter Walker, Roger Davis and Majid Khan all having a trundle before, with the total on 84-0, Tony had his chance.

He dismissed both openers – Maurice Hallam and Micky Norman – inside his first three overs and proceeded to bowl with further success for the next two and a half overs. The chance to emulate Jack Mercer in taking all ten disappeared when Ossie returned to the attack and had Jack Birkenshaw caught at bat-pad by Roger Davis. But the wickets kept tumbling at the other end and when the umpire upheld an l.b.w. appeal against Garth McKenzie, Tony had the outstanding figures of 24.4-4-49-9.

The following month Tony claimed 6/21 as second-placed Glamorgan defeated top-of-the-table Gloucestershire at Sophia Gardens having once again been belatedly introduced into the attack, as the West Country side nosedived from 78-2 to 117 all out. The tree-lined ground in Cardiff was also the scene of Tony's return of 5/42 in Worcestershire's second innings as he helped to bowl Glamorgan to the Championship crown. It was not long before his beloved record player was belting out the strains of "Oh Happy Days" and "Delilah" as Tony and his colleagues celebrated their victory with the Bajan leading the singing and dancing

His joyous jigs that afternoon – and evening - with fellow West Indian Bryan Davis in the pavillion at Sophia Gardens epitomized Tony's outlook on life as a professional sportsman. Indeed, Tony was renowned the length and breadth of the country as a cheerful and fun-loving cricketer, once fielding on the boundary whilst holding an umbrella in an away match with Essex. These were assets which proved invaluable during the Championship match with Warwickshire at Sophia Gardens in 1971 when Roger Davis, fielding at short-leg to Malcolm Nash was struck a sickening blow on his left temple. He collapsed and was given the kiss of life, with the umpires suspending play and taking an early tea as the prostrate fielder received medical treatment before being taken to hospital.

Tony Cordle with Alan Jones behind him, seen in 1989 at Sophia Gardens ahead of the game between Glamorgan and the Welsh county's Championship-winning team of 1969 which was staged as part of Rodney Ontong's Benefit Year.

When play was about to resume, Tony Cordle turned to Tony Lewis in the dressing room having purloined a white motor-cycle helmet. "I'm serious man," he said. "I'm serious. I'm your short-leg, skipper" before taking to the field and replacing Roger at bat-pad, albeit standing twice as far back as his stricken colleague would normally position himself. It was the first time in cricket history that a helmet of any sort had been worn by a fielder. The Laws may not have permitted it at the time but, after the sickening events earlier in the afternoon, the umpires – David Evans and Bill Alley – were not going to stop Tony from wearing it. Moreover, they held his headgear in between overs when he was positioned in a catching position close to the wicket.

A contractual disagreement in 1972 saw Tony leave the Glamorgan staff before being re-instated the following year. It was a wise move as he continued to be a fine all-rounder, especially in limited-overs cricket, making useful contributions with both bat and ball. 1974 saw him take 4/16 in his eight overs against Somerset in the Sunday League encounter at Swansea as well as sharing a record partnership of 87 for the ninth wicket with Malcolm Nash against Lincolnshire in the Gillette Cup match at St Helen's.

Indeed, during the second half of the 1970s Tony enjoyed some outstanding days in the shorter form of the game and, in 1976, during the match with Gloucestershire at Sophia Gardens, he became the first Glamorgan player to reach the landmark of 1,000 runs and over 100 wickets in the Sunday League. 1977 was Tony's Benefit Year and he marked it in a fitting way as the Club ended a long barren spell by reaching the final of the Gillette Cup. Throughout the tournament, he delivered a series of accurate and probing spells, concentrating on swing rather than sheer pace as Glamorgan defeated Worcestershire, Surrey and then Leicestershire *en route* to their first-ever Cup Final appearance at Lord's.

Two summers later, with Tony definitely in the veteran stage of his career, he won the Club's Player of the Year Award, and delivered more overs than any of his younger counterparts. It was not a very successful season as, for the first time in the Club's history,

Glamorgan failed to register a solitary Championship success, but Tony toiled away in his typically cheerful way and during the Sunday League match against Hampshire at Portsmouth he claimed 5/24, with four of his wickets being caught by wicket-keeper Eifion Jones. His spell also included a hat-trick, although both he and his colleagues only realized that Tony had, in fact, across the course of successive overs taken three wickets in as many balls when the Bajan was made aware of his feat by local Pressmen during the interval between innings!

This was very much Tony's final swansong as he retired from county cricket in 1980, and subsequently acted as the county's coach. His tenure ended four years later after a change in the Club's coaching structure. It was one that was not entirely to Tony's liking and was regarded by many as underserving of someone who was considered as a good Club man. It also prompted Tony's decision to emigrate with his wife Una and their young children Jeremy and Carole to the west coast of Canada, where a coaching position was on offer with the British Colombia Cricket Association, besides decent opportunities in the medical world for his wife who was a nurse.

The Cordles moved initially to Grand Prairie in Alberta before in 1986 Tony secured a position as sports coach at St Michael's University School, a co-educational independent day and boarding school on Vancouver Island. Besides coaching cricket and hockey, Tony helped the groundstaff, especially in the preparation of the school's pitches, before assisting in the running of the school shop and, prior to retiring in 2020, acting as the mail room manager.

He also took great delight in singing in concerts, held in the school's chapel besides performing in school assemblies and other gatherings, as well as giving a rendition of the Canadian national anthem ahead of the school's

Tony Cordle.

basketball matches and other major events. A measure of his popularity, both as a man and a singer, can be gauged by the fact that Tony has also sung at the weddings of the school's alumni.

His son Jeremy also attended St Michael's before representing Canada at cricket in 1991 besides winning a place in the Canadian rugby team, with the winger winning six caps between 1998 and 2001, besides being part of the support staff at the 2019 Rugby World Cup. Jeremy currently runs the Esteem Treatment Wellness Spa in Victoria. Tony's nephew Gerald was also a talented sportsman with the oval ball, playing rugby union on the wing for Cardiff RFC and rugby league for Bradford Northern, besides winning 8 caps for Wales plus one for Great Britain.

1964

The first week of August 1964 was a very special time for the town of Swansea as they hosted Glamorgan's match against the Australians at St Helen's, and the National Eisteddfod, at both Singleton Park and in the Guildhall opposite the cricket ground. The organisers of the cultural event showed great enterprise in arranging for a few televisions to be placed around the tented village, and the sets drew an ever-increasing crowd as word spread around the 'maes' of the great endeavours by Glamorgan's relatively inexperienced team, resulting in hundreds of patriotic Welshmen and women eager to catch a glimpse of the flickering black and white images, courtesy of the coverage provided by BBC Wales.

The crowd at St Helen's swarm onto the outfield after Glamorgan's victory over the 1964 Australians at Swansea.

The two teams also assembled on the stage at the Eisteddfod after play on the second day, and as Don Shepherd later recalled, "after going up on the stage, we were so full of hwyl that there was no way we were going to lose that match the following day." So it proved, as he and Jim Pressdee shared nine wickets between them as Glamorgan won by 36 runs in front of an excited and jubilant crowd of Welsh men and women, many of whom had called in from the Eisteddfod to share in a very special moment in Welsh sporting history.

It proved to be the highlight of a summer which saw the Welsh county slide down from second to eleventh in the Championship table as well as departing in the third round of the Gillette Cup. Ossie Wheatley's team won their first and last matches of the summer, but apart from the totemic victory over the Australians, there was very little for his supporters to cheer.

Although 'Shep' went past Jack Mercer's Club record of 1,460 first-class wickets and also claimed the first hat-trick of his illustrious career, he failed to take a hundred wickets, with Ossie's haul of 84 Championship wickets being the highest overall in what turned out to be a generally disappointing summer in the inter-county matches.

453
HILL, Leonard Winston.

Born – Caerleon, 14 April 1941.
Died – Newport, 10 April 2007.
Professional.
RHB, RM, occ WK.
Ed – Caerleon CS.
1st XI: 1964-1976.
2nd XI: 1964-1975.
Club and Ground: 1975.
Cap: 1974.
Clubs: Newport, Ammanford and Newport Fugitives.
Football for Lovells Athletic 1958-1962, Swansea Town and Newport County (1962-1970, 1971-1974).

Batting and Fielding Record

	M	I	NO	RUNS	AV	100	50	CT	ST
F-c	76	130	20	2690	24.25	-	14	40	1
List A	28	25	5	285	14.25	-	-	12	-

Bowling Record

	Balls	M	R	W	AV	5wI	10wM
F-c	52	1	44	0	-	-	-

Career-bests

First-class – 96* v Gloucestershire at St Helen's, Swansea, 1974.
List A – 42 v Nottinghamshire at St Helen's, Swansea, 1976.

Len Hill played both professional football and cricket, with Len representing Glamorgan between 1964 and 1976. However, his football commitments with Lovell's Athletic and Newport County meant that it was not until the mid-1970s that Len played a full season of county cricket for Glamorgan.

Born during the spring of 1942, his father – who was the caretaker of Caerleon's secondary school – and mother patriotically gave their son the second name of Winston. On several occasions whilst batting for Glamorgan, he showed the same determination and stickability as Mr Churchill. However, his father was not alive to see Len's sporting success, having died when his youngest son was only ten. It was his brother Royston, fourteen years his senior, who became the father-figure to the adolescent Len.

As he later recalled, "Royston used to take me everywhere – to watch Glamorgan's home games, as well as soccer and rugby in Cardiff and Newport. For years, he also used to bowl to me in the backyard of our home. He was a decent village cricketer and after all that had happened, I tried harder for him than I ever would for any coach."

On leaving school, Len began an apprenticeship as an electrical engineer, besides playing football and cricket in the local leagues in the Newport. His prowess as a wing-half and

Len Hill.

centre-forward in football soon attracted the scouts of Lovell's Athletic FC and, as a sportsman at heart, the teenager was able to agree semi-professional terms for the 1957/58 season before agreeing full-time terms the following season having also been chosen to play for the Wales Under18 team. Len continued to impress, besides becoming a prolific goal-scorer and it was no surprise that he joined Newport County for the 1962/63 season, although to his chagrin, his duties as a professional footballer restricted his cricket-playing from mid-May until mid-July when pre-season training began in earnest.

His batting prowess however with Newport CC saw Len make his debut for Glamorgan 2nd XI in 1964, before later that season making his first-class debut against Lancashire at the Arms Park. It proved to be an inauspicious start as he was trapped leg before by Brian Statham for one. He was also known as an agile and nimble fielder close to the wicket and during his second Championship appearance Len deputized behind the stumps when David Evans was injured ahead of Surrey's second innings in their match at The Oval. Len did not look out of place, conceded a solitary bye and deftly stumped Mickey Stewart off the bowling of Jim Pressdee.

Despite playing regularly for Glamorgan 2nd XI during his summer breaks from football, Len only made occasional appearances for the 1st XI between 1965 and 1967. He re-appeared during 1970 and 1971 and continued to post a half-century each year in Championship cricket, whilst in the latter season he also made his List A debut during the Sunday League encounter with Middlesex at Ebbw Vale.

Len had a brief spell with Swansea Town during the early 1970s before returning to Newport County. However, he quit

Len Hill (jumping right), the footballer.

professional football at the end of the 1973/74 season, having made 421 appearances for the club and scoring 74 goals, saying that he was no longer enjoying the game and wanted to focus on cricket, believing that, at the age of thirty-two, he had a few decent years remaining in county and club cricket. During the mid-1960s, Wilf Wooller and Phil Clift had each told Len that he was a good enough batsman to become a full-time cricketer and both suggested to Len that he signed full-time terms with the Club. At the time, he couldn't really decide which sport he liked most, and given his goal-scoring record and abilities in the Newport County midfield, he opted for football, but a decade later it was a very different scenario as Len switched his sporting affiliations to the summer game.

The presence of the steady right-handed batsman was a boost for the Welsh county who were re-building their batting line-up following the retirement of Tony Lewis and Peter Walker, besides losing other senior and experienced figures such as Don Shepherd. Len was the consummate sportsman, in professional terms and possessed an unflappable outlook. His gritty temperament was to the fore during August 1974 in Glamorgan's Championship match against Hampshire at Sophia Gardens – a game in which Andy Roberts, the fiery West Indian pace bowler reduced the Welsh county to 41-7 in their first innings with his spell of four wickets in five balls including that of Len who departed l.b.w to a ball from the Antiguan which kept wickedly low on the capricious surface.

Thanks to some lusty blows from a gleeful Tony Cordle, Glamorgan saved the follow-on before Malcolm Nash and Barry Lloyd shared seven wickets between them as Glamorgan were left with a target of 282 and ample time at their disposal. Even though the ball continued to dart around from the Caribbean quick bowler, the Glamorgan top order got their heads down, took few risks and patiently waited for the runs to come. Len was to the fore in this doughty riposte, and shared what proved to be a match-winning stand of 106 for the fourth wicket with Eifion Jones. In all, Len batted for five and three-quarter hours before being caught off the spin bowling of Nigel Cowley, but his efforts were not wasted as he helped the Welsh county completely turn the game around and register a four-wicket victory. His reward was the presentation shortly afterwards of his Glamorgan cap.

In early June, Len had also come close to scoring a maiden hundred in the second innings of the Championship match against Gloucestershire at Swansea. Needing 283 to prevent the West Countrys ide from recoding an innings win, the visiting attack soon made early inroads into Glamorgan's brittle top-order and Len, batting at number seven, arrived in the middle with the St Helen's scoreboard reading 47-5. Together with the lower order, he chiselled away at the deficit, showing great composure against the pace of Mike Procter and the accurate seam and swing of Tony Brown and Jack Davey.

Unruffled by the situation, Len completed a defiant half-century before heading on towards three figures, but with the total on 183-9 he was joined by Lawrence Williams, a number eleven with modest batting credentials. For once, Lawrence put bat to ball with good effect, albeit in an unorthodox way, and the last wicket pair had added 43 by the time Tony Brown returned to the attack. He duly re-arranged Lawrence's stumps and put an end to his merry spree, leaving Len unbeaten on 96 and four runs short of richly deserved century.

His county career came to an abrupt end two years later as Len became caught up in the unfortunate chain of events associated with the Club's long, hot summer of discontent. Having recorded six fifties in first-class games during 1974, Len scored two in 1975 and

Len Hill flicks a ball to the boundary during Glamorgan's match against Surrey at The Oval in 1970.

had mustered only one by the middle of 1976. He was one of several players to receive a letter from Wilf Wooller, on behalf of the Glamorgan committee, specifically about their perceived dwindling performances and tersely reminding them that, under employment law, a future contract could not be guaranteed.

Rather than remaining confidential, this information entered the public domain and, amidst allegations of mismanagement over the departure of captain Majid Khan, it made headline news in the local newspapers. Shocked at these events, the popular and unassuming man decided to leave professional sport with his final appearance for Glamorgan coming against Gloucestershire at Sophia Gardens.

Len subsequently played club cricket for Ammanford, as well as Newport Fugitives, besides focusing his efforts on his work as a self-employed builder. Len had also been a talented tennis player in his youth, and had appeared in several grass court tournaments at Rodney Parade and elsewhere. Later in life, Len became a scratch golfer and represented the Wales Over 55 team.

DAVIS, Roger Clive.

Born – Whitchurch, Cardiff, 1 January 1946.
RHB, OB.
Professional.
Ed – Llandaff Cathedral School and Blundell's School.
1st XI: 1964-1976.
2nd XI: 1963-1976.
Club and Ground: 1976-1996.
Cap: 1969.
England U25 1971, Gloucestershire 1971/72.
Clubs: Cardiff, Swansea, Llanelli, Briton Ferry Town and Bridgend Town.

Batting and Fielding Record

	M	I	NO	RUNS	AV	100	50	CT	ST
F-c	213	369	30	7363	21.71	5	32	208	-
List A	122	108	8	1730	17.30	1	6	44	-

Bowling Record

	Overs	M	R	W	AV	5wI	10wM
F-c	17208	700	7793	241	32.33	6	-
List A	2869	48	1952	71	27.49	-	-

Career-bests

First-class   134 v Worcestershire at Sophia Gardens, Cardiff, 1971.
              6/62 v Gloucestershire at Cheltenham College , 1970.
List A   91 v Northamptonshire at Wellingborough, 1975.
              4/48 v Essex at St Helen's, Swansea, 1969.

Had it not been for the actions of an off-duty doctor sitting, by chance, in the members stand at the River End of the Sophia Gardens ground, Roger Davis might have been the first county cricketer to be killed after being struck on his head whilst fielding close to the wicket during Glamorgan's Championship match against Warwickshire at Cardiff on 29 May 1971.

As usual, Roger was crouching in his customary position of short-leg with the twenty-five-year-old all-rounder having developed into a quite fearless and agile fielder close to the bat. Peter Walker had been his mentor with the pair spending hours practicing together in diving and catching exercises to improve their skills in these days before shin-pads, helmets and other associated body armour became *de rigeur*. With just a box for protection, Roger thrived at short-leg through a combination of alert reflexes, good technique and sharp instincts. But these attributes could not prevent a macabre sequence of events, with Roger perhaps crouched too close as Neal Abberley, the Warwickshire opening batsman, middled a leg glance off a rare loose delivery from Malcolm Nash.

It struck Roger a sickening blow on the temple, and the stricken fielder collapsed as an eerie silence descended over Sophia Gardens. As Roger went into violent convulsions, his legs twitching and jerking, fielders on the boundary immediately ran into the pavillion to summon medical help. Fortunately, Dr Colin Lewis sprinted out from the member's enclosure at the River End, whilst Dr Greg Brick the duty medic also came out from

the pavillion. After quickly assessing the dire situation, with Roger's face turning dark blue, Dr Lewis gave mouth-to-mouth resuscitation, and placed the stricken fielder into the recovery position. Thankfully, Roger started to breathe again as the umpires took the players off the field for an early tea. After twenty minutes, an ambulance crew from St David's Hospital in Cowbridge Road, carried Roger off the field and took him to Cardiff Infirmary.

Roger Davis (right) crouches at short-leg during Glamorgan's match against Gloucestershire at Sophia Gardens in 1968. Eifion Jones is keeping wicket and Peter Walker is at leg-slip.

As Roger later said "When the ball hit me on the side of the head I was out straight away. By chance, there was a doctor who had just arrived to pick his wife up to go to a party in the evening. After seeing what had happened, he came on and saved my life. In those days, you didn't have a doctor at each game – thankfully, they changed the rulings afterwards but, on this occasion, the doctor who later became the grandfather of Rhydian Roberts, the opera singer, he had just come by chance to watch the game with his family. It sounds dramatic, but if it weren't for him, I wouldn't be here now. He saved my life."

Having arrived at Cardiff Infirmary, it quickly became clear that Roger's head injury was life threatening and, with a hairline fracture to his skull and a blood clot developing on his brain he underwent a series of operations to heal the fracture and remove the clot. Even so, there was still some damage to his brain, as Roger recalled. "I had to learn talking and walking again. I remember shortly after the operations a doctor put a children's alphabet in front of me. I had lost my speech and everything, I couldn't even walk in a straight line and I had to do it all again from scratch – I was being taught the ABCs again, and I was calling

Roger Davis.

a dog a cat and a tree a car, and things like that. The doctors warned me never to play again, but I was eager to get back into the team and continue to play for Glamorgan. I was in hospital for about a month, and went back to training in July. That was my job, and it had to be done. Perhaps if an insurance company had turned up and offered me a million pounds to stop then I might have taken it, but it just wasn't like that then."

Three years earlier, Roger had been in the headlines once again for all the wrong reasons during the infamous County Championship match against Nottinghamshire at Swansea – the game when Garry Sobers became the first man in cricket history to hit six sixes in an over in first-class cricket. The Bajan's batting fireworks occurred on 31 August 1968 as Nottinghamshire were manoeuvering their way towards a declaration with Tony Lewis, the Glamorgan captain, bringing on Malcolm Nash at the Pavillion End to bowl a few 'experimental' overs of left-arm spin.

The first two balls disappeared high over the heads of the mid-wicket fielders and into the crowd sitting in the enclosures, before the third delivery – pushed a little wider on the off-side – was driven by Garry high over long-off where Roger was fielding and into the seating in front of the pavilion. Malcolm then dropped the fourth ball a little bit shorter, but Garry quickly rocked onto the backfoot, and pulled it square of the wicket for another six.

The fifth ball was on a good length around off stump, and Garry again played a lofted straight drive. But he did not hit the ball quite as cleanly as before, and this time it travelled high and straight towards Roger, now positioned on the boundary edge. He duly caught the ball chest high, but in so doing, tumbled backwards over the rope and into the small gulley in front of the low brick wall that ran along the perimeter of the playing area in front of the Pavillion.

Roger had done very well to ignore the cries of "Drop it, drop it!" which came from some spectators behind him and after getting back to his feet, he nodded to Eddie Phillipson, the umpire at the bowler's end that he had caught the ball. Without any hesitation Garry accepted the fielder's word and started to walk off, but the cries of "six, six, six" from the members enclosure grew louder and he halted as Eddie consulted with his colleague John Langridge. The MCC, as guardian of the Laws, had brought in an experimental regulation regarding such situations at the start of the 1968 season, with the new ruling stating that a fielder had to remain

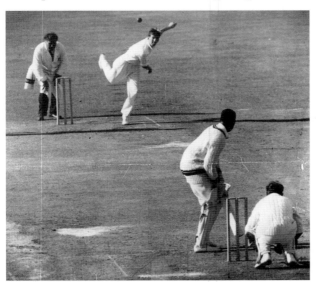

Roger Davis seen bowling against the 1966 West Indians at Swansea.

within the playing area for a catch to be made. After a quick chat, Eddie signalled six again as Gary returned to the crease. By his own admission, Roger was still feeling a little giddy after his tumble and he saw Garry ferociously pull the final ball of the over for his sixth six and a place in the record books.

Ironically, the year before, Roger had nearly conceded six sixes in an over himself at Swansea as Majid Khan, playing for the 1967 Pakistanis feasted on his off-breaks and struck him for five sixes in a dramatic over, with the balls ending up high onto the terraces of the members' enclosure, and in an innings that shortly afterwards prompted the Glamorgan hierarchy – or more correctly Wilf Wooller – to offer the graceful and willowy batsman a contract with the Welsh county.

Cricket at Swansea in August 1968 also had its own particularly sweet memories for Roger as at the start of the month Roger had been part of a very special moment in Welsh sporting history at St Helen's - and this time for all the right reasons – as he was a member of Glamorgan's team which defeated the 1968 Australians and, as Alan Jones' opening partner, the batsman played an important role in the 79-run victory. He shared in a half-century stand with Alan in the first innings besides taking a brilliant running catch at fine-leg to remove the obdurate Les Joslin in Australia's first innings, before posting a fifty of his own second time around and sharing a partnership worth exactly 100 in a shade over an hour with his Caribbean namesake Bryan.

With the tourists chasing a target of 365 on the final day, Roger was one of the gaggle of close fielders and held two smart catches as the Welsh spinners, under the direction of acting captain Don Shepherd, tricked and teased the Australian batsmen. As Alan Jones later reflected "Roger snapped up a very good catch off an inside edge to remove Barry Jarman at a time when the outcome was still in the balance. It seemed that Roger's catch inspired us even further in the field. The tension on the field of play was incredible, probably the most thrilling game of its kind I ever experienced... Roger later repeated his performance to get rid of [John] Gleeson as the game started to swing in our favour."

The following year Roger took part in another famous victory at St Helen's as, on 2 September, the off-spinner delivered the final over in the historic and narrow victory against Essex which put Glamorgan on the verge of the Championship title. Needing 190 to win on a gripping final afternoon, Roger's clever spin had already accounted for the two Keith's – Fletcher and

Roger Davis, bowling during 1975, with Ray Julian standing as the umpire.

Boyce – but, as the game approached its final conclusion, it looked as if Gordon Barker and the Essex lower-order were going to douse Glamorgan's aspirations.

As Roger later recalled, "Gordon and his team-mates seemed to have a plan – block out Don Shepherd and then gather the runs at the other end from me. Thinking that Tony would recall one of the quicker bowlers for the last over, I was a bit surprised to be honest for Tony to lob me the ball and told me to continue. The match was on a knife-edge but I held my nerve. Singles came off the first two balls before, with six to win, Gordon gave me the charge, missed and was stumped by Eifion [Jones]. Ray East was joined by last man John Lever with five needed off three balls. Two more singles were added before, from the final ball, Ossie [Wheatley] produced that brilliant piece of fielding to run out Lever and we had won by one run!"

Born in Cardiff, Roger had followed in the footsteps of his elder brother John by attending Llandaff Cathedral School before continuing his sporting education at Blundell's School in Devon. At the end of August 1964, the eighteen-year-old made his first-class debut against Kent at the Arms Park with the teenager being the fourth spinner in the Welsh county's attack after Don Shepherd, Jim Pressdee and Peter Walker. He batted at number seven in the first innings but did not feature second time around as Eifion Jones and Don Shepherd were promoted above him in the pursuit of quick runs and in what proved to be a successful run chase.

He featured next in the 1st XI during June 1966 as Alan Jones' opening partner and duly played for the next three seasons on a regular basis with the left-hander, before having a spell at number three in the line-up following the acquisition of West Indian Test openers Bryan Davis and Roy Fredericks. However, he still had stints at the top of the order and in July 1969 at Derby, Roger made his maiden Championship hundred besides sharing an opening stand of 224 with Alan. His steady batting and outstanding fielding close to the wicket made him a vital cog in Glamorgan's Championship-winning machine, with Roger claiming 33 catches in the first-class games during 1969 and deservedly winning his county cap.

The early 1970s saw Roger enjoy further success batting in the top three, as he made 134 against Worcestershire at Sophia Gardens in 1971 as well as 114 in the game with Lancashire at Old Trafford the following summer. He also proved to be a more than useful spinning foil to Don Shepherd in Championship cricket, and claimed 54 wickets at 25 runs apiece during 1970, including a career-best haul of 6/62 against Gloucestershire on the opening day of their encounter at Cheltenham College.

After fully recovering from his near-fatal injury at Cardiff in May 1971, Roger appeared four months later in an England Under-25 team which met an England XI in a three-day match at the Scarborough Festival during the first week of September. There was a strong Glamorgan contingent in the game with Lawrence Williams alongside Roger in the Under-25 team, whilst Alan Jones, Tony Lewis and Peter Walker were all in the England XI. "It was great to have returned to the Glamorgan side," recalled Roger, "and it was quite a privilege to take part, alongside my county friends, in the historic Festival. I had heard so much about the matches at Scarborough and not necessarily just the cricket. I was still, though, on strong medication and, unlike the others, I wasn't able to fully enjoy all of the social trappings associated with matches at the seaside ground in Yorkshire!"

Roger Davis pulls a ball for four during Glamorgan's match against the MCC at Lord's in 1970. Bob Taylor of Derbyshire is the wicket-keeper.

In October 1971 Roger continued his rehabilitation, alongside Don Shepherd, as both guested for Gloucestershire on their tour to Zambia. All went well and Roger continued to be a regular member of Glamorgan's line-up in both first-class and List A cricket for the next few seasons and in 1973 he hit 101 against the West Indians in their 40-over friendly at Swansea besides acting as 12th man during one of the Test Matches in England's series against the tourists. It was a proud moment for Roger to take to the field, but he still remembers the occasion more because of the fact that during the game, the Glamorgan administrators had sent a message to the ground to confirm that Roy Fredericks' contract was not being renewed for 1974 with Roger having to go into the West Indian dressing room to give his team-mate the bad news.

1975 proved to be Roger's most productive summer in a Glamorgan sweater as he amassed 1,000 first-class runs for the one and only time in his career, with his tally of 1,243 including 131 against Leicestershire at Grace Road as well as 123 in the game with Sussex at Hove. Roger also flourished in the List A matches, and struck a sparkling 91 against Northamptonshire in the televised Sunday League match at Wellingborough School as the Welsh county posted what at the time was their best-ever total in the competition as they ended their 40 overs on 266-6.

Within twelve months however his county career had come to an abrupt end. Roger lost form with both bat and ball during 1976, but given his track record at county level, it was still a huge surprise when he was one of half-a-dozen players who received mid-season a letter from Wilf Wooller, on behalf of the committee, saying that a new contract was unlikely to be offered. Like the others, he was shocked at this abrupt treatment, especially when having played for the Club on a regular basis for over ten years, he was hoping to negotiate a Benefit Year. With news of the letters being splashed all over the back pages of the local newspapers, and no progress in his efforts at securing a new contract, Roger resigned and left the Club, with his final appearance coming on 26 June 1976 in the Gillette Cup match against Warwickshire at Edgbaston.

Many were saddened by his treatment after Roger's years of proud and loyal service to the Club, as well as his decent run of form during 1975. Others felt it was an unworthy way to treat someone who had nearly given their life to Glamorgan Cricket. Roger subsequently became an estate agent, besides commentating on the Welsh county's matches on TV and radio for BBC Wales. During the 1990s he also returned to the Club as a member of the cricket committee.

1965

Glamorgan proved that their success in beating the 1964 Australians had not been a fluke as they enjoyed, by far, the better of the draw with the touring Springboks whilst as far as the Championship was concerned, they were on the coat tails of the leaders for the bulk of the summer before ending up in third place. They would also have pipped Worcestershire, the eventual Champions, had they taken maximum points from their last three games and enjoyed better weather at the Arms Park during August.

The team played positive cricket throughout with Alan Jones leading from the front with five Championship hundreds and an imposing aggregate of 1,665 runs. Ossie Wheatley and Jeff Jones also formed a spirited new ball attack, whilst Don Shepherd bowled superbly all season, bagging 107 Championship wickets at just 15 runs apiece.

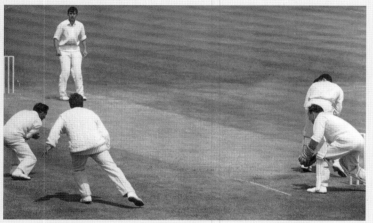

A photograph from Glamorgan's match against Kent at Swansea in 1965 with Euros Lewis removing a visiting batter thanks to a smart catch at short-leg by Bernard Hedges.

Peter Walker and Tony Lewis also passed the 1,000-run mark with the bat with Tony's finest moment, and perhaps of the team overall, coming in early August at St Helen's in the tourist match against the South Africans. On the opening day, the Cambridge graduate struck an unbeaten 146 with his four and a quarter-hour innings decorated with a series of booming off-drives and crisply struck square-cuts.

After rain delayed the start of the second day, Jeff and Ossie reduced the tourists to 117-5 before Jim Pressdee filleted the tail taking 4/11 in eight overs. Ossie then had the rare luxury of inviting the Springboks to follow-on before Jim made further inroads and fired up the romantics who had predicted another famous Welsh victory at St Helen's. But Peter van der Merwe and Richard Dumbrill defended stoutly as the South Africans were eight wickets down at the end of a match which, in the words of Wisden's correspondent had been "worthy of a Test Match."

455
LEWIS, Brian.

Born – Maesteg, 18 July 1945.
Professional.
RHB, OB.
1st XI: 1965-1969.
2nd XI: 1963-1969.
Clubs: Maesteg Celtic, Pontarddulais, Ammanford and Gorseinon.

Batting and Fielding Record

	M	I	NO	RUNS	AV	100	50	CT	ST
F-c	37	45	5	333	8.32	-	-	29	-
List A	1	1	0	4	4.00	-	-	1	-

Bowling Record

	Balls	M	R	W	AV	5wI	10wM
F-c	4021	160	2001	82	24.40	6	1

Career-bests

First-class –   38 v Nottinghamshire at St Helen's, Swansea, 1968.
        7/28 v Hampshire at Southampton, 1968.
List A –   4 v Middlesex at Lord's, 1969.

Brian Lewis, an off-spinner from Maesteg, was a member of the Glamorgan side which defeated the 1968 Australians at Swansea.

Brian had impressed as a schoolboy with his batting and bowling skills for Maesteg Celtic and, after making his 2nd XI debut for Glamorgan during 1963, he spent the following year on the MCC groundstaff at Lord's, honing his bowling skills under the watchful eye of Head Coach Len Muncer. Whilst at Lord's, Brian also made a number of appearances for the MCC in their out-games against club and school teams, as well as alongside Mushtaq Mohammad, Wes Hall and Basil D'Oliveira in their one-day friendly against Scotland.

In 1965 he joined the Glamorgan staff as an understudy to Don Shepherd and Roger Davis, and during early July, Brian – or 'Bertie' as he was known by his colleagues – made his first-class debut against Lancashire at Swansea. With the other spinners in fine and consistent form, Brian's opportunities were limited, but he got an extended run in the 1st XI during 1967 as well as 1968.

During May 1968 he helped to spin Glamorgan to victory at Southampton as he took 4/46 and 7/28 as Glamorgan defeated Hampshire by two wickets.

Brian Lewis.

Three months later he played a hand in the historic victory over the Australians, taking 4/51 in their first innings, plus three more in the second innings as he was cleverly used by acting captain Don Shepherd with the youngster's sharply spinning off-breaks finding plenty of assistance bowling into the rough during a marathon 32 over spell on the final day.

Despite missing a difficult chance to catch Paul Sheahan off his own bowling in the Australians second innings, this was a commendable haul for the young spinner in such a pressure cooker environment, and in the extreme heat of the amphitheatre-like cauldron of St Helen's. However, it also proved to be the finest hour of Brian's brief county career. Over the winter months he was encouraged by senior figures in the Club to add variety to his armoury by bowling the ball which goes straight on. However, the plan backfired as Brian subsequently lost his action. He did not make any Championship appearances during 1969, although he did play in the inaugural Sunday League match at Lord's against Middlesex. He was released at the end of the Club's Championship-winning summer.

1966

1966 saw Glamorgan play their first-ever County Championship game in North Wales as Derbyshire visited Colwyn Bay, with the Club adding Denbighshire to the list of other counties in Wales – including Monmouthshire and Carmarthenshire – where they had staged first-class cricket.

The summer also saw the Welsh county's final fixture at the Arms Park, with the match against Somerset ending in a 71-run defeat a month or so before the bulldozers and construction workers moved into the Cardiff ground as work began creating the National Stadium. All of the seats were also transported a mile or so to the north to Sophia Gardens where work had been taking place for several years in creating a new series of pitches suitable for first-class cricket.

Tony Lewis, seen on the Pavillion balcony at Colwyn Bay during Glamorgan's inaugural Championship match at the Rhos-on-Sea ground during 1966.

Whilst building work took place off the field in creating a new venue, there were few changes to the personnel on the field as, apart from Jim Pressdee, the same set of faces appeared in what proved to be Ossie Wheatley's final summer as Glamorgan captain. Fittingly, he bowed out with 100 Championship wickets to his name, whilst Don Shepherd claimed 111. On the batting front, Tony Lewis and Alan Jones were the mainstays of the Glamorgan line-up with 1960 and 1626 Championship runs respectively.

Alan's finest innings that summer came at Swansea against the 1966 West Indians and their much-vaunted pace attack led by Wes Hall. As Alan recalled, "The giant six foot two inch tall bowler was a truly frightening sight – several buttons on his shirt were undone and his gold medallion was swinging wildly and glistening in the sun. We were 15 for 2 and faced a struggle. Tony Lewis joined me and we began to get the upper hand, gradually we began to punish the bowling. I felt in control and went on to carry my bat for 161."

In the minds of many shrewd judges, this was amongst Alan's finest innings and one of the best-ever played by a Glamorgan batsman against a touring team. It might also have laid the foundation of another famous victory against a touring team as, needing 198 to win in three hours, the men from the Caribbean were 33-2 when rain washed out the final session.

456
MORRIS, Ian.

Born – Maesteg, 27 June 1946.
Professional.
RHB, SLA.
Ed – Maesteg GS.
1st XI: 1966-1968.
2nd XI: 1962-1968.
Clubs: Maesteg Celtic and Ynysygerwn.

Batting and Fielding Record

	M	I	NO	RUNS	AV	100	50	CT	ST
F-c	14	25	2	253	11.00	-	-	15	-

Bowling Record

	Balls	M	R	W	AV	5wI	10wM
F-c	168	4	141	4	35.25	-	-

Career-bests

First-class –   38 v Hampshire at Cardiff Arms Park, 1966.
2/30 v Northamptonshire at St Helen's, Swansea, 1968.

Ian Morris was a steady right-handed batsman and capable left-arm spinner who was on Glamorgan's staff for three years during the late 1960's.

The all-rounder first played for the county's 2nd XI at the age of sixteen following some decent performances for Maesteg Celtic CC. He then spent two years on the MCC groundstaff at Lord's, and following the departure of fellow left-arm spinner Jim Pressdee at the end of the 1965 season, Ian joined the county's staff in 1966.

He subsequently made his first-class debut later that summer against Hampshire at the Arms Park but, over the course of the next couple of years, he had few opportunities in the 1st XI with Peter Walker still in outstanding form, and opening batsman Roger Davis regarded as the back-up spinner. However, Ian had an extended run of nine Championship games during May and June 1968, but during this time he only scored 158 runs and claimed just three wickets.

Ian was released from the staff at the end of the season and returned to play for, and coach, Maesteg Celtic CC besides playing for Wales and the South Wales Cricket Association's representative team.

Ian Morris.

NASH, Malcolm Andrew.
Born – Abergavenny, 9 May 1945.
Died – London, 30 July 2019.
Professional.
LHB, LM.
Ed – Hereford Road Junior School, Abergavenny and Wells Cathedral School.
1st XI: 1966-1983.
2nd XI:1964-1983.
Club and Ground: 1972-1976.
Cap: 1969.
Shropshire 1984.
Clubs: Abergavenny, Crickhowell, Ebbw Vale, Worcester City, Swansea, Gowerton and Llanelli.
Hockey for Abergavenny and Wales Under 23.

Batting and Fielding Record

	M	I	NO	RUNS	AV	100	50	CT	ST
F-c	335	467	67	7120	17.81	2	25	148	-
List A	268	224	42	2256	12.39	1	4	47	-

Bowling Record

	Balls	M	R	W	AV	5wI	10wM
F-c	55158	2426	25601	991	25.83	45	3
List A	12281	360	6791	322	21.09		

Career-bests

First-class – 130 v Surrey at The Oval, 1976.
9/56 v Hampshire at Basingstoke, 1975.
List A – 103* v Hampshire at St Helen's, Swansea, 1976.
6/29 v Worcestershire at Worcester, 1975.

Malcolm Nash will always be remembered as the bowler struck by Sir Garfield Sobers for six sixes in an over during the Championship match with Nottinghamshire at Swansea during 1968 – the first time this batting feat had been achieved in professional cricket. What is often forgotten though was that Malcolm was not bowling in his usual style and, instead, was experimenting with slow left-arm as the visitors were approaching a declaration.

A more fitting epitaph would therefore be that he was one of the finest new ball bowlers from the late 1960s until the early 1980s, and a man skillful enough with the new ball to be rated by Barry Richards, the legendary Springbok batsman, as one of the most difficult bowlers he faced whilst playing county cricket with Hampshire. Had Malcolm played for a more fashionable team or one in the south-east of England, he would probably have won a string of Test caps. Garry's feat of hitting 36 runs from one of Malcolm's overs is one of three landmark performances in the UK in the history of the game and stands comparison

A cartoon montage of Garry Sobers' six-hitting feat for Nottinghamshire during their County Championship match at Swansea in 1968.

– in the record books – alongside Brian Lara's unbeaten 501 at Edgbaston during 1994, and Jim Laker's 19 for 90 in the Ashes Test at Old Trafford in 1956. In time, somebody might surpass the feats of the West Indian batsman and the English off-spinner, whilst in the modern era of free hits for a no-ball, the achievement of Garry could theoretically be overtaken. But Garry was the first to attain the maximum possible off six legal deliveries and his feat has only been equalLed in first-class cricket, including by Ravi Shastri, the Indian all-rounder during 1984/85 before also enjoying a short career in county cricket with Glamorgan.

And so to the events of that fateful over on 31 August 1968. As Malcolm later recalled, "Notts had reached a commanding 358-5 by 5pm on the first day and I had already taken four of the five wickets to fall and was bowling well. Garry was on about 40 not out. I had got his wicket a couple of times before and, as they were now seeking quick runs before a declaration, I thought I could do so again."

"The first ball I bowled to Garry during that over – around the wicket – wasn't a bad ball, on a length on the stumps, but he hit it over long-on and into the guttering on The Cricketers pub in Bryn Road. I thought 'Crikey, that's some hit', but I also thought the best way to try to get him out was to keep pitching it up and let him have a go at it in the hope that he whacks it up in the air. And that's exactly what he did, except he didn't whack it too short! He put the next one over square leg and it bounced into the road."

"Then the third went over long-off and the next one high over midwicket. I still though felt confident as he played everything off the back foot and I thought 'OK, but he's going to mishit one in a minute'. I then gave the fifth one a little bit more air, and he got underneath it, but Roger Davis at long-off overbalanced and fell over the ropes after taking the catch. For the last ball, I bowled a seamer off my short run from around the wicket – something which I'd never done before, and it was, by far, the worst ball of the day, never mind the over, and it disappeared high over mid-wicket before ending up by a bus stop way, way down the road."

Within a few minutes, the Press Association wires had transmitted details of Garry's feat, and Malcolm's bowling to the newspaper offices in Fleet Street in London as well as to other media outlets around the world. The BBC Wales footage with Wilf Wooller's infamous words accompanying the final six – "And it's gone all the way down to Swansea" were soon being shown on news programmes whilst Brian Hoey, then a BBC reporter in Cardiff and later the biographer of HRH Princess Diana, was hastily dispatched to the St Helen's ground to conduct a post-match interview with the batsman and bowler.

In 1977 when bowling in his normal style, history very nearly repeated itself during Glamorgan's Championship match against Lancashire at Swansea as Frank Hayes bludgeoned Malcolm for five sixes and a four during an over with the new ball. It was probably just as well that on that day one of the balls did not go for six as there were no television cameras present and a much smaller crowd to watch events. Another difference was that on this particular day, Malcolm had been bowling at the Mumbles Road End and, years later, he was able to ruefully reflect on having been hit for 70 runs in two overs at opposite ends of the St Helen's ground!

Had the same sentiment been shown to Malcolm as others – possibly less abrasive – had enjoyed in other counties, he would have finished his county career with over 1,000 wickets. Instead, he ended seven short in all first-class games of what would have been

a fitting milestone given his outstanding abilities with the new ball. His career tally of 991 wickets for the Welsh county places him fifth in the list of the Club's wicket-takers – a total that, since Malcolm's departure from the county game in 1983, only Robert Croft has surpassed. Similarly his career-best figures of 9/56 against Hampshire at Basingstoke in 1975 have only been bettered on eight occasions in the Club's history.

Malcolm owed his success as a left-arm bowler to having the priceless knack of being able to deceptively move the ball both ways, without any discernable change in his action, besides possessing an attacking outlook, never looking to be defensive but always looking to outwit opposing batsmen who were unsure whether the ball would be swinging in or out. Like other fine bowlers in the county game, Malcolm cared greatly about his action, the position

Malcolm Nash, as seen in 1967.

of his feet in the crease, the rotation of his hips and a high arm with his wrist cocked behind the ball. He was fortunate as well that during the peak of his career in the late 1960s and into the 1970s he had the support of a group of outstanding fielders close to the wicket, especially Roger Davis and Peter Walker in the leg-trap, Majid Khan at first slip and Eifion Jones behind the stumps.

He invariably dismissed several top-order batsmen when the shine was on the ball and, in typical fashion, dismissed Mike Brearley (at the time the England captain) with the first delivery of the Middlesex innings in the 1977 Gillette Cup Final at Lord's. As he later recalled, "the ball was in exactly the right place. From my point of view, it was the perfect away-swinger, drifting across Mike's bat. It took the edge and was enthusiastically gobbled up by Eifion behind the stumps. Mike walked. It must have been a strange experience for him, leaving the field after a first-baller and with the strains of *Mae Hen Wlad Fy Nhadau* sung with great gusto accompanying him."

Soon afterwards, Malcolm saw Man-of-the-Match Clive Radley dropped at second slip by Collis King and had the Bajan all-rounder held onto the low catch, Malcolm may have run amok through the Middlesex line-up, just as he had done on countless times in one-day games in the past for Glamorgan. Instead, it proved to be the decisive moment of the game as the Welsh county's big day out at Lord's ended in defeat.

Malcolm Nash, as seen in 1974, during his delivery stride.

Indeed, Malcolm had been a highly effective and miserly bowler in the Sunday League since the competition's inception in 1969 with the left-armer frequently delivering his allocation of eight overs straight through at the start of the opponents innings and at a minimal cost. His figures of 8-4-8-1 and 8-4-8-2 against Lancashire in 1973 and 1980 were never bettered by any other Glamorgan bowler.

Born in May 1945 into a well-known sporting family in Abergavenny, Malcolm's mother Marie was a good tennis player whilst his father Ted had enjoyed success with the town's cricket club. Being in such a sporting environment, it was no surprise that Malcolm picked up the cricket bug from an early age and gleefully joined his father on trips to Ebbw Vale to watch Glamorgan play their annual fixture at the ground. He had also visited the town from a young age to attend the coaching sessions at Glamorgan's indoor school at Ebbw Vale, and it was here where young Malcolm benefitted from the wisdom of Phil Clift, the Club's coach and 2nd XI captain, as well as the kind words of former Somerset cricketers such as Bill Andrews and Harold Gimblett, who were, in turn, the professionals attached to the Monmouthshire club.

Malcolm Nash, seen batting against Sussex during 1969.

"It was an amazing experience," recalled Malcolm about these days, "I learned so much. Harold always said 'Go for your shots' and he never tried to change anything that came naturally and worked. I remember one day when he threw a widish ball at me, just short of a length. I waited for the ball to pass me, and then flat-batted it through square cover off the front foot. He asked me if I could do it again. I said I could and then did! 'Never stop playing that shot, son' Harold instructed. Sure enough, it became a firm favourite of mine. I could play it off the back foot too!"

Aged ten, Malcolm played his first cricket match for Abergavenny and, by the age of fifteen, he had followed in his father's footsteps by regularly playing for their 1st XI. His debut came against Panteg, then one of the strongest teams in the region, and his maiden innings of 61 helped Abergavenny stave off defeat. His sporting education continued at Wells Cathedral School in Somerset, where he had plenty of opportunities to further hone his cricketing skills, besides developing into a useful hockey player. His abilities in that sport were good enough for Malcolm to later captain the Wales Under 23 team against Ireland in Dublin in 1966.

In 1962, and at the age of seventeen, Malcolm left the Cathedral School and returned to Abergavenny to train as an accountant for a builders merchants in Abergavenny as well as playing as much cricket as possible. His success in club cricket for Abergaveny, allied to his confident manner, led to Malcolm making his 2nd XI debut for Glamorgan in 1964 before the following year he completed the Double of 1,000 runs and 100 wickets in club matches for Abergavenny, besides also claiming 10/29 in a game with Lydney. His talents also attracted the attention of Worcester City, one of Abergavenny's regular opponents, and following some swash-buckling innings and probing bowling performances, Malcolm was invited to join them on their tour to the South Coast in 1965.

It was whilst based with the rest of the tour party near Portsmouth that Malcolm was approached by the Worcester officials who suggested that he switched his allegiances and played for them during 1966. As Malcolm recalled, "they also said that they could arrange for a trial with Worcestershire. It was a massive compliment and a great chance, especially as they had just won the Championship. I was a bit overawed by the idea of playing at New Road and after returning home, I eventually mentioned it to my father. 'Why don't you want to play for Glamorgan instead?' was his response."

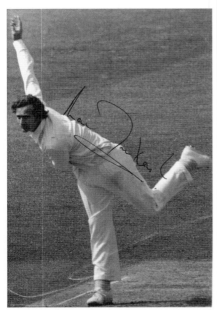

A signed photograph of Malcolm Nash in his delivery stride.

Malcolm duly wrote to Wilf Wooller, and after a successful trial in the Indoor Schools at Neath and the Arms Park, he secured a summer contract with Glamorgan at £10 per week, much to the delight of his doting father. After some decent performances for the 2nd XI, Malcolm duly made his first-class debut against Cambridge University at the Arms Park in June 1966. The following year, he joined the full-time staff and, following an injury to Tony Cordle, Malcolm made his Championship debut in an all-Welsh born Glamorgan side against Yorkshire at Harrogate where, had it not been for a dropped catch by Jeff Jones, he would have had Geoff Boycott as his maiden wicket.

1968 was a breakthrough summer for Malcolm as he claimed 55 first-class wickets besides taking 4 five-wicket hauls. The finest came at Swansea, in the Championship contest against Somerset where the visitors had eased to a first innings lead of 133 after a typically sublime 81 from Greg Chappell, their young Australian batsman. But the 23 year-old dramatically transformed the state of the game on the second evening as, bowling unchanged with the new ball, he returned figures of 13.3-7-15-7 as the West Country side were bundled out for 40. Nobody got into double figures before the following morning Alan Jones scored a fine century, his fifth against Somerset in the space of as many seasons as the left-hander led Glamorgan to a resounding nine-wicket victory, and all on the same wicket where the night before, Malcolm's swing had decimated the visiting line-up.

As Malcolm recalled, "the pitch played very differently after tea on the second day. Perhaps it was because the tide had turned after lunch and was now well on its way back in. I don't know how much difference it made to the sandy square but Wilf Wooller used to think it did. It was rumoured that Wilf never tossed at Swansea without a copy of the tide-tables in his pocket! On that particular day for me, together with the incoming tide, an onshore breeze certainly helped my lateral movement."

The following month, Malcolm took 5/28 in the first innings of the match against the 1968 Australians. It was the biggest game, so far, of his fledgling career but he stepped onto the St Helen's turf without a nervous twitch and effectively displayed his subtle arts of swing bowling against the cream of the tourist's batting. His assuredness and confidence in his own abilities was not a surprise to his colleagues, especially Tony Lewis to whom Malcolm had said the previous summer that he was quite happy to open the batting as well as the bowling, besides having a go at captaincy if Tony wanted to take a rest!

Returning to the match at St Helen's against the 1968 Australians, Malcolm was swiftly into the action at the Mumbles Road End. "They began with a careless run out with my throw from the boundary to the bowler's end seeing skipper [Barry] Jarman out by a country mile. Then I got Ian Redpath and Bob Cowper in quick succession, clean bowling Redpath and having Cowper snapped up at second slip. Our tails were up. I was certainly in the groove and getting late lateral movement." Malcolm later had both Ashley Mallett and John Gleeson caught behind by Eifion Jones to complete his 'five-for'. In the second innings, Malcolm added the scalp of opening batsman John Inverarity before the Glamorgan spinners took over and under the wise guidance of Don Shepherd, spun the Welsh county to a famous victory.

Malcolm built on this success in 1969 and became the spearhead of the Championship-winning attack, with the left-armer ending the daffodil-golden summer as the Club's leading wicket-taker, with 71 wickets at just 18 runs apiece: a performance which also saw Malcolm win his Glamorgan cap. As he later recalled, it was a joyous summer for all concerned – "the bond and team spirit was the strongest I experienced over all my Glamorgan years. We had confidence not only in our own individual abilities, but also in those of our team-mates. Our Welshness and pride in being Welsh was another significant factor in our strength as a playing unit. However, our attacking approach and quick-scoring strategy was the key, especially as it gave the bowling unit plenty of time. We ended the season as unbeaten Champions, and I took great delight that our unbeaten record was only the result of what Eifion Jones and I had achieved on the last day of our opening game of the season against Yorkshire at Swansea where we hung on for a draw."

Having got his MCC coaching badge at Lilleshall, Malcolm spent the winter of 1969/70 coaching in the Transvaal in South Africa, deputizing for Alan Jones who had coached at Springs the previous winters, before returning to the UK and continuing to spearhead the Glamorgan attack. His record for the next eight years speaks volumes for his durability and finesse with the new ball as he claimed seasonal hauls of 79 wickets, 65, 64, 80, 63, 85, 69 and 81.

In 1975 at Swansea, Malcolm also came agonizingly close to claiming a hat-trick against the Australians. Having bowled Rick McCosker, he then trapped Ian Chappell l.b.w before next ball having another appeal against Greg Chappell turned down by umpire Tom Spencer – "I'm sorry, "I couldn't do it," the long-serving umpire said to Malcolm at the end of the over. "I couldn't give two in a row. I'm in line for a Test Match!" In those days, before the advent of ICC umpires, the captains of touring teams could object to particular officials from the English panel standing in the Tests, but Malcolm left the former Kent batsman and professional footballer in no doubt about what he thought was a shocking piece of decision-making!

Malcolm though was not to be denied a hat-trick later that summer during the Sunday League game with Worcestershire at New Road. After a typically accurate six-over salvo at the start of the home side's innings, he returned later to complete his allocation. As Malcolm remembered, "I bowled Rodney Cass off the third ball. He was replaced by the skipper, Norman Gifford, who nicked his first ball to Eifion behind the stumps. Enter Paul Pridgeon – another first baller! Clean bowled. The first – and as it turned out, only – hat-trick of my professional career. It was a great feeling, even if my victims weren't front

Malcolm Nash strikes a boundary during Glamorgan's match against Surrey at The Oval in 1976.

line batsmen." Malcolm also added the scalps of Vanburn Holder and Brian Brain as in the space of seven balls, he had taken five wickets for one run.

1975 also saw Malcolm claim his career-best figures during the Championship match against Hampshire at Basingstoke. Glamorgan had been put in to bat at May's Bounty and were dismissed for 207 at tea. As Malcolm later recalled, "we felt there was something still in the wicket when we started bowling and I soon removed Gordon Greenidge and Richard Lewis in my opening spell before Trevor Jesty and Barry Richards steadied the ship. Our cause wasn't helped by Greg Armstrong sustaining a foot injury so I returned to the attack in the final hour and had one of those spells every bowler dreams about. I got another four wickets, including the prized one of Barry whilst their total moved on by nine runs to 76-6. I had taken all six wickets to fall. The following morning I continued bowling a good line and had Richard Gilliat and Bob Stephenson given out leg before as it dawned on me that a rare ten-wicket haul was a distinct possibility. But my hopes were dashed as Andy Murtagh who had joined Andy Roberts called for a crazy single to cover and was run out by a mile." Shortly afterwards, Malcolm bowled John Southern and proudly led the team off the field at May's Bounty with figures of 9/56.

Besides his accurate and probing bowling, Malcolm was a forthright batsman, capable of producing an explosive innings. Indeed, in 1976 he become Glamorgan's first centurion in the Benson and Hedges Cup, with a boundary-laden 103 against Hampshire at Swansea and also that summer struck a century before lunch in the County Championship match against Surrey at The Oval. He also once hit four consecutive balls from Somerset's Dennis Breakwell for six, besides setting a then Club record of nine sixes during a brutal innings of 89 against Gloucestershire during the Championship match at Swansea in 1973.

Malcolm was a good enough all-round cricketer to appear several times on the radar of the England selectors. When Derbyshire's Alan Ward broke down on the MCC tour of Australia in 1970/71 many thought Malcolm might get his chance, such had been his success with Glamorgan over the previous three seasons. Instead, the selectors opted for Bob Willis, then a promising quick bowler with Surrey 2nd XI. It was around this time that Alec Bedser, the England selector, told Malcolm that, in order to progress into the England team, he would have to develop an extra yard or two of pace, especially to trouble the lower-order batsmen. In his typical no-nonsense way, Malcolm replied "OK, let me focus on knocking over batsmen one to six and I'll then let the quicks deal with the rest!" He eventually won a place in the Test Trial at Bristol in 1976 and typically did not let anyone down, but it was the closest he ever came to Test honours.

As shown by his response to the Chairman of Selectors, Malcolm was a man of strong opinions, and someone who did not suffer fools gladly, but he had a shrewd cricket brain and capably led the Welsh county during 1980 and 1981. There was also a greater sense of pride and purpose when he was in charge, compared with the summer of 1979 when the Club had languished without a solitary Championship victory.

Typically, Malcolm led from the front as Glamorgan's new captain and, during his second match in charge, against Gloucestershire at Bristol, he returned figures of 5/58 and 6/72 as Glamorgan won by seven wickets – a victory celebrated in true Nashy style with a crate of champagne in the team's changing room. Indeed, he revelled in the social aspects of life on the county circuit, in these days when mixing and drinking with opponents after play was *de rigeur*. As a young player, he had relished the opportunities to mix with visiting players and umpires, and had picked up many tips from talking to them, as well as avidly watching play with his senior colleagues. Two opponents who were particularly helpful were Wes Hall and Fred Trueman who both encouraged the young colt to stick with, and treasure his action, and not to risk damaging his innate ability to swing the ball by striving for more pace.

It was no surprise that after taking over as the Club's leader, Malcolm encouraged the selection committee to seek an overseas fast bowler with whom he could share the new ball. But Malcolm's glee at securing the services of Ezra Moseley in 1980 was short-lived as the West Indian suffered a serious back injury. But Malcolm kept his sense of purpose and led Glamorgan up to 13th place besides claiming 74 first-class wickets in 1980, followed by 71 the next year as he shouldered the burden of the attack as the Club's hierarchy gave preference to the mercurial batting talents of Javed Miandad.

He returned to the role of senior professional during 1982 as Javed Miandad and Barry Lloyd shared the captaincy duties, but he continued to be full of advice for the younger players. As Greg Thomas recalled in a letter read out at Malcolm's Memorial Service. "I was mightily impressed by his never-say-die attitude such as the time when Glamorgan played the Pakistanis at Swansea in 1982. They had a fine wrist-spinner in Abdul Qadir who took five cheap wickets in our first innings and made us follow-on. I was twelfth man and vividly remember sitting in the player's area and hearing Malcolm say,' I don't know what the fuss is all about with his bowling – it's quite straight forward what he's trying to do.' Malcolm duly went in, hit a boundary and then tried to repeat the stroke but missed and ended up flat on his back as he was stumped!"

The appointment of Mike Selvey as Glamorgan captain in 1983 reduced Malcolm's opportunities in both Championship and limited-overs cricket. However, he had only claimed 38 first-class wickets during 1982 and, taking the sentiment out of these matters, there were signs that his powers were on the wane. However, Malcolm steadfastly believed that he still had a role to play, with his frugal returns in one-day cricket suggesting that he could still be a handy performer with the ball. But this was a time of re-building for the Club and looking ahead to the future. Greg Thomas and Steve Barwick, to name but two, had shown great promise. A suggestion was made to Malcolm that he could play in just the one-day games in 1984, but this did not appeal to him, and instead he agreed terms to play in Minor County cricket for Shropshire, with his last Championship appearance for Glamorgan being, quite fittingly against Worcestershire at Abergavenny in mid-June 1983.

The following summer, Malcolm was in the Shropshire team which famously defeated Yorkshire at Telford in the 1984 Gillette Cup and returned figures of 12-6-16-1. For several years, Malcolm had been running a sports outfitters in Swansea, but the end of the 1985 season, having also brought a close to his time in Minor County cricket, he emigrated to North America where he worked initially as a sports coach in Canada before working for a recycling firm in Northern California where he mixed his duties as a sales and marketing manager with coaching cricket in ten schools in the Los Angeles area.

Golf was Malcolm's other sporting passion, and he subsequently worked as an advisor to the developers of golf courses in the mid-West, before moving to Florida where he worked for a transport company in Tampa Bay. Malcolm also took great delight in visiting Barbados to play a round of golf with his good friend, Garry Sobers. After returning to the UK in 2013, he rejoined Langland Bay Golf Club, with whom he had been a member since the 1970s. After undergoing a triple heart bypass, Malcolm enjoyed playing golf with his friends at the club, where he was famed for his approach to 12th hole, where a sharp dog-leg meant most people would take two drives in order to reach the green. Not for Malcolm, and someone who in cricketing circles had seen the prefix 'Super' added to his initials M.A.N. Instead, he would regularly drive straight over the trees to land on the green in one blow, before successfully putting to go one under par!

Half a century after 'that' over at Swansea, Malcolm was still content to recall the events of that afternoon at St Helen's. It had featured prominently in his memoirs *Not Only, But Also* written in conjunction with Richard Bentley and published in 2018 by St David's Press. For a couple of years following his return from the States, Malcolm lived on the Gower Peninsula and

Malcolm Nash walks through the Guard of Honour and onto the outfield at Sophia Gardens during Glamorgan's T20 match against Gloucestershire in August 2017.

did the rounds of Cricket Societies, other organizations and cruises, promoting his book and reflecting on the six deliveries against the West Indian in 1968, as well as the other highlights of his illustrious career as a Glamorgan cricketer. Tragically, he was taken ill in late July 2019 at a function at Lord's and died in a London hospital a few hours afterwards.

On hearing of Malcolm's passing Garry Sobers said "Malcolm was a good friend – we always kept that friendship, he was a nice man. We played against each other many times, and I was fortunate to hit six sixes against him but things never changed. As far as we were concerned, we were always friends in spite of what happened on the cricket field. I don't see why it should change things if you score runs against somebody else."

"I remember him driving from Wales to London last year when I was there. He was writing his book and he asked me to sign copies. I am very shocked and it is sad to hear. When we were asked to go up to be interviewed on TV afterwards at Swansea in 1968, I looked back over my shoulder and saw him smiling. I said to him what are you smiling at? And he replied 'I want you to know you could not have achieved this without me!' "

1967

1967 saw the start of a new era in the Club's history. Tony Lewis succeeded Ossie Wheatley as the Club's captain whilst the Welsh county began playing at Sophia Gardens. Their new base in Cardiff hosted the three-day match starting on 24 May against the Indians, but the building work was not complete by the start of the game, with temporary changing and dining facilities.

There were concerns as well about the way the new drainage had been installed, with a ridge running at ninety degrees to the stumps mid-way down the pitches. As a result, the bounce was erratic, with bowlers regularly hitting the ridge, only to see the ball either fly towards the batsmen head or shoot through low towards his ankles.

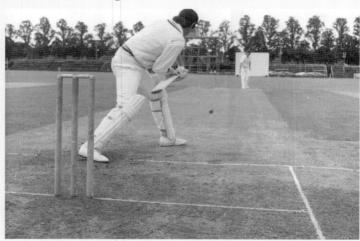

Tony Lewis, in a specially posed photograph at Sophia Gardens in 1972.

The vagaries of the pitches at Sophia Gardens were a factor behind Glamorgan remaining closer to the bottom, rather than the top of the table in 1967, but after remedial work was undertaken following advice from the MCC's Inspector of Pitches, mid-August saw Glamorgan record their first victory at Sophia Gardens as they defeated Kent by an innings after some hostile bowling by Tony Cordle and Jeff Jones.

The latter was in fine form during 1967 and prospered from a more relaxed attitude and greater accuracy with ball in hand. The fast bowler ended the summer with 88 Championship wickets to his name at 16 runs apiece, although Don Shepherd yet again claimed most wickets in the competition with a haul of 90 victims. The two Alans – Messrs Jones and Rees – enjoyed success with the bat but Tony, after his prolific form in 1966, had a relatively quiet summer with the bat as he eased into his new role as Glamorgan's leader.

458
JARRETT, Keith Stanley.

Born – Newport, 18 May 1948.
1st XI: 1967.
2nd XI: 1965-1969.
RHB, RM.
Ed – Monmouth School.
Club: Newport.
Rugby Union for Abertillery, London Welsh, Newport, Wales and British Lions. Rugby League for Barrow and Wigan.

Batting and Fielding Record

	M	I	NO	RUNS	AV	100	50	CT	ST
F-c	2	3	1	27	13.50	-	-	-	-

Bowling Record

	Balls	M	R	W	AV	5wI	10wM
F-c	72	2	76	0	-	-	-

Career-bests

First-class –   18* v Pakistanis at St Helen's, Swansea, 1967.

Keith Jarrett had a fine record as a cricketer and rugby player, initially at Monmouth School, with his success for the Welsh public school, seeing the young all-rounder play twice for Glamorgan during 1967. However, Keith went on to win greater fame on the rugby pitch, playing for Wales and the British Lions.

Keith Jarrett.

The son of Hal Jarrett (Vol. 2, p 290-291) his club rugby career had begun with Abertillery whilst he was still at Monmouth, but shortly after leaving school in 1966 he joined Newport. Some outstanding performances in the centre for the Rodney Parade club led to his selection in April 1967 for the match against England at the Arms Park. But the selectors chose him at full-back even though he had never played in that position before. A week before his international debut, the selectors also asked Newport to play Keith in this position against

Newbridge, but things did not go according to plan and he was switched back to his normal position at half-time.

Despite this, he made his debut in the number 15 shirt the following week and scored a try which is still regarded by afficionados of the oval ball game as amongst the top ten of all time for Wales. It came as Keith caught the ball, without breaking his stride, near the touchline on the halfway line after a kick through by an opposing back. He proceeded to sprint the sixty yards down the left wing, outflanking and outrunning the entire England defence to score in the corner. Just for good measure he converted his try with a booming kick, besides kicking two other penalties and five conversions in the 34-21 victory which prevented England from sharing the title with France.

The story also goes that later that night, and perhaps a little worse for wear, Keith was at Cardiff Bus Station looking to head back home to Newport. A driver recognized him and said "The last bus went a few minutes ago, but I'm going back to the depot so jump on and I'll ask the supervisor if its OK for me to take you to Newport." Permission was duly given but the driver was a bit puzzled when his superior, who had noticed Keith puffing away on a cigarette, suggested going on another vehicle instead. "But there's only the two of us," he said to which came the immortal reply "Take the double-decker over there. Mr Jarrett might want to go upstairs and have a smoke!"

There were no such tales of heroics during Keith's short cricketing career with Glamorgan. He had first come to the attention of the county's selectors in 1964 when,

aged sixteen, he had dismissed Gilbert Parkhouse, plus two others, whilst playing for Monmouth School against the MCC. Some further good performances with the bat and ball for Monmouth School saw Keith make his 2nd XI debut during 1965, with some wondering whether he could be a long-term replacement for the now retired Allan Watkins and another man of Monmouthshire. It duly led to a summer contract in 1967 with the Welsh county, with Keith playing regularly for the 2nd XI besides appearing against the Indians at Sophia Gardens and the Pakistani's at Swansea.

He did little of note in these two appearances for Glamorgan's 1st XI and, following his success in the red jersey of Wales in 1966/67, he opted to focus on his rugby-playing career. From May until August 1968 Keith toured South Africa with the British

Keith Jarrett bowling in the nets at Sophia Gardens during 1967.

Lions under the captaincy of Tom Kiernan, the Irish full-back. The young Welshman failed to make the Test team but continued to play for Wales and had won 10 caps when he agreed terms with Barrow and switched to rugby league after agreeing a signing-on fee of £14,000. Keith also played for Widnes and the Great Britain rugby league team, but during 1973, at the age of twenty-five, he suffered a stroke and was forced into retirement.

459
LYONS, Kevin James.

Born – Cardiff, 18 December 1946.
RHB, RM.
Professional.
Ed – Herbert Thompson Primary School and Lady Mary HS, Cardiff.
1st XI: 1967-1977.
2nd XI: 1963-1984.
Club and Ground: 1972-1983.
Clubs: Cardiff, Maesteg Celtic, St Fagans, Maesteg Town and Llanelli.
Glamorgan Assistant Coach 1972-1984; Coach of Worcestershire 1992-1993; Coach of
Cardiff UCCE 1999-2011; First-class umpire 1985-1991, 1994-1998.

Batting and Fielding Record

	M	I	NO	RUNS	AV	100	50	CT	ST
F-c	62	99	14	1673	19.68	-	9	27	-
List A	41	32	5	336	12.44	-	1	15	-

Bowling Record

	Balls	M	R	W	AV	5wI	10wM
F-c	487	13	252	2	126.00	-	-
List A	227	0	198	9	22.00	-	-

Career-bests

First-class –   92 v Cambridge University at Fenner's, Cambridge, 1972.
                1/36 v Worcestershire at Sophia Gardens, Cardiff, 1972.
List A –   56 v Nottinghamshire at Trent Bridge, 1969.
                4/61 v Warwickshire at Edgbaston, 1977.

Kevin Lyons, as seen in 1979.

Kevin Lyons has enjoyed a lifetime in first-class cricket – as a player, coach, umpire and talent scout – and apart from a brief affiliation with Worcestershire, he has spent nigh on forty years closely associated with Glamorgan and other teams in South Wales.

The Cardiff-born cricketer joined the Glamorgan staff in 1967 having spent the two previous years at the Welsh county's behest on the Lord's groundstaff under MCC coaches Len Muncer and Harry Sharp. He made his first-class debut against Hampshire at Swansea in May 1967 and showed promise as a top-order batsman. However, with the Glamorgan selectors opting for the West Indian duo of Bryan Davis, and subsequently Roy Fredericks to partner Alan Jones, Kevin found his opportunities restricted.

However, he was the regular 12th man during the Championship-winning summer of 1969 before having an extended run in the Championship-team during 1970 and 1971. During this time, he struck a pair of half-centuries against Hampshire as well as another against Sussex, besides playing a match-winning innings of 88 against the 1971 Pakistanis on a capricious surface at Sophia Gardens. Some felt that this would be the turning point in his career but the following year, Kevin announced his retirement from the first-class game to become the county's assistant coach and 2nd XI captain.

For the next twelve years he helped to groom the next generation of Glamorgan cricketers besides seeing his young charges win the Warwick Pool Under-25 competition in 1980 and the Second Eleven Championship the following year. Between 1969 and 1985 Kevin also coached in Cape Town, initially at Rondesbosch High School before securing a post with the University of Cape Town. He also acted as coach to the Western Province side and amongst his charges was Gary Kirsten, who later went on to fame with the South African national side as well as being coach of India's World Cup-winning team.

During his time in South Africa, Kevin played in the top-grade local league, besides being amongst

Kevin Lyons, in Worcestershire kit, during his time as coach of the West Midlands county.

the first group of white players to regularly visit the townships, such as Langa, to play with, and coach, the Black African cricketers. This period also saw Kevin return to the Glamorgan 1st XI when they were beset by injury, appearing twice in 1976 and in six first-class matches plus a handful of limited overs matches during 1977. With Alan Jones taking over the 2nd XI duties in 1984, Kevin then became a first-class umpire, but he returned to coaching in 1992 when he took over as Head Coach of Worcestershire.

Kevin then reverted back to umpiring in 1996, before in September 2000 becoming the Head Coach of the Cardiff University Cricketing Centre of Excellence based at the Cyncoed campus of Cardiff Metropolitan University. This led to him coaching future England players such as Rory Burns, Jack Leach and Heather Knight who were all students at the university. He remained in this capacity until 2012 before acting as Director of

Cricket at Cardiff CC as well as working as a talent scout for Glamorgan and more recently Warwickshire. In all, Kevin umpired 192 first-class and 187 List A games, whilst in July 2001 Kevin stood in the One-Day International at Northampton between England Women and their counterparts from Australia.

During his time with Glamorgan Cricket, Kevin also got into a couple of quite humorous scrapes. In 1977 he was arrested outside Lord's on the morning of the Gillette Cup after police believed that the man handing out tickets to friends outside the Grace Gates was an illegal ticket tout! This followed the time in September 1969 when Kevin was acting as twelfth man and, together with his friend Roger Davis, was responsible for the transfer and loading of their kit and other items. On this particular occasion,

Kevin Lyons, seen batting against the MCC at Lord's during the Champion County match in 1970.

Glamorgan were travelling home from The Oval, having acquired a couple of cases of champagne following their Championship success. As the game with Surrey petered out into a draw, Kevin dutifully ordered the taxi's back to London Paddington mindful that his colleagues were looking forward to finishing off the champagne during their train journey home.

As he still remembers, "The taxis reached Paddington two or three minutes before our train was due to depart. In the rush, I got all of our bags off the cars, counted them, made sure they were all there, tipped the drivers, got hold of a porter and got all the kit on the train. But as the train pulled off I said to Roger, 'I haven't put the champagne on!' And he said 'Who's going to tell him?' Him being Don, our senior pro. And then he came down the corridor of the train a couple of minutes later and asked where the bottles were. I said 'Err, I've got some bad news for you senior. I left them in the back of the taxi.' His face just dropped, just as it did when he was told he was coming off as a bowler!"

460
KINGSTON, Graham Charles.

Born – Newport, 1 November 1950.
Professional.
RHB, RM.
Ed – St Julian's HS, Newport.
1st XI: 1967-1971.
2nd XI: 1966-1971.
Colts: 1970.
Clubs: Newport, Swansea, Briton Ferry Town and Llanelli.

Batting and Fielding Record

	M	I	NO	RUNS	AV	100	50	CT	ST
F-c	9	15	2	161	12.38	-	-	4	-
List A	13	7	1	19	3.16	-	-	5	-

Bowling Record

	Balls	M	R	W	AV	5wI	10wM
F-c	360	12	210	4	52.20	-	-
List A	383	6	277	19	14.57		

Career-bests

First-class – 26 v Oxford University at BP Llandarcy, 1971.
2/18 v Worcestershire at The Gnoll, Neath, 1970.
List A – 9 v Lancashire at Sophia Gardens, Cardiff, 1970.
6/36 v Derbyshire at Ebbw Vale, 1969.

Graham Kingston was an all-rounder who spent five years on Glamorgan's books during the late 1960's and early 1970's.

The right-handed batsman and seam bowler had first impressed whilst playing as a schoolboy for Newport CC and Welsh Schools. In 1966 he appeared in the schools internationals against Ireland and England besides making his 2nd XI debut aged fifteen for the Welsh county. The following summer, Graham also played for Welsh Schools against their counterparts from India before making his Championship debut, still only Sixteen years and 302 days old against Worcestershire at Colwyn Bay during August 1967.

Graham had batted at number seven but did not bowl on his Championship debut before the

Graham Kingston.

following year opening the batting with Alan Jones in Glamorgan's Gillette Cup game at Northampton. In 1969 Graham also had a chance to display his bowling skills as, in his second appearance in the Sunday League, the teenager claimed 6/36 in the match against Derbyshire at Ebbw Vale. However, over the course of the next couple of years, Graham never reproduced similar figures with his seam bowling in subsequent appearances in List A games.

In 1969/70 Graham went on the county's tour of the West Indies and made a further first-class appearance against the Windward Islands. He played in three further Championship games, and appeared in seven Sunday League matches during 1970, but left the county's staff at the end of the 1971 season having only played that summer in the friendlies against both Oxford and Cambridge University.

Despite leaving professional cricket before his twenty-first birthday, Graham went on to enjoy a fine career with Newport CC whom he captained in 1974, 1975, 1984 and 1985, besides working as an estate agent in the town.

Derek Shackleton of Hampshire defends against Don Shepherd at Southampton in 1968. Eifion Jones is the wicket-keeper, Brian Lewis is at short-leg, whilst Tony Lewis is the fielder at mid-wicket.

1968

1968 was an historic summer for Glamorgan Cricket. For the first-ever time they took to the field with two overseas internationals in Bryan Davis of the West Indies and Majid Khan from Pakistan. The former only played a handful of games that summer whilst qualifying to play for the Welsh county but during August both were in the side as the Welsh county famously defeated the Australians as they became the first county to defeat the men in baggy green caps on successive tours.

The joyous crowd congregate at the foot of the Pavillion steps at St Helen's after Glamorgan had beaten the 1968 Australians.

The victory over the Australians at Swansea was one the highlights of Don Shepherd's career for Glamorgan with the off-cutter standing in as the Welsh county's captain for the unwell Tony Lewis and skilfully guiding his charges to a 79-run victory. They were always in command and never lost the upper hand after the first day when a superb 99 by Alan Jones plus a brilliant fifty in even time by Majid had put Glamorgan into the ascendancy. Some superb catches were also taken with the acting captain adding at the end of the game "we held the catches that mattered."

Later that month, Garry Sobers added to the list of record-breaking achievements at Swansea by becoming the first man to hit six sixes in an over. Like the victory over the Australians, the footage of Garry's outstanding feat was captured by a BBC Wales outside broadcast team, although in the case of the Bajan's feats it was purely by chance that the cameras were still rolling on the afternoon of 31 August 1968.

The BBC Wales crew were televising the match for the regional network besides providing training for a camera team from another part of England. "Let's carry on filming – something might happen" were the words of Wilf Wooller, who was leading the commentary team, to producer John Norman as the live transmission on BBC Wales came to an end. Although staff at one of the signal relay stations near St Mary's Hill in the Vale of Glamorgan were due for a break, John agreed and this world record was fortuitously captured for posterity by the BBC cameras.

461
MAJID, Jahangir Khan.

Born – Ludhiana, India, 28 September, 1946.

Professional.

RHB, RM/OB.

Ed – St Anthony's, Lahore; Aitchison College, Lahore; Government College, Lahore, Punjab University and Emmanuel College, Cambridge.

1st XI: 1968-1976.

Cap: 1968.

Lahore 1961/62-1982/83; Punjab 1964/65-1967/68; PIA 1968/69-1980/81; Cambridge University 1970-1972 (Blue all three years); Pakistan 1964/65-1982/83 (63 Tests); Queensland 1973/74.

Batting and Fielding Record

	M	I	NO	RUNS	AV	100	50	CT	ST
F-c	154	270	17	9610	37.98	21	47	155	-
List A	113	112	6	2543	23.99	-	16	34	-

Bowling Record

	Balls	M	R	W	AV	5wI	10wM
F-c	4341	216	1674	51	32.82	-	-
List A	1314	33	676	35	19.31		

Career-bests

First-class – 204 v Surrey at The Oval, 1972.

4/48 v Hampshire at Portsmouth, 1972.

List A – 97* v Gloucestershire at Bristol, 1975.

5/24 v Northamptonshire at Northampton, 1969.

In September 1969 Majid Khan played one of the greatest innings in Glamorgan's history as, on a pitch at Sophia Gardens which had a devilish streak, he scored 156 against Worcestershire in the penultimate Championship match of the summer. His masterful innings gave the Welsh county the foundation they needed to win both the game and the County title, but what made his majestic innings even more special was that no other batsman on either side looked at home on a surface of indifferent bounce and one pithily described by a visiting batsman as being like a small terraced house – "two up, two down!"

Despite the foibles of the pitch, the graceful Pakistani remained unruffled against the waspish new ball pairing of West Indian Vanburn Holder and Brian Brain, with Majid using his almost magical charm to play a series of perfectly timed and elegant strokes as he completely mastered the Worcestershire attack. Batting at number three, Majid had arrived in the middle after just a couple of overs with opening batsman Roger Davis having retired hurt retiring hurt following a painful blow on the elbow from Vanburn. Early in his own innings, Majid was also hit on the shoulder by a steeply rising delivery from the Bajan which prompted Alan Jones to walk down the wicket to check on the

Majid Khan pulls a ball to the boundary in 1969 during Glamorgan's Championship match with Worcestershire at Sophia Gardens.

Pakistani. "Majid, are you alright? I thought it had struck you on the head," enquired the left-handed opener, to which Majid calmly replied, "Alan, of course I am fine. Don't worry. Please go back to the other end!"

Alan duly did what he was told and, despite the hard ball rearing around dramatically, he remained unflustered and added 110 with Alan for the first wicket. Having serenely passed 50, he reached his 100 without any undue alarms but, by the time he got to 150, a series of others had come and gone at the other end, largely to the spin of Norman Gifford and in a bid to gain a single and protect one of his partner, Majid eventually played a rash stroke against the spinner and was caught by Ron Headley. With Roger unlikely to bat in Glamorgan's second innings, Majid opened the batting and when Eifion Jones was felled by another horrendous lifter from Vanburn, the Pakistani kept wicket in the visitor's second innings and claimed a pair of catches off the bowling of Tony Cordle and Don Shepherd before in the words of *Wisden's* correspondent "Sophia Gardens broke out in pandemonium."

Right from his first major game in Wales, Majid wooed the Welsh public with the grace and sheer eye appeal of his stroke-play. In 89 minutes before lunch on the final day of Glamorgan's match against the 1967 Pakistani's at Swansea, Majid struck an awesome 147 with 10 fours and 13 sixes, five of which came in an over from Roger Davis. As Tony Lewis remembered, "Majid was brilliant entertainment for the crowd, but it was impossible for any of the Glamorgan players to judge just how good a player he was. It was a bit of a slog; a glorious, savage, talented slog."

It was a joy to watch for the Club's Secretary Wilf Wooller who had been at Cambridge at the same time as Majid's father and had played for the University alongside Dr Jahangir Khan who was bowling during a match in 1936 at Lord's when the ball hit and killed a sparrow. Wilf could scarcely suppress his joy at Majid's boundary-laden innings and when a month or so later the TCCB decreed that counties could recruit one overseas cricketer by immediate registration, he swiftly struck a deal for the twenty-year-old to join Glamorgan the following summer.

Majid duly struck up a friendship with the Welsh county's captain, with the Pakistani lodging with Tony and his family, besides travelling together with him to away games. It was not long before Tony discovered Majid's love of Western films and ice-creams. Whilst the former only featured on rainy days with visits to a cinema, the latter were a common feature at county grounds and, as Tony recalled about the away game with Gloucestershire in 1969, "we did a deal at Cheltenham where I should buy him two ice-creams for a 50, four for a 100 and so on. That evening he was furious and angry with himself for failing. 'I wanted six or even eight ice-creams,' he said. 'Big ones, double 99s. But I only had a taste this time.' Yes, I had walked around the ground with him to the ice-cream van and paid up – two ices for a brilliant innings of 69, which turned out to be the top score of the whole match on either side. Next year, we played at Cheltenham again on a damp turning wicket. It was almost a benefit match for the spinners. I went out to join Majid at the crease when we had

Majid Khan relaxes in the Glamorgan dressing room at Sophia Gardens in 1969.

lost two wickets for 15 runs. David Allen bowled me a couple of balls that bit and turned and, at the end of the over, I wandered down to talk to Majid. 'We are going to get stuffed here if we are not careful, Maj.' He produced his severe schoolboy frown. 'Not if you are buying ice-creams again,' he announced!"

Born in Ludhiana in India, Majid grew up in Lahore, the capital of the Punjab in Pakistan and, as a schoolboy, showed promise as a pace bowler. He was a member of the Aitchison College 1st XI at the age of thirteen and was still at school during 1961/62 when he made his first-class debut for Lahore against Khairpur Division, scoring 111* and taking 6/67 with his fast bowling. After winning a place at Punjab University, he produced another outstanding performance against Karachi in the National Ayub zonal tournament. He batted at number five in the University line-up and arrived at the crease with the scoreboard reading 3-3. It soon became 5-4, but the unflappable Majid played himself in and went on to score an unbeaten double century and win the match.

Majid toured the UK in 1963 with the Pakistan Eaglets and had featured in a couple of games at Colwyn Bay but – despite his latent batting prowess – the selectors regarded his fast bowling as his stronger suit. To the delight of his father, who held a post with the Board of Control for Cricket in Pakistan, Majid made his Test debut against Australia in Karachi on 24 October 1964. He was eighteen-years 26 days old, making him the ninth youngest Test cricketer in the history of the game and, in his second over, he dismissed

Bill Lawry as the opener hit his wicket trying to hook a short ball from the debutant. Majid also removed Brian Booth with a bouncer, but after the game doubts were raised by the Australians over the legality of his action. He missed the tour to Australia as he re-modelled his action, and around the same time started to suffer with back problems. The upshot was that by the time Majid had joined Glamorgan, his batting had become his stronger suit and he had switched to bowling medium-pace off-cutters as well as off-spin, besides preferring to sleep on the floor rather than in the soft bed of a hotel!

Majid Khan, as seen during the Pakistan tour of the UK in 1967.

Having also struck centuries against Sussex, Middlesex and Kent on the Pakistani tour in 1967, and now having Test centuries under his belt, there were great expectations as Majid made his Championship debut for Glamorgan against Leicestershire at Sophia Gardens during the first week of May.

He did not disappoint and ended his first year of county cricket with 1,258 runs under his belt, plus hundreds against Sussex and Somerset. It was no coincidence either that Glamorgan rose from fourteenth up to third place in the Championship table, with Majid deservedly winning his county cap. It proved to be the *hors d-oeuvre* for a wonderful 1969 as he passed the 1,000-run mark again, besides scoring 147 against the touring West Indians at Swansea, plus 122 in the decisive victory against Middlesex – also at St Helen's – before his majestic match-winning and title-clinching innings against Worcestershire. Alex Bannister was fulsome in his praise of Majid's efforts and in his tribute in *Wisden*, following Majid's choice as one of the Five Cricketers of the Year, he wrote "As the 1969 season developed into a triumph for Glamorgan Majid's success was synonymous. It became almost an inexcusable cliché to describe his batting as sheer magic, but so often it was exactly that. While it is true that Glamorgan's victory was essentially one of good leadership, team-work and the ability to catch everything above ground, Majid was able to add a glow of inspired individualism. When he conjured 156 off Worcestershire in the crucial match on a none too easy pitch at Cardiff, a lilting Welsh voice was heard to exclaim: 'I'd pay five bob just to see this chap take guard!'"

At the end of the 1969 season, Majid went up to Emmanuel College, Cambridge and so began a phase in his life and cricketing career where he spent the next three years mixing his sporting commitments with his studies, besides playing on the shirt-front wickets at Fenner's until mid-summer before returning to the county game for the remainder of the season, with Glamorgan's supporters continuing their love affair with the quiet and unassuming Pakistani. Majid had been in the middle of his undergraduate studies in the Faculty of Arts at Government College in Lahore when agreeing to play for Glamorgan, and, after conversations with the Sri Lankan pairing of Manoharan Ponniah and Vijaya Malalasekera who were in the Cambridge XI during their game against the Welsh county at Colwyn Bay in 1968, Majid decided to enroll for a History degree.

He knew all about student life as Asad, his elder brother, had been an Oxford Blue during 1968 and 1969, whilst Javed Burki, a first cousin, had also been a leading batsman with the Dark Blues. It was no surprise either that Majid represented Emmanuel at cricket, hockey, squash and badminton, besides having his first taste of captaincy by leading the Cambridge X in 1971. He didn't though appreciate the

Majid Khan on-drives whilst batting for Cambridge University against Oxford during the 1970 Varsity Match at Lord's.

cold winter weather and the chill winds blowing in from the Fens, and during his first year in residence, he was very grateful that his Glamorgan colleagues, whilst playing Somerset at Glastonbury, had advised him to visit the Clark's factory shop where he bought a fur-lined coat and some warm shoes. The 1970 Varsity match saw Majid score a typically elegant double-century from 250 balls, besides sharing a 168-run stand for the second wicket with Philip Carling, who later became the Glamorgan Chief Executive.

However, the cricketing highlight of Majid's time at Fenner's was leading the University to a ten-wicket victory over the 1971 Pakistanis – the first victory by Cambridge over a touring team since their defeat of the 1927 New Zealanders. The students had a useful seam bowling attack, including John Spencer, who later played with distinction for Sussex, as well as Mike Selvey, another future Glamorgan captain, and Robert Hadley, a left-arm bowler from Port Talbot. John though was the star of the show taking 6/40 and exploiting the damp conditions besides extracting plenty of lateral movement, as the tourists were dismissed for 126 in 37 overs. Majid later admitted that he felt some of his countrymen were a bit complacent in their attitude to batting in the bowler-friendly conditions on the first morning at Fenner's. He then proved that run-scoring was not impossible as, opening the Cambridge batting, he reached 92* in three hours by the close of play as the students ended on 193-1 before the following day, amassing what proved to be a match-winning lead of 234.

Majid was the Cambridge captain again in 1972 and led the Light Blues to victory at Lord's as they defeated Oxford by an innings. If, as he freely admits, Majid was not the greatest History student to grace the walls of Emmanuel, he was one of their most gifted and naturally talented sportsman with his time at Cambridge, and exposure to English (and Welsh) conditions, helping significantly in his transformation from an opening bowler in Test cricket into a world-class batsman. This was clear to see in 1972 as he scored six Championship hundreds for Glamorgan, including a superb 204 against Surrey at The Oval, plus a rapid 113 against Warwickshire at Edgbaston with Majid's century in just seventy minutes winning him the Walter Lawrence Trophy for the fastest century of the season.

He also started to shine with the bat on the international stage with his breakthrough coming during the Test series in 1972/73 against Australia. He had arrived 'Down Under' with a modest record of a shade over 400 runs in 13 Tests but against an attack boasting Dennis Lillee, Jeff Thomson and Max Walker, he struck a classy 158 from 276 balls during the Second Test at Melbourne. Later that winter, he was appointed in place of Intikhab Alam as Pakistan's captain in their series back home against England. The MCC party were led by Tony Lewis as, for the first time in the game's history, both captains in a Test series were current Glamorgan players. It led to a few jocular comments as well as a cartoon in a national newspaper with Tony saying to Majid "Has Wilf Wooller given you his instructions yet?"

Over the winter months, Majid had also been confirmed as Glamorgan's new captain for 1973. He had deputized for Tony Lewis a couple of times in Championship games the previous summer and he returned to South Wales in early May ahead of scoring 1,433 runs in all first-class cricket that summer besides adding two further Championship hundreds to his record. As Tony Lewis recalled, "Majid swiftly earned the respect of every opposition and of his team as well. He was the

Majid Khan on-drives.

darling of the Welsh public. On top of his technique and the sheer eye appeal of his stroke-play, Majid possessed the pride of the Pathan. No pitch, not even the uneven strip at Sophia Gardens in Cardiff, would persuade him to throw away his wicket. He was at his most stubborn in a tight spot, and for the sake of the side would bowl too, even though he was always worried about a recurring injury to his back."

In 1974 he mixed his time with Glamorgan and Pakistan as they toured the UK, whilst in 1975 he also appeared in the inaugural World Cup, besides hitting a remarkable 50 from just 22 balls during the televised Sunday League match against Northamptonshire at Wellingborough School. In both 1974 and 1975 Majid passed the 1,400 run mark in first-class cricket and took his tally of hundreds in the UK since coming down from Cambridge to ten. His success was built around a fine technique and a simple philosophy. "When I go into bat" he said, "I regard it as a personal battle with the bowler. The other ten on the field are his helpers. I always believe the ball is there to be hit, and it is wrong to change techniques for different types of pitches. I feel it is the most certain way to get out to change your methods. I always try and play the way it comes naturally to me."

The Glamorgan squad which met Hampshire in their away contest during 1975. Standing – Greg Armstrong, John Solanky, John Hopkins, Geoff Ellis, Alan Lewis Jones, Gwyn Richards and Tony Cordle. Seated – Roger Davis, Eifion Jones, Majid Khan, Alan Jones and Malcolm Nash.

His star seemed to be in the ascent as he prepared to continue leading Glamorgan in 1976, but not all was well in the Welsh camp, with tensions that had bubbled away under the surface dramatically erupting, with those who had first championed his coronation now leading the calls – either in public or in private – for his dethronement. Nobody doubted Majid's silken grace with the bat or his abilities with ball in hand, but there were questions over his style of leadership, his apparent indifference to one-day games and a preference in the changing room to either sleep or read a book, rather than sit on the balcony with his young charges and chat to them whilst watching play and analysing what was happening out in the middle.

As Alan Jones later said, "As a person, Majid was likeable and liked by the players. He was a gentleman cricketer whom I feel would not have been out of place playing in the colonial India of EM Forster, an author Majid enjoyed reading. He unfortunately became a disillusioned captain, who allowed his casual manner to influence his professional attitudes, even to the neglect of his commitment to the team, the county and his fellow professionals. On many occasions, I can recall seeing Majid settling down to a good book or even a comfortable nap prior to going in to bat, or to a fielding position, perhaps at slip. More often than not this period of detached relaxation would be followed by an aggressive onslaught of the bowling. It did not always appear in this context to his team-mates, however, many of whom resented his apparent lack of interest in the fate of his colleagues. Majid was, and is, a super person, but in many ways he was the wrong man to captain the Welsh county of Glamorgan."

The early and mid-1970s had been quite difficult years in many ways for Glamorgan as they looked to rebuild after the retirement of several senior players, especially those who had been the cornerstones of the Championship-winning squad. In their place, were a group of young and relatively inexperienced cricketers with a different range of interests and a completely different outlook to life in general compared to the softly spoken Muslim. He had been in a similar position whilst captaining Cambridge during his second and third year, but that was student cricket – this was professional cricket and a very different proposition with the Welsh sporting public clamoring for further success after the glory of winning the Championship and twice defeating the Australians, besides calls for improved performances in one-day cricket.

Under Majid's captaincy, the Welsh county had finished in 11th place in 1973, followed by a slide down to 16th in 1974. They had risen up to 9th spot in 1975 but despite this yo-yo, there was still no sign of success in the various List A games, whilst the young colts were finding life hard on the professional circuit. The summer of 1975 had been the time to address the situation and as *Wisden*'s correspondent wrote "it was a pity that these insinuations were not brought out into the open at the time. Instead, in the absence of firm and decisive action, an already unpleasant situation was allowed to drift and, indeed, magnified."

Majid Khan.

So was Majid entirely to blame for what unfolded during 1976? As Tony later wrote, "Majid had plainly announced that he would lead on the field only, and wanted no part of the first-team organization or the constant speaking at dinners which others had done before him ...there was no way in which a twenty-six-year-old Muslim was going to be able to communicate with only a moderately talented Welsh county side. In these ways Majid Khan was a victim of the seventies. As criticism heaped up and the disloyalty, both of the players and of the Glamorgan administration which once wooed him, could be heard paraded on all home grounds, Majid returned to his introverted self. On the field, he thrust his hands deeply in his pockets, used his shirt collar as blinkers and carried on as best he could."

This sad episode in the Club's history ended with Majid quitting the county scene with photographers and the Welsh paparazzi following almost his each and every move as he made his farewell to a Club and its Secretary who had fêted his arrival in the first place but was now fiercely out-spoken in his criticism. He left South Wales having scored over 9,000 runs and recorded 21 first-class centuries, before continuing his outstanding career in international cricket having in August 1974 at Trent Bridge becoming Pakistan's first centurion in a one-day international, scoring 109 from 93 balls.

In the 1976/77 series between Pakistan and New Zealand, Majid became the fourth batsman in the game's history to score a century before lunch on the opening day of a Test match as he made an unbeaten 108 off 112 balls at Karachi. He also shone that winter on the tour of the West Indies with Majid scoring 530 Test runs as he fearlessly opened the batting against one of the most fearsome bowling attacks of the twentieth century, with his sublime 167 in Pakistan's second innings at Georgetown helping to save the game for his team.

As he had shown on the hard and pacy pitches in the Caribbean, Majid loved the challenge against the quicker bowlers and prospered again against Australia on the Pakistan tour of 1976/77 which saw Majid, plus his opening partner Sadiq Mohammed go head-to-head again in the proverbial lion's den against Lillee and Thomson. Majid enjoyed another fruitful series culminating in his moral victory at Sydney over Lillee who had vowed in an interview to knock off Majid's faded hat. Majid not only hooked Dennis for an effortless six in the midst of a fiery opening burst as Pakistan chased the modest target of 32 runs, but he also jovially handed over his famous gardener's hat to the quick bowler during the post-match presentation ceremony at Sydney!

Majid retired at the end of the 1982/83 series with New Zealand after winning 63 caps. In all first-class cricket, the right-hander scored 27,328 runs and hit 73 centuries, besides taking 223 wickets and making 410 catches, with the latter being testament to his outstanding abilities in the slips plus the way he made most catches look easy. Added to this impressive statistical record was Majid's well-known reputation as a "walker", thereby maintaining the standards of the game in an era when so-called professionalism was starting to affect the game's traditions and etiquette.

Therefore, Majid richly deserved the following words and description by Mohammad Naukhez Arsalan as "The El Magnifico of cricket. A cricketer and a gentleman. An aristocrat in the true sense…For those who have been fortunate enough to witness his presence on a cricketing field whether wielding his bat like a magic wand wearing that faded gardener's hat or standing serenely at first slip or delivering his innocuous looking off-breaks from a short run up with sleeves buttoned, there was be no sight more graceful, beholding and enriching. It just seemed that the ball just obeyed Majid. He caressed it ever so gently and it sped to the boundary like a Lewis Hamilton-driven F1 car. No brutal force, just hand-eye coordination and sheer timing. A joy to watch."

Majid Khan in his whites seen at Cardiff Arms Park in 1989 ahead of the televised Benefit Match between Rodney Ontong's Glamorgan side and the Welsh county's 1969 Championship-winning team at the Arms Park. Also seen are, left to right, Alun Williams, Henry Blofeld and Ossie Wheatley.

After retiring from professional cricket, Majid moved into broadcasting and became Controller of Sport for Pakistan Television, before becoming Chief Executive of the Pakistani Cricket Board during the 1990s. As a highly respected individual, both as a player and administrator, Majid also had a brief stint as an ICC Match Referee and, in this capacity, officiated in 4 Tests during the 1994/95 series between the West Indies and Australia. His son Bazid also played in one Test and five One-Day Internationals for Pakistan, making the Khan family the second, after the Headleys, to have three consecutive generations of Test cricketers.

462
DAVIS, Bryan Allan.

Born – Belmont, Port of Spain, 2 May, 1940.
RHB, OB.
Ed – St Mary's College, Port of Spain.
1st XI: 1968-1970.
2nd XI: 1968-1969.
Cap: 1969.
Trinidad 1959/60-1970/71; 4 Tests for the West Indies in 1964/65.

Batting and Fielding Record

	M	I	NO	RUNS	AV	100	50	CT	ST
F-c	60	103	3	28.48	29.87	1	22	67	-
List A	34	34	4	920	30.67	-	7	10	-

Bowling Record

	Balls	M	R	W	AV	5wI	10wM
F-c	444	17	229	4	57.25	-	-
List A	12	1	13	0	-	-	-

Career-bests
First-class –   103 v Surrey at The Oval, 1969.
　　　　　　　1 /2 v Trinidad at Port of Spain, 1969/70.
List A –　　　74 v Somerset at Glastonbury, 1970.

Bryan Davis was a member of Glamorgan's Championship winning team of 1969. The West Indian had joined the Welsh county in 1968 and, after qualifying for the Welsh county, he established himself as a reliable batsman and a very safe pair of hands in the slips.

　　Bryan had first played for Trinidad in October 1959 against Jamaica at Georgetown and, five years later, he won four Test caps for the West Indies during their series against Australia. Bryan opened the batting with Conrad Hunte in three of these games, making 54 and 58 at his native Port-of-Spain, plus 68 in the Test at Bridgetown. He then won selection for the tour to India and Ceylon in 1966/67 after a career-best innings of 188* as he carried his bat for the North against South Trinidad. However, he did not feature in any of the Tests on this tour and did not feature in any other matches for the West Indies.

　　He agreed terms with Glamorgan in 1968 and, besides qualifying for the Welsh county, he also played for the International Cavaliers in several of their one-day friendlies against county teams. Having made his Championship debut against Yorkshire in early May 1969 at Swansea, Bryan

Bryan Davis.

established himself as a swashbuckling, free-and-easy opening batsman and, after several weeks on the county cricket he found adjusting to slower pitches in county cricket quite difficult. Tony Lewis and others spoke to him about dropping down the order, but with more than half an eye on what the West Indies selectors would think about the prospects of the potential Test opener, Bryan did not like the idea at first, but he eventually agreed and blossomed lower down the order, with the right-handed batter proving to be a free scorer against the older ball.

Bryan duly amassed 1,148 first-class runs in 1969 with his tally including a century against Surrey in the final Championship match of the season, The following summer he amassed 1,532 runs, without adding to his century tally, but he passed 50 on fourteen occasions. 1970 however proved to be his final season of county cricket – his family had never really settled in South Wales, and he duly returned with them to the Caribbean. Bryan had wanted to continue playing for Glamorgan, but he failed to find a job in Trinidad that would allow him to play county cricket during the summer, so he reluctantly retired from first-class cricket.

During his time in the UK, Bryan secured his MCC advanced coaching certificate besides attending courses on umpiring and the preparation of pitches. He duly put these to good use as he helped to coach some of Trinidad's emerging players, before becoming Chair of Trinidad's selection committee and a member of the West Indies Cricket Board. Between 1996 and 2017 Bryan was the cricket administrator and technical director at the Queen's Park Oval in Port-of-Spain, besides being a respected commentator and writer on West Indies cricket.

Bryan Davis sweeps a ball against the 1968 Australians at Swansea, with his namesake Roger as the non-striker.

His son Gregory kept wicket for Trinidad during 1990/91 whilst his brother Charlie played in 15 Tests for the West Indies between 1968 and 1973. Charlie had played alongside Bryan on many occasions in domestic cricket and the pair were in the North Trinidad team which met East Trinidad in the Beaumont Cup Final during the last week of April 1971. However Bryan was injured whilst batting at number five and took no further part in what proved to be his final first-class match.

1969

It was a great year for Wales – the investiture at Caernarvon of Charles as Prince of Wales, the national rugby team winning the Five Nations and Tony Lewis leading Glamorgan to their second Championship title. There were synergies with the success of Wilf Wooller's team during 1948 (vol. 2, p385) – an effective opening batsman in Alan Jones, a group of fast-scoring middle-order batsmen who were at the top of their game, a probing and multi-faceted attack including top-quality spin, seam and swing bowlers, plus a cluster of outstanding fielders close to the wicket and a talented wicket-keeper who, at other times, might have won England honours.

There were important differences though as well between the team of '69 and their colleagues twenty-one years before. Rather than having a day of rest of Sundays, Tony Lewis' team were engaged in a series of limited-overs matches as the John Player Sunday League was introduced into the calendar, whilst there were also matches in the Gillette Cup for the Welsh county's team. In addition, they also had the services of a pair of Test players from overseas, with Majid Khan and Bryan Davis adding some flair and extra class to an already impressive batting line-up.

The victorious Glamorgan squad are seen in the City Hall in Cardiff during a special function to celebrate their Championship-winning success. Seated (left-to-right) – Don Shepherd, Tony Lewis, Sir Lincoln Hallinan (Lord Mayor), Rowe Harding and Alan Jones. Standing are – Roger Davis, Malcolm Nash, Eifion Jones, Tony Cordle, Peter Walker, Bryan Davis, Ossie Wheatley, Majid Khan and Wilf Wooller.

Whilst Wilf Wooller's team had been involved in several heated battles during 1948, none of these games had ended up with an MCC inquiry but that is what happened in June 1969 in one of the most bizarre matches in the Club's history. It concerned the match with Hampshire at Bournemouth where the two captains tried their best to set up a match before rain set in and with the precipitation still falling in mid-afternoon and Hampshire still 39 runs in arrears. Tony spoke with his opposite number Roy Marshall, and the two captains agreed to shake hands after the tea interval.

Tony duly reported back to his team and suggested they could get changed but Don Shepherd suggested checking with the umpires, Lloyd Budd and Peter Wight. The latter's response was "It is far too early to abandon the match." As the Hampshire players got changed and departed, Tony told his men to stay. An hour later the rain stopped and play resumed at 5.30pm. Tony Cordle marked out his run, the umpire called "Play" and, after the statutory two minutes had elapsed and no batsmen in sight, the umpires awarded the game to Glamorgan.

A heated debate subsequently took place about their decision, with the MCC initially upholding the decision. But Hampshire lodged an appeal, with Glamorgan graciously telling them there had clearly been a misunderstanding and that they would not object if the game was declared a draw. By this time, the Welsh county had built a decent lead at the top of the table and, in the words of one Glamorgan official "Who wants to be remembered as the side that became champions by virtue of some obscure regulation?"

Tony Cordle and the joyous Glamorgan team look down from the Pavillion balcony at Sophia Gardens after the Welsh county had beaten Worcestershire to win the Championship title.

463
WILLIAMS, David <u>Lawrence</u>.

Born – Tonna, 20 November 1946.
Professional.
LHB, RFM.
Ed – Neath County GS.
1st XI: 1969-1977.
2nd XI: 1965-1976.
Club and Ground: 1972-1976.
Cap: 1971.
England Under 25 1971.
Clubs: Gorseinon, Hoovers, Pontarddulais and Ynysygerwn.

Batting and Fielding Record

	M	I	NO	RUNS	AV	100	50	CT	ST
F-c	150	144	72	399	5.54	-	-	38	-
List A	138	56	30	103	3.96	-	-	14	-

Bowling Record

	Balls	M	R	W	AV	5wI	10wM
F-c	21214	816	9839	363	27.10	13	1
List A	5884	113	3716	194	19.15		

Career-bests

First-class –   37* v Essex at Chelmsford, 1969.
               7/60 v Lancashire at Blackpool, 1970.
List A –   10 v Kent at St Helen's, Swansea, 1973.
               5/30 v Hampshire at Bournemouth, 1972.

Lawrence Williams, the fast-medium bowler from Tonna, won a Championship medal with Glamorgan during his first-ever season as a professional in county cricket.

The 'Tonna Terror', as Lawrence was known, had been a leading bowler in club cricket for Ynysygerwn and Gorseinon, besides playing for Glamorgan's 2nd XI since 1965. However, as Tony Lewis and Wilf Wooller hatched their plans for an assault on the 1969 title, they realised that they needed to bolster their seam attack after the serious injury sustained by Jeff Jones and Ossie Wheatley's decision to go into semi-retirement. Their choice of Lawrence proved to be a shrewd one as his steady and probing seam bowling proved to be a fine foil to the left-arm swing of Malcolm Nash plus the more skiddy pace of Tony Cordle, whilst his grounding in club cricket meant that Lawrence became a very useful performer in one-day cricket.

Lawrence Williams.

After taking a couple of wickets on his first-class debut against Yorkshire at Swansea, Lawrence returned figures of 4/37 against Hampshire at Neath and 3/33 in the match against Somerset at Cardiff, before a dramatic new ball salvo at Sophia Gardens in the contest with Sussex. After Tony Lewis had wisely opted to bowl first after overnight rain, Lawrence ripped through the Sussex top-order and claimed the first four wickets as the South Coast club nosedived to 28-5. With Malcolm's canny swing filleting the lower order, Sussex were bundled out for 59 with Lawrence returning the commendable analysis of 15-4-23-4.

Glamorgan then responded on the drying surface by declaring on 325-6, with Roger Davis, Majid Khan, Peter Walker and Tony Cordle each registering half-centuries before dismissing Sussex for a second time as they completed an overwhelming innings victory. The following month Lawrence enjoyed himself again at Sophia Gardens as he took 5/30 in Gloucestershire's second innings as the Welsh county recorded a decisive victory against the West Country side who had spent much of the season on top of the table. Thanks to Lawrence's spell, and some excellent swing bowling form Malcolm, this victory over Gloucestershire provided the launchpad for Glamorgan's successful bid for the county title.

Lawrence also played an important hand a few weeks later, but this time in a more unlikely situation with bat in hand. Lawrence was a left-hander of modest pretensions

Lawrence Williams is struck by John Snow whilst batting against Sussex at Hove during 1970.

but in this era of limitless batting points he could also defend and hold up an end if partnered by a capable run-scorer. He had already shown this on a couple of occasions and, in the match against Middlesex at Swansea, Lawrence had gone in as night-watchman to open the batting with Roger Davis. Batting at the top of the order had never been in Lawrence's wildest dreams and his experience, albeit a brief one, helped him to get over the embarrassment of earlier in the day getting a bit confused when walking back to his mark and setting off from the wrong place too far back. The upshot was that he delivered the ball to Mike Smith, the Middlesex batsman from 27 yards, amidst much laughter with Lawrence saying to Tony Lewis "I'm sorry but I came to the end of my run!"

Returning to Lawrence's batting, the visit to Essex during the third week of August revealed, for once, a more assertive side to his approach. With every batting point likely to prove vital, Glamorgan had slumped to 147-9 at Chelmsford and no points accrued by the time Lawrence, batting at number ten, was joined by last man Don Shepherd. Against an attack boasting international bowlers in Keith Boyce, John Lever and Robin Hobbs, plus the wiles of stalwart spinners Ray East and David Acfield, the pair gleefully added 78 for the last wicket and helped Glamorgan secure three invaluable points. Lawrence was unbeaten on 37 when their doughty efforts finally ended as Don was caught playing an expansive blow against Keith Fletcher's occasional leg-breaks.

This was Lawrence's penultimate appearance of the Championship season as Ossie Wheatley returned to the starting eleven for the home match with Essex at Swansea, followed by the contest against Worcestershire at Cardiff, but even so, Lawrence duly ended his debut season with a highly creditable 56 wickets. He bettered this during 1970 as he claimed 61 first-class wickets, besides featuring in a Glamorgan side which recorded a rare Championship victory on Yorkshire soil.

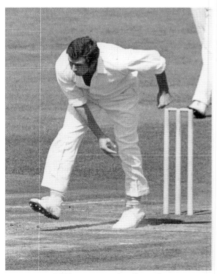

Lawrence Williams, seen bowling during 1969.

It was though a minor miracle that Glamorgan won by five wickets at Middlesbrough after a series of mishaps to the team van which was being overseen by Lawrence together with the erstwhile Kevin Lyons. All seemed to be going OK for the intrepid pair as they headed north from Birmingham after the previous match with Warwickshire. But they got lost before the van broke down on the Yorkshire Moors. The vehicle and its two weary occupants eventually reached the Acklam Park ground with half-an-hour to spare but, as fate would cruelly have it, Tony Lewis lost the toss and Lawrence had to open the bowling against the much-vaunted Yorkshire line-up. As the bowler told the local journalists, who were very interested in the nocturnal events, "Not a wink of sleep, stuck on the Yorkshire Moors overnight and then straight out of the van to bowl at Yorkshire. Where's the glamour in playing county cricket?"

1971 saw Lawrence being awarded his Glamorgan cap during a season which saw the bowler excel in the Sunday League with a Club record of 33 wickets. His *annus mirabilis* in the 40-over competition included spells of 4/21 against Leicestershire at Neath and 5/31 against Surrey at Byfleet, and may have played a role in his selection in the England Under 25 XI which met an England XI at Scarborough at the end of the season.

Lawrence took 55 first-class wickets during 1972 and the same number in 1973, plus a career-best match haul of 11/120 against Kent at Swansea where he reveled in bowler-friendly conditions at St Helen's. Like so many others of his ilk, both before and after, he found assistance in the ground's unique micro-climate on the opening day as after claiming a trio of wickets with the new ball, he returned later in the innings after the new ball had been taken and claimed three more to finish with figures of 6/67.

A violent thunderstorm broke over the ground late on the second day, leaving the entire outfield under water. Thankfully, the surface water had drained away the following morning but, with the tide coming in and warm sunshine, there was still plenty of moisture in the air to assist the bowlers as Lawrence claimed five of the first six wickets to fall as the visiting batsmen struggled for the second time in the match against the 26 year-old who had a haul of 5/53. Sensing that his bowlers would also thrive in the conditions, Mike Denness declared an hour after lunch with his side on 113-8 and left the Welsh side a target of 186 in the three remaining hours. Majid Khan, plus the fickle nature of conditions at Swansea, then made a mockery of the decision by the Kent captain with the Pakistani hitting 3 sixes and 11 fours in an unbeaten 86 as the tide went out and conditions eased with Glamorgan strolling to an eight-wicket victory.

For the third successive summer, Lawrence ended 1974 with 55 first-class wickets – it had been a season which had seen, at long last, the acquisition by the Glamorgan management of an overseas pace bowler in Greg Armstrong. It also saw Lawrence change roles to first change rather than opening the bowling, but he quickly adapted to this new role, entering the attack after an opening salvo from the West Indian and Malcolm's shrewd swing, although Greg's no-ball problem, and issues with his run-up meant, that on several occasions, not as many early wickets had fallen by the time 'The Tonna Terror' was introduced.

He only made a trio of first-class appearances during 1975 as he struggled with injuries in both his upper and lower torso. Consequently, he was only offered reduced terms for 1976, but he returned to both the Championship and one-day line-up. Nevertheless, given his decent track record in both the long and short formats of the game, he was still quite surprised to receive a letter from the Glamorgan committee midway through the summer, warning him about his performance, especially when he had taken 5/29 in a decisive spell against Hampshire at Sophia Gardens to help pave the way towards a three-wicket victory for his team, besides claiming 25 wickets in one-day games.

Several players received similar letters and, like Lawrence, they too were shocked at this quite abrupt treatment, especially when the news was leaked to the local newspapers. A match-by-match contract was subsequently offered for 1977, with Lawrence playing under this basis in a couple of one-day games during May 1977. But with no hint of a lasting contract or longer-term security, plus the presence of all-rounders Collis King, Tom Cartwright and Rodney Ontong in the Glamorgan side, Lawrence opted to call time on his county career. Had there not been so much angst off the field, and Lawrence not been troubled by some niggling injuries, he may well have had a much longer career with Glamorgan, especially in limited-overs cricket.

Lawrence returned to club cricket in South Wales and continued to be a leading performer, besides appearing in the representative matches

Lawrence Williams, seen bowling at Lord's in 1970 during the Champion County match against the MCC.

staged by the South Wales Cricket Association, and for whom he had first played as a sixteen-year-old during 1963. Between 1980 and 1985 Lawrence also played for Wales, including in the latter year, their three-day friendlies against Cambridge University at Christ College, Brecon as well as the contest against the Zimbabweans at Builth Wells.

In the game at the Brecon school, Lawrence took 4/47 in the Light Blues second innings as the Welsh team completed an innings victory over the students, with his performance both in these representative games as well as week-in, week-out in club cricket suggesting that Glamorgan could have considered offering him, at least, a contract for limited-overs cricket in 1977 and beyond. After retiring from working with the local council, Lawrence has also acted as the groundsperson at Ynysygerwn's ground north-east of Neath and close to his birthplace in Tonna.

464
THOMAS, Richard James.

Born – Griffithstown, 18 June 1942.

Non-contract.

RHB, RM.

Ed – West Mon Grammar School, Pontypool.

1st XI: 1969-1974.

2nd XI: 1965-1974.

Club: Panteg.

Batting and Fielding Record

	M	I	NO	RUNS	AV	100	50	CT	ST
F-c	1	1	1	8	-	-	-	-	-
List A	1	1	1	1	-	-	-	-	-

Bowling Record

	Balls	M	R	W	AV	5wI	10wM
F-c	62	2	40	1	40.00	-	-
List A	42	2	13	1	13.00	-	-

Career-bests

First-class –   8* v Lancashire at Aigburgh, 1974.

1/40 v Lancashire at Aigburgh, 1974.

List A –   1* v Derbyshire at Ebbw Vale, 1969.

1/13 v Derbyshire at Ebbw Vale, 1969.

Richie Thomas played for Glamorgan in a Sunday League match during 1969 as well as a Championship game five years later. He had an outstanding record in club cricket for Panteg with the right-handed all-rounder producing many fine performances for the club,

The Wales side which met the International Cavaliers at Colwyn Bay in July 1969. Sitting in the centre is Bernard Hedges, with to his right Billy Davies and Rene Clayton. Hugh Davies is stood back right next to Billy Slade with Richie Thomas standing third left in the back row.

and first appearing for the Glamorgan 2nd XI during 1965. His work commitments prevented him for playing county cricket on a frequent basis but, in 1969, Richie made his Glamorgan debut in the Sunday League fixture against Derbyshire at Ebbw Vale in 1969, and returned the typically frugal figures of 1/13 in seven overs.

Richie was also called up in 1974 when Glamorgan were beset by injuries for their Championship match with Lancashire at Liverpool. Since retiring from playing for Panteg, Richie has become a well-respected umpire in South Wales, standing in some of Glamorgan's 2nd XI matches.

465
REYNOLDS, Graham Edward Arthur.

Born – Newport, 23 September 1937.
Died – Newport, 27 February 2008.
LHB, RM.
Amateur.
Ed – St Julian's HS Newport and St Luke's College, Exeter.
1st XI: 1969-1971.
2nd XI: 1962-1977.
Club: Newport.
Football for Wales (one amateur cap in 1958/59), Newport County, Caerleon, Brecon Corries and Cwmbran Town.

Batting and Fielding Record

	M	I	NO	RUNS	AV	100	50	CT	ST
F-c	2	3	2	37	37.00	-	-	-	-
List A	11	8	5	31	10.33	-	-	2	-

Bowling Record

	Balls	M	R	W	AV	5wI	10wM
F-c	192	14	75	2	37.50	-	-
List A	492	7	347	17	20.41	1	-

Career-bests

First-class –   23* v Northamptonshire at Northampton, 1971.
                2/24 v Jamaicans at St Helen's, Swansea, 1970.

List A –   7 v Worcestershire at Stourbridge, 1969.
                5/37 v Nottinghamshire at Trent Bridge, 1969.

Graham Reynolds was a talented footballer and cricketer who briefly played for Glamorgan between 1969 and 1971.

The talented all-rounder also played football for Newport County FC, plus cricket for Newport CC. The left-handed batsman and right-arm seam bowler played the first of eleven List A games for Glamorgan in August 1969 when he played in the Welsh county's side against Worcestershire at Stourbridge as the Welsh county rested others in the big push towards the Championship title.

Graham also made two first-class appearances, against the Jamaican tourists at Swansea in 1970, and the following year in the away Championship match with Northamptonshire. However, his

Graham Reynolds.

teaching commitments in his native Newport prevented Graham from playing regularly for the Welsh county but he appeared for the county's 2nd XI from 1962 until 1977 and, as with the town's cricket club which he led for several seasons, Graham also proved to be an astute and capable captain of the county's second string.

Graham also played football for a number of Welsh League clubs including Caerleon FC, Brecon Corries FC and Cwmbran Town FC, besides winning a Welsh Amateur International cap in 1958/59. After retiring from teaching, Graham acted as Glamorgan's School Liaison Officer during the 1980s and 1990s.

1969/70

To celebrate their Championship success, Glamorgan went on their first-ever pre-season tour during April 1970 as the Welsh county visited the Caribbean for a couple of first-class games, against the Windward Islands, plus Trinidad and Tobago, as well as playing four other friendlies during a three week period.

The Glamorgan squad who played Bermuda during their tour match in 1969/70. Standing – Roger Davis, Kevin Lyons, Lawrence Williams, Bryan Davis, Graham Kingston, Malcolm Nash, Jeff Jones and Eifion Jones. Seated are Alan Jones, Peter Walker, Tony Lewis, Don Shepherd and Phil Clift, the Tour Manager.

The tour was the brainchild of Peter Walker who, together with his good friend and journalist Peter Corrigan, secured sponsorship from Rizla, the makers of cigarette papers who had a large factory in Cardiff. At a cost of just £5,000, fourteen players plus coach Phil Clift travelled to the West Indies, with Bryan Davis meeting up with the party in the Windward Islands where, like the other destinations on the tour, the cricketers stayed in small hotels or with the families of opposing players.

Three members of the tour party had already spent time overseas that winter as Tony Lewis, Alan Jones and Don Shepherd had spent February and March on the MCC tour of Ceylon, Singapore and Malaysia, Thailand and Hong Kong. The Glamorgan party also included Jeff Jones who had re-modelled his action after his injury problems and subsequent rehabilitation in 1968 and 1969. Sadly, though, it was all to no avail and it was at Gilbert Park in Trinidad on 15 April 1970 that he played his final game for the Welsh county, returning figures of 7-1-29-0 in the 40-over contest against the Trinidad Colts.

Ossie Wheatley, seen bowling during Glamorgan's tour of the West Indies during 1969/70.

1970

Amongst the many messages sent to the Glamorgan offices at 6, High Street, Cardiff following their Championship success in 1969 was one from HRH Prince Charles. The newly invested Prince of Wales congratulated the players and said "I am delighted by your splendid win, especially in this particular year. Many congratulations – do it again next year!" But Tony and his team did not obey this royal missive as they finished the 1970 season in second place in the table!

There were mitigating factors as Glamorgan were without the services of Majid Khan until the second half of the summer, whilst Alan Jones was plagued by a back ailment which forced him to take a complete break from cricket during August and September, making it a disappointing end to a year which had started with the left-hander on tour abroad with the MCC before later in the summer appearing for England against the Rest of the World at Lord's.

Glamorgan's fielding during 1970 was still of the highest order with Eifion Jones ending the summer as the leading wicket-keeper in the County Championship. His haul of 94 victims was a new Club record whilst Don Shepherd topped the national bowling averages. With 106 first-class victims to his name, 'Shep' became the most recent, and probably the very last, bowler to reach the hundred-mark in a season for the Welsh county.

But as the Club ended its 50th summer as a first-class county, there was still one dark cloud hanging over them – namely their modest record in one-day games and still no sign of success in limited-overs cricket. 1970 had seen Glamorgan exit in the second round of the Gillette Cup having travelled to Truro for the first round where, after rain interference on the first two days, they secured a 72-run victory over Cornwall, whilst in the Sunday League, they finished 16th out of 17 with just five victories in the 40-over games.

The telegram from HRH The Prince of Wales to Tony Lewis and his team after their Championship success during 1969.

466
LLEWELLYN, Michael John.

Born – Clydach, 27 November 1953.

LHB, OB.

Professional.

1st XI: 1970-1982.

2nd XI: 1969-1982.

Club and Ground: 1976.

Cap: 1977.

Wiltshire.

Clubs: Clydach, Skewen, Llangennech, Maesteg Celtic and Briton Ferry Steel.

Batting and Fielding Record

	M	I	NO	RUNS	AV	100	50	CT	ST
F-c	136	215	30	4288	23.17	3	20	87	-
List A	143	135	25	2527	22.97	-	10	41	-

Bowling Record

	Balls	M	R	W	AV	5wI	10wM
F-c	1363	62	615	23	26.73	-	-
List A							

Career-bests

First-class – 129* v Oxford University at The Parks, Oxford, 1977.

4/35 v Oxford University at The Parks, Oxford, 1970.

List A – 79* v Gloucestershire at Bristol, 1977.

Mike Llewellyn nearly became the second player in cricket history to strike a ball over the tall Pavillion at Lord's. His feat in striking the ball onto the gutter at the top of the famous and imposing building came during the 1977 Gillette Cup Final against Middlesex and was, quite literally, the high point in his thirteen-year career with Glamorgan from 1970 until 1982.

He had arrived in the middle with Glamorgan on 50-3 before, with the aid of dogged opener John Hopkins, the left-hander gave the 6,000 or so Welsh fans crammed into the ground something to cheer as the pair mounted a spirited a counter-attack. Mike was renowned for wanting to go for his shots early and, true to form, he went four, six, four from the first three balls he faced from England all-rounder Mike Gatting. He was though more guarded against the accurate off-spin of John Emburey but, in the England bowler's final over, he struck a colossal drive for six over long-on. The ball ended up in the guttering above the BBC commentary box on the top tier of the pavilion and prompted Brian Johnston, the famous *Test Match Special* commentator to wave a white handkerchief out of the window of the broadcasting box!

As Mike recalled, "I had been wanting to get after Emburey before then but I knew if I mis-hit anything it would wreck our chances of getting a total of over 150. But in his final over I had my chance and struck it clean out of the middle of my bat – it just went up and up and up. It got the loudest cheer so far and some of the Middlesex boys said 'Well done' at the end of the over. But at the end of the day, we lost the game and that was that!"

Albert Trott is the only man to have sent a ball over the pavilion, although his feat – against the 1899 Australians – came when the building did not have the modern-day top tier. Mike's blow did cause a bit of mirth within Middlesex's ranks with Wayne Daniel claiming that he had cricked his neck looking up and watching the ball sail high into the top of the pavilion, and that he would need the masseur to rub his neck before he could bowl again!

At the end of the game, many thought that Mike, rather than Clive Radley, should have been the Man-of-the-Match as his monumental blow had been the real highlight on what *Wisden's* correspondent described as "rather a dreary day's cricket." But Fred Trueman opted to go with the winning side and gave the award to the Middlesex batsman even though Clive had ridden his luck having been dropped in the slips with just two runs to name, besides surviving a couple of run out attempts as the Glamorgan fielders fumbled the ball.

Mike Llewellyn, seen batting at Lord's during the Gillette Cup final against Middlesex in 1977.

This particular day in September did not turn out the way Mike, his colleagues nor the legion of Glamorgan supporters had wanted, but a couple of weeks later there was plenty to smile about as he, Gwyn Richards and Alan Wilkins toured Canada with a party of current and former players on behalf of the Lord's Taverners as part of the charity's fund-raising activities and promotion of the game.

Mike had graduated from the Welsh Schools side of 1969 and in 1970 he made his first-class debut aged sixteen years and 202 days as a batsman and off-spinner against Oxford University at The Parks. He was one of several young spinners who were considered as potential replacements for Don Shepherd and, during 1971, he had several opportunities to display his bowling skills. Batting at number eight, the youngster failed to score on his Championship debut against Warwickshire at Cardiff and, after being taken ill during the game against the Indians at the same ground in mid-July, Mike missed the rest of the season.

The teenager returned to the 1st XI the following June for the match

Mike Llewellyn (right) alongside Gwyn Richards as Phil Clift brings on some hot drinks during Glamorgan's 2nd XI game with Hampshire at Southampton during 1973.

against Cambridge University at Swansea. After his eleven month absence, plus some decent innings for the 2nd XI, Mike's role in the team dramatically changed as, batting at number three, he became what at the time was the club's youngest centurion with an innings of 112* aged eighteen years and 213 days.

Having lost his bowling action, batting duly became Mike's forte and during 1973 he won a regular place in the Championship side. A bright future had been forecast for the blond-haired batsman but he failed to live up to his youthful promise. Despite playing some forceful cameo's, he found batting harder in Championship cricket, especially up against a diet of fast bowling, and only struck one Championship century during his career, with an unbeaten 106 against Worcestershire at Swansea in 1979. In addition, he never scored a thousand runs in a season, with 849 during 1978 being his highest aggregate in first-class games.

Mike Llewellyn congratulates Malcolm Nash after the latter's whirlwind hundred against Surrey at The Oval during 1976.

Nevertheless, he played some useful innings and during 1976 Mike was involved in an extraordinary seventh wicket stand with Malcolm Nash at The Oval. It came after Robin Jackman had wreaked havoc amongst the top-order with his five wickets seeing the Welsh county slump to 65-6. The night before Malcolm had been out with a couple of colleagues enjoying the sights and sounds of the capital city and, when Glamorgan began their innings at the start of play, he decided to take a leaf out of Majid's book and get forty winks in the changing room. But within forty minutes he, rather bleary eyed, was out in the middle. Mike was the last remaining specialist batsman and was hoping that his new partner would last longer than the others and hold an end up for him.

But Malcolm had a wild swing at the five remaining balls of the over, and prompting Mike to saunter down the wicket afterwards and admonish him by saying "What's going on, Nashy? What are you doing?" Malcolm reassured his partner that he was OK to which Mike replied "You're joking. We're lucky not to be seven down!" But Malcolm was true to his word and lived up to his nick-name of 'Superman' by blasting a six-laden century in the space of 76 minutes and went to lunch unbeaten on 119 after a fusillade of aggressive blows with Mike ironically playing second-fiddle as the pair added 171 and restored Glamorgan's fortunes as they ended on 271 with Mike's contribution being a doughty 73.

The presence of Majid Khan in Glamorgan's middle-order during 1974 and 1975 saw Mike miss out as other young batsmen were preferred to him for the Championship games. He kept his place in the one-day side and, on the back of his excellent efforts in 1977, he was awarded his county cap. By this time, he had returned to a regular berth in the three-day side but Mike lost his place in the Glamorgan side in both formats during 1981 as Javed Miandad became the Club's overseas batsman and Norman Featherstone – who had dismissed Mike in the Gillette Cup Final – was signed from Middlesex to bolster the batting line-up.

By 1982 Hugh Morris was showing rich youthful promise and, with Alan Lewis Jones' career starting to blossom, Mike was again the batsman to miss out. He duly left the staff at the end of the season and played Minor County cricket for Wiltshire during 1983. It was only though for a season – as he admitted "I was also still playing in club cricket in the South Wales leagues on the Saturday before having to drive to wherever Wiltshire were playing the next day, either home or away. Their players and officials were very pleasant but it wasn't quite the same as playing for Glamorgan

Mike Llewellyn.

week-in, week-out and playing alongside people you had known for years."

After retiring from playing as a professional in club cricket, Mike has successfully run a company manufacturing and supplying dart boards and snooker tables for pubs and sports clubs.

467
ELLIS, Geoffrey Philip.

Born – Llandudno, 24 May 1950.
Professional.
RHB, RM.
Ed – John Bright GS, Llandudno and Cardiff College of Education.
1st XI: 1970-1976.
2nd XI: 1968-1972.
Colts: 1970.
Club and Ground: 1972-1976.
Wales 1979.
Clubs: Swansea, Neath, Skewen, Llanelli, Ammanford and Mumbles.

Batting and Fielding Record

	M	I	NO	RUNS	AV	100	50	CT	ST
F-c	75	139	10	2673	20.72	1	10	24	-
List A	62	55	8	1086	23.10	-	7	15	-

Bowling Record

	Balls	M	R	W	AV	5wI	10wM
F-c	2824	105	1418	24	59.08	-	-
List A	1707	28	1214	40	30.55	-	-

Career-bests
First-class –   116 v Middlesex at Sophia Gardens, Cardiff, 1974.
              2/20 v Lancashire at St Helen's, Swansea, 1975.
List A –   97* v Yorkshire at Headingley, 1976.
              3/16 v Sussex at Hove, 1975.

Geoff Ellis.

Geoff Ellis was one of the leading schoolboy cricketers in North Wales during the late 1960's, with the Llandudno-born batsman and seam bowler also progressing from the Welsh Schools side onto the Glamorgan staff.

Having first played for the county's 2nd XI in 1968, Geoff made his debut for the 1st XI in 1970 and marked both his first-class and Championship debuts by posting assertive half-centuries opening the batting against Oxford University and Gloucestershire. The signing of Roy Fredericks, the West Indian opener as the Club's overseas player between 1971 and 1973 limited Geoff's further opportunities at the top of the batting order, but at the time he was training to be a PE teacher at Cardiff College of Education and was only available during the second half of the summer.

Geoff Ellis (left) on the player's balcony at Colwyn Bay with Alan Jones, Mike Llewellyn and Malcolm Nash.

1974 saw Geoff score his one and only Championship hundred against a high-quality Middlesex attack at Sophia Gardens and, for the next two summers, he was Alan Jones' regular opening partner in Championship cricket, besides being a member of the one-day team where his medium-pace bowling proved to be a useful asset. His best performance with the ball in these List A matches came at Hove during the 1975 Sunday League match against Sussex, with Geoff returning figures of 8-1-16-3 and also removing the home captain Tony Grieg for nought.

August 1976 saw Geoff register his highest score in List A cricket with the opener making an unbeaten 97 against Yorkshire at Headingley. At the time, it was the Club's highest-ever score in the 40-overs competition, but he was one of several players to receive letters about their future employment. With the emergence of John Hopkins as a capable top-order batsmen, Geoff left the county game at the end of 1976.

He continued to be a leading all-rounder in club cricket and played until 1988 for Wales, including appearing in the ICC Trophy during 1979. In 1983 Geoff also captained the Glamorgan 2nd XI, whilst he also played for the Wales Minor Counties team in 1988 and 1989. He also featured in the South Wales Cricket Association's representative team between 1979 and 1986, besides playing for the Wales Over 60s team from 2010 until 2015. Geoff also left teaching and followed a successful career in the pharmaceutical industry as a medical representative for Ashfield Healthcare.

468
JENKINS, Huw.

Born – Swansea, 24 October 1944.
Died – Clevedon, 21 August 2013.
Non-contract
LHB, RM.
1st XI: 1970.
2nd XI: 1966-1970.
Clubs: Gorseinon and Clevedon.

Batting and Fielding Record

	M	I	NO	RUNS	AV	100	50	CT	ST
F-c	1	2	1	81	81.00	-	1	1	-
List A	2	2	0	8	4.00	-	-	-	-

Career-bests
First-class –   65   v Oxford University at The Parks, Oxford, 1970.
List A –   8   v Gloucestershire at The Gnoll, Neath, 1970.

Huw Jenkins played for Glamorgan in two Sunday League matches during 1970, as well as their friendly against Oxford University at The Parks during the same season. He struck an attractive 65 against the students, but never appeared in Championship matches.

The left-handed batsman had a fine record with Swansea and, after some impressive innings for the Welsh Schoolboys side, he made his debut for Glamorgan 2nd XI during 1966. Huw subsequently joined the South Wales Constabulary, but he continued to enjoy much success in the South Wales Cricket Association, as well as making further appearances for Glamorgan 2nd XI.

In 1969 Huw had also been chosen by the Welsh Cricket Association in their side which met the International Cavaliers at Colwyn Bay in a special one-day game as part of the celebrations for the investiture of the Prince of Wales at Caernarvon Castle. He duly made an unbeaten 62 against a star-studded bowling attack. He subsequently moved to Somerset and played for many years for Clevedon.

Huw Jenkins.

469
HOPKINS, John Anthony.

Born – Maesteg, 16 June, 1953.
Professional.
RHB, OB, occ WK.
Ed – Ynysawdre CS and Trinity College, Carmarthen.
1st XI: 1970-1988.
2nd XI: 1967-1987.
Club and Ground: 1975.
Cap: 1977.
Eastern Province 1981/82.
Club: Maesteg Celtic.

Batting and Fielding Record

	M	I	NO	RUNS	AV	100	50	CT	ST
F-c	299	524	32	13610	27.66	18	64	210	1
List A	264	255	18	5657	23.86	2	33	69	1

Bowling Record

	Balls	M	R	W	AV	5wI	10wM
F-c	157	3	148	0	-	-	-

Career-bests
First-class   230 v Worcestershire at Worcester, 1977.
List A   130* v Somerset at Bath, 1983.

John Hopkins, as seen during 1970.

John Hopkins was born just a six hit away from Maesteg Celtic's cricket ground, so it was no surprise that he and his brother Jeff had careers as professional cricketers. Jeff acted as understudy to John Murray for a number of years at Middlesex, whilst another brother Ken won a rugby Blue at Oxford playing at full-back in the 1978 Varsity Match.

Known affectionately to all as 'Ponty', John's nickname stemmed from his successful partnership opening the batting with Alan Jones, with one wag in the Welsh county's changing room comparing the pairing to the cartoon characters 'Ponty and Pop', created by Gren of the *South Wales Echo*. Their paths had first crossed in a Benefit Match at Maesteg during 1968 when John was barely fifteen years old. The short and stocky teenager had come into bat against for the local side against the county professionals and, in what was at the time

256

his rather ungainly way garnered some runs. It led to some uncomplimentary and critical comments from Alan's colleagues in the slips, but then Bryan Davis chipped "Hang on boys, the kid is playing every ball in the middle of the bat!"

The name of the youngster from Maesteg Celtic duly went down into the coaches' notebooks and, later that summer, he played for the Glamorgan Colts in a match at BP Llandarcy. Since 1966, on the recommendation of Cyril Evans, the Maesteg club's coach, John had attended the Indoor School at Neath and had first come under the tutelage of Phil Clift. After his innings in the Benefit match, Alan and Kevin Lyons were also able to put some gloss on John's steadfast technique. His temperament remained unwavering, especially on the hard and skiddy surfaces in the Neath Indoor School as the ball flew around during the winter coaching sessions. Whereas some batsmen look good in the nets yet struggle in the middle, John remained no different outside in the fresh air and, during his early innings for Glamorgan, he won favourable comments from colleagues and opponents alike for his technique, plus his ice-cool and unflappable manner.

After a short spell on the MCC groundstaff, John made his Glamorgan debut in 1970 as a solid batsman and also an occasional wicket-keeper. Indeed, he created several records by becoming the youngest ever wicket-keeper in both the Sunday League competition and for Glamorgan in any form of cricket when he kept wicket against Northamptonshire at Sophia Gardens aged 17 years and 68 days.

There were other games where John's spritely fielding in the deep also drew praise, as in May 1971 during the Championship match against Gloucestershire at Colwyn Bay. As journalist John Billot recalled, John came running along the boundary "giving a one-man impression of the Maesteg pack hunting a nervous fly-half. David Shepherd had just tonked a delivery from Roger Davis just about as hard as he could hit anybody, aiming to send the ball soaring out into Penrhyn Avenue, but along came young Hopkins to hurl himself, like a human javelin. There did not seem a chance in a million of him getting within a yard of the ball. Yet one arm telescoped to its extremity as he slid across the turf with the ball nestling in his fingers he lay there in front of the press tent, spread out like the racing page of the *Western Mail* on the dressing room table!"

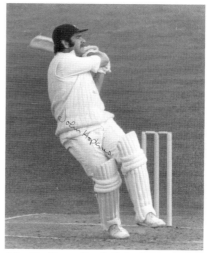

John Hopkins pulls a ball for four against Middlesex during the Gillette Cup Final at Lord's in 1977.

The regular presence of Eifion Jones behind the stumps allowed John to develop his batting skills during the 1970's as he completed his college studies in Carmarthen and started teaching. But deep down John hankered after a full-time career in county cricket so he decided to leave teaching and joined the Glamorgan staff at the start of the

1977 season. It was therefore no surprise with Roger Davis having departed the Club the previous summer that Alan approached John and asked if he would like to open the batting with him. "I've never opened an innings in my life, not even at Club level," replied John to which Alan replied "Well, now is the time to start." John duly said, "OK, I'll give it a go!"

Alan's hunch proved correct and during their partnership until Alan's retirement at the end of the 1983 season, the pair became Glamorgan's most productive opening partnership in Championship cricket since Gilbert Parkhouse and Bernard Hedges. It was also a period which saw John score thirteen hundreds, including four during 1981 with centuries against Leicestershire, Hampshire, Yorkshire and Worcestershire. His consistency duly brought the following tribute from Alan during his final summer of playing county cricket – "John is the ideal man for any situation – he's a fighter, he has a big heart and, if my life depended on it, I would always have John Hopkins as my batting partner."

During his first season as an opener, John compiled a career-best 230 against Worcestershire at New Road. At the time, it was the highest post-War Championship score for the Welsh county, and the fourth best overall, having been achieved during an opening partnership of 253 with Alan. It was also an innings which won John his county cap with the presentation taking place at lunch on the second day at Worcester with John still unbeaten.

Two months later, John was a member of the Glamorgan side which met Middlesex in the Gillette Cup Final having won the Man-of-the-Match Award after an excellent innings in the semi-final at Swansea as the Welsh county defeated Leicestershire and clinched a place in their first-ever one-day final at Lord's. It proved to be a bitter-sweet occasion for the opener as he helped Mike Llewellyn mount a rearguard action after the loss of three early wickets, but Middlesex went on to triumph by five wickets. "The support we received from the Welsh public was tremendous", he later recalled, "and it was the first, and probably only time, in my career where every run I scored was accompanied by a huge roar. It was almost like playing the final at Cardiff Arms Park! I felt dejected at the time that we had let all of those people down, but I can look back on it now as a memorable day that will live with me for the rest of my life."

By the end of the 1977 season, John had established himself as an opening batsman with a rock solid defence, allied to skilled and selective strokeplay against the new ball. On several

John Hopkins, seen batting for Glamorgan during 1985.

occasions he had shown himself to be resolute and brave when the ball was flying around at helmet height, and on one occasion was struck on the chin by Richard Hadlee of New

Zealand and continued batting until the next interval, believing that it had only left a small graze on his face. After coming off the field, the medics thought otherwise and John went to the nearest A&E to have four stitches put into the wound.

Although there were many quicker bowlers on the county circuit at the time, the New Zealander was the bowler who troubled John most of all during this time opening the batting. As John later said, "his control was immaculate. Though his pace was not frightening, it was what he did with the ball off the pitch that caused me problems."

John's powers of courage, concentration and determination also drew attention from England selectors, and in 1977/78 he won a Whitbread scholarship to play club cricket in Melbourne in Australia. Unfortunately, due to a serious family illness, he had to return home and experienced only a couple of months 'down under'. Nevertheless, at the start of the 1978 season John was also selected to play for the MCC against the Pakistani tourists, but this was the closest that he ever came to higher honours.

He duly became the sheet anchor of many Glamorgan innings, both in the County Championship and in the one-day competitions. Indeed, in 1983 he established another Club record with an innings of 130 in the Sunday League fixture against Somerset at Bath – this remained for fourteen years the highest score in the competition by a Glamorgan batsman. In his penultimate match for Glamorgan, against the 1988 West Indians at Swansea, he also produced a masterclass in how to play fast bowling as he complied a typically gritty 87 against an attack featuring Ian Bishop, Malcolm Marshall, Patrick Patterson and Courtney Walsh.

John Hopkins.

John Hopkins, Ravi Shastri and Hugh Morris on the pavillion balcony at St Helen's, Swansea during 1987.

A trademark of any innings by John was that whether he had scored 0 or 200, he would slowly walk back to the pavillion, dragging his bat behind him, and looking like the man who had chosen the winning numbers in the National Lottery but had lost his entry slip! He never smiled when he walked off the field having struck his maiden century against Warwickshire at Edgbaston in 1976, nor at Swansea against Derbyshire in 1983 when he became only the third Glamorgan batsman since the Second World War to carry his bat through a completed innings. Like at New Road in 1977 after his double-century, he merely raised hiss bat aloft to acknowledge the crowd's applause as he left the field, but his head was still bowed as if he had committed the greatest crime in the world by getting out!

John was awarded a Benefit in 1986 – a summer which saw him score his final hundred for the Club with a fine 142 against the New Zealanders at Swansea. Having trained to be a schoolteacher John followed his brother into the world of education by teaching up until 1977 when he became a full-time cricket professional. After retiring from playing at the end of the 1988 season, John opted not to return to the classroom and instead joined the Bristol and West Building Society and, for many years, was the manager of their branch in Merthyr.

470
JONES, David Aneurin.

Born – St Asaph, 21 January 1950.
Non-contract.
RHB.
Ed – St Asaph GS.
1st XI: 1970.
2nd XI: 1968-1974.
Warwickshire 2nd XI 1970; Wales 1971-1985; North Wales 1972-1975; Denbighshire.
Clubs: St Asaph, Colwyn Bay, Marchwiel, Hereford City.

Batting and Fielding Record

	M	I	NO	RUNS	AV	100	50	CT	ST
Friendly	1	2	-	29	14.50	-	-	-	-

Career-best
Friendly   20 v Jamaicans at Colwyn Bay, 1970.

David Jones was a stalwart of club cricket in North Wales during the 1970s and 1980s, with the opening batsman making one appearance for Glamorgan in 1970, besides appearing in the ICC Trophy for Wales in 1979.

Born and raised in St Asaph, David won a place in the Welsh Schools side in 1967 and 1968, besides making his debut for Glamorgan 2nd XI in the latter season. He duly won a place in the Glamorgan side which met the Jamaicans in a two-day friendly at Colwyn Bay – the two teams had met the previous week in a three-day contest at Swansea. The

David Jones.

match at the Rhos-on-Sea ground saw David open the batting with Geoff Ellis, another member of the successful schoolboys side and a fellow North Walian. The pair shared a half-century stand before David was bowled by Lyndel Wright for 20. Second time around, he was run out for 9 as the friendly ended in a draw.

Although David was never chosen again for a 1st XI match, he did appear for the next few years in the county's 2nd XI, as well as being a regular face in the Wales team. In 1979 David was a member of the Wales squad for the ICC Trophy with the right-hander playing against the Netherlands, Israel and the USA.

David was also a regular in both the Denbighshire and North Wales sides throughout the 1970s. In 1972 he appeared for North Wales against East Africa at Colwyn Bay, before three years later appearing against them for Wales in a World Cup warm-up match at Swansea. David also played basketball for Wales.

1971

The highlight of 1971 was Glamorgan's 46-run victory over the Pakistanis at Swansea. Such an outcome though had seemed unlikely on the first day as Intikhab Alam claimed 7/37 as the Welsh county were dismissed for 114. But a five-wicket haul from Malcolm Nash meant that the tourists over gained a first innings lead of 44, before a career-best innings by Kevin Lyons, who occupied the crease for three and a quarter-hours, led a Welsh rally. Thanks to useful contributions from others, the Pakistanis were left needing 279 to win on the final day but, with Don Shepherd making early inroads, their task became an uphill one and they had only reached 232 when Malcolm claimed the final wicket.

Only three Championship matches were won as Glamorgan slipped to 15th place in the table. In their defence, a spate of injuries did not help, especially the sickening blow suffered to his head by Roger Davis whilst fielding at short-leg in the game with Warwickshire. With Majid Khan at Cambridge until mid-summer and other front-line batsmen on the sidelines, the Welsh county's line-up often had an unfamiliar and inexperienced feel.

They also enjoyed a curate's egg of a summer in one-day games, starting and ending the season with some decent victories, but being erratic and inconsistent in between. At their best, Glamorgan could give any county a decent run for their money, as exemplified in the final Sunday game of the summer as the Welsh county met Lancashire at Old Trafford. The Red Roses were on the verge of winning the League, but Majid Khan helped to turn the tables on Lancashire in front of the BBC TV cameras plus a large and partisan crowd.

The Glamorgan squad of 1971 seen at Sophia Gardens. Standing – Eifion Jones, Roy Fredericks, Malcolm Nash, Lawrence Williams, Roger Davis, Kevin Lyons and Mike Llewellyn. Seated – Tony Cordle, Don Shepherd, Tony Lewis, Peter Walker and Alan Jones.

Majid began with a composed 37 whilst Tony Lewis also chipped in with 39 as Glamorgan ended on 143.

It seemed a modest total but after the dangerous Farokh Engineer departed early, Majid's accurate cutters accounted for three Lancashire men, all for just 13 runs, including West Indian Clive Lloyd who had played a series of match-winning innings earlier in the season. The visiting spinners then snuffed out the lower order as Glamorgan ended their 40-over campaign with a handsome win by 34 runs.

471
FREDERICKS, Roy Clifton.

Born – Blairmont, British Guiana, 11 November 1942.
Died – New York, 5 September 2000.
Professional.
LHB, SLA.
Ed – New Amsterdam TC, British Guiana.
1st XI: 1971-1973.
Club and Ground: 1972.
Cap: 1971.
Guyana 1963/64-1982/83; 59 Tests for the West Indies 1968/69-1976/77.

Batting and Fielding Record

	M	I	NO	RUNS	AV	100	50	CT	ST
F-c	45	80	8	2991	41.54	7	12	21	-
List A	45	45	0	1047	23.26	-	7	24	-

Bowling Record

	Balls	M	R	W	AV	5wI	10wM
F-c	1243	45	667	20	33.35	-	-
List A	41	0	35	1	35.00	-	-

Career-bests

First-class – 228* v Northamptonshire at St Helen's, Swansea, 1972.
            3/37 v Northamptonshire at St Helen's, Swansea, 1971.
List A –   87 v Hampshire at Bournemouth, 1972.
            1/17 v Nottinghamshire at Trent Bridge, 1971.

The effervescent Roy Fredericks added a touch of Caribbean flair to the Glamorgan batting during his three-year association with the Welsh county during the early 1970s and, had circumstances been different, the Guyanese left-hander might have enjoyed a longer career with the Club.

'Fredo', as he was christened by his county colleagues, joined the Glamorgan staff – on the advice of Jeff Stolmeyer – ahead of the 1971 season following Bryan Davis' decision not to return to South Wales. He had already played in fourteen Test Matches, the first of which came on the West Indies tour to Australia in 1968/69. Roy had also made a very favourable impression during the tour to England in 1969 with Glamorgan beating other teams in a race for his signature as he agreed a three-year contract with the Welsh county.

Roy Fredericks.

The short and powerfully-built batsman, blessed with good eyes, fast feet and muscular forearms duly marked his Championship debut, against Nottinghamshire at Trent Bridge, with a stunning three-hour century. Having top-scored with 66 in the first innings, and opening the batting with Alan Jones, he made an unbeaten 145 in the second. In all, he struck two huge sixes and fourteen blistering fours to cheer his colleagues on a chilly and overcast day in Nottingham. As his opening partner and room-mate on away trips later recalled "It was a superb century in totally alien surroundings, with new team mates. A remarkable performance...but Roy Fredericks had arrived! He had announced himself in the way he knew best, by scoring runs." Together with five wickets with his unorthodox wrist-spin, and a mix of googlies and chinamen, it was a performance which won Roy his Glamorgan cap.

But from the highs of Trent Bridge to the lows of Sophia Gardens as, in the following match, against Worcestershire at Cardiff, Roy was struck on his right forearm by a

Roy Fredericks and Alan Jones walking out to bat at Swansea during their record-breaking opening stand against Northamptonshire in 1972.

vicious lifting delivery from Vanburn Holder, ironically his West Indian team-mate. The blow fractured a bone and saw Roy on the sidelines until July – nevertheless, he still managed to top the Club's batting averages with 1,377 first-class runs at an average of 46. Roy continued in productive vein the following season, during which he shared a Club record first wicket stand of 330 with Alan on the second day of the match with Northamptonshire at Swansea.

Roy's innings, full of calypso cricket, showcased his talents, especially his quick-silver reflexes and ability to swifly get into position, allied to an attacking instinct, and a willingness to take on the bowlers, safe in the knowledge that he had a wide range of shots in his locker. He occupied the crease for five hours, striking 3 sixes and 32 fours as Alan Jones played the role of sheet anchor and so enraptured the Swansea faithful that a group, sat on the balcony of the Pavillion, approached Wilf Wooller, the Club's Secretary, for permission to undertake a collection from the spectators in gratitude of the batsman's efforts – and so were born the St Helen's Balconiers who since that sun-kissed afternoon overlooking Swansea Bay have supported and encouraged the Welsh county's players. His outstanding efforts though did not produce a Glamorgan victory as seven wickets tumbled for seven runs against Bob Cottam and Bishen Bedi with Glamorgan needing 42 to win in ten overs.

As well as awe, however, there was also annoyance when watching Roy with bat in hand, as in the game – also at Swansea – against Yorkshire in 1971. The Tykes had left

Glamorgan half an hour or so to bat on the opening day after centuries from Phil Sharpe and Doug Padgett had seen the visitors to 353-2. But, after a flurry of singles at the start of the Glamorgan innings, Chris Old bowled a short ball down the leg-side against which Roy, with a huge swing, pulled the ball high in the air and straight into the hands of Tony Nicholson positioned on the fine-leg boundary. Majid followed early on the second morning and, despite a resolute and unbeaten 86 from Tony Lewis, the Welsh county followed-on before rain washed out the final day's play.

However, Roy had already made Yorkshire pay for the events of Saturday evening when walking off their fielders had gleefully told Alan that they could dismiss Roy any time they fancied because he couldn't resist the temptation to hook. Alan duly told Roy the gist of this conversation, to which he replied "We'll see about that, old chap," before the following day, in the Sunday League fixture taking apart the Yorkshire attack striking 7 sixes and 8 fours in a rapid 84 as Glamorgan emphatically won by six wickets.

Nevertheless, the Championship game with Yorkshire in 1971 was an example where Roy was, perhaps, too impetuous as an opening batsman, and as *Wisden*'s correspondent wrote in 1972, "there were some who even believed that Fredericks' adventurous approach was an embarrassment. He was a law unto himself. And if he did occasionally stray from the text-book in attempting the unorthodox when the more conventional county opening batsman would have 'pushed straight down the line', let it also be admitted that Fredericks brought a breezier and fresher gust of gaiety to the cricket grounds of South Wales. His two innings at Swansea against Northamptonshire and Yorkshire in the John Player Sunday League will remain in my memory of cricket cameos for all time, if only for the joyous abandon of his batting."

There was no doubting however his commitment to Glamorgan Cricket, nor his infectious enthusiasm which made him a popular figure in the changing room. As Alan wrote, "Roy always gave 100 % for his adopted county and worried if things were not going well…. He enjoyed challenges and he certainly had plenty of those with us." But there was a lobby on the committee who reasoned that with Majid Khan having come down from Cambridge and available more frequently, they already possessed one world-class batsman but still desperately needed a top-class strike bowler. Others argued that the slow and sandy pitches of South Wales would negate even the fastest of bowlers, and argued that Roy's services should be retained. However, only by a casting vote, the committee agreed that rather than filling their second overseas berth with Roy, they should secure an overseas fast bowler instead for 1974.

Roy Fredericks, seen batting for the West Indies against Glamorgan at Swansea in 1969.

As it turned out, Roy only made a handful of appearances for Glamorgan during 1973, as he was a member of the West Indian party that were on tour and taking part in the Test series with England. Roy's final Championship appearance came at Lord's during the second week of June, with the West Indian signing-off by top-scoring with a typically breezy 60 in an opening stand of 82 with Alan. Their efforts set Glamorgan well on the way towards their target of 245 in a shade over three hours and, with 19 needed from five overs and Majid in full flow, a Middlesex defeat looked on the cards. But left-armer Dennis Marriott claimed four wickets in quick succession leaving Eifion Jones to block out the final over to salvage a draw.

Roy Fredericks.

Roy had made his first-class debut for Guyana in 1963/64, with the five-foot four-inch tall batsman making 127 and 115 in the 1967 Shell Series match against Barbados. By this time, he had given up his job as a lowly clerk in a government office to concentrate on playing cricket and becoming a professional. His reward was selection for the West Indies tour to Australia in 1968/69 as well as in 1969 to England. He subsequently became a mainstay of the Caribbean side and, on the tour to England in 1973, his 150 at Edgbaston during the first innings of the Second Test with England led to Roy being named as one of Wisden's Five Cricketers of the Year.

His eight and a half hour innings was out of character with some of his more flamboyant efforts for Glamorgan, but Roy was quick to pay tribute to the Welsh county for his success "The experience I gained playing on English county wickets helped me tremendously. I never really watched the ball until I joined Glamorgan. Playing all my cricket on flat West Indian and Australian wickets had made me a little slack. You don't have to concentrate so hard at home, once you are in and got the pace of the pitch and the bounce of the ball, only fatigue should get you out. In England, it is different. You can get a ball bowled at you when you are say 40 and set, which is totally unplayable. It's made me a lot more selfish if you like. By that I mean once I get over the initial few overs, and survive, particularly in a Test match, I try to make the most of my time at the crease and not throw it away as I used to do."

However, Roy remained happiest when going for his strokes, and few will forget the way he gleefully hooked Dennis Lillee during the opening exchanges in the inaugural World Cup final at Lord's in 1975 only to clip the stumps with his feet. Some believed Roy to have been an impulsive hooker but in making this assessment, we should not forget his 40 first-class hundreds, nor his exhilarating and courageous century off 71 balls against Australia at Perth in 1975/76. His 169, opening the batting bizarrely with Bernard Julien, rendered Dennis and Jeff Thomson almost impotent.

As Ashley Mallett remembered "The West Indians had ninety minutes to bat before lunch. Fredo hit Lillee's second ball for six, with a hook. It was some statement of intent.....Fredo smashed the ball continuously, especially when he batted at the Members' End, where he hit with the strong south-easterly that blew like a mini-cyclone. His slash through backward point travelled with the velocity of a tracer bullet and was nigh on impossible to catch. There was Lillee hurling down his thunderbolts and Thomson bowling like the wind, and Freddo cutting and pulling like a man possessed. There was many a time when he cut at lifting deliveries, and at the precise instant he struck the ball, both his feet were well clear of the ground."

Having been a member of the West Indies side that won the inaugural World Cup in 1975, Roy also joined World Series Cricket in Australia during 1977/78, with his performances confirming his status as being amongst the leading left-handed opening batsmen in international cricket. It was a time as well when Roy seemed affronted by any suggestion to don a protective helmet and, despite being struck on the head by Graham McKenzie and others, he preferred to continue batting in a cap.

His 59th and final Test cap for the West Indies had come at Sabina Park, Kingston against Pakistan in April 1977, but it was not until six years later, during 1982/83 that he retired from first-class cricket having made, at the age of forty, 217 in his final game against Jamaica. He subsequently followed a career in politics, serving as Minister of Youth, Sport and Culture in Guyana.

As a youngster, Roy had also represented Guyana in table tennis and squash, before in later life coaching and managing Guyana, besides being a West Indian selector. In 1998 he had an operation for throat cancer in the United States, but his condition worsened and sadly, two years later, he died whilst undergoing further treatment in hospital in New York.

472
RICHARDS, Gwyn.

Born – Maesteg, 29 November 1951.
RHB, OB.
Professional.
1st XI: 1971-1979.
2nd XI: 1969-1976.
Club and Ground: 1972-1975.
Cap: 1976.
MCC groundstaff 1971-1972; Wales.
Clubs: Maesteg Celtic, Briton Ferry Steel, Gowerton and Pontarddulais.

Batting and Fielding Record

	M	I	NO	RUNS	AV	100	50	CT	ST
F-c	107	174	26	3370	22.77	1	15	36	-
List A	96	83	17	1058	16.03	-	2	25	-

	Balls	M	R	W	AV	5wI	10wM
F-c	4149	134	2257	48	47.02	1	-
List A	1724	24	1213	45	26.95	1	-

Career-bests

First-class – 102* v Yorkshire at Middlesbrough, 1976.
5/55 v Somerset at Taunton, 1978.
List A – 73 v Gloucestershire at Sophia Gardens, Cardiff, 1978.
5/29 v Lancashire at St Helen's, Swansea, 1977.

Gwyn Richards was amongst a group of promising homegrown players who Glamorgan blooded during the 1970s, with the Maesteg-born all-rounder being a member of the Welsh county's team that appeared in the final of the Gillette Cup in 1977.

The off-spinner bowled several accurate spells during the competition, especially in the semi-final against Leicestershire at Swansea, where Gwyn returned figures of 12-4-17-2.

Later in the match he shared a useful partnership with wicket-keeper Eifion Jones which saw Glamorgan to their victory target with fifteen balls to go, and a place in a major one day final for the first time in the Club's history, prompting Gwyn to gleefully embrace his partner and say "We've done it, Eif, we've done it!"

The following month, Gwyn also bowled an excellent containing spell in the final at Lord's against Middlesex, conceding just 23 runs from his 12 over allocation, as well as taking the wicket of Graham Barlow. It was performances such as these which had led some to suggest that Gwyn might become a successor to Don Shepherd in the Glamorgan line-up. It was not to be however, and within a couple of years of appearing in the Gillette Cup Final, Gwyn had left the county game.

Gwyn Richards, as seen in 1971.

Gwyn had progressed from club and Welsh Schools cricket to a place on the MCC groundstaff during which time he made his first-class debut for Glamorgan during 1971 whilst still at Lord's and showed promise as a middle-order batsman. It was not though until 1976 that he won a regular place in the side but, during the summer, Gwyn hit a maiden Championship century against Yorkshire at Middlesbrough and ended the year with a tally of 774 runs at an average of 36.85 besides being awarded his county cap.

August 1978 saw Gwyn, rather unwittingly, being involved in an incident during a Sunday League match against Surrey at The Oval which ended up with Robin Jackman being 'Mankaded' by Alan Wilkins. At the time, there always seemed to be a bit of a niggle when the two teams met each other and, as this example showed, it didn't take much for matters to escalate. Gwyn was bowling to Monte Lynch, with Robin Jackman as the non-striker when things started to turn sour. Gwyn had delivered a ball to Monte and was checking with umpire Ray Julian when the return throw from John Hopkins, the stand-in wicket-keeper, struck Gwyn on his arms as he tried to cover his head. The ball ricocheted away to cover with none of the Glamorgan fielders doing anything as they believed the ball was dead. But Robin yelled to Monte "Come on, there's a run there," and the pair sprinted through for a single.

The Glamorgan squad which met Warwickshire at Edgbaston in 1976. Standing – Alan Lewis Jones, Arthur Francis, Tony Allin, John Hopkins, Barry Lloyd, Alan Wilkins, Kevin Lyons and Gwyn Richards. Seated – Eifion Jones, Tony Cordle, Alan Jones, Lawrence Williams and Malcolm Nash.

Alan Jones, the Glamorgan captain, immediately remonstrated to the umpires that the ball should have been called dead, besides exchanging a few words with the Surrey batsmen about the spirit of the game and cancelling the run. But Alan's pleas were overruled, and with Monte ready to face the next from Alan Wilkins, he dutifully instructed the bowler to run in but not to let go of the ball and whip off the bails at the non-striker's end without warning Robin and running him out as he backed up. The bowler duly did as he was instructed and Robin, much to his annoyance, was given out. Further words were exchanged with Alan saying "If that's the way you want to play the game, so can we!" It was a sour incident in a game that Surrey won by two wickets and which also saw Gwyn and his colleagues being booed off the field by the partisan Surrey supporters after their local hero had been run out.

Known as 'Spitzy' (in deference to Olympic swimmer Mark Spitz) because of his inability to swim, Gwyn subsequently lost form and confidence during 1979, and following news of the signing of batsman and off-spinner Norman Featherstone from Middlesex, Gwyn left the county's staff at the end of the summer.

Around this time, he was also asked by Welsh rugby legend JJ Williams to manage his sports shop in Porthcawl. Gwyn was so successful that within six years of leaving the county game, he had purchased the business, besides opening similar premises in Port Talbot and Maesteg specializing in the sale of sports clothing, schoolwear and personalized embroidery. In recent years, he has also acted as secretary of the Glamorgan Former Players Association and overseen their annual get-together at Sophia Gardens.

473
DAVIES, Thomas *Clive.*

Born – Pontrhydyfen, 7 November 1951.
RHB, SLA.
Professional.
1st XI: 1971-1972.
2nd XI: 1970-1972.
Colts: 1970-1971.
Clubs: Neath and Maesteg Town.

Batting and Fielding Record

	M	I	NO	RUNS	AV	100	50	CT	ST
F-c	7	6	4	9	4.50	-	-	-	-

Bowling Record

	Balls	M	R	W	AV	5wI	10wM
F-c	1267	41	625	18	34.72	-	-

Career-bests

First-class –   5 v Yorkshire at St Helen's, Swansea, 1971.
        3/22 v Leicestershire at Sophia Gardens, Cardiff, 1971.

Clive Davies.

Clive Davies was another of the many promising young Welsh cricketers during the late 1960s to spend time on the MCC groundstaff with the young spinner from the Afan Valley benefitting from the tutelage of Head Coach, Len Muncer, the former Glamorgan all-rounder and purveyor of both leg-breaks and off-breaks.

Having completed his stint at Lord's, the left-arm spinner joined Glamorgan's staff in 1971 and made his first-class debut against Leicestershire at Sophia Gardens during mid-June. He claimed five wickets in the match and kept his place in the Glamorgan line-up for the following games against the Pakistanis at Swansea and Cambridge University at Pontypridd.

The match against the tourists saw a young Glamorgan side win by 46 runs, thanks to some fine new ball bowling by Malcolm Nash and the clever off-cutters of Don Shepherd. In the Pakistanis' first innings, Clive filleted their tail after Wasim Bari and Mohammad Nazir had offered some resistance. Kevin Lyons then took centre-stage in Glamorgan's second innings with 88 before the senior Glamorgan bowlers made their way through the tourists' batting. Clive again claimed a couple of wickets, including captain Intikhab Akam and, as the Glamorgan side left the field to plenty of applause, Clive and the others could take pride in being members of only the second Glamorgan side to defeat the Pakistanis.

Clive appeared in three further games that summer, all at Swansea during July and August. However, he only made a solitary appearance the following year, again at St Helen's, against Cambridge University and claimed three wickets as Glamorgan defeated the Light Blues. Despite some decent performances in 2nd XI cricket, Clive was released from the staff at the end of the 1972 season.

474
HADLEY, Dr Robert John.

Born – Neath, 22 October 1951.
RHB, LFM.
Non-contract.
Ed – Sandfields CS and St John's, Cambridge.
1st XI: 1971.
2nd XI: 1969-1971.
Cambridge University 1971-1973 (Blue all three years); Oxbridge to Malaysia and Singapore 1972/73.
Clubs: Port Talbot and Bridgend Town.

Batting and Fielding Record

	M	I	NO	RUNS	AV	100	50	CT	ST
F-c	2	3	2	4	4.00	-	-	-	-

Bowling Record

	Balls	M	R	W	AV	5wI	10wM
F-c	197	7	93	7	13.28	1	-

Career-bests

First-class –   4* v Leicestershire at Grace Road, Leicester, 1971.
             5/32 v Leicestershire at Grace Road, Leicester, 1971.

Robert Hadley, a Cambridge Blue, played twice for Glamorgan in 1971 whilst reading Medicine at Cambridge University.

Born in Neath and raised in Port Talbot, Robert played for Welsh Schools between 1968 and 1970, as well as Glamorgan 2nd XI from 1969 before reading Medicine at St John's College Cambridge. The left-arm pace bowler duly won Cricket Blues in 1971, 1972 and 1973, opening the bowling initially alongside Sussex's John Spencer and later Middlesex's Mike Selvey,

In all, Robert claimed 47 wickets at 30 runs apiece for the Light Blues including five-wicket hauls at Fenner's and Lord's. He also did not look out of place bowling alongside others with first-class experience and against the more experienced county professionals. Majid Khan had also been impressed with Robert's bowling at Fenner's and it was on the Pakistani's recommendation that the county's selectors chose him for a couple of County

Championship matches during August 1971, against Leicestershire at Grace Road and Somerset at Sophia Gardens.

Several in the Glamorgan hierarchy hoped that Robert might be a replacement for the now retired Jeff Jones besides adding further venom to the county's attack. But despite yet another five-wicket haul at Grace Road, Robert opted against being a professional cricketer and continued his medical studies, before becoming a GP in his native South Wales.

475
HARRISON, Stuart Charles.

Born – Cwmbran, 21 September 1951.
Professional.
RHB, RM.
Ed – Abersychan GS and Caerleon College of Education.
1st XI: 1971-1977.
2nd XI: 1970-1978.
Colts: 1970.
Clubs: Panteg.

Batting and Fielding Record

	M	I	NO	RUNS	AV	100	50	CT	ST
F-c	5	6	0	32	5.33	-	-	1	-
List A	10	7	4	57	19.00	-	-	1	-

Bowling Record

	Balls	M	R	W	AV	5wI	10wM
F-c	558	15	314	7	44.85	-	-
List A	448	7	347	10	34.70	-	-

Career-bests
First-class –   15 v Derbyshire at Derby, 1971.
              3/55 v Derbyshire at Buxton, 1973.
List A –   20* v Middlesex at Sophia Gardens, Cardiff, 1972.
              3/47 v Derbyshire at Buxton, 1973.

Stuart Harrison, who played for Glamorgan during the 1970s, is the patriarch of a cricketing family from Panteg with his sons David and Adam progressing in their father's footsteps from club cricket in Monmouthshire to professional cricket with the Welsh county.

The tall seam bowler progressed from the county's Colts and Welsh schoolboy teams during the late 1960s into the Glamorgan 1st XI in 1971. He made his first-class debut that summer against Somerset at Sophia Gardens before gaining a summer contract with the Welsh county as he mixed his studies at Caerleon College of Education with playing for Glamorgan.

However, Stuart only played in one Championship match in 1972 and again during

1973, and largely played in one-day cricket during this period. He was also a member of the Glamorgan Under-25 side that reached in 1972 the final of the competition at Edgbaston where they were beaten by a more experienced Warwickshire team.

Stuart subsequently opted for a career in education and taught PE for over thirty years at Llantarnam CS in Monmouthshire where amongst his charges were former Glamorgan cricketers Huw Waters and John Glover, as well as professional footballers Danny Gabbidon and Andrew Dibble. Since retiring as Head of PE at Llantarnam, Stuart has been teaching on a part-time basis at Rougemont School in Newport.

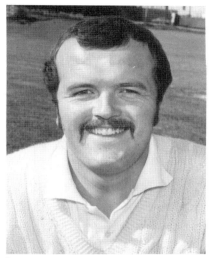

In 1977 he also re-appeared for Glamorgan in their County Championship match against Yorkshire at Cardiff when the Club were beset with injuries. He has also served on the Club's committee and remains an avid follower of the Welsh county.

Stuart Harrison.

1972

This was another nondescript summer for Glamorgan as they finished in 13th place in the Championship table and did little of real note in the Sunday League or Gillette Cup. They did however make a bright start in the newly-instigated Benson and Hedges Cup winning three of their four group games and by virtue of topping their group, they secured a home quarter-final against Warwickshire. But after overnight rain at Sophia Gardens, Lance Gibbs constrained the home batsmen, with the West Indian spinner returning the splendid figures of 11-8-5-2 as Warwickshire won by five wickets.

Tony Lewis' team only recorded a solitary Championship victory, against Hampshire at Portsmouth, and there were several occasions when they lost the initiative at vital times when they appeared to have gained the upper hand. The same happened in the closing Sunday League match against Worcestershire at Colwyn Bay where, needing three runs to win from the final over, they proceeded to lose a trio of wickets and the match by two runs.

The end of an era – Don Shepherd and the rest of the Welsh county's team in Don's final Sunday League match, against Worcestershire at Colwyn Bay. Standing – Bill Edwards, Eifion Jones, Malcolm Nash, Wilf Wooller, Roger Davis, Lawrence Williams, Roy Fredericks, Mike Llewellyn and Geoff Gadd. Seated – Majid Khan, Peter Walker, Tony Lewis, Don Shepherd, Alan Jones and Tony Cordle.

Not only was it a disappointing way to end the summer, the defeat in North Wales was not the way Don Shepherd would have wanted to bow out from the county game after twenty-three years of loyal service, with the veteran claiming the wickets of David Stewart and Norman Gifford during his final over, both with the assistance of Peter Walker who also retired from playing at the end of the summer.

These two stalwarts may have departed the county scene at the end of the season, but Wilf Wooller was still around, and ruffling a few feathers as in the rain-affected Championship game against Somerset at St Helen's. After a truncated first day, Brian Close opted to continue batting on the second before declaring in mid-afternoon, but the pedestrian pace of the Somerset innings annoyed Wilf and, as the visiting captain reached his painstaking hundred, Wilf went onto the tannoy and announced to the crowd "In view of Somerset's negative approach to this game, we are willing to refund the admission money of any spectator who wishes to call at the county office." As it happens, there were only a couple of dozen spectators in the ground, but Brian had the last laugh as Somerset the following day eased to an innings victory!

476
SOLANKY, John William.

Born – Dar-es-Salaam, Tanzania, 30 June 1942.
Died – Carrickfergus, Northern Ireland, 7 October 2003.
RHB, RM.
Professional.
Ed – Tusiime School, Dar-es-Salaam and Plymouth Polytechnic.
1st XI: 1972-1976.
2nd XI: 1971-1977.
Club and Ground: 1972-1976.
Cap: 1973.
East Africa 1963/64-1964/65; Devon 1967-1969.
Clubs: Plymouth, Torquay, Cardiff and Lisburn.

Batting and Fielding Record

	M	I	NO	RUNS	AV	100	50	CT	ST
F-c	82	134	22	2263	20.20	-	8	17	-
List A	90	75	14	1131	18.54	-	2	21	-

Bowling Record

	Balls	M	R	W	AV	5wI	10wM
F-c	9707	396	4514	176	25.64	8	-
List A	3554	58	2486	91	27.31	-	-

Career-bests

First-class –   73 v Cambridge University at St Helen's, Swansea, 1975.
        6/63 v Derbyshire at Buxton, 1975.
List A –   60 v Derbyshire at Buxton, 1975.
        4/23 v Nottinghamshire at Trent Bridge, 1973.

John Solanky, an all-rounder from East Africa, played for Glamorgan during the 1970s after a brief spell in Minor County cricket for Devon.

Born and raised in Dar-es-Salaam, John had played for Tanzania against Uganda in 1959/60 before making his first-class debut for East Africa against the MCC in 1963/64. Political unrest in Tanzania, plus the offer of a place to read engineering at Plymouth Polytechnic, led to John emigrating to the UK where he subsequently played in club and Minor County cricket in Devon.

Some excellent performances, initially for Plymouth and later Torquay in the Devon Leagues attracted the attention of talent scouts from several counties. This led to John having a trial with Glamorgan in 1971, followed by the offer of a full-time contract. The Tanzanian duly made his County Championship debut the following year against Hampshire at Neath.

John won his county cap during 1973 as he became a regular in the Glamorgan side in both three-day and one-day games. His all-round skills and capable fielding made him a very useful acquisition, especially in one-day cricket where John became a steady batsman in the middle-order with a range of wristy strokes, as befitted a talented squash player, as well as being an accurate medium-pacer with a whippy action and economical run-up.

In 1974 John also won the Gold Award in the Benson and Hedges Cup match against the Minor Counties South at Amersham having scored 47 and returned figures of 7-4-11-2. With Lawrence Williams struggling with a series of niggling injuries. John also became a useful change bowler in Championship cricket, entering the attack behind Malcolm Nash and Tony Cordle, with his nagging accuracy – after the efforts of the new ball pairing – being rewarded by a series of five-wicket hauls as well as the impressive

match figures of 9/95 against Essex at Ilford in 1973 and two years later 9/80 against Derbyshire at Buxton – a ground where he also posted his career-best score of 60 in List A games.

Over time, his bowling became his stronger suit, but John nevertheless recorded eight half-centuries and played some delightful cameos, especially in several run-chases after the two captains, as was in fashion at the time, had reached agreement on a target on the third and final afternoon of these Championship encounters. Examples included scores of 54 and 50 against Middlesex at Lord's in 1973 as well as 57 against Worcestershire at New Road in 1973.

John's county career however ended in 1977 following the emergence into the team

John Solanky.

of Rodney Ontong, plus the acquisition of West Indian all-rounder Collis King as the Club's overseas player. After briefly acting as a cricket coach and squash professional in South Wales, John moved to Northern Ireland where he played and coached with Lisburn and Cliftonville. He captained the former during 1982 and, in his new guise as an off-cutter, John formed a fine bowling partnership with Dermott Monteith, the former Middlesex off-spinner.

Having been one of the first overseas professionals to play in Ulster cricket, John also became a highly respected coach and mentor of the emerging talent. He also became renowned for his cry of "No slogging in the nets boys" as he insisted that the youngsters played properly and in the same correct manner as they would during a competitive match. During the late 1980s, John also began a second career as a Technology teacher at Hopefield High School in Newtonabbey – a position he still held until his untimely and sudden death from a heart attack with the bachelor being found dead on the floor of his flat at Greenisland during 2003.

477
WHITE, David William.

Born - Sutton Coldfield, 14 December 1935.
Died – Pulborough, 1 August 2008.
LHB, RFM.
Professional.
1st XI: 1972.
Warwickshire 2nd XI; Hampshire 1957-1971; England 1962/63 (2 Tests); International
Cavaliers to the West Indies 1964/65.
Clubs: Aston Unity, New Milton.

Batting and Fielding Record

	M	I	NO	RUNS	AV	100	50	CT	ST
F-c	1	1	0	8	8.00	-	-	-	-
List A	8	6	1	38	7.60	-	-	-	-

Bowling Record

	Balls	M	R	W	AV	5wI	10wM
F-c	106	2	32	1	32.00	-	-
List A	334	9	173	8	21.62	-	-

Career-bests

First-class –   8 v Gloucestershire at St Helen's, Swansea, 1972.
               1/32 v Gloucestershire at St Helen's, Swansea, 1972.
List A –   8 v Gloucestershire at St Helen's, Swansea, 1972.
               2/18 v Northamptonshire at Northampton, 1972.

'Butch' White joined Glamorgan in 1972 primarily to play in one-day matches, as the Welsh county desperately sought success in limited-overs cricket.

He duly appeared in eight List A games during 1972, with the veteran proving to be a useful ally to the swing of Malcolm Nash, the accurate seam of Lawrence Williams plus the skiddy pace of Tony Cordle. When the latter was injured in early July, Butch was drafted into the Glamorgan side for the Championship fixture against Gloucestershire at Swansea, but it proved to be a single innings game after torrential overnight rain and throughout the morning had flooded the St Helen's ground. With other, and younger seam bowlers emerging through the 2nd XI, this was Butch's only year with the Welsh county.

He had enjoyed an illustrious career with Hampshire that saw the fast-medium seamer play in 315 first-class

Butch White, seen bowling in the nets at Southampton where he played for many years for Hampshire.

matches between 1957 and 1971. Together with Derek Shackleton, his lively bowling helped Hampshire clinch the 1961 County Championship title. Butch took over 100 wickets in a season on four occasions during his career, besides playing in two Tests for England during the MCC tour to India and Pakistan in 1961/62.

Regarded as one of the fastest bowlers in county cricket during the early 1960s, Butch had a bustling 25-yard run ending, in the words of John Arlott, with "a mighty, convulsive heave". By the time he was playing for Glamorgan, he had lost much of this venom, but he was still a wholehearted and accurate bowler, cleverly using his ability to swing the ball in towards batsman rather than relying on raw pace.

The one blot on Butch's outstanding county career came in 1960 when he was called for throwing by Paul Gibb. The umpire later admitted that he had made a grave error, but this incident and its related furore on the South Coast was a factor behind the England selectors opting not to chose him for the national team, especially as there was plenty of controversy over the action of the South African Geoff Griffin.

Like many cricketers, golf was Butch's other great love and, after retiring from playing cricket, he moved to West Sussex, and became a marshal at Mannings Heath, where his duties included the enforcement of green fees.

478
DUDLEY-JONES, Robert David Louis.

Born – Bridgend, 26 May 1952.
RHB, RM.
Professional.
Ed – Millfield School and Cardiff College of Education.
1st XI: 1972-1974.
2nd XI: 1971-1974.
Clubs: Cardiff and Whitchurch-Heath.

Batting and Fielding Record

	M	I	NO	RUNS	AV	100	50	CT	ST
F-c	5	7	2	15	3.00	-	-	1	-
List A	5	3	0	4	1.33	-	-	1	-

Bowling Record

	Balls	M	R	W	AV	5wI	10wM
F-c	533	9	351	13	27.00	-	-
List A	175	1	131	4	32.75	-	-

Career-bests

First-class –   5 v Worcestershire at Sophia Gardens, Cardiff, 1973.
            4/31 v Hampshire at Portsmouth, 1972.
List A –   3 v Minor Counties South at Amersham, 1974.
            2/31 v Somerset at St Helen's, Swansea, 1974.

Bob Dudley-Jones was a lively right-arm seam bowler who was on Glamorgan's staff during the early 1970s.

Educated at Millfield School in Somerset, Bob played in the school's 1st XI alongside Gloucestershire's David Graveney and Jim Foat, as well as Somerset's Peter Roebuck. He subsequently progressed from the Welsh Schools team in 1971 onto Glamorgan's junior staff and in August 1972 the twenty-year-old made his first-class debut against Hampshire at Portsmouth. In his first bowl in Championship cricket, Bob took 4/31 with his brisk seamers and dismissed the dangerous Roy Marshall in each innings.

Bob Dudley-Jones.

As a result of this highly promising debut, Bob kept his place in the Glamorgan side for the remaining Championship games of the summer but he met with less success. He appeared in two further matches the following year whilst training to be a teacher at Cardiff College of Education (nowadays Cardiff Metropolitan University), but following the acquisition of Greg Armstrong, the West Indian pace bowler for 1974, Bob only appeared in a couple of Benson and Hedges games early in 1974 before opting to focus on his teaching career.

He subsequently taught at Llanishen High School in Cardiff before, in 1984, joining the brewing trade and working in Swansea as an account manager for Molson Coors, before joining the Gower Brewing Company in 2017. Bob also played rugby for both Bridgend and Cardiff, whilst his son Rob, also a back-row forward, has appeared for the Ospreys and the Wales Under 20 side, in addition to playing for Aberavon, Swansea, Esher and the Bridgend Ravens.

479
LLOYD, Barry John.

Born – Neath, 6 September 1953.
Died – Neath, 1 December 2016.
RHB, OB.
Professional.
Ed – Llangatwg CS, Neath and Bangor Normal College.
1st XI: 1972-1984.
2nd XI: 1971-1984.
Club and Ground: 1983-1996.
Cap: 1982.
MCC Young Professionals 1971-72; Wales 1984-1996; Wales Minor Counties 1988-96.
Clubs: Neath, Pontarddulais.

Batting and Fielding Record

	M	I	NO	RUNS	AV	100	50	CT	ST
F-c	147	184	47	1631	11.90	-	-	87	-
List A	94	52	18	391	11.50	-	-	24	-

Bowling Record

	Balls	M	R	W	AV	5wI	10wM
F-c	20511	779	10133	247	41.02	3	-
List A	3626	65	2397	64	37.45	-	-

Career-bests

First-class –   48 v Sussex at Sophia Gardens, Cardiff, 1982.
                8/70 v Lancashire at Sophia Gardens, Cardiff, 1981.
List A –   32 v Northamptonshire at Northampton, 1983.
                4/26 v Combined Univs. at Sophia Gardens, Cardiff, 1982.

Barry Lloyd, who shared the captaincy duties of Glamorgan during 1982 with Javed Miandad, had a fourteen year career with the Welsh county, besides being a stalwart figure in club cricket in the Neath and Swansea area.

Barry Lloyd.

He first joined the Glamorgan staff during the early 1970s following success in club cricket for Neath, with the young off-spinner being regarded as a potential successor to Don Shepherd. As a result, the Welsh county arranged for the former pupil of Llangatwg Comprehensive School to have a spell on the MCC groundstaff during 1971 and 1972.

Whilst at Lord's, Barry came under the wing of MCC Head Coach Len Muncer, another outstanding off-spinner with Glamorgan, and a measure of Barry's progress came with his debut for the Welsh county's 2nd XI in 1971, followed the next summer by his County Championship debut for Glamorgan in their end-of-season game against Gloucestershire at Bristol

After leaving the MCC groundstaff, Barry also trained as a school-teacher at Bangor Normal College, but he continued to play for the Welsh county during his vacations, and in 1973 made his debut for Glamorgan in one-day cricket in their Sunday League game against Sussex at Hove.

Having completing his studies in 1977, Barry played on a regular basis for the Welsh county in both formats of the game for the next six summers, besides helping the 2nd XI to win the Second Eleven Championship in 1980, as well as leading the 1st XI in the Tilcon Trophy games at Harrogate and winning the limited-overs competition after defeating Yorkshire and Kent. The following year, Barry claimed 53 first-class wickets at just 32 runs apiece including a career-best return of 8/70 against Lancashire at Sophia

Gardens. He then followed this in 1982 by taking 55 first-class wickets, besides claiming career-best one-day figures of 4/26 against the Combined Universities, also at Sophia Gardens.

Barry's greatest asset was his nagging accuracy and his frugal spells in one-day cricket, allied to his wicket-taking in Championship matches, led to Barry winning his county cap in 1982. It was something of a landmark summer for Barry as in 1982 he also shared captaincy duties with Javed Miandad.

With Rodney Ontong having switched to bowling off-spin, Barry had fewer opportunities during 1983 so the following year he retired from county cricket and joined the South Wales Police. Despite his new role, Barry continued to play with success in the South Wales Leagues, as well as playing for the Wales Minor County side until 1996. Indeed, his final List A appearance was for the Welsh side in 1993 in their NatWest Trophy game at Hove where Barry top-scored with an unbeaten 31 against a strong Sussex attack.

In addition, Barry played for the British Police, as well as the Welsh Cricket Association's representative team, besides appearing for Wales against both Cambridge University and Zimbabwe in 1985, plus their match the following year against Denmark. During the 1990s he also became a Coach Education tutor for the Cricket Board of Wales, and later ran Coach Development Workshops for Cricket Wales.

Despite all of these duties, Barry still found time to play on a regular basis for the Pontarddulais 1st XI from the mid-1980s until 2010. By this time, and to his great pride, his daughter Hannah had graduated from

Barry Lloyd, seen bowling against Sussex in the Sunday League game at Hastings in 1978.

playing as a young girl with Pontarddulais to being selected for the England Women's team, playing in five one-day internationals between 1999 and 2003.

1972/73

It's a quiz question that has taxed many afficionados of Glamorgan Cricket – where did Don Shepherd play his final game for Glamorgan? Many say The Oval in London, because that is where the curtain came down on his Championship career in August 1972, whilst others offer Colwyn Bay, because that's where the following month he played his final List A match for the Welsh county. However, the correct answer is Zambia because at the end of September and into early October, Glamorgan undertook a short tour of the East African country.

The visit, sponsored by the Moorwell Motor Company of Cardiff, had been the brainchild of Don himself, following a successful visit the previous autumn with Gloucestershire. His visit as a guest with the Bristol-based club also explains why the Glamorgan squad was augmented by Gloucestershire's Graham Wiltshire, plus Somerset's Brian Langford with whom Don had also played and toured overseas with for the Mendip Acorns. Several local players also helped out Glamorgan in some of their matches during their visit.

The tour itinerary included a trio of three-day matches against the Zambian national side, plus a couple of two-day games against a Copperbelt Invitation XI, with the second at Mufulira seeing Don bowl for the final time in Glamorgan ranks. There were also some one-day contests with the last being a light-hearted affair at the Shelton Oval in Lusaka as Don led a team called the Ancients and Ravens, composed of members of the local sports club plus Graham Wiltshire, against his county colleagues. After bowling eight economical but wicketless overs, Don then had a final spree with the bat hitting six fours plus a trio of sixes before being caught by Malcolm Nash off the left-arm chinamen of Roy Fredericks.

480
LANGFORD, Brian Anthony.

Born – Birmingham 17 December 1935.
Died – Taunton, 12 February 2013.
RHB, OB.
Professional.
1st XI: 1972.
Somerset 1953-1974; RAF 1954-55; MCC 1959-66; TN Pearce's XI 1972.

Batting and Fielding Record

	M	I	NO	RUNS	AV	100	50	CT	ST
Friendlies	3	2	-	61	30.50	-	-	1	-

Bowling Record

	Balls	M	R	W	AV	5wI	10wM
Friendlies	503	21	216	12	18.00	-	-

Career-bests
Friendlies –   42 v Zambia at Ndola, 1972/73.
                4/39 v Zambia at Lusaka, 1972/73.

Brian Langford.

Brian Langford, the long-serving spinner and captain of Somerset, appeared as a guest for Glamorgan on their tour to Zambia in September and October 1972.

The veteran off-spinner formed a fine pairing with Don Shepherd who led the Welsh county, besides planning the visit to East Africa, as his outstanding career came to a close. The pair had been good friends for many years with Don also playing alongside Brian for the Mendip Acorns.

At the time of his retirement at the end of the 1974 season, Brian was the third highest wicket-taker for Somerset, with a career tally of 1,390 wickets. Brian had made his first-class debut in 1953 and during his second math that year, against Kent at Bath, he took fourteen wickets in the match. In 1969 he won fame for returning the figures of 8-8-0-0 in the Sunday League match against Essex at Yeovil and he remains the only person to have bowled their full quota of overs in a List A match without conceding a run. Brian captained Somerset between 1969 and 1971, besides taking a Benefit Year in 1966, as well as a Testimonial during 1971.

481
WILTSHIRE, Graham George Morley.

Born – Chipping Sodbury, 16 April 1931.
Died – Bristol, 2 August 2017.
Professional.
RHB, RM.
1st XI: 1972/73.
Gloucestershire 1953-1960.
Clubs: Duke of Beaufort's XI, XL Club.

Batting and Fielding Record

	M	I	NO	RUNS	AV	100	50	CT	ST
Friendlies	2	-	-	-	-	-	-	1	-

Bowling Record

	Balls	M	R	W	AV	5wI	10wM
Friendlies	39	1	26	1	26.00	-	-

Career-bests
Friendlies – 1/26 v Metropolitan Sports Club at Lusaka, 1972/73.

Graham Wiltshire accompanied the Glamorgan party to Zambia in 1972/73 having toured the country the previous autumn in his capacity as Gloucestershire's coach. The former seam bowler, who was a great friend of Don Shepherd and Phil Clift, duly appeared in a couple of the one-day friendlies for the Welsh county.

He had played in 19 first-class matches for Gloucestershire between 1953 and 1960 with his finest moment coming at Headingley during 1958 when he claimed 7/52 in the rain-affected Championship match against Yorkshire. Sadly, the weather prevented the West Country side from capitalizing on his efforts as the contest ended in a soggy draw.

Graham coached Gloucestershire from 1962 until 1984, and enjoyed a Benefit Year in 1973, followed by a Testimonial in 1995.

Graham Wiltshire.

482
RUZIKE, Zivanayi Leslie.

Born – Zambia, 1955.

Non-contract.

1st XI – 1972/73.

Zambia 1972-1976; Warwickshire 2nd XI 1975-1976.

Club: Roan Antelope.

Batting and Fielding Record

	M	I	NO	RUNS	AV	100	50	CT	ST
Friendlies	2	4	1	80	26.67	-	-	2	-

Career-bests

Friendlies – 36 v Copperbelt Invitation XI at Chingola, 1972/73.

Zed Rusike.

'Zed' Ruzike was a highly promising schoolboy batsman who assisted Glamorgan during their two-day matches against a Copperbelt Invitation XI at both Chingola and Mufulira. The young opening batsman cut a favourable impression and subsequently played for Warwickshire 2nd XI whilst studying accountancy at Birmingham University.

He also played in representative cricket in Zambia before moving to work and live in Zimbabwe where he has subsequently enjoyed a highly successful business career. He is currently Chair of Dulux Paints Zimbabwe having been Managing Director of United Builders Merchants and Tractive Power Holdings. Zed has also been Chair and President of the Confederation of Zimbabwean Industries.

483
WATTS, Peter David.

Born – Henlow, Bedfordshire, 31 March 1938.

Non-contract.

LHB, LBG.

Ed – Bedford Modern School.

1st XI – 1972/73.

Bedfordshire 1955-1971; Northamptonshire 1958-1966; MCC 1960-1963; Nottinghamshire 1967; Shropshire 1969.

Club: XL Club.

Batting and Fielding Record

	M	I	NO	RUNS	AV	100	50	CT	ST
Friendlies	1	-	-	-	-	-	-	-	-

Bowling Record

	Balls	M	R	W	AV	5wI	10wM
Friendlies	72	2	35	2	17.50	-	-

Career-bests
Friendlies – 2/26 v Copperbelt Invitation XI at Chingola, 1972/73.

Peter Watts assisted Glamorgan in their two-day friendly against the Copperbelt Invitational XI at Chingola. A few days later, the leg-spinner played for the Invitation XI against the Welsh county at Mufulira with the former Northamptonshire cricketer claiming 5/38 in the two-day contest.

Born and educated in Bedfordshire, Peter had first played for his native county in Minor County cricket whilst still at school. He subsequently enjoyed a nine-year career with Northamptonshire, with the highlight being a return of 13/140 against Hampshire at Bournemouth during 1962, before spending a year with Nottinghamshire Peter subsequently played for Shropshire before returning to play for Bedfordshire. It is believed he was coaching in Zambia at the time of his selection as a guest with Glamorgan.

A postcard of Peter Watts.

He was the elder brother of Jim Watts who enjoyed a long and successful career with Northamptonshire.

484
McLEOD, Hamish G.

Non-contract.
LHB, WK.
1st XI – 1972/73.
Zambia 1968-1975/76; East Africa 1975.

Batting and Fielding Record

	M	I	NO	RUNS	AV	100	50	CT	ST
Friendlies	1	1	1	11	-	-	-	1	-

Career-bests
Friendlies – 11* v Copperbelt Invitation XI at Mufulira, 1972/73.

With Eifion Jones having sustained a minor injury in the third and final representative match against Zambia, the Welsh county borrowed Hamish McLeod, the regular wicket-keeper for the East African side, for their two-day friendly against a Copperbelt Invitation XI at Mufulira. Hamish also kept wicket for Zambia in all three of the representative matches during the Welsh county's tour, besides appearing for the Ancients and Ravens in the closing match at Lusaka.

Hamish McLeod.

Hamish had first played for Zambia against Kenya at Nairobi during September 1968 before winning selection in the East Africa team which played in the ICC World Cup during 1975. During the competition, Hamish appeared in two One-Day Internationals, each at Edgbaston against New Zealand and England. Ahead of the inaugural competition, Hamish had also featured in three warm-up games, one of which was against Glamorgan at Sophia Gardens, with the others being against Somerset at Taunton and Berkshire at Reading.

485
GREEN, B.

Non-contract.
1st XI – 1972/73.

Batting and Fielding Record

	M	I	NO	RUNS	AV	100	50	CT	ST
Friendlies	1	-	-	-	-	-	-	1	-

Bowling Record

	Balls	M	R	W	AV	5wI	10wM
Friendlies	36	-	19	-	-	-	-

He opened the bowling with Lawrence Williams for Glamorgan in the two-day friendly against the Copperbelt Invitation XI at Mufulira but did not take a wicket in his three-over spells in each innings.

1973

1973 was a year of firsts with Majid Khan becoming the first-ever overseas cricketer to be appointed as the Club's captain, whilst the summer also saw the inaugural One-Day International staged on Welsh soil. The game in question was on 18 July as England met New Zealand at Swansea as the TCCB experimented by staging matches in the Prudential Trophy series at non-Test Match venues.

From Glamorgan's perspective, the match at St Helen's proved to be a successful experiment as a crowd of just over 10,000 were present, with the Welsh county augmenting the facilities at the ground with a new scoreboard erected at the top of the bank on the eastern side and replacing the two-sided structure adjacent to Gorse Lane, besides building a new press box alongside the Pavillion and erecting five marquees on the rugby pitch in order to provide dining and catering facilities for the crowd, VIP guests and sponsors.

The new scoreboard and seating area for spectators adjacent to Bryn Road created for the One-Day International at Swansea in 1973 between England and New Zealand.

They duly saw England win by seven wickets with Dennis Amiss nominated as the Man of the Match after scoring a century. He received the award at the post-match presentations from Cyril Walters, the former Glamorgan, Worcestershire and England batsman (Vol. 2, p83-87), with the man who in 1934 had been the first Welshman to lead England in a Test Match, also adding "we are all grateful to the authorities for bringing the England side to Wales for the first time. I hope they will do it frequently in the future." He duly got his wish, but not until twenty-six years later!

With Peter Walker and Don Shepherd having retired, Tony Lewis sidelined by injury and with Roy Fredericks away on international duty, a number of Glamorgan's highly regarded colts had an extended run in the 1st XI during 1973. In all, four Championship matches were won, with the Welsh county finishing in 11th place in the table. But yet again, they had a very modest record in the one-day games and suffered nine successive defeats from 13 June until 12 August.

486
FRANCIS, David _Arthur_.

Born – Clydach, 29 November 1953.
Professional.
RHB, OB.
Ed – Birchgrove Comprehensive School, Swansea.
1st XI: 1973-1984.
2nd XI: 1971-1984.
Club and Ground: 1976.
Cap: 1982.
Wales Minor Counties 1986-1992.
Clubs: Clydach and Briton Ferry Steel.

Batting and Fielding Record

	M	I	NO	RUNS	AV	100	50	CT	ST
F-c	138	237	36	4938	24.57	3	23	62	-
List A	100	90	12	1275	16.34	1	3	36	-

Bowling Record

	Balls	M	R	W	AV	5wI	10wM
F-c	30	0	31	0	-	-	-

Career-bests
First-class – 142* v Kent at Canterbury, 1982.
List A –   101* v Warwickshire at Edgbaston, 1980.

Arthur Francis spent a dozen years on the Glamorgan staff and played in a total of 238 matches for the 1st XI from 1973 until 1984.

The right-handed batsman did not play any cricket at school, and it wasn't until the age of fifteen, through the Clydach club that he played his first organized game and subsequently received coaching. Despite his relatively late entry into the game, the blond-haired youngster showed sufficient promise to win a place in the Welsh Secondary Schools team, before being invited to Glamorgan's winter nets at the Indoor School in Neath. This duly led to an offer to join the MCC groundstaff for two years, and he duly spent 1971 and 1972 at Lord's furthering his cricketing education.

After some promising innings for the county's 2nd XI, Arthur was initially drafted into the Glamorgan side for the Sunday League match with Essex at Ebbw Vale during late May 1973. With Roy Fredericks' departure to join the West Indian tour, the nineteen-

Arthur Francis, as seen in 1973.

289

year-old made his first-class debut three weeks later against Lancashire at Swansea. He was run out for a duck in his maiden innings, but made an unbeaten 21 in the second innings and duly kept his place in the side throughout July. He had further opportunities in both three-day and one-day matches during 1974, with his swift running in the field and ambidextrous ability to throw with either arm winning favourable comment from spectators and the Media alike.

1974 also saw Arthur score his maiden half-century against Leicestershire at Sophia Gardens, with his efforts coming during a stand of 111 with John Solanky for the seventh wicket. At the time, young Arthur was batting at number seven or even number eight in the order, but it was still a steep learning curve with the loss of several experienced players all within the space of eighteen months. As he later said, "We had to play rather than being brought in quietly. It was a big jump into the 1st XI because there was such a gap between 2nd XI and first-class cricket. There were not many second chances if you made a mistake whilst batting in Championship cricket. Phil Clift helped us a lot – he kept telling us that we were good enough to make it. My problem, though was although I could play myself in, when I got bogged down, I would get myself out."

Arthur Francis, seen batting at Edgbaston during Glamorgan's Championship match with Warwickshire in 1977.

The solution to Arthur playing through sessions and building an innings was a move up the order to the number three berth. "Don't worry about playing a rash shot, just bide your time," were the words of encouragement from Phil and in 1977 Arthur made his maiden century with an innings of 110 against Warwickshire at Nuneaton. But a run of low scores and a modest summer with the bat in the Sunday League saw Arthur miss out on a place in the starting eleven for the Gillette Cup Final at Lord's, despite having scored an unbeaten 62 and being adjudged the Man of the Match in the second round victory over Worcestershire.

His form continued to be erratic for the next few seasons, but confirmation of his batting abilities came on a sunny afternoon at Edgbaston in 1980 as, in the televised Sunday League contest against Warwickshire he scored an unbeaten 101 and became only the second Glamorgan batsman in the 40-over competition to score a century. By this time though the acquisition of Javed Miandad and the signing of Norman Featherstone from Middlesex meant that Arthur had lost his place in the Championship line-up.

He bounced back in 1982 following the retirement of Norman and realizing that his career lay in the balance, Arthur enjoyed his most successful summer in first-class cricket,

Arthur Francis, as seen in 1982.

amassing 1,076 runs, and won his Glamorgan cap after making 127 against Somerset at Taunton, an unbeaten 142 against Kent at Canterbury and passing fifty on seven other occasions. The extended run in the team bolstered his confidence, but despite making 903 runs in 1983, Arthur failed to score any more hundreds in Championship cricket. With Hugh Morris and other young batsmen showing rich promise in the 2nd XI, Arthur lost his place in the 1st XI and left the county's staff at the end of the 1984 season.

Arthur continued to play with success in the South Wales Cricket Association, besides representing Wales Minor Counties until 1992. In his younger days, Arthur had also been a strong-running centre or fly-half with Vardre RFC.

487
FRANCIS, Kenneth McKoy Valentine.

Born – St Kitts, 14 March 1950.
RHB, RFM.
Professional.
1st XI: 1973.
2nd XI: 1972-1973.
Worcestershire 2nd XI 1975-1977.
Clubs: Progressive.

Batting and Fielding Record

	M	I	NO	RUNS	AV	100	50	CT	ST
List A	1	1	1	0	-	-	-	1	-

Bowling Record

	Balls	M	R	W	AV	5wI	10wM
List A	48	1	25	1	25.00	-	-

Career-bests

List A –   0* v Surrey at Sophia Gardens, Cardiff, 1973.
            1/25 v Surrey at Sophia Gardens, Cardiff, 1973.

Kenny Francis was a brisk medium-pace bowler who was on Glamorgan's staff in 1972 and 1973. During this time, he played in one Sunday League game, against Surrey at Cardiff in 1973, but the West Indian did not appear in any first-class matches.

Born and raised in St Kitts, Kenny's family moved to South Wales when he was fourteen. Success in club cricket in the Cardiff area, saw Kenny join the Glamorgan staff but apart from the Sunday League game against Surrey, he chiefly played for the Club's 2nd XI and Under-25 team.

He subsequently moved to the West Midlands and played for Worcestershire 2nd XI between 1975 and 1977, before returning to play in club cricket in Cardiff. After retiring from playing cricket, Kenny returned with his wife Jasmine to St Kitts where he is now the owner of El Fredo's, a highly successful restaurant in Basseterre. Given Kenny's background in cricket, you could be forgiven for thinking that the name of the popular eating place stems from a link with Roy Fredericks, the Caribbean batsman who was on Glamorgan's books at the same time as Kenny, but the name actually stems from various members of his family!

Kenny Francis.

488
JONES, Alan Lewis.

Born – Alltwen, 1 June 1957.
Professional.
LHB.
Ed – Ystalyfera GS and Cardiff College of Education.
1st XI: 1973-1986.
2nd XI: 1972-1986.
Club and Ground: 1996.
Cap: 1983.
DH Robins' XI to New Zealand 1974/75 and 1979/80.
Clubs: Gowerton and Neath.
Father of MA Jones.

Batting and Fielding Record

	M	I	NO	RUNS	AV	100	50	CT	ST
F-c	160	278	24	6548	25.78	5	36	104	-
List A	112	104	4	2047	20.47	-	9	35	-

Bowling Record

	Balls	M	R	W	AV	5wI	10wM
F-c	95	0	152	1	152.00	-	-
List A	4	0	5	0	-	-	-

Career-bests
First-class – 132 v Hampshire at Sophia Gardens, Cardiff, 1984.
          1/60 v Yorkshire at Sophia Gardens, Cardiff, 1984.
List A – 82 v Warwickshire at Edgbaston, 1982.

The phrase "promising young colt", coined so often during the 1960s and 1970s by Wilf Wooller during his time commentating for BBC Wales during their television coverage of Glamorgan's home matches, seemed perfectly appropriate for Alan Lewis Jones, a talented left-handed opening batsman who had made his 1st XI debut for Glamorgan, aged just sixteen years and 99 days old, in the end of season County Championship match against Gloucestershire at Bristol in 1973.

Alan Lewis Jones, as seen in 1970.

But this tag hung around his neck for the next ten years before the long-awaited award of his county cap in 1984. But professional cricket can be a cruel game and, having seemingly turned the corner, Alan suffered a career-ending injury the following summer.

Alan had been the leading batsman in the Welsh Schools teams of 1972 and 1973, besides winning selection in the National Association of Young Cricketers team in both seasons, with the latter also seeing Alan appear against Indian Schools. In 1974 Alan confirmed his rich promise by sharing a stand of 107 for the second wicket in the space of 19 overs as Glamorgan defeated Worcestershire in the Sunday league encounter at Cardiff. The following year, the eighteen-year-old hit a rapid 55 against the Australians at Swansea and shared another century partnership as he opened the batting with his older namesake. To the delight of a large and partisan crowd at St Helen's, the teenager repeatedly hooked and pulled the experienced Aussie pacemen to the boundary, and all whilst wearing *a la* Majid Khan a white sunhat.

During July and August 1976 Alan was also chosen in the England Young Cricketers parry which toured the West Indies, with the Welshman appearing in the only One-Day International of the tour alongside David Gower, Chris Cowdrey, Bill Athey, Mike Gatting, Ian Gould and Paul Allott, all of whom went on to win full England honours.

The young left-hander was regarded as the long-term successor to Alan Jones and was also given the nickname of 'Posh' (simply for having a middle name!) in order to distinguish him from his illustrious partner. After completing his studies at Cardiff College of Education (now Cardiff Metropolitan University), he had an extended run in the 1st XI during 1979 and struck half-centuries against Hampshire, Leicestershire and Derbyshire besides making 83 against Worcestershire at New Road and might have reached three figures had he not been stumped by wicket-keeper David Humphries advancing down the wicket to Dipak Patel.

Ironically, the Worcestershire spinner became soon afterwards a colleague of Alan's as the pair were both chosen for the tour to Australia and New Zealand which had been organized by Derrick Robins, the Midlands-based businessman, who besides being Chairman of Coventry City FC organized a series of overseas tour for emerging county players. Alan duly furthered his cricketing education by playing alongside, amongst others, Kim Barnett, Nick Cook, Tony Pigott, Kevin Sharp and Gladstone Small.

The decision by the Glamorgan hierarchy to sign Javed Miandad and Norman Featherstone for the 1980 season meant that Alan played chiefly for the 2nd XI over the next couple of years before returning to the 1st XI, eager to prove that the selectors should have had faith

Alan Lewis Jones is presented with the Warwick Pool Under-25 competition trophy at Edgbaston in 1980.

his abilities rather than hiring players from other counties. He duly struck his best List A score, with 82 against Warwickshire in their Sunday League encounter at Edgbaston, plus six other fifties in first-class games, including 88 against Northamptonshire at Swansea

Alan Lewis Jones unluckily deflects a ball onto his stumps whilst batting at Swansea during 1979.

before being trapped l.b.w. by Tim Lamb, when seemingly on the verge of his maiden century.

He continued to make headway in both formats in 1983, and struck eight half-centuries in the first-class games, besides being awarded his Glamorgan cap. But again Alan agonizingly missed out on reaching his hundred, this time by the slender margin of a solitary run as he departed for 99 having been caught by Somerset wicket-keeper Trevor Gard off the spin bowling of Jeremy Lloyds in the Championship match at Swansea before trudging dejectedly back up the long flight of steps to the St Helen's pavillion and words of consolation from colleagues and supporters alike.

It was a different story a year and ten days later at the same ground, as Alan returned to the

Swansea pavillion, smiling broadly and proudly holding his bat aloft having scored his second Championship hundred for Glamorgan as the veritable floodgates opened having shed this particular monkey off his back. His maiden hundred had come a few weeks earlier at the end of May against Gloucestershire at Sophia Gardens, where he and fellow centurion John Hopkins had added 240 for the first wicket with Alan making 129. He then made 122 against Middlesex at St Helen's, plus 114 in the match with Essex at Southend-on-Sea, 100 against Somerset at Taunton and 132 against Hampshire at Cardiff.

Alan ended the 1984 season with a career best tally of 1,811 runs in first-class cricket and deservedly won

Alan Lewis Jones cover drives a ball during a County Championship match at Sophia Gardens in 1984.

Glamorgan's Player of the Year Award. He seemed poised to confirm his potential, but in May 1985 he badly dislocated his right shoulder whilst diving to stop the ball in the opening Sunday League match with Kent at Sophia Gardens. He duly spent several months on the sidelines but having returned to the side, he suffered further discomfort and found it difficult to throw the ball. Having decided to only appear in Championship matches, Alan duly underwent a second operation on his shoulder and underwent another period of rehabilitation, but to no avail and was forced to retire at the end of the 1986 season.

Alan retained his link with Glamorgan by captaining their Colts team in the South Wales Cricket Association during 1987 besides playing for Wales Minor Counties the following summer. He subsequently joined a well-known Building Society before becoming the manager of their branch in Maidenhead. His son Matthew was a member of the Glamorgan Academy in 2005/06 besides playing for the county's 2nd XI and the Cardiff MCCU team, in addition to playing Minor County cricket for Berkshire and Buckinghamshire.

1974

1974 was another difficult summer for Glamorgan as they ended up 16th out of 177 in the Championship table, and with just two victories to their name, plus a chastening defeat at Swansea to Lincolnshire in the Gillette Cup.

The embarrassing loss to the Minor County side came in bowler-friendly conditions at St Helen's with the Lincolnshire captain winning a decisive toss and then, despite a long drive to South Wales the previous day, their bowlers reduced Glamorgan to 59-8. As the tide went out in Swansea Bay, batting became easier allowing Malcolm Nash and Tony

The Glamorgan squad which played Hampshire at Basingstoke in 1974. Standing – Gwyn Richards, Kim Norkett, Barry Lloyd, Lawrence Williams, Alan Lewis Jones, Len Hill and Arthur Francis. Seated – Roger Davis, Tony Cordle, Alan Jones, Eifion Jones and Malcolm Nash.

Cordle to share a ninth wicket stand of 87. But the eventual target of 156 in 60 overs proved to be insufficient as Martin Maslin struck an unbeaten 62 and led Lincolnshire to a six-wicket victory.

For much of 1974, the Glamorgan side lacked balance and experience, whilst Majid Khan, their talismanic batsman and Club captain, only played in six Championship matches before joining the Pakistan touring party for the Test and One-Day International series with England. Some had hoped to have seen him and his colleagues in action on Welsh soil in the one-day series, but despite the success of the game the previous summer with New Zealand at St Helen's, Glamorgan's hopes of staging further games were dealt a blow as the TCCB opted to host these matches at the traditional Test Match ground.

The Club's hopes of securing the services of a high-class overseas fast bowler were also dealt a series of blows after plenty of heated discussion in the committee room. Glamorgan courted Greg Armstrong, the West Indian paceman, but he only appeared against the Pakistanis during August. The absence of a top-class strike bowler, as well as a leading spinner, was magnified by the fact that only Malcolm Nash and Lawrence Williams claimed over 50 first-class wickets, whilst in Majid's absence for much of the summer, Alan Jones – who also stood in as acting captain – was the only batsman to score 1,000 runs in Championship cricket.

489

ARMSTRONG, Gregory de Lisle.

Born – Bank Hall, Barbados 11 May, 1950.

RHB, RFM.

Professional.

1st XI: 1974-1976.

2nd XI: 1974-1976.

Club and Ground: 1976.

Barbados 1973/74-1977/78; West Indies Board President's XI 1973/74.

Batting and Fielding Record

	M	I	NO	RUNS	AV	100	50	CT	ST
F-c	30	42	11	426	13.74	-	1	10	-
List A	33	20	11	115	12.77	-	-	7	-

Bowling Record

	Balls	M	R	W	AV	5wI	10wM
F-c	655.3	122	2423	72	33.65	2	-
List A	1465	18	1102	44	25.04	-	-

Career-bests

First-class –   64 v Leicestershire at St Helen's, Swansea, 1976.

6/91 v Warwickshire at St Helen's, Swansea, 1975.

List A –   28* v Surrey at Byfleet, 1976.

4/28 v Worcestershire at Ebbw Vale, 1976.

After years of waiting to hire a genuinely quick international fast bowler, there was great excitement in Glamorgan ranks when Greg Armstrong, their soon-to-be recruited overseas player, dismissed Majid Khan with the third ball of his opening over as the Barbadian made his debut for the Welsh county against the 1974 Pakistanis at Swansea.

The following summer, his colleagues were smiling as well when the Bajan managed to frequently hit the ridge which ran mid-pitch across the square at Sophia Gardens causing balls to rear up sharply. In fact, in one match against Hampshire, Greg bowled a viciously lifting delivery to Barry Richards which struck the peak of the South African's cap and sent it spinning back-to-front. But the laughter amongst Glamorgan ranks soon turned to despair as Greg was plagued by problems with his run-up causing him to deliver a plethora of no-balls. Some claimed that this stemmed from the fact that Greg had not previously played before on such lush green turf whilst others questioned whether his stuttering run-up was because Greg was not wearing the right length of spikes in his boots!

Wilf Wooller also had his two pennyworth and personally oversaw a series of special sessions in the nets at Sophia Gardens in the hope of helping Greg to develop a more rhythmical run-up and without bowling no balls. But not even 'The Skipper' could sort out the problems and having taken 45 first-class wickets in 1975 followed by just 25 during 1976, the Welsh county opted to look elsewhere and hired fellow Bajan Collis King for 1977.

It was all rather embarrassing in 1975 for Glamorgan's administrators who faced mounting criticism for letting go Roy Fredericks, who by now was one of the world's finest opening batters and starring in the World Cup, and instead hiring a rookie fast bowler who had just five first-class appearances under his belt and had developed a no-ball problem. The red faces increased when a story leaked out about events relating to Greg coming to Glamorgan's attention in the first place and the advice given to committee member Bill Edwards when visiting the West Indies during 1973/74.

Greg Armstrong.

For many years, Bill ran a highly successful sports shop in Swansea, just a six hit away from St Helen's, and supplied kit and equipment for many county players as well as international teams including the West Indies. Bill's excellent links with the hierarchy of West Indian cricket – as well as other Test-playing nations – had proved to be very helpful with the recruitment of overseas players, and, like officials in other counties, the MCC winter tours to the Caribbean provided an ideal opportunity to scout for fresh talent. But, on this particular occasion, there may have been a case of mistaken identity or the wrong name being given to Bill when he was watching the match at Bridgetown between a West Indies Board President's XI and the touring MCC.

Greg had made a highly encouraging first-class debut the week before during Barbados' match against Trinidad, and on the strength of his return of 4/45, plus some fiery performances in club cricket, Greg was selected to open the bowling with Andy Roberts for the President's XI. But Greg went wicketless as the MCC rattled up 511-4, with Geoff Boycott also making an unbeaten 261 against an attack which also featured Michael Holding. The young Jamaican fast bowler delivered a typically waspish spell as first change, but when Bill returned to the UK and met up with his fellow Glamorgan officials, it was Greg who he recommended they signed.

As Malcolm Nash succinctly said "Greg was someone who could bowl very quickly and with hostility, though unfortunately, not always accurately." But when Greg got it right, his speed through the air could flummox the finest of opposing batsmen and his best figures for Glamorgan, both in first-class and List A cricket, came on the notoriously sluggish surfaces at Swansea and Ebbw Vale.

There were times as well when the ridge at Sophia Gardens, which had been the bane of so many batsmen in the early years of cricket at Glamorgan's new ground in Cardiff, bizarrely came to the Welsh county's aid, although there were also occasions when it added a touch of comedy to proceedings as some umpires deemed the balls going high over the batsmen's head should be called wide, whilst at other times, the balls evaded the outstretched gloves of wicket-keeper Eifion Jones whose tally of byes conceded rose when the Bajan was bowling.

He returned to the Caribbean having failed to reproduce his West Indian form and bowl with the consistent hostility shown by other overseas players who were plying their trade at the time on the county circuit. Nevertheless, Greg continued to play in Shell Shield cricket and in 1977/78 he struck a career-best 93 for Barbados, batting at number nine against a Combined Leeward and Windward Islands side at Castries.

This proved to be his final season in the Barbados side, and it was not until early in the 1982/83 season that he featured again in major games, having taken part in a charity tour organised by a Caribbean XI in Guyana. Later that year, he hit the headlines again when Greg acted as the Assistant Manager of the so-called 'rebel' West Indian team to South Africa. With Ali Bacher, the former South African captain, unable to set foot in the Caribbean, Greg's role was more than just managing the players on the tour itself, as the Bajan undertook the recruitment of the players and helped oversee the appointment of Lawrence Rowe as captain of the tour party.

He was also heavily involved in other decision-making, such as the time when the South African Cricket Union informed Greg that there was a lack of commercial support behind

the tour. He duly got together with Lawrence, as well as Alvin Kallicharran and Albert Padmore, to enlist the help of an agent to find their own sponsors. A series of heated exchanges took place over the situation shortly before the first One-Day International, with the West Indians taking to the field in whites, rather than the maroon-coloured clothing which they had been given as a protest at the way they had been treated.

Eventually, a deal was struck with Yellow Pages, but the plans which Greg had discussed for the West Indian tours being an annual event for the next five years were scrapped. There was dissatisfaction amongst the party about the

Greg Armstrong, seen bowling at Swansea in 1975 and watched by umpire Peter Wight.

congested itinerary as well as some of the umpiring, especially their interpretation of short-pitched deliveries. If Greg didn't already have enough on his hands, he was also pressed into service in the 50 overs match against Griqualand West at Kimberley. Batting at number ten he scored a typically cavalier 16 besides returning figures of 6-0-24-2 in what proved to be his last major match.

Greg returned to Barbados having gained a degree of financial security but his career in cricket was over as he, like the rest of the party, was banned for life by the West Indian authorities for having taken part in the tour. He has subsequently worked for the Barbados Tourist Authority, but others in the party faced a difficult time blending back into Caribbean society, besides being beset by personal problems. He is currently a successful businessman in the construction trade in Barbados.

490
NORKETT, Kim Thomas.

Born – Malta, 24 December 1955.
Professional.
RHB, RM.
Ed – Monmouth School and Durham University.
1st XI: 1974.
2nd XI: 1974-1975.
Clubs: Chepstow, Ebbw Vale.
Rugby for Newport and Ebbw Vale.

Batting and Fielding Record

	M	I	NO	RUNS	AV	100	50	CT	ST
List A	1	1	0	0	0	-	-	-	-

Bowling Record

	Balls	M	R	W	AV	5wI	10wM
List A	48	0	34	1	34.00	-	-

Career-bests
List A –   1/34 v Hampshire at Basingstoke, 1974.

Kim Norkett played in one Sunday League match against Hampshire at Basingstoke in the penultimate game of the 1974 season. Having replaced John Solanky in the Welsh county's line-up, he bowled an accurate spell of seam bowling, opening the bowling with Malcolm Nash and dismissing Gordon Greenidge. He was set to keep his place for the final match of the summer, but the contest – against Sussex at Cardiff – was called off twenty-four hours before the game after the Sophia Gardens ground was flooded.

Raised in Chepstow and educated at Monmouth School, the all-rounder impressed for Welsh Schools, before securing a place on Glamorgan's staff whilst reading History at Durham University. However, he did not make another 1st XI appearance and focused instead on his rugby-playing career. Kim was a talented scrum-half and played for Newport, Durham University, English Universities, Durham, Newcastle-Gosforth, Pontypool and Ebbw Vale.

Kim Norkett.

He also taught and coached rugby at Christ College, Brecon as well as Stonyhurst College in Lancashire where amongst his young charges was Kyran Bracken, the future England scrum-half. Kim also had a spell as Director of Coaching at Blackburn RFC before returning to Wales and working for the Welsh Rugby Union as the community development officer for Pembrokeshire. His daughter also played rugby for the Welsh Women's team but tragically Elli was killed in a car crash in 2017 whilst a student at Cardiff Metropolitan University. His eldest daughter Lowri has also represented Wales at both netball and rugby.

Kim currently lives in the Swansea area and has created a company specializing in digital media and software development.

1975

Glamorgan continued to show a Jekyll and Hyde character across all competitions during 1975. At times they were very, very good, and in the County Championship they rose up to 9th place in the table with seven victories, including wins against Lancashire, Hampshire and Kent who all finished in the top five of the table.

There were signs of promise as well from several of the young batsmen whilst Majid Khan, Alan Jones and Roger Davis all passed the 1,000-run mark in the Championship. All three also featured prominently in an extraordinary Sunday League match at Wellingborough School where Majid plundered fifty off 22 balls. Roger continued the assault before falling nine runs short of a deserved century, and then claimed three wickets with his off-spin as Northamptonshire subsided to 66-6, chasing 267 to win.

With a victory firmly in their grasp, Majid duly called up Alan for a few overs of off-spin. He claimed three wickets whilst Eifion Jones also took off his wicket-keeping pads to deliver a couple of overs, as the brothers made a rare appearance as bowlers in tandem!

But there were days, especially in limited-overs cricket, when Glamorgan were very, very poor. They departed early in both the Gillette Cup as well as the Benson and Hedges Cup, whilst they finished bottom of the Sunday League despite the batting fireworks in Northants. The continued lack of success in one-day cricket attracted plenty of adverse comments from journalists with *Wisden's* correspondent writing how "Glamorgan have never got to grips with the new formula, and their innings were never properly phased. Things were just allowed to happen without rhyme or reason. There was no policy."

The Glamorgan playing squad at the annual photocall in 1975. Back row (left to right) – Len Hill, Kim Norkett, John Solanky, Greg Armstrong, Gwyn Richards and Arthur Francis. Middle row – Kim Davies, Lawrence Williams, Rupert Hill, Mike Llewellyn, Geoff Ellis, Alan Lewis Jones, Rodney Ontong, Tyrone Powell and Roger Davis. Front row – Malcolm Nash, Tony Cordle, Majid Khan, Alan Jones and Eifion Jones.

491
HILL, Rupert Knight.

Born – Kingston, Jamaica, 14 August 1954.
Professional.
RHB, RM.
1st XI: 1975.
2nd XI: 1974-1977.
Clubs: Briton Ferry Town, Newport, Maesteg Town and Blackheath.

Batting and Fielding Record

	M	I	NO	RUNS	AV	100	50	CT	ST
F-c	1	-	-	-	-	-	-	-	-
List A	1	1	1	2	-	-	-	1	-

Bowling Record

	Balls	M	R	W	AV	5wI	10wM
F-c	74	8	58	1	58.00	-	-
List A	48	0	39	1	39.00	-	-

Career-bests

First-class – 1/34 v Cambridge University at St Helen's, Swansea 1975.
List A – 2* v Derbyshire at Buxton, 1975.
1/39 v Derbyshire at Buxton, 1975.

Rupert Hill was a medium paced seam bowler who was on Glamorgan's staff during the mid 1970s.

Born in Jamaica and raised in South Wales, Rupert played against Cambridge University in 1975 besides appearing in one Sunday League game that summer away to Derbyshire. Despite a good record in club cricket for Newport, Maesteg Town and Briton Ferry Town, he never made any other 1st XI appearances, and left the staff at the end of the 1976 season.

He subsequently became a social worker and moved to Kent where he played for Blackheath, one of the premier clubs to the south-east of London. In 1981 he opened the bowling for the Kent club against Scarborough at Lord's in the final of the John Haig Final. Despite delivering a frugal new ball spell, he ended up on the losing side on his big day at the famous ground in St John's Wood. He also guested for several wandering teams as well as for HSBC in their annual matches in the Kent area from 1981 until 2008.

Rupert Hill.

492
DAVIES, Morean Kimsley ('Kim').

Born – Clydach, 13 October 1954.
Professional.
LHB, WK.
Ed – Cwmtawe CS.
1st XI: 1975-1976.
2nd XI: 1972-1976.
Club: Clydach.
Rugby for Aberavon.

Batting and Fielding Record

	M	I	NO	RUNS	AV	100	50	CT	ST
F-c	2	2	1	14	14.00	-	-	2	2

Career-bests

First-class – 12 v Cambridge University at St Helen's, Swansea, 1975.

Kim Davies was Eifion Jones' understudy as Glamorgan's wicket-keeper during the mid-1970's. Eifion's success and durability behind the stumps meant that during Kim's time on

Kim Davies.

the Glamorgan staff he only played twice for the 1st XI, each time against student opposition, appearing against Cambridge University at Swansea in 1975 and Oxford University at The Parks in 1976.

The left-hander had joined the Welsh county's staff after impressing keeping wicket for Welsh Schools and the National Association of Young Cricketers during the early 1970s as well as in club cricket for Clydach. Kim made his Glamorgan 2nd XI debut in 1971 aged sixteen and still at school, before joining the Club's staff in 1973.

Kim was also a talented rugby player and played as a full-back for Aberavon, besides acting as coach to Trebanos. Since leaving the world of professional cricket, Kim has been the owner/manager of Sportscene and Scholars Schoolware in Morriston who, besides selling clothing and equipment for a wide variety of sports, have been the official suppliers of kit for the West Wales Football Association.

His brother Malcolm also played for Glamorgan 2nd XI during the 1970s, whilst his son Sam played for Glamorgan 2nd XI between 2009 and 2014, as well as for Cardiff MCCU during 2013 and 2014.

493
NEEDHAM, Patrick John Easthorpe ('Ricky').

Born – Canton, Cardiff, 6 December 1951.
Amateur.
LHB, RM.
Ed – Harrow School.
1st XI: 1975.
2nd XI: 1973-1975.
Wales 1975-1986.
Clubs: St Fagans, MCC, XL Club.

Batting and Fielding Record

	M	I	NO	RUNS	AV	100	50	CT	ST
F-c	1	1	0	4	4.00	-	-	1	-

Bowling Record

	Overs	M	R	W	AV	5wI	10wM
F-c	41.5	11	105	2	52.50	-	-

Career-bests

First-class – 4 v Cambridge University at St Helen's, Swansea, 1975.
1/49 v Cambridge University at St Helen's, Swansea, 1975.

Ricky Needham, a well-known figure in club cricket in South Wales and the West Country, played once for Glamorgan during 1975.

Ricky had been in the Harrow XI between 1966 and 1970, besides captaining the side in 1969 and 1970. The hard-hitting left-hander and right-arm seam bowler also played for Welsh Schools before making his 2nd XI debut in 1973. He was also a member of the county's Under-25 side which met with success in the one-day competitions.

With Glamorgan struggling at the time in the various limited-overs competitions, Ricky's name was mentioned as someone who could be drafted into their Sunday League team, especially given his success in club cricket for St Fagans. In 1975 Ricky made his 1st XI debut in the three-day friendly against Cambridge University at Swansea but he had little impact with either bat or ball.

Despite never appearing again at 1st XI level, Ricky continued to be a decent performer in 2nd XI as well as club cricket and led St Fagans to victory in the 1991 Haig Village Final at Lord's. He played for Wales

Ricky Needham.

between 1975 and 1986, appearing in their match at Swansea in 1975 against East Africa as they warmed-up for the World Cup, as well as the contest in 1985 against Argentina at Builth Wells. Ricky also appeared on a regular basis in The Cricketer Cup for Harrow Wanderers as well as being selected for the Western League's representative side. In 1995 he was also in the MCC party which undertook a very sociable tour to France.

Having qualified as a solicitor in 1981, Ricky has been a senior partner in the practice of Davies, Prichard and Weatherill in St Andrew's Crescent in Cardiff. He also served for many years on the Glamorgan committee and, in recent times, sat on the ECB's Disciplinary committee.

494
ONTONG, Rodney Craig.

Born - Johannesburg, South Africa, 9 September 1955.
Professional.
Ed – Selbourne College.
RHB, RM/OB.
1st XI: 1975-1989.
2nd XI: 1974-1989.
Cap: 1979.
MCC Young Professionals 1971-1973; Border 1972/73-1975/76; Middlesex 2nd XI 1973-74; Surrey 2nd XI 1973; TN Pearce's XI 1976; Transvaal 1976/77-1977/78; Northern Transvaal 1978/79-1981/82; Border 1982/83-1987/88; Impala's 1984/85; MCC 1987; Northern Transvaal 1988/89-1994/95.
Clubs: Swansea, Cooke Collegians, Cregagh.

Batting and Fielding Record

	M	I	NO	RUNS	AV	100	50	CT	ST
F-c	257	413	65	10825	31.11	18	53	116	-
List A	227	201	30	4454	26.04	1	19	71	-

Bowling Record

	Balls	M	R	W	AV	5wI	10wM
F-c	34259	1285	17279	531	32.54	20	4
List A	9250	139	6392	203	31.48		

Career-bests
First-class – 204*   v Middlesex at St Helen's, Swansea, 1984.
             8/67   v Nottinghamshire at Trent Bridge, 1985.
List A –   100   v Northamptonshire at Abergavenny, 1982.
             5/30   v Somerset at Taunton, 1985.

Rodney Ontong was a gifted all-rounder, who led Glamorgan between 1984 and 1986, and had it not been for an horrific car crash which ended his professional career, he might have won Test honours with England as a combative batsman and astute off-spinner.

The South African-born cricketer had initially come over to the United Kingdom at the age of sixteen to have football trials with Chelsea. Having also been a talented schoolboy cricketer at Selbourne College, Rodney also joined a cricket club in London, besides visiting Lord's to watch cricket at the famous ground. During the visit he had seen young cricketers training on the Nursery Ground, so when Chelsea's youth coaches told him that they were not going to offer him a contract, Rodney headed to Lord's to enquire about any opportunities.

Rodney Ontong.

With favourable comments from the club for whom he had been playing, plus an impressive trial with bat and ball in the indoor nets, Rodney duly secured a place on the MCC groundstaff and spent the next three summers at the St John's Wood ground along with other talented young cricketers such as Ian Botham. The pair became firm friends, to the extent that they also shared a flat and enjoyed everything that young and single sportsmen could discover in London, both by day and especially by night!

Having opted to become a professional cricketer rather than a footballer, Rodney also developed his cricket career when back home in South Africa and in 1972/73 he made his first-class debut for Border aged seventeen years and seven months and acquired the nickname of 'The Kid'. Later that year, Rodney made his debut for Middlesex in both their 2nd XI and Under 25 teams with the all-rounder, in particular, impressing with his technically correct batting and ability to bowl at a lively pace from an accelerating run-up and smooth high action. In a match against Surrey 2nd XI Rodney took 6/44 but with the likes of Mike Gatting and others already ahead of him, it was no surprise when Middlesex opted against offering the young South African a summer contract.

He also played for both Surrey 2nd XI, and their Under-25 side during 1973, and with Rodney desperate to break into professional sport, Len Muncer, the MCC Head Coach and former member of the Welsh county's Championship-winning team in 1948 (Vol. 2, 365-369) suggested to Glamorgan's officials that they should have a look at the all-rounder and consider offering him terms. He duly made his 2nd XI debut for Glamorgan during 1974 and, after agreeing a development contract with them, he made his first appearance the following year against the 1975 Australians at Swansea scoring 4 and 15, besides claiming the wicket of Rick McCosker whom he trapped l.b.w.

By this time, Rodney already had a first-class hundred under his belt, having made 106 for Border against Transvaal B in 1974/75, whilst in his first full year on the Glamorgan staff in 1975 he scored centuries for their 2nd XI against both Somerset and Warwickshire as he spent a couple of years qualifying as an English player. Even so, he still returned home during the winters and, after recording figures of 7/60 for Border against Northern Transvaal and 7/118 against Griqualand West, Rodney was chosen in March 1976 in a series of games for both a Multi-Racial XI and the South African Board President's XI which met the International Wanderers, captained by Greg Chappell.

Also in the President's team were other South Africans who were familiar faces on the county circuit including Ken McEwan, Kepler Wessels and Kenny Watson, whilst the International side included Glenn Turner, Mike Denness, Phil Edmonds, Bob Taylor, Derek Underwood and Ashley Mallett. Rodney did not, however, look out of place alongside such experienced names, claiming 7/83 for the multi-racial team in the one-day match at Pretoria before claiming 6/52 in the Wanderers second innings of the three-day contest at Port Elizabeth.

The domestic season of 1976 saw Rodney continue his qualification period, playing club cricket for Swansea, besides playing regular 2nd XI cricket as well as appearing for the 1st XI in the friendlies against Oxford University and the West Indians. He also played against the latter at Scarborough for TN Pearce's XI prior to returning to South Africa for the 1976/77 season. That winter Rodney played for Transvaal, alongside Clive Rice, the combative all-rounder who enjoyed a long and successful career in county cricket for Nottinghamshire. It was not long before Clive was highly impressed by Rodney's talents with both bat and ball, and later wrote "he is an incredibly talented sportsman... and I would have him in my side anywhere in the world... As the opposition captain for many years at Nottinghamshire, Rodney has been my main worry in the Glamorgan batting line-up"

In early May 1977 Rodney made his Championship debut for Glamorgan and having completed his qualification period, the all-rounder subsequently won a regular place in the side and impressed many with his stylish batting in

Rodney Ontong pulls a ball for four at Lord's.

the middle-order, as well as his brisk seam bowling, with Rodney claiming his maiden Championship five-for against Hampshire at Sophia Gardens. These all-round skills also proved invaluable to the Welsh county in the limited-overs games, and his emergence in the team, allied to the Caribbean flair of Collis King and the nous of veteran Tom Cartwright were key factors behind the Welsh county enjoying a successful run in the Gillette Cup. However, the final at Lord's was a game to forget for Rodney as he didn't bowl and, batting at number four, lasted just five balls before being caught by wicket-keeper Ian Gould off the bowling of Mike Gatting.

He duly put aside these disappointments in 1978 and registered his maiden Championship hundred, with an unbeaten 116 against Essex at Sophia Gardens, followed by 116 against Surrey at The Oval. That winter, he also made his debut for Northern Transvaal and in one game in Pretoria, he came in for some light-hearted comments from a spectator as he was delivering, for once, an expensive spell of seam on a sweltering hot afternoon. The verbal barrage from the well-lubricated supporter began as a series of wide half-volleys were effortlessly dispatched to the cover boundary by the grateful batsman. "You couldn't bowl cherries!" shouted the spectator, followed by a few other more coarse remarks before, as Rodney trudged back to his bowling mark desperately seeking any solace he could find, yelling out "Hey, Ontong. You're bowling like my biltong – a piece of dried up s**t!" Rodney smiled genially at the fellow, whilst his colleagues grinned and laughed but, for the next few years, 'The Kid' had become 'The Biltong Bowler'!

Three more centuries followed in Championship games in 1979, against Warwickshire, Leicestershire and Gloucestershire, whilst the latter must have been fed up with the sight of him batting and bowling as Rodney also won the Gold Award against the West Country side in their Benson and Hedges encounter at Swansea. Given performances such as these, it was no surprise that Rodney won his Glamorgan cap during 1979. The following year, he moved up the batting order to the number three berth, and in 1981 shared a third wicket stand of 270 with Javed Miandad – once again against Gloucestershire – with Rodney making another unbeaten 116 as he enjoyed batting alongside the mercurial Pakistani.

A few weeks earlier, Rodney had enjoyed another large stand, this time at Swansea and with a more unlikely partner in the shape of veteran leg-spinner Robin Hobbs. The pair had become good friends, both on and off the field, with Rodney enjoying Robin's wit and humour. Indeed, there were plenty of smiles on their faces as they frustrated the Hampshire attack in adding an unbeaten 140 for the last wicket in the course of 39 overs and batting throughout the final session before Glamorgan declared on their overnight total of 317-9.

Robin initially blocked for all his might as Rodney, who had been on 87* when his pal arrived in the middle, completed his sixth Championship hundred for Glamorgan. As their part-nership continued, Rodney unfurled a series of his trademark cover drives and other firm blows in an arc from backward point to mid-wicket,

Rodney Ontong seen bowling against Worcestershire at Neath during 1986.

with Robin also using some cross-batted blows against a weary attack-ending unbeaten on 49 with Rodney having reached the 150-mark in the final over of the day.

1981 saw Rodney claim his first ten-wicket haul for Glamorgan, taking 10/107 against the Sri Lankans at Sophia Gardens. During his spell in both innings against the tourists, Rodney also bowled a few overs of off-spin. For several years, he had dabbled with spin-bowling, often coming on out of necessity for Glamorgan in a bid to break a partnership or simply for the sake of variety in the hope of getting a wicket. He was a big spinner of the ball and so impressed was Wilf Wooller when watching Rodney in the nets at Sophia Gardens that the Club's Secretary told him that he would take far more wickets as a spinner rather than a seamer. Rodney ignored this well-meaning advice, revealing, as in these large batting partnerships, the stubborn side to his nature.

He therefore continued as a seam bowler and claimed his first ten-wicket haul in Championship cricket, returning figures of 10/126 against Gloucestershire at Bristol in 1982. He ended the summer with 64 first-class wickets – a feat which saw him win the county's Player of the Year Award for the first-ever time – besides enjoying plenty of success for Border, who he joined at the start of the 1982/83 season. But by the time he returned to the UK for the summer of 1983, the situation at the Welsh county was starting to change. Rodney had been suffering niggling injuries in his right shoulder and left knee, whilst Glamorgan had strengthened their seam bowling options, having secured the services of Winston Davis, the West Indian fast bowler, as well as having Mike Selvey as their new captain for 1983.

Realising that he might get greater opportunities as a spinner, and experience fewer niggles, he bowled more and more spin as the 1983 season unfolded. Rodney also sought advice from Don Shepherd, another man to switch from pace to spin, whilst his transition was also eased by some advice from Fred Titmus, the former Middlesex and England spinner in the pre-season sessions during the spring of 1984.

Besides having decided to become a full-time purveyor of off-breaks, 1984 was an important season in other ways for the all-rounder as he was also appointed as vice-captain to Mike Selvey. The appointment of the seemingly laid-back South African raised a few eyebrows in some quarters, but those close to the team knew that Rodney was a deep thinker on the game and had an astute cricket brain. Some had even suggested in 1982 that he should share the leadership duties with Javed Miandad rather than Barry Lloyd.

His latent talents as a leader had also been recognized in South Africa where he was appointed as captain of Border for 1983/84, before leading the Impalas in the Benson and Hedges series in 1984/85, where he played alongside his young Glamorgan team-mate Greg Thomas who was honing his skills as a fast bowler with a winter in the Cape.

Returning to matters with Glamorgan, Rodney's appointment as vice-captain for 1984 was a clear indication that he was being groomed for higher honours. But his elevation came far sooner than either he, and most others, had anticipated with Rodney taking over as caretaker captain at the end of July following Mike's resignation before being appointed on a full-time basis at the end of the summer. It prompted a re-shuffling of the batting order as Rodney, in his new role as captain and off-spinner dropped down from number three to five, ironically having made a career-best and unbeaten 204 in a five and three-quarter hour innings against Middlesex at Swansea during late June.

1984 proved to be Rodney's best-ever summer with the bat as he amassed 1,320 first-class runs, but the shift down the order and the duties of captaincy saw him pass the thousand run mark for the fifth and final time in 1985. Having already made fourteen hundreds, Rodney only made a further four in the rest of his career, although it should not be forgotten that from 1985 onwards, Glamorgan did have a stronger line-up with more prolific batsmen above him in the batting order.

However, 1986 saw Rodney's batting form dip and, without a century to his name, plus a seasonal tally of just 744 first-class runs, it was no surprise that he contacted David Lewis, the Chairman of the cricket committee and said that he did not want to captain the side in 1987 as the stress of dealing with matters, both on and off the field, was affecting his own game. After a lot of quiet discussion, Rodney agreed that it would be in the best interests of his successor if he stepped down immediately with Hugh Morris taking over from 23 July at Leicester.

Rodney's bowling had gone from strength to strength since switching to spin, with his first-class tally rising from 56 wickets in 1983 to 74 in 1984 and 64 in 1985. The latter season also saw Rodney become only the second Glamorgan cricketer to achieve the feat of making a century and taking ten wickets in a first-class match, scoring 130 and returning match figures of

Rodney Ontong, seen in the Glamorgan offices at Sophia Gardens on his appointment as Glamorgan captain in 1984.

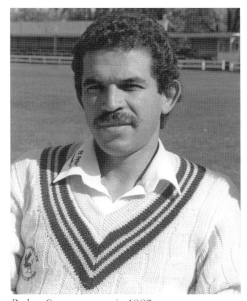

Rodney Ontong, as seen in 1987.

13/106 in the Championship match at Trent Bridge. His feats with bat and ball won him the Cricket Society's Wetherall Award as the leading all-rounder in county cricket, besides the Glamorgan Player of the Year Award for a second time.

The Glamorgan captain began his almost one-man demolition job of Nottinghamshire with a spell of four wickets in five overs, without conceding a run, before sharing a jaunty fifth wicket stand with the teenage Matthew Maynard, hitting 14 fours and a six in his four and a hour stay at the crease. He then, in the space of 111 balls, took 8/67 as the home side nosedived from 59-1 to 120 all out as Glamorgan secured an emphatic innings victory.

The following September, Rodney took thirteen wickets again against Nottinghamshire as, in the match at Sophia Gardens, he returned figures of 5/26 and 8/101 although, this time, it was not enough to secure a Glamorgan victory as Nottinghamshire won by 24 runs on a spin-friendly surface. Nevertheless, it confirmed his standing as one of the leading off-spinners in the country.

With his name being mentioned in high circles as a potential England cricketer, it was around this time that Rodney said no to the offer of playing for South Africa in their series against Kim Hughes's Australians. The chance of batting alongside such greats as Graeme Pollock must have been very tempting, but confirmation of Rodney's high standing came in April 1987 as he was chosen by the MCC in their annual game against the champion county at Lord's. The traditional curtain-raiser to the season, against Essex, duly saw Rodney go wicket-less in five overs, besides making unbeaten scores of 63 and 46.

He was also tipped by several journalists as a candidate to play for England during October and November 1987 in the ICC World Cup, with the Pressmen arguing that with the competition being staged in India and Pakistan, his nagging off-spin and forceful batting would be an asset to Mike Gatting and his team. But just when he seemed destined to be poised for higher honours, Rodney's form deserted him in 1987 whilst he suffered a series of niggling injuries and missed several matches. He ended the season with just one Championship score of over fifty, plus a modest tally of 488 runs to his name at 25 runs apiece. Nevertheless, on 18 August he scored his 10,000th first-class run for the Club during the 418th innings of his career with the Welsh county.

His bowling though remained potent, as shown in the rain-affected match with Yorkshire at Sophia Gardens where, in the visitor's second innings, Rodney bowled Glamorgan to victory with a return of 6/91. The summer had also seen Rodney form an effective partnership with Ravi Shastri, the Indian slow left-armer, whose nickname from his Welsh colleagues was 'The Prince'. Whilst being delighted to have the opportunity to bowl in tandem with a world-class spinner, Rodney was less amused when his team-mates started calling him 'The Princess'!

Rodney continued to bowl alongside Ravi in 1988, and it may have been no coincidence that his batting form returned, with four half-centuries plus a handsome and unbeaten 120 against Kent at Sophia Gardens to remind the England selectors of his capabilities after a barren spell with the bat. But on the evening of 19 August, he and Steve Barwick were involved in a crash as they were heading along the M1 from

Rodney Ontong receives the St Helen's Balconiers Player of the Year in 1987 from Gordon Lewis.

the drawn Championship match against Essex at Colchester to the next game against Northamptonshire at Wellingborough School. In swerving to avoid a lorry, their car went through the central reservation and badly damaged Rodney's right knee.

He missed the rest of the season and underwent reconstructive surgery before embarking, with his typical enthusiasm and self-mindedness, a lengthy period of rehabilitation. He re-appeared in five Championship matches but suffered a reaction each time after playing. With great irony, 1989 was also his Benefit Year but, after discussions with a consultant, he regretfully announced in July that he had lost his battle to stay in county cricket.

With his Benefit Year having raised £72,000, Rodney left Glamorgan at the age of thirty-three with arguably his best years as a spin bowler still in front of him. He returned to South Africa and twice tried to resurrect his playing career with Northern Transvaal – firstly during 1989/90 and later in 1994/95 as an amateur but each time his efforts were to no avail. He also coached the Northern Transvaal team besides serving as the Director of Coaching at Gauteng, before going into sports marketing as well as broadcasting with SABC. Rodney currently lives near his son in Belfast where he has continued to play as an amateur, besides coaching, at various clubs in the Ulster Senior League. Rodney is not related to South African Test cricketer Justin Ontong.

POWELL, Tyrone Lyndon.

Born – Bargoed, 17 June 1953.
RHB, OB.
Ed – Heretunga College, Upper Hutt.
1st XI: 1975-1976.
2nd XI: 1975-1976.
Club and Ground: 1975.
New Zealand Under-23 1971/72; Norfolk 1982-1986.
Clubs: Hutt Valley, Cardiff, Hawke's Bay.

Batting and Fielding Record

	M	I	NO	RUNS	AV	100	50	CT	ST
F-c	1	2	0	0	-	-	-	-	-

Tyrone Powell only played one first-class match for Glamorgan. That came in 1976 against the West Indies at Swansea, but the young colt bagged a pair as he was dismissed by their fearsome pace bowlers without scoring in both innings.

The right-handed batsman had been born in South Wales, but was brought up in New Zealand, where he played for Hutt Valley before making his debut for the Wellington Under 20s in 1971/72. On 4 February 1972 the right-handed opening batsman duly made his first-class debut for the New Zealand under 23 side against Otago at Dunedin and scored 14 and 10.

He subsequently joined Cardiff CC in 1974 and, after some decent innings in club cricket, Tyrone played for Glamorgan's 2nd XI during 1975, besides appearing in Glamorgan's limited-overs friendly against East Africa at Sophia Gardens as the tourists warmed up for the World Cup. The 60-overs contest saw Tyrone open alongside Alan Jones and he made 20 before being caught by Jawahir Shah off the bowling of Ramesh Sethi who subsequently had a decent career in Minor County cricket for Shropshire.

Tyrone Powell.

Tyrone was chosen again as Alan Jones' opening partner for the match at Swansea against the 1976 West Indies but made a duck in the first innings as he was bowled by Wayne Daniel. Unfortunately, Tyrone caught a stomach bug during the game and, when Glamorgan batted for a second time the next day, Majid Khan replaced the youngster at the top of the order. His condition eased by the final morning allowing him to bat at number eight but, once again, he failed to score as he was bowled by Michael Holding. After being released by Glamorgan, Tyrone continued to play in provincial cricket in New Zealand, as well as in club cricket in the UK in East Anglia. Tyrone subsequently played in Minor County matches for Norfolk between 1982 and 1986, with his top score being 115 against Suffolk at Lakenham.

1976

For cricket-lovers and supporters in Wales the long, hot summer of 1976 will be remembered not as the year when a drought saw the turf at St Helen's and Sophia Gardens turn from a verdant green into a parched and abrasive surface the colour of straw, but one of discontent and deep, sadness for the Club's captain Majid Khan who quit the Club mid-season after what had been private discontent amongst senior players and the Club's administrators over his style of leadership became made public knowledge.

There was no disputing Majid prowess with bat, or his calm and determined manner when batting under his faded white sun hat. But tales of the Club's captain arriving late at games and apparently not looking at the pitch or consulting with others before going out to toss, seeped out from the changing and committee room and into the columns of local newspapers. As Tony Lewis wrote, "the public which had crowned him in 1969 were now prepared to crucify."

Besides the departure of Majid, the newspapers were also full of stories about the six Glamorgan players who had received letters from the committee warning them that if their performances did not improve they would not secure extensions to their contracts. One Glamorgan member also scurried around the grounds at Cardiff and Swansea seeking votes for an EGM and a vote of no confidence in the Club's committee. It was like 1958 all over again, as a lot of dirty washing was unnecessarily given a public airing.

Majid's last appearance for Glamorgan came on 7 August as the Welsh county met

Majid Khan, centre, flanked by Ossie Wheatley (left) and Bill Edwards.

the West Indians at Swansea. It was a game which the tourists comfortably won by an innings after a world-record double-hundred from their captain Clive Lloyd as the Caribbean side amassed 554-4 in 83.3 overs. The game drew a massive crowd — for many spectators, it was their first major match at St Helen's and, as one onlooker later wrote, "I'd never seen so many people before as we sat on the old, slatted benches that pinched your backside at Swansea. I remember the shrill cries of the men selling newspapers. I remember Viv Richards flicking and pulling balls from outside off-stump, high over square-leg and mid-wicket. I remember my father standing up to applaud Clive Lloyd reaching his hundred, then heading off to the toilets, queuing up and eventually returning with Clive on the verge of his double-hundred!"

496
ALLIN, Anthony William.

Born – Barnstaple Hospital, 20 April, 1954.
Ed – Belmont College, Barnstaple.
RHB, SLA.
Professional.
1st XI: 1976.
2nd XI: 1976.
Devon 1975-1998; Minor Counties 1980-84.
Clubs: Bideford, Cardiff.

Batting and Fielding Record

	M	I	NO	RUNS	AV	100	50	CT	ST
F-c	13	16	8	108	13.50	-	-	3	-
List A	3	2	1	8	8.00	-	-	-	-

Bowling Record

	Balls	M	R	W	AV	5wI	10wM
F-c	2001	95	1011	44	22.97	4	1
List A	106	0	88	3	29.33	-	-

Career-bests

First-class –   32 v Somerset at Weston-super-Mare, 1976.
                  8/63 v Sussex at Sophia Gardens, Cardiff, 1976.
List A –   8* v Kent at Canterbury, 1976.
                  1/22 v Kent at Canterbury, 1976.

Tony Allin almost made a remarkable rise from Minor County cricket to Test cricket in the space of eighteen months following some fine performances with his left-arm spin for Glamorgan during 1976. It proved not to be with the long and hot summer being his one and only year of top-level cricket. Sadly, 1976 was not an easy summer for Glamorgan and, had he joined the Welsh county at a happier time, Tony would probably have enjoyed a longer career in county cricket and perhaps won honours with England.

Tony had first played for age-group teams in Devon during 1972 before securing a place in their Minor County Championship side during 1975. His regular wicket-taking drew the attention of Glamorgan's talent scouts, and he agreed terms with the Welsh county for 1976. The farmer's son made his first-class debut against Essex at Swansea in May 1976 and a measure of his rapid headway can be gauged by a haul of seven wickets against Gloucestershire at Cheltenham, before taking 8/63 against

Tony Allin.

Sussex at Cardiff in late July, with his victims including England captain Tony Greig who was completely bamboozled by Tony's subtle flight and guile.

With the drought of 1976 continuing into August, and the pitches being dry and conducive to spin bowling, Tony continued his dramatic entry into county cricket with returns of 6/133 and 5/95 in Glmaorgan's Championship match with Middlesex at Swansea, followed by 6/24 in the match against Worcestershire at Sophia Gardens as he filleted the visitor's innings by taking the last six wickets. His wicket-taking ability and accuracy had also seen Tony win a place in Glamorgan's one-day team and in the Sunday League match in mid-August at Headingley he added to his illustrious list of scalps by clean bowling Geoff Boycott.

By this time, Tony's name was being touted by such eminent journalists as Robin Marlar for a place on England's winter tour to India. However, he was not included in the tour party and, at the end of the summer, he opted not to continue with the Welsh county,

Tony Allin demonstrates his bowling action at Swansea in 1976.

having been disenchanted with life as a professional cricketer after all the bickering and back-biting within the dressing room

Having opted for a more peaceful life on his father's dairy farm near Bideford and playing for Devon, Tony continued to be a prolific wicket-taker in the Devon League as well as in the Minor County Championship. His success duly saw Tony play for the Minor Counties representative side against the 1980 West Indians at Jesmond, the 1982 Pakistanis at Slough, the 1983 Indians at Monks Risborough and the 1984 West Indians at West Bromwich.

Tony became a stalwart of Devon cricket, playing for the Minor County until 1998, with his sons Matthew and Tom also following in their father's footsteps by playing for Devon. Matthew, a right-handed batsman and wicket-keeper played for Devon in 2002 and 2003, whilst Tom was a fast-medium seamer who played for Devon from 2007, besides appearing for Cardiff MCCU from 2008 until 2010, and securing a contract with Warwickshire from 2011 until his premature death in 2016.

Since leaving county cricket with Glamorgan, Tony has overseen the running of the family's farm at Bucks Cross at Northam, to the north of Bideford. During 2013, he took advantage of generous government subsidies to diversify and switch away from dairy farming, having been disappointed by the constant fall in milk prices. As a result, Tony's farm became the largest producer of worms in the UK, with Tony also overseeing the conversion of other buildings as holiday cottages before retiring as a farmer. Tony has also become a decent golfer and has enjoyed plenty of success at the Royal North Devon Golf Club in Westward Ho!, which is one of the oldest courses in England.

497
WILKINS, Alan Haydn.

Born – Rhiwbina, Cardiff, 22 August 1953.
Ed – Rhiwbina PS, Whitchurch HS, Polytechnic of Wales and Loughborough.
University.
Professional.
RHB, LM.
1st XI: 1975-1983.
2nd XI: 1975-1983.
Gloucestershire 1980-1982; Northern Transvaal 1981/82.
Clubs: Cardiff, Cowbridge.
Rugby for Cardiff, Bristol and Glamorgan Wanderers.

Batting and Fielding Record

	M	I	NO	RUNS	AV	100	50	CT	ST
F-c	65	73	22	502	9.84	-	2	19	-
List A	65	20	7	48	3.69	-	-	9	-

Bowling Record

	Balls	M	R	W	AV	5wI	10wM
F-c	7514	234	4204	135	31.14	6	-
List A	2724	58	1845	84	21.96		

Career-bests

First-class – 70 v Nottinghamshire at Worksop, 1977.
             6/79 v Hampshire at Southampton, 1979.
List A   5* v Worcestershire at Worcester, 1978.
             5/17 v Worcestershire at Worcester, 1978.

Alan Wilkins was a member of the 1977 Glamorgan side that played in the Gillette Cup Final at Lord's before becoming a broadcaster and commentator on a wide variety of sports, including cricket.

His father was Haydn Wilkins (Vol. 2, p347), a stalwart of Cardiff CC who played for Glamorgan towards the end of the Second World War and a long-serving Glamorgan committee member. Through there connections, young Alan was able to be on fringe of the formal celebrations at several historic Glamorgan matches, including being in the players' area after the victory over the 1968 Australians at Swansea and on the pavillion balcony at Sophia Gardens the following year as the Welsh county defeated Worcestershire to clinch the county crown.

Alan represented Wales Schools at both cricket and rugby, with his first, and quite unexpected 'appearance' for Glamorgan coming completely out of the blue in mid-July 1971 when the seventeen-year-old was drafted in as an emergency fielder during the Welsh county's friendly against the Indians. Alan had been sitting on the benches in front of the Sophia Gardens pavillion that morning watching the tourists bat, as well as

Alan Wilkins.

soaking up the sun, when Wilf Wooller approached him during the lunch interval and said: "Young Wilkins, do you have any cricket kit with you?" Alan replied in the negative before being ushered upstairs by the Glamorgan Secretary and into the home team changing room where he was given some kit. "We have a few sick players and we are short of a twelfth man," added Wilf. "So you are going to play for us this afternoon. Go out there and enjoy yourself!" Wearing borrowed clothes plus Tony Lewis' spare boots. Alan duly went out and did what Wilf had instructed, and just for good measure, also got a bout of heatstroke!

Owing to an oversight with his UCCA form, and failing the Cambridge entrance exams, Alan had a year out after leaving Whitchurch High School. He briefly attended a computer sciences course at the Polytechnic of Wales at Treforest before joining the groundstaff at Cardiff Athletic Club where he helped prepare the pitches at the Arms Park and Sophia Gardens – where he had played cricket for Cardiff since his early teens. He also played as an outside half for Cardiff 2nd XV (known as The Rags) before in September 1973 starting his B.Ed. course at Loughborough University.

Whilst at Loughbourough, he played a good standard of rugby and cricket, with fixtures in the latter as part of the UAU tournament as well as friendlies against Nottinghamshire and Leicestershire. As Alan recalled, "in the game at Trent Bridge, I managed to trap Derek Randall l.b.w. during a lengthy spell from the Pavillion End. In the evening over drinks and food, I was approached by the Nottinghamshire captain, Mike Smedley. He asked if I was contracted to any county. Naively I said no, leading to discussions of a possible professional contract with them. News of this reached the *Western Mail* in Cardiff. I thought this looked rather good, but did not consider what Glamorgan would say. I soon knew. Wilf Wooller contacted me on my return to Cardiff and let me know in no uncertain terms that I would not be playing my cricket for Nottinghamshire!"

A year later, Wilf was on the phone again to Alan, saying that owing to an injury to Tony Cordle he would be playing the following day in the Sunday League match against

Somerset at Taunton. He had impressed playing for the 2nd XI, and travelling down by car with his parents, the twenty-one year-old had plenty of time to think about how he would bowl against the likes of Viv Richards and Ian Botham. It proved to be a thrilling game as both sides made 188-8 with Alan claiming the wickets of Peter Denning and Derek Taylor in the tied contest.

Having completed his studies at Loughborough, Alan got a further taste of 1st XI action during 1976, and even had an opportunity to act as a substitute fielder for the West Indians in their three-day game at Swansea. The following summer – his first as a full-time professional – Alan bagged the wickets of two of these Caribbean stars, Viv Richards and Joel Garner, during the Championship match at Sophia Gardens, although he was very grateful that Malcolm Nash at third man was able to take a fine one-handed catch to remove Viv. Alan also yorked Ian Botham to claim a third wicket, before further adding to his stock in the next match at Worksop as he made 70 as night-watchman in the Championship match against Nottinghamshire.

Alan's decent form, and that of Glamorgan, continued in the early rounds of the Gillette Cup with Alan playing a hand in the victories over Worcestershire and Surrey, returning figures of 12-3-33-2 against the latter besides joining in with some of the verbal jousts with the batsmen from the South London club. There were some heated incidents as well in the semi-final against Leicestershire at Swansea – a contest which ran into three days because of rain. Firstly, Alan incurred the wrath of visiting captain Ray Illingworth after taking a low catch at extra-cover as David Gower drove at a ball from Gwyn Richards. As Alan later recalled, "I dived forward and got my fingers under the ball and claimed the catch. In that split second, David Gower just stood there, looking at me and asked 'Alan, did you catch that?' I replied immediately that I had and to his credit, David walked off. "Watching from afar, Ray thought differently and when he eventually came in to bat his mood had not improved as he became involved in a very animated conversation with umpire Ken Palmer.

Alan was bowling from the Mumbles Road End and remembers how a ball immediately found the outside edge of Ray's bat. "We all heard a noise. Eifion and the three slips and I all went up in unison appealing. But Ray just stood there and starred at me. I made a second appeal to [umpire] Bill Alley but he shouted back 'Not Out'. I was livid. We all knew Ray had got an edge and he knew it as well, but for some reason – maybe Bill thought I hadn't taken the David Gower catch cleanly – my appeal fell on deaf ears." Despite having returned figures of 12-5-34-3, Alan was still fuming the next day. But his mood lifted as Glamorgan – to the delight of the large and partisan crowd at St Helen's – completed a successful run-chase the following day to clinch a place in the final at Lord's.

His mood darkened again on the eve of the final against Middlesex when he arrived at the team hotel in Maida Vale only to find that a committee member had taken his room and that there were no other spare rooms in the hotel. When trying to sort things out with Ossie Wheatley, the Club's Chairman, a cousin of Alan's who lived in Beaconsfield suggested that he stayed with him and drove Alan to the ground the following morning. The journey though the next morning took longer than expected thanks to roadworks,

The Glamorgan squad which played in the Gillette Cup final against Middlesex at Lord's in 1977, as seen at Swansea. Back row (left to right) – Alan Lewis Jones, Tom Cartwright, Rodney Ontong, Mike Llewellyn, Collis King, Alan Wilkins, Arthur Francis, Frank Culverwell (scorer). Front row – John Hopkins, Malcolm Nash, Eifion Jones, Alan Jones, Gwyn Richards and Tony Cordle.

so having agreed to be at the ground by 9a.m, Alan was fifteen minutes late and was admonished for his late arrival – not the best way for Alan to start the biggest match of his life.

It turned out to be an emotional, but ultimately disappointing day for the Welsh contingent as Alan remembered "The singing under the Lord's Tavern rang out with songs that only Welsh sporting fans can sing, but I didn't think that we got our act right. We changed our bowling formula on the day and I was called upon to bowl as Glamorgan's sixth bowler, when the match had gone away from us. I thought I should have bowled much earlier than I did, and as I'd done in the earlier rounds of the competition. My return was a less than impressive six overs for 27 runs and I didn't look like taking a wicket...Nevertheless, I ended up top of the Club's bowling averages with 47 wickets at 23 apiece. I felt I belonged in the company of professional cricketers, even if I couldn't get into the team hotel with my own team for the biggest game of my life!"

After a brief visit to Canada with the Lord's Taverners, Alan spent the winter teaching PE and History at Newbridge Comprehensive School and playing rugby for Glamorgan Wanderers. The following summer, Alan took his best-ever List A bowling figures during the Benson and Hedges Cup match at Worcester, albeit in quite unusual circumstances as Glamorgan won by 27 runs. Alan had been troubled by a hamstring twinge in the days leading up to the match but had assured Alan Jones as captain and Tom Cartwright, who was now coach and manager, that he was fit enough to bowl. Running in for his first delivery at New Road, Alan stopped in his run-up as he felt a shooting pain in his right leg. Aware that he had made a pledge to his colleagues that he was OK, he proceeded to bowl his eleven overs straight through and from the shorter run-up he used on a Sunday. Remarkably, he returned figures of 5/17 and had his last ball, a thick outside edge through the slips for four, been caught it would have been 6/13!

Alan spent the winter of 1978/79 in South Africa, acting as coach of Springs High School Old Boys and following in the footsteps of Don Shepherd and Alan Jones by working with the club some 50 kilometres east of Johannesburg. However, he had accepted the appointment against the advice of Tom Cartwright, who held strong views about sporting links with the country under Apartheid. As the summer of 1979 unfolded, Alan's relationship with the manager-coach, which had never been great at the best of times went from bad to worse. The pair had polar opposite attitudes on many things with Alan, in his gregarious and confident manner, not being afraid to speak his mind if he felt slighted in any way. It had always been a potentially volatile mix and, despite a return of 6/79 against Hampshire, Alan lost his place in the 1st XI and became disenchanted about playing for Glamorgan.

A chance conversation with several Gloucestershire players, including Mike Procter, whilst Alan was doing 12th man duties against the West Country side at Sophia Gardens, led to an offer to move across the Severn Bridge to Bristol with Alan duly agreeing a three-year contract with Gloucestershire. He duly made his Championship debut for them against Worcestershire at New Road, but not before another winter in South Africa, playing in the North-Eastern Transvaal League and coaching in the various schools around Springs.

Alan Wilkins.

Alan enjoyed something of a renaissance to his career with Gloucestershire during 1980, recording five-wicket hauls in the Championship matches against Hampshire and Sussex, besides delivering a series of probing spells with his left-arm swing against the West Indians in their friendly at Bristol. His efforts also prompted a back-handed compliment from Ted Dexter, the Chairman of Selectors who, after play, said "Well done, a fine bowling display Alex. Keep it going!"

During the winter months, Alan also worked in the marketing department of Gloucestershire, besides playing rugby for Bristol and appearing over the Christmas period in an Overseas XI in a five-day match at Calcutta arranged by the Cricket Association of Bengal to celebrate their Golden Jubilee. Led by Mike Brearley, the batsmen included Wayne Larkins, Alan Butcher and Frank Hayes, whilst the other bowlers included Mike Selvey, Simon Hughes and John Lever, the experienced left-arm bowler with Essex.

It was especially pleasing for Alan to play and mix with the latter as John had been extremely helpful, advising him about different grips, slower deliveries and other nuances. This had been in stark contrast to the approach of some of his Glamorgan team-mates, including Malcolm Nash, as Alan later wrote in his autobiography *Easier Said Than Done*— "Nashy was something of a strange personality. He was a genuinely talented crickteer, but I found him no help when I started at Glamorgan. He never once offered advice on how to swing the ball, something that I had to work on...That an opponent [such as John] gave me advice when a teammate offered nothing illustrated the insecurities of professional cricketers, who protected their patch with zealous fervour."

Having taken 52 first-class wickets for Gloucestershire during 1980, Alan took the same number again the following summer, besides claiming a career best 8/57 against Lancashire at Old Trafford in the first innings of the penultimate Championship match of the summer opening the bowling with Australian Mike Whitney. With both Mike Procter and Brian Brain on the injury-list, Alan was the senior bowler, and, as he recalled, "the ball did everything that I hoped it would do. It swung and it seamed, but it was not enough for us to press for victory as Lancashire mounted a recovery mission second time around."

1981/82 saw Alan head back to South Africa where he coached at Pretoria High School, and played for their Old Boys team, besides appearing once again alongside Rodney Ontong for Northern Transvaal in the Datsun Shield and Currie Cup. It was whilst he was in the Cape that Alan first experienced pain in his left shoulder and, after further excruciating spasms during pre-season nets at Bristol, Alan was diagnosed with Adhesive Capsulitis, or Frozen Shoulder Syndrome. A manipulative operation followed but he spent almost the entire season on the sidelines, save for a handful of 2nd XI matches where he bowled around 100 overs of innocuous left-arm seam and swing at well below his normal pace.

With his contract up, and doubts over his (and others) long-term fitness, it came as no real surprise when Gloucestershire's officials told him that they would only offer him terms for 1982 if he regained full fitness and full pace. Unsure of what the future might hold, Alan returned to Pretoria over the winter months to continue his rehabilitation. News that he was playing, and bowling again at something like his normal pace, reached Glamorgan and after discussions with their new management team of Secretary Phil Carling and captain Mike Selvey, Alan signed a new three-year contract back at Glamorgan.

Alan Wilkins – the TV presenter.

He made a dramatic return claiming the wicket of Essex's Brian Hardie with his first ball back in a daffodil sweater in the opening Championship match at Cardiff. As it turned out, Alan only played one season back in Wales, during which he added a further 12 first-class wickets to his tally, as he struck up a friendship with Ron Jones, the cricket and football commentator for BBC Wales. Whilst in South Africa the previous winter Alan had played alongside Trevor Quirk, a well-known media personality and, on several occasions, he had visited the broadcaster in his offices at SABC. Ron encouraged Alan to think about this as a new career, as well as arranging for some training in the art of commentary. Alan's training and experience as a teacher meant that he already had a good and strong voice, whilst he also possessed a good ear and had been renowned as a great mimic and impersonator in the dressing room banter that is part and parcel of life on the county circuit.

Alan took to this new work like a duck to water, so whilst spending the winter of 1983/84 in Johannesburg, playing and coaching at The Wanderers Club, he made further contact with SABC and accepted their offer to become a sports reporter and announcer. Realising that this would provide greater long-term security rather than trying to, soldier on in county cricket, he contacted the Glamorgan office to confirm that he had decided to retire from professional cricket.

He duly spent four years in South Africa covering a wide range of sports, besides doing shifts in the studio, writing scripts and learning the skills of live broadcasting. In 1988 Alan returned to the UK and became the presenter of BBC Wales' *Rugby Special* programme. He also worked on other TV and radio output from both Broadcasting House in Llandaff, as well as BBC Network in London, besides working for SABC, fronting their coverage of the Proteas cricket tour to the UK in 1995 as well as the 1995 Rugby World Cup.

After a dozen years with the BBC, Alan subsequently worked for TWI and ESPN Star Sports, based in Singapore, on a variety of sporting events with Alan commentating on, as well as presenting, coverage of Test Matches, One-Day Internationals and T20 matches all over the world, including the Indian Premier League, as well as other global events in golf and tennis, plus the Olympic Games in London in 2012 and Rio de Janeiro in 2016. Not bad for a man who came on to bowl as fifth change in the 1977 Gillette Cup Final!

1977

'Taffs against Toffs' was the headline in one tabloid as Glamorgan met Middlesex at Lord's in their first-ever one-day cup final at Lord's. Leading the side out at Lord's was another highlight in the long and distinguished career of Alan Jones. "Playing for England at Lord's in 1970 was great," recalled Alan, "but it was something else to lead out the Glamorgan team for the 1977 Gillette Cup Final, with our arrival onto the outfield being greeted by a huge roar from our supporters, as well as songs more reminiscent of Cardiff Arms Park on a rugby international day... There were Welsh flags, many huge red dragons, blue and yellow sun hats galore and plenty of banners and flags in both English and Welsh... we may have lost the battle, but we had won the war. A great day for Glamorgan and Wales."

It was certainly a watershed year for the Club as their successes in the Gillette Cup, plus better performances in the 40 and 55 overs competitions helped them shake off the malaise that had previously affected their performances in limited-overs cricket. Only four players – the Jones brothers plus Malcolm Nash and Tony Cordle – remained from the team that had won the County Championship eight summers before, whilst a series of new faces, including Collis King and Tom Cartwright, had been recruited specifically with one-day games in mind.

Both were in the Welsh county's line-up in late July as Glamorgan took county cricket to Aberystwyth as Vicarage Field hosted the Sunday League game with Essex as part of the university town's 900th anniversary celebrations. Apart from the result, the game was a huge success with receipts exceeding £2,000, with the crowd being treated to some Caribbean flair as Collis led the run chase after Graham Gooch had underpinned the Essex innings with 80 in even time.

1977 was also the final year of Wilf Wooller's tenure as Secretary with his retirement opening up a new chapter in the Club's history, with Ossie Wheatley acting as the Chair of a new and streamlined administration who were eager to shake off the troubles that had seen the previous summer degenerate into one of misery and despair. Having

Wilf Wooller (third left) on his last day in the Glamorgan offices during 1977. Also seen are Phil Clift, Les Spence and Bryn Thomas.

been the laughing stock of the county circuit in 1976, Glamorgan supporters had to pinch themselves in 1977 as John Hopkins posted a magnificent 230, Leicestershire were defeated in the Gillette Cup semi-final at Swansea, and Mike Llewellyn almost sent the ball over the pavilion at Lord's – to have done so, would really have been the stuff of dreams!

498
KING, Collis Llewellyn.

Born – Christ Church, Barbados, 11 June 1951.
Professional.
RHB, RM.
Ed – Metropolitan HS, Bridgetown.
1st XI: 1977.
West Indies 1976-1981 (9 Tests); Barbados 1972/73-1981/82; DB Close's XI 1982-
1986; Worcestershire 1983-1986; Natal 1984/85-1986/87.
Clubs: Nelson, Colne, Pontblyddyn, Oldham, Dunnington.

Batting and Fielding Record

	M	I	NO	RUNS	AV	100	50	CT	ST
F-c	16	27	1	811	31.19	-	6	13	-
List A	21	21	0	391	18.61	-	3	5	-

Bowling Record

	Balls	M	R	W	AV	5wI	10wM
F-c	1555	58	730	20	36.50	-	-
List A	818	15	565	17	33.23		

Career-bests

First-class –   78 v Surrey at Sophia Gardens, Cardiff , 1977.
        4/31 v Worcestershire at New Road, Worcester, 1977.
List A –   66 v Essex at Vicarage Field, Aberystwyth, 1977.
        2/17 v Derbyshire at Ilkeston, 1977.

Collis King was Glamorgan's overseas player in 1977 and appeared for the Welsh county against Middlesex in the final of the Gillette Cup at Lord's.

With Glamorgan looking for greater success in one-day cricket, and in the wake of Majid Khan's departure as overseas player, the Club's administrators signed the Bajan all-rounder who had made his Test debut during the 1976 West Indies tour of England and had struck an impressive 163 in their match against Northamptonshire.

Compared with other overseas all-rounders on the county circuit at the time, Collis failed to score a century for Glamorgan, or take a Championship 'five-for', and many Glamorgan supporters – rather unfairly – still remember him as the man who dropped the catch offered by Clive Radley in the Gillette Cup Final. Putting this to one side, Collis proved to be a useful acquisition and, after the upheavals of the previous summer, he proved to be a popular figure with his colleagues. There were occasions when Collis was hampered by a series of niggling injuries but, when fully fit, he gave several glimpses of his international pedigree with both bat and ball, scoring 70 and 67 in the match with Sussex at Eastbourne, besides making 74 and taking 4/31 against Gloucestershire at Abergavenny, as well as a return of 4/37 plus a combative 68 earlier in the season against Somerset at Sophia Gardens.

Collis King, seen practising at Swansea during 1977.

The following summer, Collis enjoyed a stellar season playing in the North Wales Premier League for Pontblyddyn. His all-round performances for the village club near Mold have gone down in the annals as amongst the finest by anyone in a single season in Welsh cricket – in a dozen matches, Collis hit 74 sixes and 92 fours as he amassed 1,115 runs at and average of 139, besides claiming 44 wickets at just four runs apiece.

The summer of 1979 saw Collis hit the international headlines with a scintillating and match-winning innings for the West Indies in the World Cup final at Lord's. Batting at number six, Collis arrived at the crease with England having reduced the Caribbean side to 99-4. With Collis known as a flamboyant striker of the ball, and Geoff Boycott bowling a spell of nagging seam, Viv Richards strolled down the wicket to greet his new partner and said "Hey man, take it easy – we have plenty of time." Collis duly replied "Smokey, I ain't gonna let Geoffrey do this. In the League there would be no mercy, so why should this be any different?"

Viv strolled back to his crease, but the usually merciless Antiguan was reduced to being a bit-part player as Collis plundered 86 off 66 balls with 10 rasping fours and 3 huge sixes as the pair shared a 138-run stand. Viv went on to remain unbeaten 138 and won the Man-of-the-Match award, but it was Collis who had played the innings of the day as his side strolled to victory by 92 runs. After his hurricane hitting, and the West Indians victory, Collis could have forgiven for being wrapped up in the joyous celebrations with Clive Lloyd and his colleagues, but the story goes that an hour or so after the presentation ceremony ended, Collis phoned up his friends at Pontblyddyn to find out how the North Wales club had fared in their league match!

Born and raised in the Christ Church district of Barbados, Collis had made his first-class debut for his native island at Bridgetown in January 1973 before securing a regular berth in the Barbados side. 1976 saw Collis win the first of his 9 Test appearances for the West Indies, with the highlight being the Second Test of the series against New Zealand at Christchurch in 1979/80 when he scored an unbeaten 100. Collis also appeared in 18 One-Day Internationals, besides appearing in World Series Cricket between 1977 and 1979, before going on the 'rebel' West Indian tours to South Africa during 1982/83 and 1983/84. He hit 101 at Johannesburg in the second 'Test' of the 1982/83 series with his classy efforts prompting four young spectators to run onto the outfield with a banner reading 'Coll Is King'.

By this time, Collis was also enjoying a successful time in the Lancashire Leagues, having first played for Nelson in 1974. He was attached to Colne but, during May 1983, Collis helped out Worcestershire and marked his Championship debut for the West Midlands side by scoring 123 against Somerset at New Road. He maintained his allegiance with them until 1985, but largely played in one-day matches.

In subsequent season, Collis has given loyal service to Dunnington for whom he has played well into his sixties in both the York and District Secnior League as well as the Yorkshire Premier League North. Sadly, during 2018 bureaucratic issues saw the sixty-seven-year-old briefly deported back to Barbados after a technicality on his application for a spousal visa to live in the UK alongside Beverly, his English wife, despite the fact that Collis had spent forty-four years in the country.

Collis King, seen batting for the West Indies during 1979.

499
CARTWRIGHT, Thomas William MBE.

Born – Aldermans Greens, Coventry, 22 July 1935.
Died – Neath, 30 April 2007.
RHB, RM.
Professional.
Ed – Foxford School, Coventry.
1st XI: 1977.
2nd XI: 1978-1983.
Warwickshire 1952-1969; England – 5 Tests 1964/65; Somerset 1970-1976.

Batting and Fielding Record

	M	I	NO	RUNS	AV	100	50	CT	ST
F-c	7	11	2	76	8.44	-	-	2	-
List A	19	8	4	32	8.00	-	-	2	-

Bowling Record

	Balls	M	R	W	AV	5wI	10wM
F-c	789	52	258	10	25.80	-	-
List A	912	26	503	17	29.58	-	-

Career-bests

First-class –   22* v Kent at St Helen's, Swansea, 1977.
                 4/46 v Yorkshire at Sophia Gardens, Cardiff, 1977.
List A –   10* v Derbyshire at Sophia Gardens, Cardiff, 1977.
                 3/17 v Northamptonshire at Northampton, 1977.

Tom Cartwright was one of the finest medium pace bowlers in county cricket during the late 1950s and 1960s – a period that saw him play for Warwickshire before spending six years with Somerset and one year playing for Glamorgan. Although he only claimed 27 wickets for the Welsh county, Tom left a lasting legacy on Welsh cricket by being an outstanding Director of Coaching for the Welsh Cricket Association from 1977 unto 2000, besides creating a coaching framework across the Principality.

Tom's association with Glamorgan, and *inter alia* Wales, quite bizarrely began in a toilet in Weston-super-Mare during August 1976. This was the location for a heated exchange between Tom and the Somerset Chairman, Herbie Hoskins, a farmer from Yeovil. At the time, Somerset were riding high in the Sunday League and looking like clinching their first-ever title. Tom though was on the sidelines with a damaged right shoulder and had just started out on the comeback trail by taking 6/24 in a 2nd XI match against Shropshire at Bath.

Herbie was desperate for the experienced seamer to return to 1st XI action as soon as possible, and with Tom at the Clarence Park ground for the match against Lancashire, Herbie suggested a chat in the pavillion. The only space though in the tiny pavillion was in the toilet area and it was here that a furious row unfolded. Herbie told Tom that he was keen for him to return to 1st XI action and said that the club doctor had told him that Tom was fit enough to return. Tom insisted however that he was not yet fit to bowl, with their argument continuing for around ten minutes. In the days that followed, a committee meeting was held which resulted in Tom, who was in the final year of his contract being told that his contract was not going to be renewed.

Matters were not helped firstly, when a story started circulating saying that Tom had refused to play or secondly, when Somerset needing to

Tom Cartwright.

win or tie their final game against Glamorgan at Sophia Gardens, were beaten by one run in a pulsating finish at a ground where over 90% of the crowd were from Somerset, prompting Alan Gibson to write "Sophia Gardens might have been Bridgwater Carnival!" Despite the result, the Somerset committee did not change their decision with Tom finding himself out of work. His good friend John Arlott came to the rescue and wrote to Ossie Wheatley, the newly appointed Chairman of Glamorgan suggesting that Tom could do a job coaching and, if fit, playing for the Welsh county.

Ossie relished John's approach, especially given the parlous state of the Club after the events of 1976, the plethora of young and inexperienced players, plus the team's modest record in limited-overs cricket. He also knew of Tom's success in grooming a number of young players for Somerset, including Ian Botham, as well as the complete absence of a coaching framework in Wales. Ossie therefore met up with Tom and, with the committee's blessing, proposed that he spent the summer acting as Glamorgan's player/coach before starting work over the winter as Director of Coaching to the Welsh Cricket Association. With his wife Joan having been born in Neath, Tom readily agreed and, together with his family, he moved back to the town where the pair duly spent the rest of their lives.

By sheer coincidence, Tom made his debut for Glamorgan in their Benson and Hedges Cup match in April at Edgbaston – the ground where he had first played for Warwickshire Schools back in 1950. He began with the fine return of 8-0-25-3 as the Welsh county comprehensively won by 92 runs. The following week, he was back in action in the double-header against Worcestershire at Swansea, followed by the Sunday League encounter with Gloucestershire at Bristol. Once again, he returned the outstanding figures of 11-5-26-2 at Swansea as Glamorgan won by six wickets before the next day seeing his new county beat Gloucestershire by three wickets, thanks to decent performances from two of his young charges, as Mike Llewellyn made an unbeaten 79 whilst off-spinner Gwyn Richards took 3/20. It was a handsome start to the summer for Glamorgan who had lurched from

Tom Cartwright, at first slip appeals as Mike Brearley edges Malcolm Nash into Eifion Jones' gloves during the 1977 Gillette Cup Final. Collis King also appeals at second slip.

defeat to defeat the previous year, but their bubble burst at the end of May as they lost their Championship encounter with Yorkshire by ten wickets at Cardiff, despite Tom returning figures of 31-15-46-4.

July and August saw Tom being part and parcel of Glamorgan's winning run in the Gillette Cup, starting with figures of 12-6-29-0 in the victory over Worcestershire at New Road, followed by 12-2-43-2 in the quarter-final victory over Surrey at Cardiff. The semi-final saw Tom in equally miserly mode at Swansea, returning the analysis of 11-1-34-0, before completing figures of 12-2-32-1 in the final against Middlesex at Lord's. Given his parsimony, it was no surprise that Glamorgan's committee offered him fresh terms to carry on playing in 1978, but Tom knew that the time was right to hang up his bowling boots once and for all, and he accepted instead the new role as the Club's cricket manager.

After the dream start to his time with Glamorgan during 1977, things became much more difficult over the course of the next couple of years. Not all of the younger players appreciated his style of management, especially Alan Wilkins who left the Club at the end of 1979 having clashed swords on several occasions with Tom. Alan later wrote in his autobiography that "I was not the only young player in that Glamorgan team who felt that way about his lack of empathy with a team that needed collective responsibility, a group of young players who needed more encouragement, not the autocratic style which Tom brought to the club which I felt was archaic and not suited to this team." With Glamorgan failing to win a single Championship match during 1979 for the first time in their history, there was an overhaul of the Club's coaching structure with Tom devoting his energies on his work with the Welsh Cricket Association and junior age-group teams, with Tom, from 1980, running the under-16 team – a role he continued until 2006 and after his retirement from the Director of Coaching post.

Tom proved himself to be an outstanding coach and his tireless hours of effort and wise guidance helped to produce a steady stream of talented Welsh cricketers, several of whom went to win honours for both Glamorgan and England. He fully deserved all the plaudits he received, including the MBE on his retirement in 2000. In the words of Robert Croft, "Tom's been superb. He's got a fantastic technical knowledge of the game and a very good eye for talent. For all of us guys who've come through into the Glamorgan team, he's been a real influence; he's added an extra edge of discipline and professionalism."

Having joined the Warwickshire staff aged sixteen, Tom made his first-class debut in 1952 and in the space of ten seasons with Warwickshire, he took over a thousand wickets, despite rarely using, or wanting, the new ball. His repertoire of in-swingers and subtle changes of place also won him 5 Test caps in 1964/65. Tom played for Warwickshire until 1969 when he joined Millfield School as their coach and began his career with Somerset.

Tom's career best figures were 8/39 for Warwickshire against Somerset at Weston-super-Mare in 1962, whilst his best match figures were 15/89 against Glamorgan at Swansea in 1967. He was also an effective batsman, scoring, in all, seven first-class centuries. His highest score was 210 for Warwickshire against Middlesex at Nuneaton in 1962, and that season, he also completed the coveted 'Double' of 1000 runs and 100 wickets.

500
CROWTHER, Peter Gwynne.

Born – Neath, 26 April 1952.
Professional.
RHB, OB.
Ed – Cwrt Sart School, Neath Grammar School and Aberystwyth University.
1st XI: 1977-1978.
2nd XI: 1971-1978.
Wales 1974-1976.
Clubs: Maesteg Town, Neath and Briton Ferry Town.

Batting and Fielding Record

	M	I	NO	RUNS	AV	100	50	CT	ST
F-c	9	14	0	185	13.21	-	1	3	-
List A	1	1	1	0	-	-	-	-	-

Bowling Record

	Balls	M	R	W	AV	5wI	10wM
F-c	42	1	22	1	22.00	-	-

Career-bests

First-class –   99 v Cambridge University at Fenner's,1977.
1/22 v Cambridge University at Fenner's, 1977.
List A –   0* v Derbyshire at Ilkeston, 1977.

Peter Crowther was a highly talented young batsman with Neath and Maesteg Town during the 1970s, but had the misfortune to score 99 on his first-class debut for Glamorgan, against Cambridge University at Fenners in 1977. Sadly, the right-handed batsman never got another chance to score a hundred for the Welsh county as, after suffering health problems the following summer, he asked to be released from his contract. He had first played for Glamorgan 2nd XI in 1971 after a brief spell on the MCC groundstaff at Lord's under the tutelage of Head Coach and former Glamorgan cricketer Len Muncer. Peter then attended Aberystwyth University and, as an undergraduate, made his debut for Wales in 1974 in their Triple Crown game against Ireland.

Peter Crowther.

During June 1975 Peter featured in the Wales team which met East Africa in their World Cup warm-up game at Swansea, whilst the following year he played again for Wales against Scotland in the Triple Crown competition.

After some decent innings in 2nd XI games, Peter appeared in three Championship games during June 1977 before doing the same the following year. But in a total of nine innings against county opposition he only amassed 32 runs. After leaving Glamorgan, there was talk of Peter having a trial with Worcestershire, but he opted against trying to pursue a career in county cricket.

1978

Many thought 1978 would be the dawn of a new era following Glamorgan's appearance at the Gillette Cup Final in 1977, plus the appointment of Phil Clift as Wilf Wooller's replacement as Secretary and Tom Cartwright becoming the Club's first-ever Cricket Manager. It did not materialize though and, for the umpteenth time during the 1970s, the phrase "we are in transition" was trotted out by the administrators, although as Peter Walker candidly observed "there were many players and other officials who were unsure where the Club were transitioning to or from!"

Glamorgan rose up one place in the County Championship table, but dreams of another decent run in the Gillette Cup were quickly snuffed out by a 70-run defeat to Somerset in the second round of the competition. Early in the season, the Welsh county enjoyed decent form in the Benson and Hedges Cup and appeared in the quarter-final at Edgbaston. But Warwickshire won by 46 runs to end Glamorgan's dreams of another trip to Lord's and putting right what had happened the year before.

Six out of sixteen games in the Sunday League were won, including the contest with Gloucestershire at Sophia Gardens where Alan Jones became the Club's first centurion in the 40 overs competition. There might have been victories in other

Alan Lewis Jones receives a presentation flanked by Phil Clift (extreme right) and Judge Rowe Harding, the Glamorgan Chairman (third left).

matches as, like in the Championship, Glamorgan lost the initiative at vital times and let a possible victory slip from their grasp. The weather also played a hand, and during the first half of the so-called summer 30 out of 40 playing days were affected either in part or in full by rain and bad light.

The loss of match days meant that gate receipts fell and, over the winter months, the Club's administrators took steps to rectify both the financial position and strengthen the playing resources. Membership fees duly rose but, without any financial clout behind them, the Club's officials – despite lofty ambitions of signing high-profile players and promising talent at other counties – were unable to net a big fish.

501
SWART, Peter Douglas.

Born – Bulawayo, Rhodesia, 27 April 1946.
Died – Cape Town, 13 March 2000.
Professional.
Ed – Que Que Junior School; Jameson HS, Gatooma, Rhodesia.
RHB, RM.
1st XI: 1978-1979.
Cap: 1979.
Rhodesia 1965/66; Western Province 1967/68-1980/81; Lancashire 2nd XI 1969; South African Invitation XI 1973/74; Cambridgeshire 1974-1976; DH Robins' XI 1974-1976; Boland 1981/82-1982/83; Western Province 1983/84-1984/85.
Clubs: Accrington, Haslingden, East Lancashire, VRA Amsterdam.

Batting and Fielding Record

	M	I	NO	RUNS	AV	100	50	CT	ST
F-c	44	73	8	1996	30.70	4	9	34	-
List A	40	39	8	1077	34.74	-	9	10	-

Bowling Record

	Balls	M	R	W	AV	5wI	10wM
F-c	3555	123	1785	64	27.89	-	-
List A	1585	24	1052	41	25.65	-	-

Career-bests

First-class –   122   v Worcestershire at St Helen's Swansea, 1979.
                4/24 v Middlesex at St Helen's, Swansea, 1978.
List A –   85*   v Surrey at The Oval, 1978.
                4/35 v Essex at Chelmsford, 1979.

Peter Swart was Glamorgan's overseas player during 1978 and 1979 having enjoyed much success in Lancashire League cricket and in domestic cricket in South Africa since the late 1960s.

The Rhodesian all-rounder proved a useful acquisition, especially in one-day games, where his hard-hitting batting and accurate medium pace bowling delivered with a slingy action, were particularly useful, drawing on his many years of experience in League cricket as well as in domestic cricket in South Africa for Western Province. As befitted a man with an upright stance whilst batting, Peter's quick eye and long levers also allowed him to unleash some flowing drives, especially through the offside.

His miserly bowling made an immediate impact in the List A matches and made up for the retirement of Tom Cartwright, whilst against a strong Combined Universities team at The Parks in May 1978 Peter won the Gold Award after making an unbeaten 83 followed by figures of 10-0-34-1. He also made valuable contributions in Championship matches during 1978, amassing 1,078 runs in first-class games, besides making 115 against Oxford

University at The Parks, 102* against Northamptonshire at Sophia Gardens, and 103 against Sussex at Swansea. Some felt though that given his impressive record in South Africa, Peter should have scored more runs in both formats of the game, with some critics believing that perhaps Peter should have shown more restraint at crucial times of an innings and resisted going for an aggressive stroke. There were mutterings as well from some quarters about his heavy drinking and a negative impact on the younger players.

Peter failed to pass a thousand in 1979, although had it been a better summer collectively for the Club, he would probably have had greater chances to improve on his tally of 918 first-class runs and one century. Nevertheless, the summer did see Peter record career-best performances with 122 against Worcestershire at St Helen's,

Peter Swart, as seen at Swansea during 1979.

plus figures of 4/35 in the List A encounter with Essex at Chelmsford. It was though a largely unproductive season for the Welsh county, with the lack of success, as well as the financial constraints frustrating Peter, who left the county at the end of the season, but not before telling a journalist about his angst and how better treated other overseas players were at other counties, before firing off a broadside alleging that Glamorgan were "a fish and chip county rather than being the real deal!"

As well as his outstanding record in League and South African cricket, Peter's combative approach and competitive instincts were highly valued in the Glamorgan changing room, especially given what was, on several occasions, a quite inexperienced line-up. His forthright and brash character did however lead to a few clashes of personality, notably with Rodney Ontong and coach Tom Cartwright. Nevertheless, Peter's sheer love of the game led to him giving plenty of generous advice to the junior professionals. Alan

Wilkins was one of the youngsters at that time who benefitted from Peter's honest words – "he helped me with my bowling, using different grips, using different types of deliveries and just talking to me about the craft of pace bowling, which none of my Glamorgan teammates had done with the exception of Tony Cordle."

Kevin Lyons, who also coached in Western Province, had spoken up in favour of Peter's acquisition, aware of his fine record and, like the rest of the Glamorgan administrators, was unaware that Peter had agreed to return to play for Haslingden in the Lancashire League. In these days before agents, misunderstandings were commonplace, and the outcome was that Haslingden agreed to release Swart with Glamorgan offering compensation to them.

Born and raised in Rhodesia, Peter's father was a cricket fanatic who played and coached for around fifty years. To his delight, young Peter had shown immense promise as an all-rounder whilst at senior school and played as a teenager in the Logan Cup competition as well as for Mashonaland Country Districts. His athletic fielding also impressed, especially his ability of throwing accurately with either arm.

Peter Swart in bowling action for Glamorgan.

His prowess as a youngster drew comparisons with Colin Bland whilst during his time with Glamorgan, Peter completed what Alan Jones described as the finest catch he had ever seen. It came during the match at New Road against Worcestershire as Glenn Turner top-edged a ball from Andy Mack high in the air towards deep backward point, only for Peter to sprint some thirty yards from second slip to catch the ball as it dropped over his shoulders and into his out-stretched hands. As John Billot reported in the *Western Mail*, "to retain the ball in his grip as Swart hit the ground in a fast free-fall with a shattering thud that must have virtually loosened his teeth was the *piece de resistance*. His Glamorgan team-mates went chasing towards him like a pack of hounds to shower their congratulations as he untangled himself from a spread-eagled position on the turf."

Peter had made his first-class debut for Rhodesia in the Currie Cup against Natal at Pietermaritzburg in December 1965 before undertaking his military service and then heading to Cape Town where he started playing for Western Province. He duly enjoyed a highly productive career for them in domestic cricket, including winning the Currie Cup in 1974/75 under Eddie Barlow. Indeed, it was on Eddie's recommendation that in 1969, Peter headed to the UK where he played in the Lancashire Leagues for Accrington until 1973, prior to having a stint with Haslingden from 1974-1977.

The tradition in the Leagues of a collection being made for anyone who made a half-century greatly appealed to Peter and his colleagues recalled how he would gleefully use the money to purchase plenty of beer and, as befitted someone who was a chain-smoker, a stack of cigarettes. As well as his habit of walking barefoot around Accrington, Peter's team-mates also recalled one of his special party pieces with fags. "He used to hold a block of ice between his thumb and forefinger for ten minutes," said one, "resulting in them turning completely numb and would then light a cigarette and allow it to burn against his skin until only a stub end remained."

During 1969, Peter also played in 2nd XI cricket for Lancashire besides having a three-year association with Cambridgeshire in the Minor County Championship. In September that year, Peter also appeared for the International Cavaliers against Barbados at Scarborough, whilst in 1973/74 he was also chosen for a South African Invitation XI, led by Eddie Barlow and including Barry Richards, Graeme Pollock, Mike Procter and Vincent van der Bijl which played a series of matches against DH Robins' XI. Peter also played for Derrick's team in the UK, appearing against Oxford University in 1974 and Middlesex during 1976.

After leaving Glamorgan, Peter returned to League cricket and played for East Lancashire from 1980 and 1982 before spending a couple of years playing in Amsterdam where he enjoyed the Dutch lifestyle and everything that the famous city had on offer. Having also had a spell with Boland during the early 1980s, Peter returned to Western Province for 1983/84 and played for two more seasons until retiring, but not before having become one of the few players to complete the Currie Cup career double of over 2,000 runs and 200 wickets.

After retiring from playing, Peter became a groundsman at Newlands in Cape Town, as well as at Paarl in Border where he oversaw the relaying of a trio of what had hitherto been quite difficult pitches. He had previously worked as a salesman for Stellenbosch farmers Winery, where Eddie Barlow was his boss. Never short of a few words, Peter took great delight in selling a cheap white wine, with his sales pitch being "The best in the west, for the throat and the chest!"

Perhaps though Peter's best one-liner related to his liking for a brand of cigarettes called 'Life', with Peter telling anyone who would listen "I smoke these because they give you life!" Sadly, however, in March 2000 Peter died in his sleep at the age of fifty-three, at his home in Newlands, Cape Town from a suspected heart attack.

502
MACK, Andrew James.

Born – Aylsham, Norfolk, 14 January 1956.
Professional.
LHB, LM.
1st XI: 1978-1980.
2nd XI: 1978-1980.
Surrey 2nd XI 1973-1977; Surrey 1976-1977; Norfolk 1989-1991; Minor Counties
1990-1991.
Clubs: Norwich Barleycorns, XL Club.

Batting and Fielding Record

	M	I	NO	RUNS	AV	100	50	CT	ST
F-c	21	23	10	60	4.61	-	-	4	-
List A	26	13	10	16	5.33	-	-	5	-

Bowling Record

	Balls	M	R	W	AV	5wI	10wM
F-c	2113	70	1129	37	30.51	-	-
List A	1156	18	856	24	35.67	-	-

Career-bests

First-class –   18 v Indians at St Helen's, Swansea, 1979.
                4/28 v Worcestershire at New Road, Worcester, 1978.
List A –   3* v Essex at Chelmsford, 1980.
                3/24 v Middlesex at Sophia Gardens, Cardiff, 1980.

Andy Mack spent three years on Glamorgan's staff during the late 1970s, after spending two years on Surrey's books.

The tall left-arm seamer had first played for Surrey 2nd XI during 1973, before appearing in five Sunday League matches for Surrey during 1975, starting with the game against Hampshire at Southampton. He then joined their staff and made his first-class debut against the 1976 West Indians at The Oval. Andy subsequently made two appearances in Championship games during 1976, but he was unable to command a regular first team place and in 1978 moved to South Wales hoping to play more first-class cricket.

However, Andy continued to struggle with form and fitness whilst with Glamorgan and, despite an ability to bowl a nasty short ball, the left-armer did not win a regular place in the 1st XI line-up. In all formats, he claimed a total of 61 wickets with his best performance coming on his

Andy Mack

Championship debut for the Welsh county at New Road during June 1978. Entering the attack as first change after Malcolm Nash and fellow left-armer Alan Wilkins had shared the new ball, Andy returned figures of 3/24 and 4/28 with Worcestershire dismissed for 95 in their second innings as Glamorgan completed a 175-run victory.

Andy ended the 1978 season with a tally of first-class wickets at just 12 apiece, but his 14 scalps during 1979 came at a cost of 41 runs. In 1980 he enjoyed an extended run from mid-July until late August in Glamorgan's Championship line-up, but in eight first-class appearances, Andy only took 7 wickets at 51 runs apiece and with injury concerns still plaguing him, he was released from the Welsh county's staff in 1980

Andy Mack, seen bowling for Glamorgan at Swansea.

Andy subsequently joined the Metropolitan Police and represented the British Police from 1982 besides returning to club cricket in his native Norfolk. In 1989 Andy also appeared in Minor County cricket for Norfolk with his lively left-arm bowling winning him a place in the Minor Counties squad for the Benson and Hedges tournament the following year. 1990 proved to be something of a renaissance for Andy as, despite a ten-year absence from the county circuit, he returned the commendable figures of 11-2-47-2 against Middlesex at Lord's before taking 2/36 against Sussex, 2/22 in the match with Somerset and 2/49 against Derbyshire.

Andy retained his place in the Minor Counties squad in the Benson and Hedges Cup for 1991 and re-appeared for them against Glamorgan at Trowbridge. He went wicketless in the game against his former employers, as well as the contests against Hampshire and Yorkshire which both ended in heavy defeats for the Minor Counties. Andy continued to play for the British Police until 1995, whilst in 2006 and 2007 he played for the Norfolk Over 50s.

503
HOLMES, Geoffrey Clarke.

Born – Newcastle-upon-Tyne, 16 September 1958.

Died – Cardiff, 23 March 2009.

Professional.

RHB, RM.

Ed – West Denton HS.

1st XI: 1978-1991.

2nd XI: 1977-1991.

Club and Ground: 1989-1996.

Cap: 1985.

Northumberland 1974-1977; Border 1989/90.

Clubs: Jesmond, Cardiff and Neath.

Batting and Fielding Record

	M	I	NO	RUNS	AV	100	50	CT	ST
F-c	203	325	50	7529	27.38	9	34	82	-
List A	181	165	29	3474	25.54	-	18	53	-

Bowling Record

	Overs	M	R	W	AV	5wI	10wM
F-c	6932	223	3963	88	45.03	2	-
List A	4232	42	3430	136	25.22		

Career-bests

First-class – 125* v Somerset at Sophia Gardens, Cardiff, 1990.

5/38 v Essex at Colchester, 1988.

List A – 73 v Warwickshire at Edgbaston, 1984.

5/2 v Derbyshire at Ebbw Vale, 1984.

Geoff Holmes was a talented all-rounder who played in over 200 first-class matches for Glamorgan between 1978 and 1991, before serving as the Director of the Cricket Board of Wales and painstakingly overseeing a host of developments in cricket at grass roots level across the Principality.

Born in Newcastle in September 1958, he soon developed a love of sport, fanatically supporting the city's football team during the winter and playing cricket during the summer. Indeed, Geoff caught the cricket bug at a young age, playing his own version of Test matches by bowling a ball up against a wall in his back garden and then batting against the rebound, whilst at the same time providing

Geoff Holmes.

his own running commentary on the progress of his England team! Born Geoffrey Holmes, his fanatical love of cricket also saw the youngster add 'Clarke' as a second Christian name, believing that all respectable cricketers had a middle initial. Geoff Boycott soon became his batting idol, simply because of their shared Christian name. It proved a wise choice because, after several years of modelling his skills on the great Yorkshire and England batsman, the teenager won selection in the Northumberland junior teams, before securing a place on the MCC groundstaff.

The coach of Jesmond, Geoff's junior team, was also a Welshman and he set the ball rolling by organizing a trial for Geoff with Glamorgan 2nd XI during April 1977 against the MCC Young Professionals at Uxbridge. He impressed both parties and after playing for the MCC side, plus further positive comments coming from Len

Geoff Holmes on-drives a ball at Sophia Gardens during a Championship match in 1989.

Muncer, Glamorgan's former all-rounder who served as the MCC's head coach, Geoff was offered terms by the Welsh county for 1978.

At the end of August 1978, Geoff made his first-class debut against Warwickshire at Sophia Gardens. He soon confirmed his rich potential by scoring a century against Gloucestershire at Bristol the following year in only his third Championship match and all against a lively attack that included the waspish pace of Mike Procter having arrived at the crease with the South African on a hat-trick and his team in all sorts of trouble on 39-5. His Northern grit, plus great tenacity and application saw him reach three figures after five hours at the crease with Glamorgan recovering to 327.

Whilst his next Championship century did not come until 1985, with an unbeaten 112 at Leicester, Geoff subsequently developed into a highly effective batsman, and also a great team man, who was prepared to bat anywhere in the Welsh county's line-up from number three to six in Championship games whilst also opening the batting in one-day games. He also had a short spell opening the batting in Championship matches during 1985 whilst on three occasions – 1984, 1985 and 1986 – Geoff scored 1,000 runs in the season. In 1988 at Taunton, he also scored a century in each innings with scores of 100* and 107 and became only the seventh Glamorgan batsman to achieve the feat.

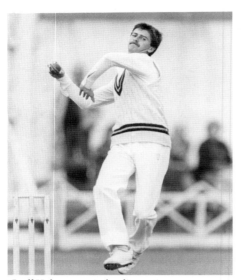
Geoff Holmes, seen in bowling action.

Whilst others were more flamboyant in style, Geoff became a steady accumulator, cleverly working the ball into gaps in the field, and then running like a whippet in between the wickets. Indeed, in his early years on the county's staff, his scampering with the likes of Pakistani maestro Javed Miandad frustrated a number of opponents, whilst his refusal of another quick single was always accompanied by a cry, in lilting Geordie tones, of "Weet".

1988 saw Geoff make 117 against Gloucestershire at Bristol and 108 against Somerset at Sophia Gardens, with the latter match seeing him share a stand of 216 for the fourth wicket with Ravi Shastri. This was one of many sizeable partnerships in which Geoff participated with others including an unbeaten 199 with Javed Miandad for the fifth wicket against Leicestershire at Swansea in 1984, 234 with Matthew Maynard for the fourth wicket against Oxford University at The Parks in 1986, plus 180 for the third wicket with John Hopkins against the 1986 New Zealanders at Swansea.

Geoff's most productive season from a batting point of view in Championship cricket was 1985, when he amassed 1,129 runs and won his county cap. Three years later, he ended the domestic season with an aggregate of 999, but in typically cheerful fashion, he did not dwell for too long on his misfortune of missing out on a thousand, and was very grateful for getting so close. In all, he scored nine first-class hundreds, with his career-best score being 182 for Border against Western Province B in 1989/90 – one of several winters when Geoff played and coached in South Africa.

His athleticism saw Geoff develop into a livewire in the field, whilst he also became highly adept at bowling nagging medium pace, delivered with a slingy action modelled on another Jeff – Australian Jeff Thomson. Admittedly, Geoff's bowling was somewhat slower than his bowling idol, but even so, he produced some fine spells in limited overs cricket during the 1980's – an era during which the Welsh county, at long last, found their feet in the shorter form of the game – with his returns including a remarkable 5/2 in the Sunday League match with Derbyshire at Ebbw Vale in 1984, as well as a hat-trick at the same ground in 1987 during the Sunday fixture with Nottinghamshire as he returned figures of 5/27. Two years before, he also claimed 5/16 in the Sunday League match against Yorkshire at Swansea as well as 5/24 in the NatWest Trophy contest with Scotland at Edinburgh – a performance which deservedly won Geoff the Man-of-the-Match Award.

Alan Wilkins, a long-standing friend and colleague of Geoff's summed up his attributes "he is your archetypal 'bread and butter' county professional upon whom the more glamorous cricketers depend week in and week out. He has batted in virtually every position for the county and has been called upon to bowl when he was least expecting to. Never a murmur, he would simply get on with the job his captain asked of him."

A back injury forced Geoff to retire from county cricket at the end of 1991, which was also his Benefit Season. He subsequently joined a leading Building Society, and his excellent inter-personal skills and organisation saw him quickly rise to a management position. In 2005 he returned to the cricket world succeeding Mark Frost – his former county colleague – as Director of the Cricket Board of Wales.

For the next few years, he tirelessly promoted cricket at grass roots level in Wales and helped establish a coaching and development framework which has become the envy of many counties. Amongst his many achievements for the CBW was overseeing the introduction of the Chance to Shine initiative in Wales and bringing in a capping system for the junior Welsh sides, with Geoff – as befitted a proud family man – taking great satisfaction in the achievements of the young players and their progression through the various national squads. His son Greg duly followed this pathway and played for Glamorgan 2nd XI between 2011 and 2016, besides representing Cardiff MCCU and Wales Minor Counties before becoming the captain of Cardiff CC.

Tragically, Geoff died suddenly during March 2009 after being taken ill whilst working at the Sophia Gardens ground. The healthy state of Welsh cricket at junior and club level at the time of his sudden and untimely death was a lasting legacy to the outstanding efforts of a hard-working and loyal man who was a great servant to cricket in Wales.

Geoff Holmes on-drives the ball at Sophia Gardens during 1989.

1979

As *Wisden*'s correspondent wrote "if 1978 was never an easy summer then 1979 was a disaster for Glamorgan." They failed to win a Championship match for the first-ever time in their history and only won a handful of one-day matches. Whilst Glamorgan progressed to the quarter-final stage of the Benson and Hedges Cup, they only reached the last eight and had a home quarter-final with Derbyshire at Sophia Gardens, after Somerset had been thrown out of the competition following their decision to declare their innings after just one over against Worcestershire at New Road.

Whilst Somerset's decision caused a furore amongst the corridors of power at Lord's, more than a few eyebrows had been raised earlier in the year by Glamorgan's decision to replace Alan Jones as captain for 1979 by signing Robin Hobbs, the former Essex and England leg-spinner. After everything which had gone on during the previous few years, Alan had the confidence and support of the team, but Tom Cartwright, the Cricket Manager, believed Alan to be a reluctant captain. The committee backed Tom

The Glamorgan playing squad for 1979. Back row – John Derrick, Michael Thornton, Geoff Holmes, Jeremy Newman, Andy Mack, Neil Perry, Mark Davies, Arthur Francis and Alan Lewis Jones. Front row – Rodney Ontong, Mike Llewellyn, Peter Swart, Robin Hobbs, Tony Cordle, John Hopkins and Gwyn Richards.

and authorized a change in leadership, but it was yet another decision made by the administration without confiding in the senior players.

As Alan recalled. "I was therefore disappointed to hear rumours that the Club were actively searching for a new captain in 1979. I had packed my bags for [another coaching stint in] South Africa hoping that this was just idle gossip. It was only when I was 4,000 miles away that the decision was made not to retain me as captain." If the left-hander had not been such a proud Welshman and loyal to the county he had served for over a quarter of a century, he could have easily stayed put in the Cape, or join another county. It was a sign of his professionalism that he put these disappointments to one side and, together with John Hopkins and Rodney Ontong, passed the 1,000-run mark.

As it turned out, Robin was only in charge for one summer with 1979 proving to be the nadir in Glamorgan's recent history. Steps were subsequently taken to improve matters with top-class international players being signed, rather than journeymen from overseas. In addition, a new crop of promising homegrown players emerged during the 1980s who, unlike their counterparts in the 1970s, established regular berths in the Glamorgan side, besides meeting with much success in county cricket and, in several cases, playing for England as well.

504
HOBBS, Robin Nicholas Stuart.

Born – Chippenham, 8 May 1942.

RHB, LBG.

1st XI: 1979-1981.

2nd XI: 1980-1981.

Cap: 1979.

Ed – Raines CS, Stepney.

Essex 1961-1975; MCC to East Africa 1963/64, to South Africa 1964/65 and to Pakistan 1966/67 and 1968/1969; England (7 Tests) 1967-1971; Suffolk 1976-1978.

Batting and Fielding Record

	M	I	NO	RUNS	AV	100	50	CT	ST
F-c	41	44	19	246	9.84	-	-	20	-
List A	14	5	1	26	6.50	-	-	3	-

Bowling Record

	Balls	M	R	W	AV	5wI	10wM
F-c	4641	204	2370	65	36.46	2	-
List A	132	1	98	4	24.50	-	-

Career-bests

First-class –   49* v Hampshire at St Helen's, Swansea, 1981.

5/67 v Worcestershire at Hereford, 1981.

List A –   12* v Kent at St Helen's, Swansea, 1979.

3/41 v Derbyshire at Sophia Gardens, Cardiff, 1979.

Robin Hobbs.

Robin Hobbs, the former Essex and England leg-spinner, captained Glamorgan in 1979 having been signed by the Welsh county after the Chippenham-born leg spinner had enjoyed an illustrious career with Essex besides winning seven Test caps for England.

His signing – on a three-year contract – came as something of a shock, especially as he had not played in county cricket since 1975 and had started working for Barclaycard. It was said though by Glamorgan officials that there were several good, young cricketers in the Club's ranks who did not seem to be getting anywhere so they wanted somebody in charge, with plenty of experience who would, at least, help them to develop and also enjoy their cricket.

By signing him, the Glamorgan committee were taking a big gamble, opting for a larger-than-life captain with an out-going personality in the hope that Robin's enthusiasm would be infectious. He proved to be a most likeable and popular figure in the changing room. "Everyone warmed to him because he was such a genuine person, "said one player. "He called it as he saw it, pulled no punches and was absolutely straight down the line with all of us." But, as *Wisden*'s correspondent succinctly wrote "he tried very hard but found the task beyond him. He did not bowl a great deal, scored very few runs and the side slipped away. The senior players were getting older, the younger players lost form and the coach was unable to arrest the decline."

A far more harsh assessment came from a comment passed on by a spectator to Surrey's Pat Pocock during a Sunday League match at Ebbw Vale towards the end of June. The Surrey captain Roger Knight was putting in a decent all-round performance, bowling accurately, and hitting a stylish half-century. In contrast, Robin did not bat or bowl in the contest, with the disgruntled spectator saying to the spinner "You're very lucky with your captain. He bats and bowls. Our one does bugger all!"

When speaking to the Press at the start of the season, Robin told the journalists that he'd be disappointed if the Welsh county didn't win six Championship matches. These words came back to haunt him as Glamorgan became the first county since Northants in 1938 not to win a single Championship game all summer. Less attention though was paid to his words about looking after the young spinners – "when we are bowling for a declaration and the flog is on, I shall make sure that I get it and not the young spinners. It's my job to take that. I've gone past the stage of worrying about figures of 0 for 80!"

Robin was true to his word and, on several occasions, he bore the brunt of a second innings onslaught. As Alan Wilkins recalled, there were other occasions as well when he still proved that, despite four years out of the game, he had the skills for first-class cricket. "He bowled with menace, with great experience and thought," said Alan, "and he never looked out of his depth. Make no bones about it. Robin Hobbs was still, in 1979, a top-class leg-spin bowler."

But there was no getting away from the lack of quality at his disposal, especially with Malcolm Nash on the sidelines, as well as the absence of the winning touch. As Robin later wrote "we were a poor side and it was hard work playing a whole county season without winning a match although we very nearly won one." This was the contest in early July against Gloucestershire at Sophia Gardens. Set a target of 324 to win, Glamorgan had already removed the likes of Mike Procter, Sadiq Mohammad and Zaheer Abbas, with the visitors on 206-9 when their last pair of David Graveney and John Childs came together still with an hour to go. Robin again – "how we didn't win I'll never know. David wasn't a bad player but John couldn't bat. I just couldn't get our bowlers to bowl quick enough at him."

At thirty-six, going on thirty-seven, Robin's fielding also became suspect at times, and in the Benson and Hedges Cup game against Gloucestershire at Swansea, he dropped Mike Procter on four occasions, and later recalled "Everywhere I went in the field, Mike hit the ball to me. I kept dropping it but we won the game. God knows how!" With his knees also playing up, Robin sat out some of the one-day games from mid-July, with Alan Jones and Malcolm Nash taking over the captaincy. It also necessitated Robin having two cartilages removed at the end of the season in hospital in Carmarthen.

By the time the surgery was being undertaken, the Glamorgan committee were mulling over their plans for 1980, including the captaincy. Robin had made it clear that unless new players – and new overseas players in particular – were signed, he wasn't prepared to lead the side. As it turned out, Javed Miandad and Ezra Moseley were signed as overseas players, whilst Norman Featherstone moved from Middlesex to Glamorgan. But the committee opted against offering him the captaincy, with Malcolm taking over the baton.

Robin Hobbs, seen bowling in the nets at Sophia Gardens during 1980.

With his knees still playing up, Robin played more 2nd XI than 1st XI cricket during 1980 but had the consolation of seeing the young side win the 2nd XI Championship. The following summer, he appeared in 15 of Glamorgan's 21 Championship matches and claimed 35 wickets at a fraction under 33 runs apiece, including an eight-wicket match haul as Glamorgan met Worcestershire at Hereford Racecourse. Robin also shared in two important tenth wicket partnerships during 1981 – the first with Rodney Ontong against Hampshire at Swansea, with the pair adding a record 140 for the last wicket, whilst the second came with his room-mate that summer, Javed Miandad, against Somerset at Taunton on Royal Wedding Day, July 29.

As Robin recalled, "we were 295-9 when I walked out to the middle with Javed unbeaten on 170. He said to me 'Hobbsy, I will not let you face [Joel] Garner, you just take [Colin] Dredge.' He was as good as his word because I only faced two balls from the great West Indian. Javed went on to reach a double-century and my share of our 41-run stand was three not out, but I considered it a privilege to be at the other end and witness another brilliant double-hundred."

The pair joined forces again later in the year at Colchester where the Pakistani played what is acknowledged by those who saw it to have been one of the greatest modern-day innings by any Glamorgan batsman. Set 325 on a spiteful pitch at Castle Park, Essex had reduced the Welsh county to 44-4 before Javed led a remarkable fightback on the turning surface and where earlier in the day Robin had finished with figures of 5/85. Almost single-handedly, he had taken the total to 227-7 when Robin joined him out in the middle. The pair added 42 of which Robin's contribution was nought from 20 balls as Javed wristily manoeuvred the ball around and adroitly farmed the strike.

As John Lever recalled, the Essex side were almost in despair – "it seemed like forever that Hobbsy didn't face a ball as Javed kept getting a single or three off the last ball of the over. We thought 'we're never going to bowl at Hobbsy' and kept going with the spinners as we were trying to hold back the quicker bowler in case Hobbsy, by chance, got to face the beginning of an over." As it turned out David Acfield eventually had Robin caught in the slips with the total on 270. With the help of Malcom Nash and Simon Daniels, Javed helped Glamorgan to garner another 41 runs and reach another double-hundred before Simon was adjudged l.b.w. to John Lever with Glamorgan 14 runs short of their target.

This remarkable game proved to be Robin's final first-class appearance as shortly afterwards, Glamorgan confirmed that they would not be offering him a new contract. He was approached by Surrey who discussed a one-year contract but, after careful thought, Robin confirmed his retirement from the first-class game and bowed out with a career tally of 1,099 wickets at an average of 27. He duly returned to his job with Barclaycard and had another season with Suffolk before hanging up his boots once and for all.

Robin Hobbs, seen at Lord's, batting for Essex against Middlesex during 1971.

Having made his first-class debut for Essex in 1961, Robin had won the first of 7 Test caps during 1967. He made three appearances that summer against India, and once against Pakistan, before touring the West Indies the following winter alongside Jeff Jones. Whilst in the Caribbean, Robin played in the Test at Port-of-Spain, before touring Pakistan in 1968/69 and playing in the Third Test at Karachi which had to be abandoned because of riots. His final Test appearance also came against Pakistan, at Headingley during 1971.

At his peak, he bowled his leg-breaks and well disguised googlies from a moderate run-up, with plenty of flight. He was a batsman of quite modest pretensions and fittingly once quipped. "Similarities with Sir Jack ends with the last name!"

A smile was never too far away from his face as he proved in a remarkable innings in 1975 at Chelmsford where he struck a 44-minute century for Essex against the touring Australians. His innings came against their spinners Ashley Mallett and Jim Higgs as Essex were plummeting to a heavy defeat and with two men injured. Having reached his 50 off a relatively modest 30 balls with a flurry of cover drives, Robin then raced to his 100 off the next fifteen balls, dispatching Ashley for 27 in one over from the River End and sending a delivery from Jim for six through the window of a house at the Hayes Close End.

With Robin having reached his remarkable century, Rod Marsh, the tourist's acting captain, sauntered up to him and said "OK mate – we've had f***ing enough of you, you've had your fun, now get out otherwise I'm going to bring back [Jeff] Thomson!" Robin promptly skied the next ball into the hands of long-on and walked off to a standing ovation. As he pithily reflected later, "I can say that I batted against Australia when he was playing, but I wasn't going to face Mr Thomson – Sod that!"

505
SMITH, Christopher Lyall.

Born – Durban, South Africa, 15 October 1958.
Professional.
RHB, OB.
Ed – Northlands HS, Durban.
1st XI: 1979.
2nd XI: 1979.
Natal 1977/78–1982/83; Hampshire 1980-1991; DH Robin's XI 1980; England 1983-1986 (8 Tests); MCC 1984; Lavinia, Duchess of Norfolk's XI 1984; England B 1985/86.
Club: Swansea.

Batting and Fielding Record

	M	I	NO	RUNS	AV	100	50	CT	ST
F-c	1	2	1	81	40.50	-	1	1	-

Career-bests

First-class – 67 v Sri Lankans at St Helen's, Swansea, 1979.

Chris Smith was coached in South Africa by Alan Jones, who invited the promising top-order batsman to play in club cricket in South Wales, and hopefully join Glamorgan. He duly followed Alan's advice and also played in 2nd XI cricket for the Welsh county besides appearing, as an overseas player, in Glamorgan's friendly against the 1979 Sri Lankans at Swansea.

Glamorgan knew that 'Kippy' would, at some date in the future, qualify for British

Chris Smith.

passports through his father having been raised in the West Midlands and his mother being Scottish, but other counties were more proactive in accelerating matters and getting him considered as a home-grown player rather than an overseas player. Hampshire were amongst this group, with their interest in signing 'Kippy' stemming from an innings of 124* he made against them in a 2nd XI match at Bournemouth. Fortune had been on his side from the outset, having been a late call-up to the team, besides edging the first ball he faced into the wicket-keeper's gloves, but being adjudged not out by the umpire.

At the end of the match, 'Kippy' had a chat with Peter Sainsbury, Hampshire's coach, about his intentions for the future and the upshot was that in 1980 he joined the South Coast club and qualified as a homegrown player

before, with great irony to Alan and others, making his Test debut in 1983. What also irked them was that his talented younger brother Robin also joined Hampshire before playing in 62 Tests and 71 One-Day Internationals for England.

As far as 'Kippy' was concerned, he duly played in eight Tests for England and also enjoyed a highly successful career with Hampshire, scoring over 18,000 runs at an average of 44, and revealing a textbook technique, an iron will and unshakable concentration. He retired at the end of the 1991 to become the Marketing Manager of the Western Australian Cricket Association. He was one of *Wisden's* Cricketers of the Year in 1984.

506
THOMAS, John Gregory.

Born – Trebanos, 12 August 1960.
Professional.
RHB, RF.
Ed – Cwmtawe HS and South Glamorgan Institute of Higher Education.
1st XI: 1979-1988.
2nd XI: 1978-1984.
Colts: 1978.
Club and Ground: 1976.
Cap: 1986.
Border 1983/84-1986/87; England 1985/86-1986 (5 caps); Eastern Province 1987/88; Northamptonshire 1989-1991.
Club: Swansea.

Batting and Fielding Record

	M	I	NO	RUNS	AV	100	50	CT	ST
F-c	106	139	24	2137	18.58	2	4	38	-
List A	104	90	19	895	12.60	-	-	19	-

Bowling Record

	Balls	M	R	W	AV	5wI	10wM
F-c	13439	386	8230	256	32.25	9	1
List A	4470	63	3319	121	27.42		

Career-bests

First-class –   110 v Warwickshire at Edgbaston, 1988.
                6/68 v Nottinghamshire at Sophia Gardens, Cardiff, 1988.
List A –   37 v Nottinghamshire at Trent Bridge, 1983.
                5/17 v Sussex at Sophia Gardens, Cardiff, 1985.

Greg Thomas was the first fluent Welsh speaker to play Test cricket and earned the tag of "the fastest white man" in English cricket in the mid 1980s after some fiery spells for Glamorgan and Border. His skiddy pace and hostility won him a place on England's tour to the Caribbean in 1985/86 and, in the First Test, he nearly took a wicket with his first two deliveries in Test cricket, as Desmond Haynes edged his first ball over the head of first slip, before being dropped in the gully off Greg's second delivery.

This was the first of five Tests and three One-Day Internationals in which Greg appeared during a ten-year career with Glamorgan that had begun with Thomas making his first-class debut against the Sri Lankans at Swansea during July 1979. Three years before, he was still a sixteen-year-old pupil at Cwmtawe High School when he played for the Welsh county in a Benefit match at Pontarddulais. His raw pace, allied to his forthright batting in schoolboy cricket had prompted an invitation to the county's Indoor School at Neath,

and following some decent performances for the Welsh Schools, Greg made his debut for Glamorgan 2nd XI in 1978.

His College studies and training as a Science and Maths teacher, plus some niggling injuries to his ankle, meant that the tall and powerfully-built youngster did not play his first County Championship match until August 1981 when he took 4/65 against Lancashire at Sophia Gardens. The following summer he completed his studies and impressed with a dozen wickets in his first two Championship appearances, besides claiming a maiden 'five-for' with 5/61 at Derby as well as displaying his credentials with the bat with a withering 84 against Surrey at Guildford.

However, a stress fracture in his back meant that Greg was unable to immediately build on his rich promise but, after undergoing surgery, he continued

Greg Thomas.

his rehabilitation by spending the winter of 1983/84 in the sunshine of South Africa, playing for Border alongside Glamorgan team-mate Rodney Ontong. Greg returned to the UK in 1984 a much stronger and more mature cricketer and appeared in 20 first-class matches for the Welsh county besides impressing a number of good judges with his pace and hostility. It was his county captain Mike Selvey who called him "the fastest white bowler in Britain" whilst others in the Welsh media labelled him 'The Trebanos Terror' after the area in the Swansea Valleys where he had been raised.

Another winter in South Africa then followed before a series of rasping spells in Championship cricket during the opening months of the 1985 season, plus a number of high-profile scalps. His purple patch began when he clean bowled Mike Gatting, the Middlesex captain at Cardiff before, in the next match starting on 25 May at Southampton he matched the fiery bowling of Malcolm Marshall the Hampshire and West Indies paceman, and all in front of England selector Alan Smith.

Greg began by being sharp enough to capture Gordon Greenidge's wicket as the Caribbean opener, was too late on an attempted pull to a ferocious short ball. Soon afterwards, Mark Nicholas was completely beaten for pace as he fended off a sharply lifting delivery into the hands of John Steele, prompting the delighted Welshman during his follow through to mock the departing captain by saying "Come on Marshy, come on Marshy, you don't like it when its short stuff to you!" Just for good measure he also had

Robin Smith caught behind as the name J.G. Thomas went into the selector's notebook for serious consideration for the winter tour to the West Indies.

Another ferocious new ball salvo came at Sophia Gardens during the NatWest Trophy game against Sussex with Greg returning figures of 7-2-17-5 and winning the Man-of-the-Match Award for his efforts. However, the wear and tear prompted some new niggles in his groin and right hamstring and, after the match against Kent at Swansea in early August, Greg didn't bowl another ball in the Championship for the remainder of the season and started to make plans to play in Tasmania over the winter months.

However, without any further contact from the selectors or advance warning, Greg was chosen for the England tour to the West Indies in 1985/86 and became Glamorgan's first representative on a full England tour since Tony Lewis led the MCC in India and Pakistan in 1972/73. At twenty-five years of age, he also found himself being what the Media described as 'the great white hope' of the English attack and charged with the responsibility of answering, in kind, the thunderbolts of Messrs Marshall, Garner, Holding, Patterson and Walsh.

Having been given a special programme of fitness training over the winter months, plus some net sessions with Bob Willis, Greg made his England debut in the opening One-Day International in mid-February at Kingston and claimed the wicket of Gordon Greenidge having opened the bowling with Les Taylor.

Greg Thomas.

Three days later, Greg made his Test debut at the Jamaican ground and after being bowled first ball by Joel Garner, he took the new ball alongside Ian Botham. The Welshman removed Desmond Haynes who was caught by wicket-keeper Paul Downton during his second spell before returning later in the innings to wrap things up by having Jeff Dujon caught by Graham Gooch. Greg nearly took the first and last wickets once again in the Second Test at Port-of-Spain where he had Gordon Greenidge caught in the slips before returning to dismiss Courtney Walsh.

The Third Test, at Bridgetown, saw Greg return figures of 4/70 with his impressive bag of wickets featuring Viv Richards, Larry Gomes, Michael Holding and Joel Garner. But from the highs of Barbados to the lows of Trinidad where Greg bowled poorly in the Fourth Test, returning figures of 15-0-101-0 as the home batsmen feasted on a diet of short, wide deliveries. Greg had also played in the Third One-Day International at Barbados and also went wicketless and few were surprised when he was dropped for the final Test in Antigua. But long-serving journalist John Thicknesse, writing in *Wisden*, had been impressed by Greg's efforts, saying "he bowled with a bit of pace and no lack of

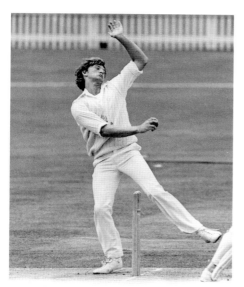

Greg Thomas in bowling action during 1984.

heart. Picked on debatable credentials – a succession of injuries and only 34 wickets in the Championship for Glamorgan in 1985 – he vindicated the selectors' judgement."

Flushed by this success, Greg returned to South Wales, won his Glamorgan cap and delivered another series of feisty spells. One of these came at Taunton in the Championship encounter with Somerset where Greg twice beaten the outside edge of Viv Richards' bat during an over. It was quite a rarity for the great West Indian to play and miss, and the fast bowler – after England's humbling in the Caribbean – was not going to waste the opportunity of having a few words with the Master Blaster so after delivering another short ball which went past Viv's cap, he walked down the wicket and said the immortal words "It's red, it's round and it's fast."

But Viv made the perfect response as, to the next ball, he unfurled a superb lofted drive that sent the ball back over the bowler's head, high over the stand for six and into the graveyard of the church which adjoined the County Ground. As the ball disappeared out of sight, Viv sauntered up the wicket and said to Greg "Hey man, you know what it looks like, you go and find it!"

1986 also saw Greg play again for England, appearing at Trent Bridge in the Second Test of the series against New Zealand. He claimed the wickets of Bruce Edgar and Richard Hadlee as he shared the new ball with Gladstone Small in a revamped England bowling line-up in the absence of Ian Botham. However, he again featured in a losing Test team as the Kiwis won by eight wickets and did not feature in the Third and final Test at The Oval. An indication though that he still remained in the selector's thoughts came from his selection for an England XI in their short one-day series against the Rest of the World at Jesmond.

After another winter in South Africa playing for Border, Greg was eager to play more international cricket and in May 1987 he was chosen in the England squad for their One-Day International series against Pakistan. His inclusion was chiefly because of doubts over Graham Dilley's fitness and, when the Worcestershire paceman dropped out of the third match of the series, Greg returned to the international fold. Once again, he made a dramatic start removing Mudassar Nazar and Mansoor Akhtar in his first over as the tourists slipped to 0-2 after three balls.

Javed Miandad, Greg's Glamorgan colleague, then led a counter-attack as England were left a target of 214 to win the game and the series. It proved to be a dramatic and jittery run-chase, and when Greg, at number eleven, strode out to the middle, England were on 209-9 needing to score five from the remaining eleven balls. He defended stoutly, and, after his partner Neil Foster, had survived a run-out attempt, Greg brought the scores level with a scrambled leg-bye before Neil thick-edged a ball for four through the slips.

As it turned out, it proved to be Greg's final appearance at international level but, at the time, he was eager to feature in more Tests and One-Day Internationals. His erratic form with Glamorgan in both Championship and one-day cricket ignited a few tensions back home – there was no doubting that Greg could deliver the ball at blistering pace, but he became frustrated by the slow Welsh wickets which he felt were hindering his claims of regaining a Test place.

Greg duly asked to be released from his contract for 1988 but the Glamorgan committee refused his request and insisted that he honour the final year of his commitment to the Welsh county. It was a year which saw him enjoy his most productive summer in the Welsh county's ranks with 48 first-class wickets at an average of 31, as well as a pair of lusty centuries with scores of 100* against Worcestershire at Abergavenny followed by a quickfire 110 against Warwickshire at Edgbaston.

Greg Thomas and his sponsored car as a capped Glamorgan player.

His final appearance for Glamorgan came in September 1988 at New Road where Greg took three wickets during an innings defeat to Worcestershire. During a winter in South Africa playing for Eastern Province, Greg agreed terms with Northamptonshire for 1989, and it looked for a while as if his switch may re-ignite his international aspirations as he took 67 first-class wickets for the East Midlands county, with hauls of 5/87 against Gloucestershire and 6/53 against Leicestershire, besides being chosen in England's party for the short visit to Holland.

However, Greg was overlooked by the England selectors for the tour of the West Indies in 1989/90, with preference being given instead to Devon Malcolm and Gladstone Small, plus the all-round talents of Chris Lewis and Greg's Northamptonshire team-mate David Capel. Instead, the winter months saw Greg play for Mike Gatting's 'rebel' England tour to South Africa, besides playing in domestic cricket in the Cape for Eastern Province. The following summer, Greg took a career-best 7/75 against Glamorgan at Northampton, but his former employers won the game by six wickets following second innings hundreds by Matthew Maynard and Viv Richards.

1991 saw Greg win his Northants cap, but he also sustained a pelvic injury and was forced to retire at the end of the season. He has remained living in the Northampton area where Greg has subsequently become a successful businessman specializing in insurance claims, working initially for Claims Direct before in January 2009 creating his own company called Legato Legal services. His son Will played in age-group cricket for Northamptonshire as well as for their 2nd XI during 2015 and 2016. Greg is also an accomplished after-dinner speaker yet he still possesses the unassuming nature that led one journalist to write, after he had returned from the West Indies in the spring of 1986, "one of his endearing qualities is an almost boyish unawareness of exactly what it is that he has achieved and of the fact that he himself now becomes part of the fabric of Test cricket."

507
DAVIES, Terry.

Born – St Albans, 25 October 1960.
RHB, WK.
Professional.
Ed – Townsend SS, St Albans.
1st XI: 1979-1986.
2nd XI: 1978-1983.
Cap: 1985.
Clubs: Watford, Maesteg Celtic, Ammanford, Western Creek, Bathurst and Bankstown.
Football for Watford Youth, West Ham Youth and Tottenham Hotspur Youth.

Batting and Fielding Record

	M	I	NO	RUNS	AV	100	50	CT	ST
F-c	100	121	36	1775	20.89	-	6	165	27
List A	75	48	19	446	15.37	-	-	66	25

Career-bests
First-class – 75 v Middlesex at Sophia Gardens, Cardiff, 1985.
46* v Kent at Sophia Gardens, Cardiff, 1983.

Terry Davies succeeded Eifion Jones as Glamorgan's first-choice wicket-keeper between 1983 and 1986, before emigrating to Australia where he has subsequently become a leading administrator and stadium manager.

Terry made his debut for Glamorgan 2nd XI and Under 25 team in 1978 whilst on the MCC groundstaff having also had football trials as a mid-fielder with West Ham, Tottenham Hotspur and Luton Town. His sporting hero however was Alan Knott, the Kent and England wicket-keeper, with Terry owing his place at Lord's to David Cooper,

Terry Davies

Terry Davies, keeping wicket during 1986.

his former geography teacher at school in St Albans who knew Len Muncer, the former Glamorgan cricketer who was the MCC's Head Coach. A phone call duly secured a trial for Terry in a game at Finchley CC and he subsequently headed to Lord's where he became great friends with all-rounder Geoff Holmes, who also secured a place on Glamorgan's books.

Some decent performances for the MCC Young Professionals led to Terry getting offers of trials from several counties including Surrey and Glamorgan. However, Terry's father who was born in Llanelli, told the young wicket-keeper that if he was going to play county cricket it would have to be for the Welsh county after impressing behind the stumps, Terry accepted an offer to join the Glamorgan staff in 1979 as Eifion Jones' understudy. In July that year he also made his first-class debut, playing against the Sri Lankans at Swansea, before in August keeping wicket for the MCC against Scotland at Aberdeen.

May 1982 saw Terry make his Championship debut against Gloucestershire at Swansea owing to Eifion being injured and he had an extended run in the 1st XI as the veteran gloveman completed his rehabilitation. From mid-July 1983 Terry became Glamorgan's first-choice wicket-keeper and soon proved himself to be a neat and agile wicket-keeper in both Championship and limited-overs matches, besides winning his county cap in 1985 during the Club's match against the Australians at The Gnoll in Neath.

On five occasions, he kept a clean sheet as far as conceding byes were concerned in completed innings in Championship matches, whilst his ratio of byes conceded to total runs scored in Championship matches (1.15%) was lower than his predecessors Eifion (1.54%), David Evans (1.70%) and Haydn Davies (2.23%).

Terry was also a more than useful lower order batsman who, on several occasions acted as night-watchman. Indeed, it was in this role that Terry made a gritty and career-best

75 against Middlesex at Sophia Gardens in 1985 – the summer when he amassed 503 first-class runs and also won his Glamorgan cap, besides taking four catches in Scotland's innings during their NatWest Trophy game at Edinburgh. In 1986 he also equaled Eifion's record for the most number of dismissals in a List A game, making four catches again, besides completing a couple of stumpings in the NatWest Trophy match against Staffordshire at Stone – a feat which Colin Metson also equaled during 1993 and 1995, but no other wicket-keeper has surpassed for the Welsh county.

In 1982, and on his Championship debut, Terry had also taken part in a remarkable tenth wicket partnership of 143 with Simon Daniels against Gloucestershire at Swansea. Their efforts still stand as Club record for that wicket with Terry, typically being a fleet of foot runner, nudging and nurdling the ball around and playing the perfect foil to his partner who used the long handle to bludgeon the West Country bowlers into more distant parts of the St Helen's outfield. Terry's contribution was an unbeaten 66, whilst Simon made 73 before being bowled by Phil Bainbridge.

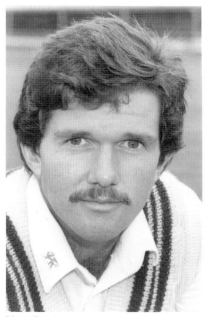

Terry Davies.

Throughout his playing career with the Welsh county, Terry spent the winter months playing grade cricket in Australia, initially for Western Creek CC in Canberra and then Bathurst CC in Sydney. At the end of the 1986 season he emigrated with his Sydney-born wife Noelle to Australia, and subsequently captained Bankstown CC (who included both Mark and Steve Waugh in their line-up) to a pair of Sydney Grade Premiership titles.

Terry continued playing for Bankstown until 2001 before becoming a state selector with New South Wales and then Marketing Manager for South Australia. He subsequently became Deputy Chief Executive of the South Australian Cricket Association and helped to establish the Adelaide Oval as one of the leading sporting and entertainment venues with the ground staging concerts by the likes of AC/DC and Fleetwood Mac, as well as hosting international rugby sevens.

In 2011 Terry became the General Manager of the Etihad Stadium in Melbourne before becoming Event Strategy Manager for the South Australia Tourism Commission. Since 2014 Terry has been Chief Executive of Dunedin Venues in New Zealand – the premier event facility on South Island including the Forsyth Barr Stadium and the Dunedin Centre, which is a multi-purpose entertainment, conference and events hub.

508
PERRY, Neil James.

Born – Sutton, Surrey, 27 May 1958.
Professional.
RHB, SLA.
1st XI: 1979-1981.
2nd XI: 1978-1981.
Surrey 2nd XI 1974-1978; MCC Young Cricketers 1977-1978; Essex 2nd XI 1978; DH
Robins' XI 1978.
Clubs: Sutton, MCC, Neath and Gowerton.

Batting and Fielding Record

	M	I	NO	RUNS	AV	100	50	CT	ST
F-c	13	12	4	19	2.37	-	-	9	-

Bowling Record

	Balls	M	R	W	AV	5wI	10wM
F-c	1695	73	919	21	43.80	-	-

Career-bests

First-class –   6 v Warwickshire at Edgbaston, 1980.
                 3/51 v Indians at St Helen's, Swansea, 1979.

Neil Perry, a left-arm spinner, played in 13 first-class matches for Glamorgan between 1979 and 1981, but did not appear in any one-day cricket whilst associated with the Welsh county.

The Sutton-born spinner had first played for Surrey 2nd XI and their Under 25 team during 1974, before spending a couple of years on the MCC groundstaff at Lord's. In 1978, Neil also played for Essex 2nd XI, besides appearing for DH Robins' XI against Cambridge University at Eastbourne.

On the recommendation of Len Muncer, the MCC Head Coach, Neil also had a trial with Glamorgan during 1978 and immediately impressed by taking 6/20 against Gloucestershire 2nd XI at Chepstow, before taking thirteen wickets in the match with Yorkshire 2nd XI at Sophia Gardens, with Neil claiming 7/45 in the Tykes first innings followed by 6/55 in their second.

This outstanding performance helped to secure Neil a contract with Glamorgan for 1979 and he continued to impress in 2nd XI cricket, returning figures of 21-14-18-5 against Warwickshire 2nd XI, again at Cardiff. Neil subsequently made his first-class debut against

Neil Perry.

the Sri Lankans at Swansea in July 1979, before ten days later also appearing against the Indians at the same venue.

Immediately after the game with the Indians, plus some further advice from Bishan Bedi – their outstanding spinner – Neil made his Championship debut for Glamorgan against Lancashire, again at the St Helen's ground. He appeared in three further Championship matches at the end of the 1979 season and bowled in tandem with off-spinner Barry Lloyd following Robin Hobbs being sidelined with a knee injury.

However, with Glamorgan further strengthening their spin-bowling resources in 1980 by signing Norman Featherstone from Middlesex, Neil failed to command a regular place in the 1st XI and did not improve on the figures of 3/84 which he had recorded against Kent at Sophia Gardens the previous September. Neil played in six Championship matches during 1980 but only claimed a further six wickets and was released by the Welsh county at the end of the 1981 season having made a solitary Championship appearance that summer against Worcestershire at Swansea – a match in which he took just a couple of wickets.

509
MIR, Parvez Jamil.

Born – Sutrapur, Pakistan, 24 September 1953.
RHB, RM/OB.
Professional.
Ed – Lahore University.
1st XI: 1979.
2nd XI: 1979-1980.
Rawalpindi 1970/71; Lahore 1971/72 ; Punjab 1972/73 - 1975/76; Universities 1973/74 -1974/75 ; Pakistan 1975-1976 (3 One-Day Internationals); Derbyshire 1975 ; Habib Bank 1975/76 - 1980/81 ; Lancashire 2nd XI 1977; Norfolk 1981-1985.
Clubs: Crompton, Egerton, Walkden, Kearsley, Ingham, Vauxhall Mallards, MCC, Horsford, Swardeston, Waltham.

Batting and Fielding Record

	M	I	NO	RUNS	AV	100	50	CT	ST
F-c	1	2	0	16	8.00	-	-	-	-

Bowling Record

	Balls	M	R	W	AV	5wI	10wM
F-c	24	0	21	0	-	-	-

Career-bests
First-class – 10 v Indians at St Helen's, Swansea, 1979.

Parvez Mir, who played in three One-Day Internationals for Pakistan, made one appearance for Glamorgan, against the Indian tourists at Swansea in 1979.

The all-rounder had previously played for Derbyshire against Oxford University at Burton-on-Trent during 1975, and he owed his selection in the Glamorgan side to a brief but successful trial with the county's 2nd XI during which he scored 203* and 80 against Gloucestershire 2nd XI at the Nevil Road ground in Bristol. He appeared again for the Welsh county's 2nd XI during 1980 and took 5/44 against Somerset 2nd XI at the Imperial Ground in Bristol but, with Javed Miandad and Ezra Moseley successfully occupying the overseas berth he did not appear again for Glamorgan's 1st XI.

Parvez had captained Rawalpindi Under 19s before making his first-class debut for Rawalpindi during 1970/71, He subsequently played in domestic cricket in Pakistan for Lahore, Punjab, Universities and Habib Bank, with the all-rounder being a member of the Pakistan squad for the 1975 World Cup. He duly played in the group matches against the West Indies at Edgbaston and Sri Lanka at Trent Bridge, and became the first Bangladesh-born player to appear in the competition, before a series of decent performances in domestic matches saw Parvez re-appear for Pakistan in the opening One-Day International of their series with England at Sahiwal in 1977/78.

Parvez Mir.

By this time, Parvez had also started a successful career in the Central Lancashire and Bolton Leagues before moving to East Anglia with Parvez also playing for Norfolk between 1981 and 1985. He also represented the Minor Counties in their game against Sri Lanka as part of the warm-ups ahead of the 1983 World Cup, as well as later in 1985 against Lavinia, Duchess of Norfolk's XI at Arundel.

Parvez subsequently played in club cricket in the Home Counties besides appearing for the MCC against Scotland, Cambridge University, and the Combined Services between 1989 and 1993. He subsequently moved to the USA and, as Director of the North American Cricket Authority, he arranged exhibition matches involving teams from England and the West Indies.

He has subsequently become a journalist and broadcaster based in London and Lahore with ARY News, specializing in programmes on politics and current affairs, whilst in 2007 he also acted as Media Manager for the Pakistan team at the ICC World Cup in the West Indies. His brother Shahid Mir was a left-arm spinner and batsman in domestic cricket in Pakistan between 1975/76 and 1980/81.

CORRECTIONS AND AMENDMENTS

TO VOLUME ONE

P42 HB Letcher

He also played rugby for Swansea RFC between 1890/91 and 1893/94, chiefly for the Club's 2nd XV.

P43 WH Gwynn

Bill played 122 times for Swansea RFC, between 1876/77 and 1887/88, and captained the team in 1884/85 and 1885/86.

P48 E Reid

Edgar won a hockey cap for Wales during February 1899 when he led the team in their contest against Ireland. It ended though in a 4-0 defeat for Wales with Edgar also sustaining a bad cut to his hand.

P68 G Storer

This was Arthur William Storer (born January 1867 in Manchester). He had initially played League cricket in Lancashire and Yorkshire, where he held a professional appointment with Skipton from 1888 until 1890, before moving to South Wales after securing a position as professional / groundsman at the Arms Park following the previous incumbent, Oswald Mettam, being signed by Somerset to work at the County Ground in Taunton. Arthur only stayed one year in South Wales before returning to Yorkshire where he secured a similar position with Driffield CC. He later moved with his wife, Mary Ann, to Northumberland and worked as a groundsman in Newcastle-upon-Tyne where he died prematurely at the age of thirty-seven on 19 December 1904.

P76 GE Bowen

George played for Swansea RFC between 1883/84 to 1894/95.

P129 A Wolfe

He was educated at Uplands School, Swansea, Swansea Collegiate School and St David's College, Lampeter. Arthur was also a fine full-back for Swansea RFC between 1885/86 and 1890/91, having also represented St David's College, Lampeter. He was the son of Rev. Edwin Wolfe who was curate of St Helen's, Swansea from 1867 until 1873, before serving as Chaplain of the St Nicholas Seamen's church in Swansea from 1877 until 1899.

P161 T Arkell

The player who appeared for Glamorgan in 1898 was TM Arkell and not TN Arkell. The statistics are as printed but the biographical details and profile are as follows:

ARKELL, Trevor Miller   ('Bob')

Born – Swansea 1878
Died – Cardiff, 2nd June 1901

Bob Arkell had a brief county career, playing twice as an amateur for Glamorgan during 1898, but tragically three years later, he died from TB at the age of just twenty-three. He was the son of Charles Arkell, a bootmaker from Gloucester, who had moved to South Wales during the 1860s to set up an outfitter's business in Swansea. He subsequently moved to Cardiff to open premises at the Bute Docks, and it was in the coal metropolis where Bob was raised before training to be an accountant.

Bob showed great prowess at cricket from an early age, playing initially for Cardiff Electrics and Cardiff Windsors in the Cardiff and District League with his prowess as a wicket-keeper drawing the attention of the town club, with Bob making his debut aged seventeen for Cardiff 2nd XI in 1895. That summer he also guested for Lansdown CC when the Bath-based club, under the captaincy of EM Grace, arrived at the Arms Park without three players for their match against Cardiff.

He subsequently played for the 1st XI the following summer and became the Club's regular gloveman for the next four summers. His neat glovework also impressed the Glamorgan selectors and during August 1898, the twenty-year-old appeared twice for the Welsh county, starting with the match at Penzance against Cornwall and followed by the contest with Monmouthshire at Rodney Parade. Sadly, Bob was diagnosed with TB the following year and, in 1900, he spent time at a convalescent home in Pentyrch. He never recovered and died the following June having also been diagnosed as suffering from heart problems.

P161 DJ Smith.

Douglas Smith died peacefully during the early hours of 14 August 1949 of broncho-pnemonia and aplastic anemia. This is the date given on his tombstone, although his death certificate gives the following day. Douglas' first professional engagements had been with the Bank of England Club at Alexandra Park in London, and subsequently the Meigle club in Scotland. Whilst playing for Yeovil in 1895 he had scored 155* against Dorchester, 122* against Weymouth and 122* against Stoke in three successive matches. In 1902 he was also approached by Surrey to  join them for a trial, but Worcestershire refused to release him. The incorrect image was also published in Volume One of this series – the correct photograph is shown here.

P295 AE Thomas.

This is the incorrect photo, instead showing AE Thomas who played one match for Glamorgan in 1925.

P269 GL Robathan

Lionel Robathan completed his sixth form studies in Kent at Cranbrook School where he won his cricket colours. He subsequently taught in Sandwich and Margate and, whilst in the latter town, he played both cricket and association football. In one season, his batting average was in excess of 100 and he was offered a trial with Kent. However, Lionel declined the approach and spent time instead working in Germany and France before returning to South Wales and joining the staff of Llandaff Cathedral School.

p328-29 AEO O'Bree.

Arthur O'Bree also played cricket for St Fagans and Margam, besides playing rugby for Aberavon. During September 1914 Arthur travelled to France with the 3rd Battalion of the Welch Regiment and took part in the Battles of Mons and Ypres. At the end of October he sustained shellshock and returned to England where he received treatment at Guy's Hospital in London. After returning to his home in Port Talbot, Arthur took part in the recruitment campaign and gave several rousing speeches at various meetings.

During 1915 Arthur was appointed Assistant Instructor in Officer Training and served in Leeds and subsequently London, before during June 1916 he returned to France as Brigade Major of the 180th Infantry Brigade. He remained in France for the rest of the War, before in February 1919 being promoted to Lieutenant Colonel and becoming officer in charge of the repatriation records office in Winchester. He retired from the Army on 8 April 1920.

TO VOLUME TWO

P111   MJL Turnbull

He was also *Wisden's* Schools Cricketer of the Year in 1925.

P135   JT Morgan

He was not a full-time pupil at Christ College, Brecon.

P291   BHS Davis

He played for Buckinghamshire between 1928 and 1937, and never represented Berkshire.

P363   WMS Trick

SA Trick attended Merchant Taylors' School in Northwood and was *Wisden's* Schools Cricketer of the Year for 1902.

P370   DC Good

He died in Oakville, Ontario on 26 June 2021.

Index

Acknowledgements

As with the previous editions, this book, would not have been possible without the kind assistance of a number of people, cricket clubs and other organizations. Images have been made available via Glamorgan Cricket's fantastic archive of photographs, held in conjunction with the CC4 Museum of Welsh Cricket. The author would also like to thank, in particular, the following for their assistance with research queries and/or photographs – Philip Bailey; Martyn Bevan; the late John Billot; the late Jeff Bird; Katrina Coopey; Tony Davies; Susan Edwards; Gerald Gabb; Roger Gibbons and the GCCC Heritage Trust, the late Bob Harragan; Stephen Hedges; the late David Herbert (senior); Stephen Hill, Lawrence Hourahane; Philip Hutchinson; Jane James; John Jenkins; Bryn Jones; Mike and David Knight; Jon Lloyd; Richard Miller; Richard Miller; Bob Mole; Amber Nash; Tony Peters; Duncan Pierce; Gwyn Prescott; Andrew Radd; Peter Roderick; Mark Shepherd; Edwina Smart; the late Wayne Thomas; Anthony Woolford; the family of the late Peter Walker; John Williams, and the Wooller Family, plus the Archivists at Glamorgan Archives, West Glamorgan Archives, Cardiff Local History Library and the National Library of Wales.